THE GREAT PHILOSOPHERS

THE GREAT PHILOSOPHERS

An Introduction to Western Philosophy

BRYAN MAGEE

Oxford   New York

OXFORD UNIVERSITY PRESS

Oxford University Press, Walton Street, Oxford OX2 6DP

Oxford New York Toronto
Delhi Bombay Calcutta Madras Karachi
Petaling Jaya Singapore Hong Kong Tokyo
Nairobi Dar es Salaam Cape Town
Melbourne Auckland

and associated companies in
Berlin Ibadan

Oxford is a trade mark of Oxford University Press

Text © Brian Magee 1987

Illustrations:

All illustrations © except:
25 Mansell Collection; 96–97 Laurie Sparham/Network;
103 Mary Evans Picture Library; 135 National Portrait Gallery, London;
144–145 Attila Kirally; 168–169 Laurie Sparham/Network;
197 & 203 Mansell Collection; 210–211 Laurie Sparham/Network;
219 Archiv für Kunst und Geschichte, Berlin;
259 & 262 Bildarchiv Preussischer Kulturbesitz, Berlin;
282 Historical Pictures Service, Chicago;
287 BBC Hulton Picture Library/The Bettmann Archive;
292 Historical Pictures Service, Chicago;
305 Archiv für Kunst und Geschichte, Berlin; 331 Popperfoto;
333 Archiv für Kunst und Geschichte, Berlin.

First published 1987 by BBC Books
First issued as an Oxford University Press paperback 1988
Reprinted 1988 (twice), 1989, 1990 (twice), 1992

British Library Cataloguing in Publication Data
Magee, Brian
The great philosophers: an introduction to Western philosophy.
1. Western philosophy—Critical studies
I. Title   190
ISBN 0-19-282201-2

Library of Congress Cataloging in Publication Data
Data available

Printed in Great Britain by
Richard Clay, Ltd
Bungay, Suffolk

CONTENTS

PREFACE *8*
Bryan Magee, Honorary Senior Research Fellow in the
History of Ideas, King's College, University of London

Dialogue 1 PLATO *12*
Myles Burnyeat, Professor of Ancient Philosophy,
University of Cambridge

Dialogue 2 ARISTOTLE *32*
Martha Nussbaum, Professor of Philosophy and Classics,
Brown University

Dialogue 3 MEDIEVAL PHILOSOPHY *56*
Anthony Kenny, Master of Balliol College, University of
Oxford

Dialogue 4 DESCARTES *76*
Bernard Williams, Professor of Philosophy, University of
California, Berkeley

Dialogue 5 SPINOZA AND LEIBNIZ *96*
Anthony Quinton, Chairman of the British Library

Dialogue 6 LOCKE AND BERKELEY *118*
Michael Ayers, Fellow of Wadham College, University of
Oxford

Dialogue 7 HUME *144*
John Passmore, Emeritus Professor of Philosophy,
Australian National University

Dialogue 8 KANT *168*
Geoffrey Warnock, Principal of Hertford College,
University of Oxford

Dialogue 9 HEGEL AND MARX *188*
Peter Singer, Professor of Philosophy, Monash University

Dialogue 10 SCHOPENHAUER *210*
Frederick Copleston, Emeritus Professor of the History
of Philosophy, University of London

Dialogue 11 NIETZSCHE *232*
J. P. Stern, Professor of German, University of London

Dialogue 12   HUSSERL, HEIDEGGER AND MODERN
               EXISTENTIALISM   252
               Hubert Dreyfus, Professor of Philosophy, University of
               California, Berkeley

Dialogue 13   THE AMERICAN PRAGMATISTS   278
               Sidney Morgenbesser, Professor of Philosophy,
               Columbia University

Dialogue 14   FREGE, RUSSELL AND MODERN LOGIC   298
               A. J. Ayer, formerly Professor of Logic, University of
               Oxford

Dialogue 15   WITTGENSTEIN   320
               John Searle, Professor of Philosophy, University of Cali-
               fornia, Berkeley

               Index   348

*It is owing to their wonder that men
now begin, and first began, to philosophise.*
ARISTOTLE
*This sense of wonder is the mark of the
philosopher. Philosophy indeed has no other origin.*
PLATO

PREFACE

BRYAN MAGEE

PREFACE

In the English-speaking world philosophy is not part of the mental furniture of most people, even most of those educated at universities. I suppose a majority of intelligent men and women regardless of education read novels and see plays; they take a newspaper-reading interest in politics, and through that and their work-experience pick up some economics; many of them read biographies, and thereby learn some history. But philosophy remains a closed book, except to the few who make a study of it. Partly this is due to the fact that in the twentieth century the subject has become professionalised and technical. Partly it is due to excessive specialisation in all subjects – British education in particular is open to the criticism that it does not carry general education to a high enough level. Partly it is due to Anglo-Saxon pride at not being too concerned with abstract ideas. Whatever the reasons in full, most well-read Anglo-Saxons are familiar with the names of the great philosophers throughout their adult lives without ever knowing what their fame rests on, what indeed any of the famous philosophers is famous *for*.

Why are Plato and Aristotle household names more than two thousand years after their deaths? A similar question can be asked about certain philosophers of more recent times. The answer, of course, is that their work is part of the foundations of Western culture and civilisation. But how? This book offers the beginnings of an answer to that question.

If you were to go to a university to study philosophy you would almost certainly find that the core of the curriculum was about the nature, scope and limits of human knowledge, something which – after the Greek word 'episteme' meaning knowledge – is called epistemology. For most of the subject's history, certainly in recent centuries, this has constituted its main preoccupation, and for that reason it dominates university courses, and dominates this book. But subsidiary branches of philosophy can be fascinating too. For some people the most interesting of all are moral and political philosophy; but there are also aesthetics, logic, and philosophy of language, philosophy of mind, philosophy of science, philosophy of religion, and many others. Several are touched on in this book; but in the nature of things it has not been possible to do justice to them all in so short a space; so for clarity's sake I have stayed close to the central stream of the subject's development and followed that through, and looked at subsidiary aspects of it only when they compelled attention. Resisting temptations to digress was difficult, for there were so many things I would like to have included but, alas, could not find the space for.

The book is based on a series of television programmes first transmitted by the BBC in 1987. It does not consist merely of transcripts of the programmes: the contributors and I started with those but then treated them with the irreverence that we would treat any first draft. The chief point which I as editor reiterated was that the book would have a life of its own independent of the television programmes, and therefore that we should take the trouble to make it as good as we could in its own right, unconfined by what we had said on the screen. The contributors responded with improvements at every level, from detailed polishing to radical restructuring. The need to publish the book at the time that the television programmes went on the air meant that the complete manuscript had to be rushed to the publishers immediately after the last of the programmes, which happened to be the one on the American Pragmatists, had been put on tape. This was particularly hard on the protagonist in that programme because he wanted to recast his whole contribution, whereas the exigencies of time were such that responsibility for seeing it to the press had to be undertaken immediately by me in London, he being in New York. He gave me detailed notes and guidelines, and I did my best, but that is the one discussion in the book for which we would have liked more time.

The television series was prepared and put on tape over a period of two and a half years, but the most important decisions were the earliest: how to divide up the subject matter and which contributors to invite. Different and equally defensible answers were available to both questions, and on both I went through changes of mind. During this period I conducted running consultations with a private think-tank consisting chiefly of Bernard Williams and Isaiah Berlin but including also Anthony Quinton and John Searle. As often as not these four gentlemen would give me four incompatible pieces of advice on the same issue, and for that reason alone they can none of them be blamed for the decisions I actually took. But their help was beyond price, for it meant that every decision was subjected to critical evaluation by someone other than myself and compared with viable alternatives before being adopted. I extend my warmest gratitude to them all. I want to thank also the producer of the series, Jill Dawson, who managed the very extensive administrative arrangements involved, as well as directing studio crews and cameras in most of the programmes. Lastly I would like to thank Susan Cowley for her typing of the manuscript and David Miller, of the University of Warwick, for his reading of it and his many useful suggestions.

Bryan Magee
March 1987

PLATO

Dialogue with
MYLES BURNYEAT

INTRODUCTION

Magee Any attempt to tell the story of Western philosophy should begin
with the ancient Greeks, who produced not only the first but some of the
very greatest of Western philosophers. The one whose name is most
familiar is Socrates, who died in the year 399 BC. But there were outstanding Greek philosophers before him, some of whose names are also widely
known, for instance Pythagoras and Heraclitus. And there were others
too of comparable calibre – the first of all being Thales, who flourished in
the sixth century BC.

If the pre-Socratic philosophers can be said to have had one common
concern it was an attempt to find universal principles which would explain
the whole of nature. In today's language, they were as much concerned
with 'cosmology' or with 'science' as with 'philosophy'. Socrates was in
conscious rebellion against them. He maintained that what we most need
to learn is not how nature works but how we ourselves ought to live, and
therefore that what we need to consider first and foremost are moral
questions. He never, so far as we know, wrote anything: he did all his
teaching by word of mouth. Since none of the writings of any of the
pre-Socratic philosophers has come down to us directly, this means that
all we know of any of the philosophers I have mentioned so far is what has
come to us second-hand, through the writings of others – though I ought
to stress that this does include some long summaries and a good many
direct quotations. Even so, the first philosopher who *wrote works which
we actually now possess* was Plato. He was a pupil of Socrates: in fact it is
from Plato's writings that most of our knowledge of Socrates derives. In
his own right, however, Plato was beyond any question one of the
greatest philosophers of all time – some think the greatest. Therefore, if
we have to pick an arbitrary starting point in what is after all a continuous
story, a good one to choose is 399 BC, with the death of Socrates and the
subsequent writings of Plato. Let us, then, begin there.

Plato was about thirty-one when Socrates died, and lived to be eighty-
one. During that half-century he founded his famous school in Athens,
the Academy, which was the prototype of what we now call a university,
and also produced his writings. Nearly all these take the form of dialogues, with different arguments being put into the mouths of different
characters, one of whom, nearly always, is Socrates. Most, although not
all, of the dialogues are called by the name of one of the people to whom
Socrates is talking in them: thus we have the *Phaedo*, the *Laches*, the
Euthyphro, the *Theaetetus*, the *Parmenides*, the *Timaeus*, and so on.
There are more than two dozen of them – some of them twenty, some
eighty, a couple of them 300 pages long. The most famous of all are the
Republic and the *Symposium*, but all the most interesting ones are
available nowadays in paperback translations. The best are regarded not
only as great works of philosophy but also as great works of literature:

Plato was an artist as well as a thinker – his dialogues have aesthetic form and dramatic quality, and many connoisseurs regard his prose as the finest Greek prose ever to have been written. Discussing his work with me is one of the leading authorities on Plato in the English-speaking world, Myles Burnyeat, Professor of Ancient Philosophy in the University of Cambridge.

DISCUSSION

Magee You regard, I know, Plato's whole career as a creative philosopher as having somehow been launched by Socrates's death. How did that come about?

Burnyeat I think that Socrates's death in 399 BC must have been a traumatic event for a lot of people. Socrates had been a spell-binding presence around Athens for many many years, much loved, much hated. He had even been caricatured on the comic stage, at a public festival, in front of the whole populace of Athens. Then suddenly the familiar figure is not there any more. The reason he is not there is that he has been condemned to death on a charge of impiety and corrupting the young; the cause of his death was even more distressing for those who loved him than the death itself. He had had a lot of devoted followers and some of them, amongst them Plato, began writing Socratic dialogues: philosophical conversations in which Socrates takes the lead. It must have been like a chorus of voices saying to the Athenians, 'Look, he's not gone after all. He's still here, still asking those awkward questions, still tripping you up with his arguments.' And of course these Socratic dialogues were also defending his reputation and showing that he had been unjustly condemned: he was the great educator of the young, not the great corrupter.

Magee The death of Socrates was not just something that got Plato going and then, later, was put behind him, was it? In a sense the whole of Plato's career has to be explained with reference to Socrates – or, at least, it *can* be.

Burnyeat I think it can. To keep alive the Socratic spirit for Plato meant to go on doing philosophy in the way Socrates had done it. The first result is a group of early dialogues – the most important of them are the *Apology, The Crito,* the *Euthyphro,* the *Laches,* the *Charmides,* the *Protagoras* and the *Gorgias* – which depict Socrates discussing the sorts of questions he was interested in, very largely moral questions. But then, since to do philosophy in the Socratic way means to do it by thinking philosophically, the process gradually leads Plato to develop his own ideas both in ethics and in other areas of philosophy. So there is an evolution in the picture of Socrates. From the gadfly questioner of the early dialogues he gradually turns into someone who expounds weighty theories in politics, metaphysics and methodology. That's the Socrates of the middle-period dialogues: the *Meno*, the *Symposium*, the *Phaedo* and the *Republic*.

Magee In short, in the early dialogues Plato is dealing with subjects that interested Socrates, dealing with them in Socrates's way, and very often, no doubt, putting into Socrates's mouth what Plato knew to be Socrates's opinions. But as the years go by the momentum of Plato's enterprise carries him into dealing with subjects that interest him, Plato, and dealing with them in his own way, and expressing his own opinions – but still mostly through the mouth of Socrates.

Burnyeat I think that's right. Wherever he can plausibly present the ideas as the outgrowth of thinking about Socrates's ideas, they get put into the mouth of Socrates. And I think it's very important that the historical claim that Plato makes about Socrates is that this is a man who thought for himself and taught others to think for themselves. So if you want to be a follower of Socrates, that means thinking for yourself and, if necessary, departing from ideas and areas that Socrates had marked out as his own.

Magee Those early dialogues, in which Socrates is dealing with moral questions, have a certain characteristic pattern. Socrates finds himself talking to some interlocutor who takes it for granted that he knows the meaning of a very familiar term, something like 'friendship' or 'courage' or 'piety'; and by simply quizzing him, interrogating him, submitting him to what has become known as 'Socratic questioning', Socrates shows this person, and, even more importantly, the onlookers, that they do not at all have the clear grasp of the concept which they thought they had. This practice itself has played an important role in philosophy ever since, hasn't it?

Burnyeat Yes indeed. And these very works are still widely used to teach philosophy, and to introduce philosophy to people who want to know something about it. You start with a familiar and important concept – it's always a concept that is important in our lives – and you get people to realise that there are problems in that concept. They try to think about it; they produce an answer; Socrates shows the inadequacy of the answer. You end up not with a firm answer, but with a much better grasp of the problem than you had before. Whether you are a twentieth-century reader or an ancient reader, you have been drawn into the problem; you are left still wanting to get the answer, and feeling that perhaps you can contribute.

Magee It has to be said that after more than two thousand years we are still puzzling about the meaning of 'beauty', 'courage', 'friendship' and other such terms. Have we made any progress?

Burnyeat 'Yes and no' must be the reply, mustn't it? Plato, I think, would be very firmly insistent that even if he did know the answers, if he told us them they wouldn't do us any good. I mean, it's in the nature of these questions that you have to puzzle them out for yourself. An answer is worth nothing unless it has come through your own thinking. And that's why these dialogues are so successful as instruments for drawing you into philosophy.

Magee In those early dialogues (to which we are still confining ourselves, for the moment) one thing Socrates keeps saying is that he has no positive doctrines to teach – that all he is doing is asking questions. There seems to me something disingenuous about this claim: certain unmistakable doc-trines do, it seems to me, emerge from below the surface of these dialogues. Would you agree?

Burnyeat Some doctrines do emerge, not very many. One highly signifi-cant group of ideas comes out in the *Apology*, for instance, when Socrates claims that to a good man no harm can come either during his life or after his death; and again in the *Gorgias* when he argues at great length that injustice harms the doer and justice benefits the doer. What Socrates is saying is that the only real harm is harm to the soul. You may lose all your money or be paralysed by disease, but that is nothing compared to the damage done – by yourself to yourself – if you lead an unjust life. Conversely, there is no gain like that which a good man has from the practice of the virtues, and consequently no loss that he would reckon as harm except the loss of his virtue.
  Now this is a group of ideas which Socrates is very emphatic about; on certain points he will even claim to have knowledge. It is also an area where Plato never reneges on Socrates. He remains convinced of the truth of the proposition that injustice harms the doer and justice benefits him.

Magee So provided your soul remains untouched, worldly misfortunes can't do you any damage of really deep and lasting significance.

Burnyeat That's right. But there is another group of ideas where Socrates does not claim knowledge and where Plato eventually is going to renege on Socrates. This is the group of ideas summed up in the statement that virtue is knowledge. In these early dialogues, when somebody is asked 'What is courage?', 'What is piety?', 'What is justice?', sooner or later as the discussion proceeds the idea emerges that this virtue, be it courage, piety or justice, should be regarded as a kind of knowledge. This suggestion is as strong and paradoxical as the first group of ideas, because common sense – and I mean common sense then as now – ordinarily supposes that it is one thing to have the wisdom to know what it is best to do in a given situation, quite another to have the courage to do it if it involves danger and difficulty, or to have the temperance to resist an easier option instead. Wisdom is one virtue, one quality to admire in a person, courage is another, and temperance a third. And a man may have one of these and not the others, or each of them to different degrees. But if courage just is this knowledge of what it is best to do, then that kind of contrast cannot arise. If I do not do the right thing, it cannot be that I knew what I should do but lacked the courage to carry it out. Rather, if I lacked the courage, I lacked the knowledge; I did not know what the right thing to do was. So any wrongdoing that I do is done in ignorance: done because I did not know it was not the best thing to do. But anything that is done in ignorance is done involuntarily. So, to sum it all up in the slogan for which Socrates is famous, 'No one does wrong willingly'.

Magee For us living in an age after Freud it is scarcely possible to believe that all the sources of action are in the conscious mind, or are even in principle available to the knowledge of the agent. So I don't think anyone nowadays could believe in that particular doctrine of Socrates's.

Burnyeat Well, I think the first thing to be said is that most people did not believe it then either. Socrates was deliberately and knowingly going against common sense. In the *Protagoras* he actually describes his position on courage as one that is contrary to the belief of all mankind. The other side of the coin, though, is that still today there are philosophers who argue vividly that the only thing we have, as it were, to put us into action is our beliefs about what is good and bad; if they won't do the job, what else can there be? There are a lot of people who still find it very hard to acknowledge that there is such a thing as the will or other forces than the cognitive at work in human action.

Magee The dialogue form in which Plato chooses to write gives rise to two important but perhaps insoluble problems. First, to what extent is this the historical Socrates whose views we are being given, and to what extent a dramatic character created by Plato? After all, every one of the dialogues was written after Socrates's death. Second, what are the author's own views? Virtually every opinion expressed is put into the mouth of a character other than Plato.

Burnyeat I think that there is a sense in which we need to worry about

Socrates (c.469–399 BC)

these questions and a sense in which we don't. The sense in which we don't need to worry is that Plato's portrait of Socrates makes the claim: here is a man who thought for himself and who could overthrow long-cherished conclusions if it turned out that they were wrong, and he taught others to do the same. So, if Plato comes to think there is more to virtue than knowledge, though knowledge remains the most important factor – and he does come to think this – then it is completely in keeping with the Socratic spirit to throw over the doctrine that virtue is knowledge and produce a better view of his own in the *Republic*. On the other hand – and this is the sense in which we do need to worry about the questions you raised – it is most important that we notice what is happening when Socrates in the *Republic* says something incompatible with what Socrates said in the *Protagoras*. It is vital to notice that we are getting a new view and how it connects with all the other concerns of the *Republic*: how it makes for a much more complicated picture of moral education, and how it makes possible a new vision of an ideal political society. The important thing is the search and the process of inquiry, but the process must be followed with an alert understanding of where we've got to from where.

Magee In other words, because our assumptions and beliefs are open to perpetual questioning, 'conclusions' don't have any special status. They are merely staging posts on the road to further inquiries.

Burnyeat Yes, I think that is something Plato believed very strongly.

Magee And is demonstrating to us by his practice.

Burnyeat Exactly. And I think he would claim that that was what it was to keep the Socratic spirit alive.

Magee As happens more often with creative artists than with philosophers, it is usual to divide Plato's output into three periods: early, middle and late. So far in this discussion we have confined ourselves to the early dialogues. If we now move forward to the middle period we find Plato for the first time beginning to put forward positive ideas of his own, and of course to argue for those ideas. Which would you say are the most important of Plato's positive doctrines?

Burnyeat I think one has to single out two above all: one is the Theory of Forms, the other is the doctrine that learning is recollection, the idea that to learn something is to recover from within your mind resources of knowledge that you had before you were born.

Magee Let us take the second of those first. A lot of people, when they first hear the suggestion that we are born knowing things, will think it sounds bizarre. But ideas closely related to that have been permanent in our Western culture. Modern idealist philosophers have argued that there must be innate knowledge, or innate ideas. Most of the great religions, I take it, believe something of the sort. Today we even have an eminent thinker such as Chomsky arguing that we are born with a whole grammar programmed into our minds. So a belief of this kind, if seriously argued, is entitled to serious consideration. What was Plato's version of it?

Burnyeat Plato's version was that the knowledge is part of the essential nature of the soul. It is knowledge which your soul possessed before you were born. (This was the period in which he came to believe that the soul exists before birth, its embodiment in our present world being just one of a series of reincarnations.) But I think that to understand the theory of recollection it is necessary to go back to those early Socratic discussions about the definitions of moral concepts.

Let us take the *Laches*, where the question is 'What is courage?'. Laches, the general whom Socrates has asked for a definition of courage, suggests that courage is a kind of endurance. Socrates then asks him some further questions, as he always does when he has been given a definition. He says, 'Is courage invariably a fine and admirable quality?' 'Yes,' says Laches. And then Socrates takes him through a number of examples of endurance where Laches agrees that endurance is not admirable at all, maybe very foolhardy . . .

Magee Pig-headedness, for example . . .

Burnyeat Yes, pig-headedness. Or it may just be morally neutral as when a financier keeps on spending money, enduring the losses because he knows he is going to get a profit in the end. So if endurance can be bad or morally neutral, but courage is always good, then courage cannot be equated with endurance; not even with endurance guided by knowledge. That is a typical pattern of Socratic discussion.

Logically, all that has happened is that Laches has been shown that his beliefs are inconsistent. If we take all his answers together, they contradict one another. This means that they cannot all be true, but it does not by itself tell us *which* of Laches's answers is false. Yet Socrates typically presents the situation as one in which the definition proposed by his interlocutor – here, Laches's proposal that courage is a kind of endurance – has been refuted and shown to be false. In practice, therefore, he takes Laches's secondary answers as either true or somehow nearer the truth than the definition. They are made the basis for refuting the definition and saying 'That's the answer which must be discarded as false'.

Magee You've said something now that is of permanent importance to all serious thought. We all tend to make the assumption that discussion can get at the truth, yet it has no special power to do that. The most that discussion can show us is that our conclusions either are or are not consonant with our premisses. However, even if they are, it still does not follow from this that they are true.

Burnyeat I suppose we are very attached to the idea that by discussion we can get at the truth, although if you think about it, it is actually quite hard to justify. Socrates does not try to justify it. He just asks his questions, gathers the answers to reveal a contradiction, and claims to have refuted the definition. But if one set out to give a theory of what he is doing, then one would have to produce something like the idea we have both pointed to, that everyone has within him the means for making the true vanquish the false. And that is exactly what Plato does in the *Meno*. He produces, as it were, a theory of Socratic or philosophical discussion according to which we all have latent within our minds the knowledge of the correct answers to these questions 'What is courage?', 'What is justice?' and the rest. That knowledge, deep back within us and not immediately accessible, is what enables us to knock down all the wrong answers and show that they are wrong. That knowledge is what is gradually emerging in the stretch of discussion where, as we saw, one thing that Laches says is used to show that some other thing that Laches says must be false.

Magee From previous conversations with you I know that, in your opinion, the doctrine you've just expounded yields the basis for the other of the two most significant doctrines of Plato's middle period, the Theory of Forms. This is far and away the most influential of all Plato's doctrines; indeed, it is what the word 'Platonism' has largely come to mean. Can you explain it?

Burnyeat These Socratic discussions we have been talking about are centred on the quest for a definition: What is the definition of courage? of beauty? of justice? Now, if we have latent within us the knowledge of the answers to these questions, and we have that knowledge independently of and prior to our experience of the world we live in, the world where we use our senses and go around from place to place; if our knowledge is prior to all that, and independent of all that, then surely *what* we know – justice, beauty, courage – must itself be independent of and prior to the empirical world we are now existing in. This latter thesis is the fundamental assertion of the Theory of Forms: justice, beauty and the like exist independently of and prior to all the just actions and just persons, all the beautiful objects and beautiful persons you can find in the sensible world. Beauty and justice exist on their own and apart. That is the Theory of Forms.

Magee The theory that there is another world than this, an ideal world in which everything exists that gives value and meaning to our present world, has had incalculable influence on the whole of our culture, hasn't it?

Burnyeat Yes.

Magee On Christianity, to take only the most important example: the influence of Platonism on Christianity has been prodigious.

Burnyeat That's correct, yes. But I think one should be careful of using phrases like 'the world of Forms' or 'another world'. Plato uses them but the contrast he has in mind is not, as one might have thought, a contrast between one set of particular things and then another set completely like it except more perfect, more abstract and located somewhere else, in some heaven somewhere. His contrast is between the particular and the general. Those questions, 'What is justice?', 'What is beauty?', etc., are general questions, questions about justice and beauty in general. They are not questions about the here and now. That is the contrast we need to understand.

There is a passage in the *Phaedo* where Socrates maintains that to do philosophy is to rehearse for death. It is in fact to practise being dead. [Laughter] Why? Well, because being dead is having one's soul separate from the body, and in doing philosophy you are, so far as you can, separating the soul from the body, precisely because you are not thinking about the here and now where the body is. For if you are asking 'What is justice?' with reference to justice anywhere, any time, justice in itself, you are not asking 'Who did me wrong today or yesterday?' If you are asking 'What is beauty?', you are not asking 'Who is the most beautiful person in this room?' And if you are not thinking about the here and now, then, in the sense Plato is interested in, you are not here and now. You are where your mind is, not because you are in some other particular place but a better one, but because you are not in place in that sense at all. You are immersed in generalities. So, it is all right to use the phrase 'the world of Forms', provided one understands it to mean the realm of invariable generalities.

Magee These middle-period dialogues we're talking about now – the *Meno*, the *Phaedo*, the *Republic*, the *Symposium*, the *Phaedrus* – were written by Plato at the height of his powers. So I think this is a good moment for us to pause and consider their literary and other aesthetic qualities. Why are they regarded as supreme works of literary art?

Burnyeat They are so alive. Other philosophers have tried writing dialogues, in both ancient and modern times – Xenophon, Cicero, Augustine, Berkeley, Hume. But the only name on the list who comes anywhere near Plato is Hume. And I think this is because for Hume, like Plato, it's the process of philosophical thinking that counts at least as much as the answers. With Xenophon or Berkeley it is all too clear that you are reading somebody who cares about the answers, not the process of journeying toward them. Where Plato is concerned, we have to add his great mastery and range of language, from high-flown, imaginative descriptions to austere analysis or jokes and witty repartee. Add that he is terribly good at making crystal clear the most difficult thoughts. You can go on adding. In the end one is left saying that he is an artistic genius as well as a philosophical one.

Magee Do you share the traditional view that his masterpiece is the *Republic*?

Burnyeat Yes, I do.

Magee Why?

Burnyeat I think because it is in the *Republic* more than anywhere else that Plato makes good his belief that every question is connected with every other; the inquiry need never stop, because every 'conclusion for now' leads on to the next problem. Thus he begins with a straightforward question, 'What is justice?', a familiar Socratic kind of question. That leads on to the question 'Is justice a benefit to its possessor?' The central task of the *Republic* is in fact to show that justice is a benefit to its possessor; it is what you need most of all if you are to be happy, whereas the unjust man is the most miserable of all creatures.

But to show all this he finds that he has to give a theory of human nature. He divides the soul into three parts: this is where he reneges on Socrates's thesis that virtue is knowledge. Virtue turns out to involve more than knowledge, though knowledge must be in control. And the idea that knowledge is something that can and should be in control of the non-rational factors in the soul also makes possible the idea of a whole society in which knowledge is in control. So we get a political theory which depicts a new and better way of life in society. At the same time, the emphasis placed on the idea of knowledge being in control raises the question, 'What knowledge should be in control, and what is knowledge anyway, and why is it better than opinion?' So we are given a theory of knowledge, and the theory of knowledge broadens out to become an inquiry into the sciences. There is an elaborate discussion of mathematics. A whole vision of what it would be to have a full understanding of the

Plato (c.427–347 BC)

world we live in is produced in order to support the claim that this understanding really is what should be in charge of ourselves, both individually and in society; this understanding will bring the benefits of justice both to the individual soul and to society at large.

With so much growing out of this one question 'What is justice?', the only natural conclusion is the vision of the after-life and the myth of Er at the end of the book. You might say that the *Republic* enacts a conviction that inquiry really does not cease until death.

Magee The *Republic* is such a rich book that it is not feasible for us in this discussion to pursue the individual strands that go to make it up. But it is unquestionably one of the most influential books in the whole history of our culture, and I hope our discussion will stimulate some people to read it.

Let us move on now to Plato's later dialogues. Just as the move from the early to the middle-period dialogues revealed one change of character, so the move from the middle to the late dialogues reveals another. Suddenly, they become less literary, less dramatic, less colourful, and more what we in our own time might call analytic, even academic. Why is that?

Burnyeat In my view they are not actually less dramatic. What happens is that the irony and imagery and other artistic resources which in previous works went into depicting the people undertaking the discussion are now devoted to bringing alive the ideas and arguments themselves. Very often they are ideas and arguments that are familiar to us from Plato's own earlier works, such as the *Republic* or the *Phaedo*. One of the extraordinary things about Plato – he may have been the first writer in history able to do this – is that he established a relationship with his readers such that when writing one work he can take it for granted that his readers have read his previous works. He uses the relationship not only to make allusions and build up resonances, but also to create surprises when he departs from his readers' expectations. But what he most splendidly does with it is conduct a sort of public self-scrutiny of his own earlier ideas, relying on us the readers to recognise them, but saying, so to speak, 'Don't get too enthused by the *Phaedo* and the *Republic*. It was all very fine stuff, I know, but those truths, if truths they were, are no good to you or to me if we can't defend them against criticism. And maybe they weren't truths anyway. Maybe they were all wrong. So let's take a few of them and subject them to really hard analytical criticism.'

Magee If you had to single out one of the later dialogues for special mention, which would it be?

Burnyeat The prime example is the *Parmenides*, where the tables are turned on Socrates. Socrates puts forward the Theory of Forms as he stated it in the *Phaedo*. It is unmistakably the *Phaedo*, not only from the content, but also because there are verbal echoes of the *Phaedo* which Plato clearly expects his readers to pick up and say to themselves, 'Gosh, the Socrates of the *Phaedo* is now on the receiving end of the questions.' And in fact old Parmenides, who is quizzing Socrates in this dialogue, produces a series of objections and criticisms of the Theory of Forms which many philosophers, from Aristotle onwards, have thought to be quite devastating. But Plato does not tell us the answer. He produces the criticisms, through the mouthpiece of Parmenides, and leaves us to decide for ourselves whether they are fair or unfair, and if they are fair, what we should do with the Theory of Forms.

Magee A dialogue which some people think is late and others think is of the middle period is the *Timaeus*. It stands aside from the others, partly because it contains more cosmology and science than philosophy, but mostly because it also contains a wonderfully poetic creation myth – not all that dissimilar to the one in the Book of Genesis. Why did Plato produce such a thing? What I have chiefly in mind in asking that question is this: do you think he believed in his creation story literally, in the way one must assume the ancient Hebrews believed in the Book of Genesis?

Burnyeat I myself think that he did not believe it literally. The question was controversial in ancient times, but Plato's closest associates took the view that Timaeus's narrative of the divine craftsman imposing order on chaos is a vivid way of presenting an analysis of what Plato took to be the fundamental structure of the whole universe. He wanted to see the entire universe as the product of order imposed on disorder, and by order he meant above all mathematical order. This, of course, is very different from the Book of Genesis. Plato's divine craftsman is mathematical intelligence at work in the world.

Magee So it's really a poetic way of explaining the intelligibility of the world, which has been a mystery for reflective human beings from the earliest times until now?

Burnyeat Right. And of course such a very general proposition as the proposition that the whole universe is the product of imposing order on disorder is not something you can prove either in general or in all its detailed ramifications. Plato is well aware of this; it is a further reason for his clothing the proposition in a myth. All the same, the myth served as the guiding inspiration for something that Plato was very serious about indeed: a research programme for which he enlisted at the Academy the leading mathematicians of his day. Every advance in geometry, in mathematical astronomy, in mathematical harmonics, even a medical theory which exhibits disease and health as resulting from the proportions between the constituent elements in the body – each such step forward is further proof of something Plato cared deeply about, the idea that mathematical regularities and harmonies and proportions are what explain things. And since these mathematical harmonies and proportions are for Plato the prime examples of goodness and beauty, this is a scientific research programme which is designed to show that goodness and beauty are the fundamental explanatory factors in the world at large.

Magee How does this fit in with the *Republic*? I ask that because when you were talking about the *Republic* a moment ago, one of the things you brought out very clearly was that it constituted, in a sense, a fully worked-out philosophy. If this is so, how does what Plato says in the *Timaeus* fit into it?

Burnyeat I think it fits as a hand fits into a glove. What you have in the *Republic* is the sketch of a programme for a scientific, above all a mathematically scientific, understanding of the world. In the *Timaeus* Plato begins to carry it out, do his share of the work. Indeed the *Timaeus* was the dialogue people went to for *the* statement of Plato's philosophy both in antiquity and for a long time afterwards. It is a comparatively more recent trend to take the *Republic* to be the major work of Plato. For a long time it was the *Timaeus*.

Magee The cosmology and science in the *Timaeus*, then, are the practical working out of some of the possibilities canvassed in the *Republic*?

Burnyeat Yes. The *Timaeus* presents itself in its introduction as a discussion which, dramatically speaking, is a continuation of the discussion in the *Republic*. What is more, the research programme, as I called the *Republic*'s recommendations for progress in the mathematical sciences – this programme was actually carried out by the leading mathematicians whom Plato gathered in the Academy to demonstrate the power and scope of mathematical order. From their efforts stem many of the greatest achievements of Greek mathematical science down to Ptolemy. Ptolemy's astronomy is the ultimate descendant of the astronomy done in the Academy with the backing of Plato's recommendations for the sciences. And since mathematical order is the expression for Plato of goodness and beauty, these sciences which show us the world as mathematically intelligible are simultaneously sciences of value. That is how the metaphysical aspects of the *Republic* – everything that makes up the content of the understanding which the philosopher-rulers must acquire – can simultaneously be the foundation for a radical new kind of politics.

What the philosophers are learning before they come to rule the rest of us are sciences of value as well as fact.

Magee You are known as an expert on one of the later dialogues in particular, the *Theaetetus*. Why do you take a special interest in it?

Burnyeat Because I find it endlessly exciting and I have never plumbed to the bottom – every time I go back to it there seems to be more to discover. It is a dialogue which Leibniz translated, Berkeley wrote quite a lot about, Wittgenstein quoted – in short, a dialogue which philosophers have always found stimulating.

Magee What is it about?

Burnyeat The question is 'What is knowledge?' and the dialogue is the kind of Socratic discussion that went on in the earlier dialogues, but on a much grander scale. Three answers are given: knowledge is perception, knowledge is true judgment, knowledge is true judgment together with an account. Each of these answers is knocked down in true Socratic style. We are not told what Plato thinks knowledge is at the end, but we have learnt such an enormous amount about the problem and about the ramifications of the problem that we go away feeling the richer rather than the poorer.

Magee No consensus has been reached to this day as to what the precise nature of knowledge is; but I suppose the nearest we come to a generally accepted view is remarkably close to what you have just said: the judgments that constitute knowledge must be derived ultimately from perception, but we also have to be able to provide a rational justification for them.

Burnyeat Ah. You have now produced an interesting solution to the problem we are left with at the end of the dialogue, when all of those answers have been knocked down one by one. Socrates has refuted the thesis that knowledge is perception, refuted the thesis that knowledge is true judgment, refuted the thesis that knowledge is true judgment with an account. And now you are suggesting that perhaps we can get a definition of knowledge by somehow putting all the elements of the three separate definitions together into one, making a theory of knowledge yield the definition of knowledge. That would be a highly suitable response to this kind of dialogue – to suggest a definition of one's own in terms of what one has learnt from the dialogue.

Magee Before we bring this discussion to an end we must say something about the after-life of Plato's ideas. His philosophy, after all, has been as influential as any in the whole of history. Can you give some indication of what the main lines of that influence have been?

Burnyeat I think it is important to remember that in the ancient world there were two philosophies opposed to materialism. Materialism itself took the form of the Atomism held by Democritus and later by Epicurus. Plato and Artistotle are both anti-materialist philosophers. Both are opposed to the idea that everything – life, order, mind, civilisation, art, nature – can be explained as the outcome of the movements of particles of matter subject just to the laws of motion and their own nature. But Aristotle's opposition carries the war so far into the enemy camp that it is actually very hard to reconcile the Aristotelian philosophy with the modern scientific enterprise, which has much to say about atoms and the movements of particles of matter and the like. Presumably it was no accident that when the modern scientific enterprise got going, it did so by throwing away the Aristotelianism which had so dominated the Middle Ages. Platonism, by contrast, is much easier to reconcile with the modern scientific enterprise, which is why, I think, Platonism lived on in the Renaissance and later, after the death of Aristotelianism. Platonism is a philosophy you can use or be influenced by if you are seeking to show how scientific and spiritual values can be reconciled. If you want to do justice to the complexities, where materialism is giving too simplistic a story, Plato is the philosopher you can go to for ammunition and help.

Magee For us in the twentieth century there is something peculiarly contemporary about the fact that, in the programme it puts forward for acquiring an understanding of the world, Plato's philosophy gives a central role to mathematical physics.

Burnyeat Yes. What Plato aspired to do, modern science has actually done. And so there is a sort of innate sympathy between the two which does not hold for Aristotle's philosophy.

ARISTOTLE

Dialogue with
MARTHA NUSSBAUM

INTRODUCTION

Magee Our view of the philosophy of the ancient world is dominated by the writings of two figures, Plato and Aristotle. Plato is the first philosopher whose works have come down to us in the form in which he wrote them, and Aristotle was his star pupil. There is an extraordinary line of personal succession here, for just as Aristotle was a pupil of Plato, so Plato had been a pupil of Socrates. It is doubtful whether there has been to this day another philosopher whose influence has exceeded that of any one of these three.

Aristotle, son of the court physician to the King of Macedon, was born in Stagira in 384 BC. He was sent to Athens to be educated, and at the age of seventeen became one of the pupils at Plato's Academy. He stayed there for twenty years, until Plato's death in 347 BC. He was then uprooted, and spent his next twelve years in political exile. During this period he was primarily absorbed in biological researches (and was even, for a short period, tutor to Alexander the Great). Then he returned to Athens, and for a further twelve years taught at a school which he founded himself, the Lyceum. Then he had to go into exile again – but died only a year later, in 322 BC, at the age of sixty-two.

Only about one-fifth of Aristotle's work has survived, but even that fills twelve volumes and touches on the whole range of the available knowledge of his time. Sadly, all those works which he himself prepared for publication – and which were praised throughout antiquity for their beauty of style – have been lost. All we have is what he wrote up from his lecture notes, and this has none of the literary art of what we possess of Plato's writings. Even so, there can be no doubting the quality – or the influence – of its content. Discussing it with me is someone who established a reputation very young in Aristotle scholarship, Professor Martha Nussbaum, of Brown University in the United States.

DISCUSSION

Magee Perhaps the best way to start is by your quickly drawing a sketch-map for us of the ground covered by Aristotle's output as a whole.

Nussbaum We have here a philosophical achievement of tremendous range and complexity. We have fundamental work in logic and all the sciences of his day, including especially the science of biology, where his contribution was unmatched for a thousand years. Then work on the general foundations of scientific explanation; work in general philosophy of nature; work in metaphysics, including the questions of substance, identity, and continuity; work on life and the mental faculties. And finally we have terrific work in ethics and political theory, and work in rhetoric and the theory of literature.

Magee It is an amazing fact, isn't it, that over this incomparable range he was regarded as *the* authority for hundreds of years during the Middle Ages? In fact the greatest philosopher of the late Middle Ages, Thomas Aquinas, used to refer to him simply as 'the philosopher'.

Nussbaum Yes; and I think this gives us a great difficulty in approaching Aristotle's thought. We're so used to thinking of him, as you say, as an Authority, as *the* philosopher, Dante's 'master of those who know', sitting on his throne. And I think this prevents us from seeing that Aristotle was really one of the most flexible and open-ended of philosophers, one who sees philosophy as an ongoing attempt to attend to all the complexities of human experience, who never rests content, but is always searching for ever more adequate ways to bring that complexity into his thought.

Magee Across this great range of output, is there any unifying factor, any consistent mode of approach, that one can point to?

Nussbaum Yes, I think there is. Aristotle tells us that 'in every area' the philosopher has got to begin by setting down what he calls the 'appearances'; then, after working through the puzzles that these present us with, he must come back to the 'appearances', saving, as he puts it, the 'greatest number and the most basic'. To show you what this means, let me give you an example. Suppose you're a philosopher working on the problem of time. Now what you'll do, according to Aristotle, is begin by setting down the 'appearances' about time, that is, what appears to us to be the case concerning time. Under this heading he includes not only our perceptual experience concerning temporal succession and duration, but also our ordinary beliefs and what we say concerning time. It's important to stress this, since his notion of 'appearances' has sometimes been misinterpreted in a rather narrow way: he has been taken to mean data of perception merely, or 'observed facts'. Unfortunately, this misunderstanding has made its way into many standard English translations, so that it's hard for the reader to appreciate sufficiently Aristotle's tremendous interest in ordinary language and belief. Now: you'll set all this down, then you'll see whether it presents you with any contradictions. If you find contradictions there, then you go to work sifting and sorting things out. If you can't remove the contradictions, you'll try to decide which of our beliefs are actually more basic and more central than others; and you'll preserve those and then get rid of the ones that conflict with them, so you come back in the end to ordinary discourse with increased structure and understanding.

Magee Time, or anything else, isn't the same as what we say about it.

Does Aristotle make a clear distinction between the world and our discourse about the world?

Nussbaum Well, as I said, his notion of 'appearances' is a broad and general notion of experience, of how the world strikes us. This covers both our perceptual experience of the world and our ordinary sayings and beliefs. It's a broad conception, and one that admits of a lot of further subdivisions; certainly Aristotle is perfectly prepared to say that sometimes we will rely more on the experience of our senses and sometimes more on ordinary beliefs and sayings. But I think he's right to think that there's a general unifying notion here. His idea, which I believe to be a very plausible one, is that perception, like belief, is interpretive and selective; the way we perceive things is an inseparable part of our conceptual framework, and of the manner in which, as human beings, we make sense of the world.

Magee Isn't there a danger that this approach might turn out a little unadventurous? If he always starts from the familiar, and always returns to it in the end, isn't the whole of his philosophy confined to the surface of things – the surface both of the world and of our experience – when what we need is more like what Plato gives us, a philosophy that gets behind the surfaces (or below the surfaces) to a deeper, more underlying level, compared with which the surface is, indeed, superficial?

Nussbaum I think you're right to bring Plato in here. It's certainly true that for Plato, and a great part of the Greek philosophical tradition that preceded Plato, the dominant image of philosophy is one of 'going behind' or getting 'out there'. Plato imagines the philosopher's mind walking to the rim of the universe and staring beyond at a transcendent reality that's above and beyond our experience. But Aristotle would, I think, have two things to say about that. First of all, he would say that our ordinary experience is an object of tremendous wonder, richness and beauty in its own right. We do not *need* to go beyond it in order to find something that's worth doing philosophy about. Then, second, he would say that actually we never can coherently go beyond our experience: the only project that we can really undertake and meaningfully pursue is the investigating, the mapping, of the sphere of our experience. Now let me give you an example of how he argues this point. There is a fundamental principle in Aristotle's thought which he calls the Principle of Non-Contradiction. This is the principle that contradictory properties cannot apply to the same subject at the same time in the same respect. For example, my dress cannot be both blue and not blue at the same time in the same place in the same respect, and so forth. Now Aristotle says, plausibly, that this is a very basic principle; in fact, 'the most secure starting point of all'. It's so basic that we seem to use it whenever we think and speak. Now how do we go about justifying such a fundamental principle, one that is the most basic of all, as he puts it? If we can see how he handles this problem, we can get a clearer understanding of his claim that philosophy must confine itself to experience. In *Metaphysics* IV he tells us that we can't justify the Principle of Non-Contradiction from outside our experience because we use it in all our experience, in sorting out experience. But, he now says, suppose that an opponent challenges it. There *is* something we can say to such a person. First of all, Aristotle says, you must find out whether the opponent is prepared to say anything to you, anything definite at all. Now, suppose he doesn't say anything: well then, Aristotle says, you can dismiss that person: because 'a person who doesn't say anything, in so far as he doesn't say anything, is pretty well like a vegetable'. Well now, he continues, suppose on the other hand the opponent does say something, and it's something definite. Then, says Aristotle, you can show that person that in saying anything definite at all he or she is in fact making use of the very principle that is being challenged – because in order to make a definite assertion you've got to be at the same time ruling something out, at the very least the contradictory of what you asserted in the first place.

Magee It is easy to see how fundamental logical principles such as this are inherent in all our discourse, but not how they could provide a foundation for the kind of knowledge about the world that Aristotle was seeking.

Nussbaum What Aristotle is eager to say here is only that we cannot provide, for any principle, a foundation that stands altogether outside of our discourse and our conceptual scheme. If the very most basic principle is internal to experience in this sense, and not, as Plato would have it, 'out there', then this must all the more be true of principles we use that are less firmly grounded than the basic ones. Principles are justified by their position in experience, by the role they play inside experience, not by anything completely external. What is completely external cannot enter into our discourse and thought, and thus cannot be anything to us at all. Aristotle gives further support for this position when he elaborates his general account of discourse. This account holds that we can designate a thing in speech only when it has actually impinged on the experience of one of us, of at least some part of our linguistic community. For example, he says, we can designate thunder in speech (refer to it, we might say) only when someone has heard a noise in the clouds. At that point, on the basis of that experience, we are able to use the name 'thunder' to refer to that noise, even if we don't yet know anything about what the noise is and what caused it. And from that starting point we can begin asking 'What is that noise we have been hearing there? What explains it?' And we can then go on to inquire about what it really is. But now suppose we tried to stand altogether outside of our experience and to talk about, even to base our inquiries and explanations upon, some entity or entities that actually had never entered the experience of any human being at all. Then, says Aristotle, the problem will be that because these items do not have any connection with experience, we cannot refer to them or talk meaningfully about them. Let's take for example Plato's Forms. These are entities that exist completely on their own; as such, in their own pure nature, they have never entered our experience. And yet all genuine understanding of the world is supposed to be based on them. To criticise this enterprise, Aristotle takes as his example the Form of White, which is said to be just pure whiteness: not the white *of* anything, not the colour *of* any body, but just unattached pure white, out there, 'itself by itself'. To go on talking like that, Aristotle now says, is not only unhelpful and unexplanatory, it is meaningless nonsense talk. We cannot refer to pure unattached whiteness, since white in all our experience is the colour *of* some body. At this point he gets rather rude with Plato and brusquely says, 'So goodbye to Plato's Forms. For they are no more meaningful than singing "La la la" – they have nothing to do with our speech.'

Magee If Aristotle thinks that profitable inquiry has to confine itself solely to the world of actual or possible experience, what, specifically, is 'philosophical' about it? Does not the whole of his programme fall under the rubric of what we now call science?

Nussbaum Well, Aristotle does not in fact make a sharp distinction between science and philosophy. But he believes that there is a general search for explanations, and a general account of the structure of explanation, that are common to all theoretical inquiries. (Here he explicitly excludes ethics and politics, which do not, in his view, have this same hierarchical structure.) In his work the *Posterior Analytics*, he provides an account of how the philosopher will search for what he calls *episteme*, or scientific understanding, in every area. In every area of theoretical investigation the philosopher is supposed to find certain principles that are prior, more basic, more securely known than the others; from these, as conclusions of a deductive argument, the conclusions of that science will follow. He believes that we have a faculty by which we are equipped to have insight into the fundamental first principles. I want to pause here for a minute because I think this is also something that has been badly misunderstood about Aristotle. This is a faculty which is called intellect or *nous*, *nous* being one of several Greek words for intellect or mind – a word that is usually associated with intuitive understanding or insight, rather than with discursive reasoning. Aristotle says that it is with this faculty of mind that we grasp first principles. Now for centuries this was thought to be a special faculty of pure intellectual intuition by which we could step outside the sphere of our experience and apprehend, as it were prior to all experience, the first principles of science. Now I think you can see already why I believe that Aristotle would be opposed to that kind of foundation for science. But in fact recently people who have been working on the interpretation of the *Posterior Analytics* have argued quite successfully that it is also a bad reading of the text – that, in reality, what *nous* is is a kind of insight we get into the explanatory role, the fundamental status, of a principle by our experience in using it to give scientific explanations.

Magee   Aristotle was the first major Western thinker to try to map out the separate sciences – in fact he gave to some of them the names which we use to this day.

Nussbaum   Yes, I think that's true, and I think his work has still been of importance for people working in those sciences, particularly in the science of biology, where his work on explanation has recently come to be recognised as extremely important and interesting.

Magee   Can you give an example of the way he would go about identifying and isolating a subject area as a single field of inquiry?

Nussbaum   I'm going to give an example not from one of the sciences, as we think of them, but from a very general inquiry that he conducts in his work on metaphysics: the inquiry into what he calls substance.

Magee   Can you first explain the word 'metaphysics', which is bound to crop up in subsequent discussions?

Nussbaum   Well, its origin is disappointingly trivial. In an ancient edition of Aristotle's work, the editor put the work that now has the title *Metaphysics* after the work that was called *Physics*: and the editor gave it the title *Metaphysics* because in Greek that simply means what comes after the work called *Physics*.

Magee   'The book after the book on physics'. But because of the contents of that book the word 'metaphysics' has since come to have a special meaning in philosophy, hasn't it?

Nussbaum   Well, it's hard to give a single account of this. But roughly one might say, I think, that what metaphysics does is not to isolate one range of things and inquire into just those, but to pursue some perfectly general questions that might be asked about anything whatever. Questions about identity, continuity, logical form and so forth.

Magee And also questions about such fundamental constituents of our experience as space, time, matter, causality, and so on . . .

Nussbaum Yes . . . questions that pertain to any object at all – whatever exists. Now central in this whole project is the question which Aristotle calls the question about substance.

I want to start here by trying to ask what this question means, because I think we don't very naturally have an intuitive sense about what a question about 'substance' could possibly be. Now if we read what Aristotle writes and try to reconstruct what his questions are, I think we find that there are really two questions which he holds together quite closely in the substance inquiry. The first is a question about change, and the second is a question about identity. The question about change is this. In our experience we come in contact all the time with things that are changing. A leaf unfolds, is green, turns yellow, then withers; a child is born, matures, grows older, finally dies. Now the question is: if we're to talk about these changing things, there still must be some *It* that remains the same while the attributes of the thing are changing. Otherwise it will be very difficult for us to talk about change at all. Change, paradoxically, requires stability. So the question that Aristotle asks here is, what are the more continuous, more persisting things on which we can anchor our discourse about change, things which themselves persist while properties or attributes are changing?

Aristotle's second question is the one that he calls the 'What is it?' question; I've called it the question about identity. It goes like this. Suppose I point at some object in my experience, say Bryan Magee, and I say: 'All right, what is this really?' What I am asking here is: Which among the many properties of you that impress themselves on my senses are the most fundamental ones, the ones that you couldn't cease to have without ceasing to be yourself? Now clearly you could change your jacket, put on a different colour of clothing, and you would still be Bryan Magee. On the other hand it's not so clear that you could cease to be human or cease to be made of flesh and blood without ceasing to be yourself, without in fact being dead. So Aristotle's question about identity is the search for the parts or elements in the thing which do play that very fundamental role, which are what it is to be that thing.

Magee The same parts or elements have to play two roles, don't they? Let me reverse the order of your questions. Question one is: Which are the characteristics that are fundamental and indispensable to any object, in that it is they that make it the object that it is? Question two is: What

Aristotle (384–322 BC)

are the characteristics of an object that persist through change, so that the object, though changing, remains the same object?

Nussbaum Yes. Aristotle wants to hold these questions tightly together. And I think there's a good reason for that. As he sees it, to single out what it is that underlies change, that persists through change, you have to single out something with a definite identity, something about which you could answer the 'What is it?' question, something that is structured enough, definite enough, to be the subject of some discourse about change. On the other hand if we're going to talk about the 'What is it?' question we'd better have as our answer something that itself is persistent enough, not always going out of existence while we're actually talking about what it is. Now early philosophers before Aristotle had not always held these questions so closely together: frequently they had focused on one and given strange answers, as a result, to the other. Let me give you two examples. Some early natural philosophers were led to say that what things really are is matter, just because it looked to them as if matter was the most persistent stuff. They could see that trees, children, animals were born out of material stuff and that when they died what was left around was again material stuff. From this they concluded that matter was the basic underlying principle of change; and then they seemed to conclude from this that matter was also what things really are in some fundamental way. So they took an answer to the first question and then without much further reflection they applied it, plugged it in, to the second one. Now on the other side is an explanation given by some Platonist theories – I won't say by Plato himself, but it is one that Aristotle finds in Plato's school – which focuses on the identity question and tries to explain the identities of things in terms of their relation to certain stable immaterial objects, the famous Platonic Forms, in something like this way. They'll say, for example: you, Bryan Magee, are brown in colour because of your relation to the Form of the brown; you are human because of some relation in which you stand to the Form of the human, and so forth. These Forms are universals, abstract objects existing apart from the particulars they explain. Now it's Aristotle's view that we've got to start, in answering this second person – I'm going to talk about the second person, the Platonist, first and then come back to the materialists – we've got to start by distinguishing two kinds of properties: properties you *have*, and properties that are what it is to *be* for you. The property of having brown colour on you is a property that, precisely, you *have*: brown colour is just *on* you, residing with you; it isn't *you*. That is, it is an attribute that you could easily lose without ceasing to be yourself; whereas the property of being human is not like that. It's not one that you could lose without ceasing to be yourself. If you changed into a baboon, you would no longer be yourself. So in Aristotle's early work, the *Catego-*

ries, he distinguishes these two sorts of properties, the ones that are simply 'in' the subject and the ones that, as he puts it, reveal the being, the what-is-it, of the subject.

Magee Can I make an interpolation here? I think it's worth interrupting at this point to bring out the fact that the overall approach we are considering is one which, on the face of it, makes it possible to describe any reality. First of all you pick out something, anything – it can be a dog, a table, a person, any material object, anything else you like: you identify something, and then you say something about it: either you attribute characteristics to it or you describe it as doing something (or as having something done to it). This subject-predicate approach – first identify a subject, then predicate something of it – has been believed by many people since to make possible the description of everything. In fact for a long time it seemed to be built into both our language and our logic. I know this isn't the point you were making, but I mention it here because it has been important in philosophy ever since.

Nussbaum Yes, but I think what Aristotle here wants to insist on is that not all predicates are on the same level; that there are some which are predicated of a subject that we've already picked out and identified, just as I pick you out, then predicate 'brown' of you. But there are these other ones, like 'human being' or 'dog' or 'tree', which are fundamental in identifying the subject in the first place. We cannot, he thinks, pick out a bare subject and tag predicates on to it. The subject itself has to be identified and picked out under some description, which so to speak reveals what that thing is; and it's natural kind terms that play the fundamental role here. It's only when I have picked you out as a human being that I can go on to say what else is true of you: that you are wearing brown, sitting on a couch, and so forth. I could not begin by picking out the brown, or the sitting, all by themselves, without attaching them to some definite kind of thing like a human being.

But of course we still haven't answered the materialists at this point. And we still haven't said, *in* the notion of human being, what is the fundamental analysis of that notion that will really give us the what-is-it of the subject. We have not yet ruled out the possibility that the proper analysis of what it is to be human will be along lines that the materialists would favour; that to be human is to be made up out of such-and-such materials. In short, we have so far said nothing about matter and its relation to other aspects of humanness, such as structure and activity. So Aristotle turns next to this problem.

Magee And of course the 'What is it?' question also applies to everything, doesn't it? It is Aristotle's attempt to discover the true nature of the identity of things, including us.

Nussbaum Yes, it is. And I think living substances and to some extent also artefacts play a very central role here, as the most basic, most definite, unitary, persisting *and* identifiable subjects. What he wants to ask now is: all right, we've gotten to the point where we see that concepts that we call natural kind concepts, concepts like human being, dog or tree, say, play a fundamental role in identifying subjects in the world. Now we have to ask more precisely what they *are*. What is it to be a human being? Is it to be a certain sort of material? Or is it to be a certain structure? And in the *Metaphysics* he argues that what a substance is is fundamentally not some material stuffs or constituents, but rather a certain sort of order or structure, which he calls its form. Now by that he doesn't mean simply shape or configuration, but he means in the case of, say, Bryan Magee, the way you're organised to function. Your form is an organised set of functional capabilities that you've got to have so long as you're in existence.

He gives us three reasons for thinking that your materials couldn't be what it is to be you.

First of all, in the case of you and other living things, matter is always going in and out, it's always changing. And of course you do change your material constituents very often without ceasing to be yourself. But second, even if that's not the case, say with an artefact, our conception of an artefact is that so long as its functional structure remains the same we *could* always replace bits of the matter without having a different thing on our hands. We could take a ship and replace some of its planks. So long as it remained that same continuous functional structure, serving the function of a ship, we would still have the same entity on our hands. Finally he argues that matter is just not definite enough to be what a thing really is. Matter is just a lump or heap of stuff, and so we couldn't say *you* are some stuff or other: it's only when we've identified the structure the stuff constitutes that we can even go on to say something intelligent about the stuff itself.

Magee Aristotle's arguments here are of such fundamental and permanent importance that I'd like to go over them again. His first argument applies to individuals as individuals, and for his example he points to Socrates the man. Socrates, he says, cannot consist of the matter that goes to make up his body, because this is constantly changing – in fact it changes in its entirety several times during the course of Socrates's life. Yet he goes on being the same Socrates throughout that life. So he cannot be just the matter of which he consists. Aristotle's second argument applies to individuals as members of a species. A dog cannot be a dog in virtue of the matter of which it consists, because different dogs consist of different matter. Furthermore they are of different weights, different shapes, different sizes, different colours, and so on, each of which characteristics has a material basis; and yet they are all dogs. So they cannot be dogs in virtue of the matter of which they consist. And Aristotle's third argument is that a heap of matter without any formal qualities such as organisation or structure is not a person or a dog at all. It is not any *thing*, it is just a heap. Things can be things at all only by virtue of their differentiating structure. And that again is what Aristotle calls their form.

Nussbaum   Your second point adds a further argument that I didn't mention. But it's one that certainly might be used to support Aristotle's position. And there's some evidence that he actually does use that argument as well. Yes, the different species members are all differently constituted materially. Spheres can be made, as Aristotle once said, of bronze, of wood, of many different materials. The same is true of most artefacts: so long as the material is suitable for the thing's function or activity, it doesn't matter what it is. Being made of wood, as Aristotle again says, is no part of what it is to be a bed. In a much more limited way, the same seems to be true of living things: their material composition varies from individual to individual. No two dogs have precisely the same amounts of the different materials in them, and so *no list of materials will tell us exactly what it is to be a dog*. We can make the same point by focusing on particular functions of living things. What it is to see red, to think of Aristotle's *Metaphysics*, to want a steak, will be made up *out of* matter every time it is realised in a living creature; but the precise material formula will vary, in such a way that no list of specific materials will give us, across every case, exactly what it is to see red, to think of Aristotle's *Metaphysics*, to want a steak. All this seems to Aristotle to show that being bronze, or wood, or whatever, cannot be an essential part of what it is to be a certain sort of thing. What things are, is form or structure. Matter is what constitutes them, or makes them up.

But now I wanted, with *my* second argument, which was different from yours, to add another point. That even when the matter of a thing does not vary during the course of its career – or, we might also add, even when all the existing members of a certain type are in fact made of the same matter – still, our conception of what it is to be a certain sort of thing, say a ship, doesn't identify it with the matter. We can see that by performing a thought experiment. Imagine replacing the material bits of a thing gradually, while preserving continuity of functional capability. Then I think we will agree that you continue to have one and the same thing on your hands.

Magee   Doesn't this bring Aristotle dangerously close to Plato's Theory of Forms – which he has rejected? Is he not saying that a dog is a dog by virtue of its canine Form? And that this canine Form is one and the same thing common to all dogs, the single entity by virtue of which they *are* dogs, and are *all* dogs?

Nussbaum Well, of course here we get to a very difficult area about what exactly Form is; and I think no two philosophers are going to be in precise agreement about the interpretation of Aristotle on this question. The textual evidence presents many problems. But let me try to say what I think. I think that first of all it's quite clear that, unlike Plato, Aristotle makes the Form something immanent to the particular. It does not exist as a thing apart from that particular perceptible dog in some heavenly realm of dogness, but it's just there; it's what in fact the dog is. It's not separate from the dog. This, I think, is uncontroversial if anything on this topic is.

Magee So the dog's Form does not exist in some other-worldly dimension inhabited also by other Forms.

Nussbaum Right. It's there; it's what the dog really is. It *is that dog*. Now the second thing, which is vastly more controversial: I believe that Aristotelian Forms are individuals. That is, they are particulars and not universals. That is to say, even though the definition of the doggy Form of each dog will be the same, so that if I take five dogs, I'm going to get only one definition of what it is to be a dog for all of them, still, if I ask how many *examples* of doggy Form I have here, well, the answer is five. I mean, just as many dogs as there are. Each one, although quite like in its essential quality, in Form, will be exactly 'one in number', as he puts it. We count Forms by counting the number of substances that we have on our hands.

Magee Even well over two thousand years later it seems to me that the best of Aristotle's arguments against materialism are devastating. Do you think they have ever been effectively answered by materialists?

Nussbaum No, I don't think they have. And what I find so powerful about these arguments is that Aristotle starts arguing against materialism not only within the context of philosophy of mind, and not only by picking out some special characteristics of the mental which make it different from everything else, but precisely here in general metaphysics, by developing these general theories of identity and substance which show why for things quite generally, including artefacts, material reductionism is not a good way to go.

Magee Can you now give us an example of an area in which Aristotle puts this approach to work, and identifies in some specific field what sorts of things there are?

Nussbaum Well now I think we can turn to an area that's very close to his general metaphysics, since his general metaphysics is already concerned quite centrally, as we have seen, with things like human beings, dogs and other natural entities: that is, to the area of philosophy of nature. Here Aristotle has many different interests. In his work *Physics* we find powerful analyses of time, of space, of the nature of motion. But one of his most central interests in this area is to talk in a general way about explanation in nature, to tell us what types of explanations the philosopher of nature can give and to give an account of the relative usefulness and importance of these different types of explanation. In the *Metaphysics* he remarks that philosophy in fact begins with a sense of wonder before the world of nature; that when we see the world we're struck by awe and wonder because we see these wonderful things going on and we can't understand why they work as they do. He says it's rather like seeing a puppet show where you see these objects moving as if by themselves and you know that behind them there must be some mechanism that explains why they move as they do. But you don't know yet what it is. You want to search and find out. Now the question is, what kind of explanation are you searching for when you ask this Why question? Why do things work as they do? Here Aristotle thinks that lots of philosophers have been too simple because they failed to notice how many different ways we ask and answer these Why questions. In both the *Physics* and the *Metaphysics* he wants to insist that there is not just one kind of explanation that is useful but quite possibly an open-ended list. At any rate, at least four types seem to him to be quite important. Now these are of course the famous 'Four Causes'. We hear about Aristotle's Four Causes. I think it's important to say that those are really four kinds of *explanations*.

Magee Four *be*-causes.

Nussbaum Four *be*-causes, yes – that's good. Four kinds of answers to Why questions. They are called the Material Cause, the Formal Cause, the Efficient Cause and the Final Cause. Suppose we take the question, why does a tree grow as it does? The material explanation (the Material Cause) will say the tree grows as it does because it's made of such and such materials. Now that form of explanation is very useful and interesting, but we can already guess that Aristotle's going to think it can't do the work alone, since a list of materials by itself does not tell us what the thing *is* whose growth we are trying to explain, what structure these materials go to constitute. For this, as you can guess, he thinks we need a further sort of explanation, the formal explanation (the so-called Formal Cause). This says the tree grows as it does because it is structured in such and such a way that is its form. So you see here the link with the metaphysical arguments. Then there is a third kind of explanation called the Efficient Cause, or Efficient Explanation. This says that the tree grows as it does because various things from the environment push it from outside in certain ways, for example the incoming materials or the earth and so on. Then the last one, which I think has been the most misunderstood one, is the form of explanation that he calls the Final Cause. We often call this the teleological form of explanation, because it refers to an end or *telos* towards which the thing moves. Now this says the tree grows as it does for the sake of becoming a certain sort of mature tree. In other words, the things in nature are always moving towards the flourishing of their adult condition.

Magee On the face of it there seems to be a mystical, almost magical element in that last one that doesn't appear in any of the others.

Nussbaum There *seems* to be – but I believe that's a big misunderstanding. First of all, Aristotle is not saying that there's anything magical out there in the future that goes down and pulls the tree towards its future form, as it were, exerting a causal pull from the future. No, it's all quite natural. It's all happening within the tree itself. It's a way of talking about the plastic and resourceful behaviour of living things. It's a way of offering a unified account of the way things like trees, in a variety of different natural circumstances, always move in the ways that promote their continued life and their development towards their mature form. So you see it's saying that, in a variety of different climates and weathers, the tree will always move towards the sun and its roots will go towards water and the source of nourishment, wherever that happens to be. And that's a perfectly general explanation which will give us a way of understanding the variety of the different things that the tree does. It is more simple and unified than a conjunction of descriptions of what happens 'from behind' in each case. If we grasp it, we can go on to predict that in some new case that we haven't seen yet the tree will move towards light and nourishment *wherever* those should happen to be. And we couldn't have that predictive power without mentioning an end. So you see in *that* there's nothing supernatural. There also isn't anything that refers to powers of mind or desire inside the tree itself. The tree does not have goals or ends in that sense. It's just a way of talking about the resourcefulness of natural movement.

Magee But a lot of scholars have in fact accredited to Aristotle the notion that there are souls in everything. Do you think they have understood him correctly?

Nussbaum No. I think they have misunderstood the way he uses teleological explanations. He clearly denies again and again that there are souls in everything. And I think he uses teleological explanations only for living beings. I don't think he uses teleological explanations at all for things like eclipses, thunderstorms and so on. In fact he says explicitly that an eclipse is not 'for the sake of' anything, is not teleologically explained. But in the case of living beings it's not a matter of mind or of soul in *our* sense, where that seems to imply some power of mind; it's a matter of the general character of what has life. Now we must turn here to his work on life, in order to be able to say more about these questions. Aristotle wrote a work that was called *On Psuche*, which really means On Life or the Principle of Life, and it's usually translated in English as *On the Soul*. Now our word 'soul' contains so many connotations of spirituality and mentality that it's quite misleading to use that word here. We would do better to think of this as a general inquiry into life and the living. What has *psuche* is what is alive – and this, for Aristotle, includes all plants and animals, including human animals. What Aristotle tries to do in this work is ask and answer the question: what is the animating principle in living things of many different kinds, including plants, animals, human beings? Can we give some general account of what it is to be alive? And the answer he gives is that the animating principle is, to put it quite generally, the form of a living body that's potentially organised so as to function, exercise the functions of life. Now by form, of course, he means not mere shape or configuration. As we've already seen, he means a kind of functional structure or organisation. He spells this out by coining a new word for the type of structure or form he has in mind. It is the word 'entelechy', which seems to mean an organisation in virtue of which a thing is capable of functioning in the ways that are characteristic of its particular type of life-activity – of achieving the way of acting that is its *telos* or end. So what it would be for you, Bryan Magee, to be alive would be to be organised so that you can nourish yourself, so that you can perceive, think, exercise all those functions that are characteristic of your type of life. And what Aristotle is saying is that this is an organisation *of* matter, *of* the body. It has necessarily to be realised in some matter at every point. But still, it's that organisation that's your life. It's not the matter that makes it up. So it's when you lose those functional structures that you would be dead.

Magee He applied the same principle to non-living things, didn't he? I remember a passage in his writings where he says that if an axe had a soul, that soul would be cutting. What he is saying is that the essence of even an object like an axe is what it *does*, its function. Isn't that right?

Nussbaum Yes. Now he uses that example, of course, counterfactually; he says if it had a soul, that's what it would be. And the way he uses this example is to illustrate the point I just mentioned: that by form or organisation he doesn't just mean the axe-like shape, and he doesn't mean that in fact it's made of such and such metal; he means the power to exercise certain functions. So this is a way of giving us some insight into the more mysterious case of the living creature. The analogy tells us that what it would be for that creature to have a certain animating principle is of course not for you, Bryan Magee, to have exactly a certain shape, because of course you could change your shape without being dead . . .

Magee . . . I do it only too frequently . . .

Nussbaum Nor is it to keep precisely the same bits of matter. Because of course no one does. What it is, is to have, and to continue to have, the power to function in various ways; and to have that power because of the way that you yourself are organised. It's if you lost that organisation to function that you would be dead.

Magee We have covered a lot of ground, yet even so we have touched on only a fraction of Aristotle's output. That is inevitable, I'm afraid, in the short time we have. But I hope we have succeeded in giving people an idea of the *sort* of thing to expect from this marvellous philosopher. Before we end I'd like us to take a little time to step back from what we've been talking about and draw some of the implications it has for modern philosophy. What philosophical concerns among our own contemporaries are directly influenced by Aristotle's work?

Nussbaum Well I think one is the one we've just been discussing – the philosophy of life. In contemporary philosophy we tend to call this area the philosophy of *mind*, cordoning off in a way that Aristotle wouldn't the mental powers of perception and thought from the rest of the functions of life. But in his general work on life Aristotle has some very important conclusions for a contemporary philosophy of mind. He tries to show us why a materialistic reductionism that says that perception (to take just one example) is simply a material process of a certain sort must be inadequate to explain the complex functional characteristics of life. His arguments here – the ones I gave earlier – seem compelling and still valid. On the other hand his position shows us that in order to reject materialistic reductionism we don't have to introduce some mysterious, immaterial entities. What we ought to say is that perception cannot be reduced to a material process – first, because it's realised in always different matter, and also because the notion of intentionality and active outward focusing is fundamental to the correct characterisation of the sort of awareness perception is. But on the other hand perception is not anything mysterious or separate from matter either. It is a function that's always, as he puts it, constituted in matter, realised in some matter or other.

Magee We have here an idea of fundamental significance which still seems insufficiently understood – not about perception, necessarily, but about alternatives. We are not confronted with a choice between either being materialists, on the one hand, or believing in some spiritual or abstract realm on the other. There is a third way of explaining our experience – and as you have suggested, it is a way which Aristotle pioneered.

Nussbaum Yes.

Magee Before we finish altogether we must say something about Aristotle's ethics. I do not think it would be any exaggeration to say that he is the most influential moral philosopher there has ever been. Can you give us an indication of where his gigantic influence in this field springs from?

Nussbaum Yes. Here I'm sorry we have so little time to discuss this, because it's an area that I like particularly. But I think his influence springs first of all from the question he begins with. Many moral philosophers begin by making a sharp distinction between the sphere of the 'moral' and all the rest of human life. They begin ethics with the question, 'What is my duty?' or 'What is my moral duty?' Now Aristotle begins instead with a much more general question, that is: What is it to lead a good human life? This allows him to investigate the areas that we would associate with 'the moral' alongside and in their relation to other areas of human life, such as intellectual commitment, personal love and friendship, and to ask subtle questions about their interrelationships, and what it would be to construct a good life out of all these elements.

Magee So he has a rich sense of what morality consists in. That differentiates him sharply from some other famous moral philosophers. The Utilitarians, for example, thought there was a single measure of all moral behaviour – happiness and unhappiness – so they believed you could chart the desirability or non-desirability of all moral actions on one and the same measuring rod. Aristotle was very alive to the fact that you can't, wasn't he?

Nussbaum Yes. You've mentioned the image of the measuring rod. That's a very important one for Aristotle. It's not only that he refuses to reduce the many things of value to one single measure. He also wants to say that even in each area you can't approach a complex context with a straight-edge, so to speak. He uses this image: he says that just as an architect is not going to try to measure a complex fluted column with a straight ruler, so too the ethical judge is not going to take a simple and inflexible set of rules into the complexities of a practical situation.

Instead, just as the architect measures with a flexible strip of metal which, as Aristotle puts it, bends to the shape of the stone and is not fixed, even so you or I, coming into a complex ethical situation, have to have our faculties open and responsive, ready to shape ourselves to the complex, perhaps unique and non-repeatable, demands of this particular situation. And, as he says, the discrimination rests with the 'perception' of that situation, by which he means a responsive attunement to it in both thought and emotion. And this perception is prior to any rules at all.

Magee Another thing that impresses me powerfully about Aristotle's moral philosophy is his firm grasp of the fact that we don't control our own moral environment, and therefore that we cannot be, as the Stoics wanted us to be, self-contained moral entities. Nor can we be, as perhaps the Epicureans wanted, detached moral entities. We live in a moral environment which buffets us about, and Aristotle seems to have understood that.

Nussbaum Yes, I think he understood it better than almost any philosopher who has written in this area; that the good life for a human being, if it's to be rich enough to include everything that's of value – say, for example, personal love and friendship – has got to be vulnerable to many factors that we don't altogether control; and that any attempt to close off those areas of vulnerability is going to result in an impoverishment of our lives.

Magee Do you think he had anything approaching the concept of 'moral luck' which philosophers have written of in recent years?

Nussbaum Yes, I think he does. That is, he certainly does ask which features of the good life are not under our control, and how can not only our ability to act virtuously but our virtuous character itself be shaped and altered by factors that we don't control. Now I think myself he doesn't go quite far enough here because he's so interested in describing a good life that's harmonious and balanced. That is, his image is always of a life where there are many components, that's very rich in different sorts of value, but where everything is engineered and balanced together in harmony. And I think this prevents him from doing justice to the way that certain constituents of a life, if properly pursued in all their depth, actually can have it in them to challenge and call into question all the others. Take for example the way that deep love can sometimes threaten and oppose virtue. This is something that Aristotle is very silent on. It's an area of 'moral luck' which I would regard as very important and he says nothing about. In fact he has almost nothing at all to say about erotic love

– I think because he's so interested in giving us an image of a life that's harmonious and balanced.

Magee Up to this point in our discussion we have been concerned first and foremost to communicate some of Aristotle's fundamental ideas, and we have not as yet paused to evaluate them critically. But you have just put your finger on an aspect of his thought which in your view constitutes a shortcoming. Can you mention one or two other major respects in which Aristotle is open to important criticism?

Nussbaum Well, I think one of the major areas is his political theory. I think there are a lot of good things here, and among the good things is an account of the proper function of government or politics as the provision to each citizen of all the necessary conditions for the living of a rich and good human life. This he combines with an account of the good life in terms of a variety of different functionings that are the component parts of such a life. This view seems to me well worth examining today, as an alternative to views that see the job of government in connection with the maximisation of utility. But the problem comes with his account of who it is who is to be a citizen. Here he has a very narrow-minded attitude towards the foreigner, and towards women, and he is perfectly happy to offer an account of political citizenship that excludes all but a small number of elite leisured males. He doesn't even want farmers or traders or sailors. And of course there is a reason for this, because he thinks that in order to have a good life you have to be able to reflect about its structure; and you cannot reflect well if you are engaged in certain forms of debasing labour. But I think myself he goes vastly too far when he says that a farmer or a peasant craftsman is engaged in a debasing form of labour that couldn't possibly open that person to the possibility of practical wisdom and a good life.

Magee But surely it's anachronistic, and therefore unfair, to criticise Aristotle along these lines? It may look to us, from our position in the twentieth century, as if he undervalued women and the lower social orders and foreigners, but didn't more or less everyone in his position at his time think in the same way?

Nussbaum No, I don't think so. Certainly on the issue of slavery he's opposed to some more radical positions that held that all slavery is unjust. He knows those positions, he argues against them. On farmers and sailors – well, the actual practice of Athenian democracy is what he is opposing when he says that these should not be citizens. And in the case of women, well, first of all, in his biology of women he rejects theories that are vastly more informed and more correct than his about the contribution of women to reproduction. You know, he thinks that a woman doesn't actually contribute any formal characteristics to the offspring, only its unformed matter. And in political discussions of women's role, of course, Plato had shown himself able to free himself from prevailing conventions and to rethink the whole question of women's education. And Plato had come to the conclusion that we'd better educate each individual person in the state according to that person's personal capabilities; that meant that women ought to be given the chance to be assessed as individuals and to be educated accordingly.

Magee Now you, in spite of all your objections to Aristotle's views, have devoted many years of your life to studying him, and you have published a substantial book about his work. You also teach it to students. And obviously you feel all this is hugely worthwhile. Why? What, for example, do you expect your students, nearly all of whom are not going to be professional scholars or philosophers, to get out of reading him?

Nussbaum Well I think the most basic thing is his general approach to philosophy and what philosophy could be, his idea that the philosopher must be someone who's attentive to and almost humble before the variety of human life and its great richness. But at the same time one who is committed to giving explanations, one who is committed to mapping that richness in a perspicuous way. In every area he strikes a kind of balance: between oversimplifying theorising that takes philosophy too far from the richness and complexity and even messiness of ordinary discourse and ordinary life, and, on the other hand, a kind of negative or deflationary philosophising that says theorising is all houses of cards and there's no point in asking for and giving explanations. I think Aristotle has found the right balance, and has probably the best conception of the philosophical task that one can give to a student.

MEDIEVAL PHILOSOPHY

Dialogue with
ANTHONY KENNY

INTRODUCTION

Magee For purposes of teaching it is customary to divide the history of the West into broad periods which we label Ancient, Medieval and Modern; and we do the same with Western philosophy: we talk of Ancient Philosophy, Medieval Philosophy and Modern Philosophy. Published histories of philosophy are often divided into these three sections and, as I have just indicated, universities make common use of those categories for teaching purposes.

Ancient philosophy is dominated by the writings of two people, Plato and Aristotle. It goes without saying that there were other important and interesting philosophers in the ancient world, not only before them but also after. But none has left writings in any way comparable in their combined quantity, calibre and influence. So great is the predominance of Plato and Aristotle that anyone going to a university to study ancient philosophy finds himself spending nearly all his time, perhaps literally all of it, on the work of those two.

If such a person wanted then to continue the study of philosophy he would probably find himself required to skip straight from Aristotle to modern philosophy, jumping over the medieval period entirely. Medieval philosophy – and we are talking, after all, of the philosophy of a thousand years or more, from the fall of the Roman Empire to the Renaissance – has been the victim of extreme neglect in recent generations. The chief reason, I think, is that throughout the Middle Ages virtually all important philosophers were religious scholars, nearly all of them Christian ecclesiastics, whereas in the century or two leading up to our own time there has been a widespread reaction against religion, and especially against its hold on thought. During that reaction medieval philosophers fell under suspicion of not pursuing the truth wherever it might lead but rather looking for good reasons for what they believed already. However, like most reactions, including healthy ones, this one went too far. The greatest medieval philosophers were true giants. They were doing genuine philosophy as we understand the term today. And we can still learn from them.

As in the case of ancient philosophy, among the medieval philosophers there are two figures who stand out from all the rest, although in this case they are at almost opposite ends of the period. The earlier is St Augustine, who was born in North Africa in AD 354 and died there, though having travelled widely during the course of his life, in 430. Two of his books are universally acknowledged as being among the world's great literature: *The Confessions* and *The City of God*. The later figure of comparable stature is Thomas Aquinas, who was born in Italy in 1225 and died there in 1274. Aquinas was a more technical sort of philosopher altogether than Augustine, and his most famous works are two enormous compendia written for students, one called *Summa Contra Gentiles* (translated into English under the title *On the Truth of the Catholic Faith*) and the other *Summa Theologiae*, *Summary of Theology*.

The death of St Augustine and the fall of the Roman Empire were followed by the period we dub the Dark Ages. During those centuries it was as much as the literate and learned of Western Europe could do to cling to the remnants of civilisation in the teeth of repeated pagan invasions and occupations. In these circumstances they saw their function as above all preservative, and for a long time scarcely any new intellectual work of lasting importance was done: during the seven hundred years from Augustine to Anselm there was only one philosopher of the front rank, John the Scot, who lived in the ninth century. However, once we get to Anselm in the eleventh century we embark on a continuous succession of significant thinkers – for example, Abelard in the twelfth century, Roger Bacon and Thomas Aquinas in the thirteenth; then Duns Scotus, followed by William of Ockham; by which time the medieval period itself is approaching its end.

To discuss this long but unfamiliar and fascinating period in phil- osophy's history I have invited Anthony Kenny, Master of Balliol College, Oxford. He is one of the few contemporary philosophers to have written extensively about medieval philosophy, and was himself once a Roman Catholic priest.

DISCUSSION

Magee Before we address ourselves to specific aspects of medieval phil- osophy, would you like to fill out a bit further the sketch-map of the period as a whole which I have just outlined?

Kenny I'd agree with your choice of two philosophers to sum up the achievements of the Middle Ages – Augustine and Aquinas. But they are two very different people. Augustine is a solitary thinker, somebody whose best-known work is an autobiography. His *Confessions* is a book which draws on his own meditation, his own reading of the Bible, his own interior life. Aquinas is very different: he is not a solitary figure but somebody right in the middle of a religious and academic tradition. He was one of the great Order of Dominicans. He lived his life within communities of friars. He was also a university teacher. One of his great achievements was the production of two magnificent university text- books. All this makes a great contrast with Augustine, who was such a lonely scholar that at the end of his life, when a bishop, he was the only man in the whole town who had any books at all.

Magee They are in fact excellent examples of the two main types of philosopher who have always existed, from ancient times until the present day: on the one hand the lonely, isolated, introspective thinker, and on the other the institution man, most typically the university teacher.

Kenny Throughout the history of philosophy you find people falling into these two classes. In the pattern of Augustine you have the solitary geniuses like Descartes and Spinoza, spinning their thought out of their own meditations. You also have the learned university professors like Kant and Hegel developing systems to be handed on and modified by pupils and later generations of philosophers.

Magee Our talking of university teachers prompts the reflection that it was in the Middle Ages that universities were invented; and their very coming into existence had an enormous effect on philosophy. Can you say something about that?

Kenny That is one of the most important contributions of the Middle Ages to philosophy: the invention of the university. By a university I mean a corporation of people engaged professionally, full-time, on the teaching of a corpus of knowledge, handing it on to their pupils, having an agreed syllabus, having agreed methods of teaching, and having professional standards. It's a very remarkable thing how very *professional* philosophy was in the Middle Ages. First of all there was the enormous output of the philosophers. Aquinas wrote, at about the lowest estimate, eight million words. There are a number of disputed works which might bring it up to eleven million. Now eight million words is a lot to write. The whole of the surviving works of Aristotle are only a million words. The whole of the surviving works of Plato are only half a million. Aquinas, in quite a short lifetime, writes eight million words – and they are not words just tossed off, they are words that scholars to this day can find depths of meaning in.

If the output is enormous, the rigour is equally great. Aquinas's works bear the stamp of the medieval technique of Disputation. This was one of the great medieval methods of teaching. The teacher would put up some of his pupils – a senior, and one or more junior ones – to dispute. The senior pupil would have to defend some particular thesis – for instance, that the world was not created in time, or, for that matter, that the world *was* created in time. This thesis would be attacked, and the opposite thesis presented by the other pupils. In arguing the matter out with each other they had to argue according to strict logical rules. Then the teacher would settle the dispute, trying to bring out what was true in what had been said by one, what was sound in the criticisms made by the others.

If you open St Thomas's *Summa Theologiae* you find that though not itself a record of live disputations it bears the stamp of the method. Whenever Aquinas is going to present a particular doctrine or philosophical thesis, or theological thesis, he begins by presenting three of the strongest arguments he can think of against the truth of his thesis. The method is a marvellous intellectual discipline which prevents you from taking things for granted. It makes you ask yourself: 'Who have I got to convince of what, and what are the strongest things they could say on the other side?'

Those are two of the things characteristic of medieval philosophers – the voluminous output and the rigorous method of presentation. A third medieval innovation is the syllabus. A university syllabus means that there are set topics, which anybody going to university is expected to learn. There is a corpus of knowledge that the student is expected to master before going on to add his own little stone to the cairn of the scientific edifice. There is a tradition which must be preserved, and then handed on to pupils, enhanced, one hopes.

In the Middle Ages the syllabus is set especially by the surviving works of Aristotle. At the beginning of the high Middle Ages Aristotle's works were translated into Latin. Very few of the great medieval philosophers could read Greek, but they had good Latin translations; and they worked away to assimilate all the knowledge that it was possible to extract from Aristotle, and then develop it.

Magee Before we come to the most important matter of all, namely the content of all this work, there's a question I'd like to put to you which might sound parochial and yet which might elicit an interesting answer. Any British person coming to the study of medieval philosophy is bound to be struck by how many of the leading figures either came from the British Isles or spent a significant portion of their careers there. That would apply to more than half the individuals I named in my introduction: John the Scot, Anselm, Roger Bacon, Duns Scotus, William of Ockham. . . . Is that sheer coincidence, or is there an interesting explanation for it?

Kenny It is a striking fact, but I think that it is a deceptive one if it suggests that there was something especially British about philosophy in the Middle Ages.

Magee I certainly wasn't suggesting that!

Kenny It's true that many of the philosophers spent some of their time in Britain, and that some of them were British by birth. But, after all, Anselm was an Italian; and Duns Scotus and William of Ockham spent quite a lot of their time on the Continent. If you picked any country in Western Europe you would be able to say that quite a number of the great philosophers spent time there. That is because the university community in

St Augustine (354–430)

the Middle Ages was very much a European community: Christendom, the nations of Christianity, formed a single academic community. Somebody graduating in one university would go and teach in another – all the universities spoke a common language, the Latin of the Church, and there was a great deal of academic migration. This was true of the early Middle Ages. Later on you get nationalistic wars, like the Hundred Years War between England and France, and these wars mean an interruption of travel. Later, too, there is a development of the vernacular literatures, which means that even if people go on speaking Latin they are beginning to think in, say, English. It is a significant fact that the last of the really great medieval philosophers was John Wyclif, just after William of Ockham, and he is also well known for inspiring the first translation of the Bible into English. Wyclif stands at the beginning of the end of the international Latin academic community, the first stage of the gradual fission of the different national cultures in diverse languages.

Magee Let us now turn to the philosophy itself. One preoccupation that ran throughout the whole of the Middle Ages was the desire to reconcile the great classic philosophers of ancient Greece with the Christian religion. In the earlier part of our period they were chiefly concerned with Plato, but in the later, as you have just said, it was Aristotle, but in any case the desire for reconciliation was pervasive. Can you say something about it?

Kenny Reconciling Aristotle with Christianity was a particular concern of Aquinas and those who succeeded him. Augustine was much more interested, I think, in the philosophy of Plato than that of Aristotle, and as a source of knowledge and information he was very much more interested in the Bible than he was in any philosopher at all. Augustine's presence broods over the whole of the Middle Ages. The later medieval philosophers regarded him as almost a codification of the religious knowledge to be found in the Christian tradition through the Bible. But when Aristotle was translated into Latin, in the twelfth and thirteenth centuries, scholars saw that beside the Christian tradition there is another corpus of information about the world, about human beings, about what kind of beings we are and what kinds of things we should do. This is to be found in the philosophy of the ancients, and especially of Aristotle. Aristotle was a genius in many different ways. He founded many of the disciplines that later grew into branches of philosophy, and some of them later still into branches of science; I am thinking of Logic, Metaphysics, Biology, Psychology, Botany, Meteorology. Those and other sciences began with Aristotle, and the most mature version of them available to the early Middle Ages was still Aristotle's presentation of them.

Magee I don't know quite how to word this question without its sounding flippant, but there's a serious point to be raised: given the wholehearted commitment of medieval philosophers to the Christian faith, and to a belief in the divine inspiration of the Bible, and to a belief in the unique authority of the Church as being God's representative on earth, why did they care at all what the ancients said? Were not the teachings of the Church the ultimate authority on every point? Had not that *superseded* the ancients?

Kenny   Christianity, they believed, provided them with enough knowledge for salvation. The humble washerwoman who knew the truths of the Christian faith and was completely ignorant of the science of the ancients had no less chance of getting to heaven and living in glory with God than somebody as learned as Thomas Aquinas. But it would be quite wrong to think of people like Aquinas as having an eye only on religion. They were men of intellectual curiosity who wanted to know all they could about human beings and about the world. Of course they were interested in human beings and the world *as God's creatures*, but they thought that God had things to tell us about the world not only through the Sacred books, like the Bible, but also through the story of the Creation.

Magee   When I first came to medieval philosophy one of the things that surprised me was how much of it was *not* connected with religion. There is a great deal of linguistic and conceptual analysis of a modern-seeming kind and of the subtlest sophistication. There is a lot of genuinely solid work in logic. There is – perhaps most surprising of all – interesting and sometimes innovative work across the whole gamut of the sciences from mechanics to psychology. The range is astonishingly wide, and the interest of much of it astonishingly timeless.

Kenny   In medieval philosophy we find the germ of many of the sciences which set up as disciplines on their own after the Renaissance: they are all to be found, as it were, as children growing up in the great household of philosophy in the Middle Ages. The titles of some of the professors of the ancient universities echo this: in Oxford there is a professor of mathematical physics whose title is Professor of Natural Philosophy. That was how the discipline of physics began, as the study of natural philosophy, which was itself a programme set by the text of Aristotle called the *Physics*.

The Aristotelian works themselves traced out the syllabus for the Middle Ages. The syllabus began with the logic which Aristotle created but which grew enormously in the Middle Ages. This was one of the first things which anybody going to a medieval university would learn. In recent years we have rediscovered many highly refined theorems and techniques of logic which were quite familiar to undergraduates towards the end of the Middle Ages. At the Renaissance and the Reformation, logic was cut off short, and only a truncated torso of the subject was taught in most European universities until the end of the nineteenth century. At the end of the nineteenth century a new generation of mathematical logicians, people like Gottlob Frege in Germany, Bertrand Russell and Alfred North Whitehead in England, came to logic from a different viewpoint, a mathematical viewpoint, wanting to trace mathematics back to origins in logic. These logicians set on foot a great rebirth of logic; one of its flowerings was *Principia Mathematica*, the great work in which Whitehead and Russell tried to show that the whole of arithmetic could be derived simply from pure logical truisms if you studied them systematically enough. This rebirth of logic at the beginning of the present century led to the rediscovery, before and after the Second World War, of branches of logic which had been totally lost since the Middle Ages. It is only in my own generation that people have begun to put the two together and realise that some of the most modern ideas of logic were things that were well known in the Middle Ages.

Magee When I discovered philosophers such as Duns Scotus and William of Ockham I was unexpectedly reminded of my studies some years ago in twentieth-century logic. I had expected to encounter writers distant and strange, even alien, but instead I found individuals engaged in an activity with which I was thoroughly familiar. Even their tone of voice was sometimes familiar. Would it be true to say that philosophy, at least as taught and studied in Western Europe, was logic-centred in the Middle Ages, is logic-centred now, but was not logic-centred for most of the period in between?

Kenny Yes, and that is why one sometimes gets an extraordinary feeling of sympathy and familiarity, coming from a modern philosophical background to read later medieval texts. But after the Middle Ages people lost interest in logic, and to a great extent lost interest in the philosophical study of language. They were, of course, very interested in the rhetorical and literary study of language, but lost interest in the relation of language to logic. From Descartes onwards philosophers placed epistemology in the centre of their discipline. Epistemology is based on the question: How do we know what we know? How *can* we know what we know? Epistemology placed language and logic in the background. Since Frege and Russell up to the present generation, particularly in Britain and America, logic and language are in the forefront of philosophy. The philosophers' great question in recent years has been not 'What do you know?', but 'What do you mean?' The insistence that any question, whether in science or mathematics or anything else, must be accompanied by a very careful awareness of what we mean by asking it, is something that was very typical of the Middle Ages and is typical of philosophy again now.

Magee As I mentioned in my introduction to this discussion, the commonest charge levelled against medieval philosophy in general is that its practitioners were committed to a detailed set of beliefs concerning total reality before they even started, so instead of being engaged in impartial inquiry they were looking for good reasons for what they already believed. How would you answer that accusation?

Kenny It is not necessarily a serious charge against a philosopher to say that he is looking for good reasons for what he already believes in. Descartes, for instance, sitting beside his fire wearing his dressing gown, was looking for good reasons for believing that that was what he was doing, and he took a remarkably long time to find them. Bertrand Russell accused Aquinas of not being a real philosopher because he was looking for reasons for what he already believed. It is extraordinary that that accusation should be made by Russell, who in the book *Principia Mathematica* takes hundreds of pages to prove that two and two make four, which is something he had believed all his life.

Magee Here you've said something of the utmost importance which I think people don't readily realise, so it's worth driving the point home. Any philosopher of any significance must hold at least some beliefs which differentiate him from everyone else, otherwise he would not be significant. Over the millennia almost every imaginable variety of philosophical belief has been held by some philosopher or other. What differentiates a reputable philosopher from disreputable ones is not that there is some 'correct' canonical set of beliefs which he holds but that, whatever his beliefs, he is prepared to put up reasons for them and to see those reasons subjected to scrutiny of the utmost rigour, and to abide by the outcome. He subjects his concepts *and* his arguments *and* his methods to critical analysis, not only on the part of others but on his own part, and lives with the consequences. Provided he does this with full intellectual honesty he can be a Christian or a Hindu or an atheist or anything and be a proper philosopher. Of course, there are some beliefs which have been shown by analysis to be so flawed – incoherent, perhaps, or self-contradictory – that it is now no longer possible, as it might once have been, for someone who is both intelligent and intellectually honest to hold them. The abandonment of such beliefs is part of what constitutes intellectual advance.

Kenny Certainly you can be a very good philosopher and believe very strange things. A philosopher's principal task is to tell good arguments from bad, and the difference between good and bad arguments does not depend on the starting or ending point. Indeed, the distinction that you and I have just made between what you believe and the reasons for which you believe it is something very relevant to medieval philosophy. It was very clearly brought out by Thomas Aquinas, perhaps more than by any other philosopher. He was committed to many beliefs as a believing Christian, but there were many other things which he believed because he had read Aristotle and followed his arguments. He is very careful to make a distinction between these things: a distinction between his beliefs as a theologian and his beliefs as a philosopher. He sees his job as a theologian as being to articulate, make explicit and defend the revelation of the history of the world, the salvation of the world and the future of the world, contained in the Sacred books of Christianity and in the teaching of the Church. As a philosopher, his job is to get as far as he can in discovering what kind of place the world is, and what truths we can know which are necessary truths about the world and about thought, discoverable by unaided reason, without appealing to any alleged Divine Revelation.

Magee One example of his admirable self-awareness about this distinction sticks in my mind. In his work *On the Eternity of the World* he says that as far as philosophical considerations go there is no reason why the universe should not have existed always and go on existing for ever, but that as a Christian he does not believe this: as a Christian he believes that God created the universe out of nothing and will one day bring it to an end.

Kenny That's a very good example. There were a number of Christian philosophers who thought that you could prove that the world must have had a beginning. They thought this because they didn't believe in certain kinds of infinite series. Aquinas shows the flaws in their arguments, and argues that there is nothing self-contradictory in the idea that the world has gone on for ever and will go on for ever, as Aristotle believed. Aquinas thinks that with the unaided human reason you cannot prove that the world had a beginning. Equally, he believed you can't prove that it had no beginning, and he objects to Aristotle who thought you could. Aquinas as a philosopher is more agnostic than Aristotle, and says you can't prove it either way. Why then did he believe that the world had a beginning? In answer he would have appealed to the Book of Genesis in the Bible. But that was something he believed as a Christian, as a theologian, not as a philosopher.

At the beginning you mentioned his two great works, the *Summa Contra Gentiles* and the *Summa Theologiae*. The *Summa Contra Gentiles* is meant as a philosophical work; it is directed to people who are not Christians, who may be Muslims or Jews or atheists. It aims to present them with reasons – reasons that any human being of goodwill can see to be good reasons – for believing that there is a God, that the soul is immortal, and so on. The *Summa Theologiae* is very different. It is addressed to Christians, and it accepts statements in the Bible as good starting points for arguments. But there is an enormous amount of philosophical reflection contained in that work too, even though its title describes it as a book of theology.

Magee Let us focus on one particular philosophical question, and let us take one which is fundamental, and was of concern to philosophers throughout the Middle Ages. Let us take the question whether the existence of God can be proved by rational argument, and if so what that argument is. But first let me add a word to what you just said about medieval churchmen addressing themselves to unbelievers. Some saw this as part of their Christian duty. And they recognised that in arguing with unbelievers there was no point in appealing to the authority of the Church or the New Testament – their interlocutors did not accept those authorities. So they had to rely solely on arguments which carried their own credentials. And they realised that there would be no point in their being self-deceiving about the quality of these arguments, because poor arguments would soon be routed by clever sceptics. So we find good medieval Christian philosophers subjecting even arguments for the existence of God to devastating criticism – which, as we were saying a moment ago, is among the things Christian philosophers ought to be doing.

   Now I suppose the most famous argument in the history of philosophy for the existence of God is the so-called ontological argument. Not only was it thrashed over in the Middle Ages; it crops up again in Descartes, in Spinoza, in Leibniz, in Kant – in fact it's even of interest today. Its classic formulation was by Anselm in the eleventh century. Can you explain to us what it was?

Kenny Yes, but perhaps before I do that I ought to explain to the people following our discussion what an ontological argument is – the word 'ontological' may be puzzling. In the Middle Ages and later there were two different kinds of arguments offered for the existence of God. Arguments of one kind – the best-known are the Five Ways of St Thomas Aquinas – take as their starting point some feature of the external world. They start from some very obvious feature of it, such as that some things move from place to place, or that some things come into existence and go out of existence. Starting with those, and a few universal truths of philosophy, St Thomas will offer to prove to you that there is something which is recognisable as what all men call God. These proofs are called 'cosmological arguments' because they begin from the cosmos, from the world around us. But an ontological argument is the kind of argument

St Thomas Aquinas (c. 1225–74)

which starts out just from the notion of God, from the very concept of God. You don't have to go outside the realm of ideas to get to its starting point.

The most well-known formulation of this argument is that of St Anselm – indeed, St Anselm seems to have been the inventor of the ontological argument, whereas the other arguments are developments of ideas to be found in Aristotle. Anselm's argument is very ingenious. It takes as its basis a definition of the word 'God'. God, Anselm says, is something that you can't conceive anything greater than. Now that seems a pretty harmless definition of God, and somebody who didn't believe in God might accept it as a definition of God. After all, if you don't believe in something you'll need a definition of what it is you don't believe in. And so atheists might agree to a definition of God as something that you can't conceive anything greater than. If so, Anselm will say to the atheist: 'Well let's suppose that God exists only in the mind and not in reality. You have got to agree that God exists in the mind because you are thinking of God at this very moment, and that's what it is for something to exist in the mind. But now if God existed only in the mind and not in reality, then you could conceive of something greater than God: you could conceive of something that was exactly like the God you are just thinking of, only existing in reality as well as in your mind, and thus greater. Therefore there would be something conceivable greater than God. But God, we agreed, was something than which you could conceive nothing greater; and you've just conceived of something greater than God. That's an absurdity – something self-contradictory. Now what led us to this contradictory result was the assumption that God existed only in the mind and not in reality. Therefore we have to say that God exists in reality as well.'

Magee It's an abnormally disconcerting argument, that, because anyone who hears it, at least nowadays, is bound to feel there's something wrong with it, and yet when you try to put your finger on precisely what it is that is wrong with it you find it startlingly difficult to do so.

Kenny I agree. I'm one of those who think there's something wrong with that argument. But it's not any particularly modern trend of philosophy that makes people think there's something wrong with the ontological argument. St Thomas Aquinas took some trouble to prove that there was something wrong with it – he wasn't convinced by it either. But the most interesting thing is that while many great philosophers through history have thought there was something wrong with the ontological argument they all give different reasons for saying that it goes wrong. To this day there is no consensus about what is wrong with it; indeed, there isn't any consensus that there is something wrong with it at all. Recently there has grown up in America a group of philosophers of religion, using the latest techniques of mathematical logic, who have revived the argument, and tried to present it in a way which is convincing within the background structures of contemporary logic. It would take too long to spell out how they do it. But an argument which twenty years ago was thought as dead as the dodo is now alive and well and living in Indiana and California.

Magee You have drawn a number of striking parallels between medieval philosophy and our own contemporary philosophy. Both, you said, are logic-centred, whereas philosophy in between was not. Both proceed to an important degree by linguistic analysis, whereas philosophy in between showed nothing like the same concern with language. And now you have made the point that both even concern themselves with the ontological argument! There is another similarity which is worth stressing. Both are concerned with first-order problems, that is to say with problems of living as directly encountered, as well as with the second-order problems presented by discussions of them in language – concepts, arguments, methods, and so on.

Kenny This is a fairly recent change in Anglo-American philosophy. At the time when you and I were starting analytic philosophy we would be told that it was not the task of the moral philosopher to tell you whether it was ever permissible to tell lies, or whether there was anything wrong with adultery, or what were the criteria by which you would decide whether a war was being justly waged. These were matters of importance, of course, but were not regarded as the special business of the philosopher. The philosopher's task was a second-order task: it was to analyse the language and concepts which we use in making these first-order decisions. In the last decade there has been a great swing of interest back to the live moral questions. It is now recognised that they concern philosophers as philosophers, not just as citizens or moral human beings. For instance, philosophers have made a great contribution to questions of medical ethics. They are consulted about questions concerning the preservation of life, questions such as when it is right to turn off life-support systems. In Britain it was a philosopher who chaired the committee of inquiry into the question whether it was right to experiment on embryos. There has also been a great interest in the relationship between moral philosophy and the waging of warfare.

Magee I'd like to pick up that last instance and use it as our example. You yourself wrote a book recently about nuclear deterrence, and in it you addressed yourself to the question whether there are any imaginable circumstances in which the waging of a nuclear war could be morally justified. In doing so you called into play the whole tradition of theorising, from the Middle Ages onwards, about the so-called 'just war'; and you said, quite rightly, that the arguments involved ought to be of interest to every intelligent person. Can you tell us something about what they were?

Kenny The theory of the just war is something of which there is the germ in the Middle Ages, in Aquinas, and which is further developed after the end of the Middle Ages in the post-medieval scholastics. The question is twofold. In what circumstances is it morally right to wage war? And, if you do go to war, what moral constraints are there on the way in which you wage the war – for instance, what can you choose as targets, or what can you do with prisoners?

The theory of the just war is a theory in the middle, between two opposing views. On the one hand there is the pacifist view that there is no such thing as a just war: all wars are immoral and wicked, no matter how noble the causes are for which they are waged. On the other hand there is a view that though war is a terrible thing, once you get into war there are no moral rules at all: the only moral imperative is to win the war by the most effective possible means. Now the tradition of the just war says that neither of those opinions is true. There are some values that are more important than life itself, and therefore values for which you can legitimately make war. But there are limits to the justification of war. There has to be a good reason for going to war – the values for which you go to war have to be ones important enough to defend in that way. When you go to war there are constraints on what you choose as targets: there must be no deliberate killing of the innocent, whether by the innocent you mean civilians not involved in war-making or ex-combatants who are now prisoners. This medieval 'just war' tradition lies behind two of the most significant contributions to the recent debate about nuclear weapons: in Britain, the Church of England book *The Church and the Bomb*, and in the United States the Pastoral Letter of the American Catholic Bishops on Nuclear Weapons and Nuclear Deterrence.

Magee Some of what you were just saying derives from Aquinas. Is it not the case that Aquinas is today regarded as what one might call the official philosopher of the Roman Catholic Church?

Kenny We have, in fact, just come to the end of the period in which that could have been said. Before the nineteenth century, though Aquinas was held in enormous respect, he was not in any way the official philosopher of the Roman Catholic Church. He was perhaps the official philosopher of the Dominican Order, but that's only a small part of the Catholic Church. Then in the late nineteenth century, Pope Leo XIII wrote an Encyclical Letter giving him a special place in the teaching of philosophy and theology in Catholic seminaries and universities. Since the Second Vatican Council I have the impression that Aquinas's influence on Catholic institutions has become much looser. He has been replaced by a variety of other and lesser philosophers. By contrast, the reputation of Aquinas in the non-Catholic world has gained from the fact that he is now no longer seen as the spokesman for a party line. Particularly in the United States, there is a growing interest in his work among people who are not Catholics, perhaps not Christians at all, but who are impressed by the sheer philosophical genius of the man.

Magee I'd like to put another philosophical crux to you for comment; and again I would like to choose one which is of interest today just as it was in the Middle Ages. All reflective people are interested in the problem to what extent we have free will, and it is a problem which obviously has important practical implications. One reason why it mattered especially to philosophers of the Middle Ages had to do with the Christian doctrine of Divine Grace. According to the doctrine of Divine Grace it is not open to any human being to secure his own salvation by his own efforts, he needs also the grace of God. But if this is so, to what extent do we have free will in any respect that really matters?

Kenny There were two problems in the Middle Ages, interwoven, one of them a philosophical problem and one a theological problem. The philosophical problem was the problem of reconciling divine foreknowledge and human freedom. Not only medieval philosophers but many Greek and Islamic philosophers who had considered the nature of God thought that one of the things we knew about God – if we knew anything about him at all – was that he could foretell the future, that he knew what was going to happen. Now if you and I are free, it looks as if what you and I decide to do today is what determines what's going to be the future tomorrow, but if God already knows what you and I are going to do tomorrow how can we be free to decide that today? That is a problem which arises for anybody who believes in an omniscient God at all, whether or not they believe in anything the Bible says about God.

But there was a special problem for Christians, especially the Christians who took the version of Christianity presented by St Augustine, because St Augustine, particularly in his later days, lays enormous emphasis on the doctrine that nobody achieves salvation and goes to glory in heaven unless they are predestined to do so by God. So that was an extra problem for Christians.

A great deal of patient work was done by theologians and philosophers in the Middle Ages, unravelling the concepts of freedom and prescience, to try to show that the two can be reconciled. What is interesting philosophically is that these efforts are replicated, often in ignorance, by people today who are not interested in God at all but are interested in scientific determinism. The actual logical moves which somebody in the twentieth century will use to reconcile physical determinism with our experience of freedom will be, as often as not, the same steps gone through by people in the fourteenth century trying to reconcile divine predestination with human freedom.

Magee If, as I hope it will, our discussion has the effect of stimulating some people to read some medieval philosophy for the first time, where would you advise them to start?

Kenny There are not many medieval works which are easy for beginners. This is because, as I said, most of the great works of medieval philosophy were written within a university tradition. They are highly technical university textbooks. However, there are two short books that one could pick up. The first is the one you yourself began with, Augustine's *Confessions*.

Magee That is, I think, a truly wonderful book. And very easily available nowadays in paperback.

Kenny It is indeed one of the greatest autobiographies of all time. It is probably the first autobiography in the modern sense ever written at all. It is full of personal reflection, of tender memory of his family, of insight into his own childhood and his own development. But it also moves on to the most abstract levels of philosophising. At the end it raises questions about the nature of time which are still very much alive in philosophical debate.

The other book which I would recommend is *The Proslogion* of St Anselm. That is the book in which he presents the ingenious argument for the existence of God which I tried to paraphrase earlier on. Newcomers might find it interesting to look at that – it takes only an afternoon to read – and see whether I presented the argument rightly. And see whether they find it convincing.

Magee In my introduction to this discussion I said something to the effect that medieval philosophy had in recent generations been the Cinderella of the subject's history. But I'm also beginning to get the impression that this situation may at last be changing. More and more distinguished philosophers are taking a public interest in it – you are an example. Is there, do you think, a large-scale revival of interest in medieval philosophy on the way?

Kenny Of course it is true only in the Anglo-American tradition that medieval philosophy has been a Cinderella. On the continent of Europe medieval philosophy has been thriving as a subject of study for quite a long time. In America at present there is a great revival of interest in all things medieval, not just in medieval philosophy.

DESCARTES

Dialogue with
BERNARD WILLIAMS

INTRODUCTION

Magee When the term 'Modern Philosophy' is used in universities it is normally to make the distinction from Ancient and Medieval Philosophy. So it does not mean the philosophy of the twentieth century; it means philosophy since the Reformation. In fact, there is one man who is generally, and I think rightly, regarded as the inaugurator of modern philosophy: Descartes. In clearer terms, then, what the term 'Modern Philosophy' means is 'philosophy from Descartes onwards'.

René Descartes was born in France in 1596. He received an unusually good education, but he also had unusual independence of mind, and while still a student he perceived that the various authorities he was studying often put forward arguments that were invalid. As a young man he became a soldier, and travelled widely in Europe, though without seeing any fighting; and he was struck by the fact that the world of practical life was as full of contradictions as the world of books. He became fascinated by the question whether there was any way at all in which we human beings could get to know anything for certain, and if so how. He stopped travelling, and went into seclusion in Holland, the country in which intellectual life in those days was at its freest. And there, during the twenty years from 1629 to 1649, he produced work of the profoundest originality in mathematics and philosophy and also did a great deal of work in science. (Philosophy and science had not yet been clearly demarcated, and were not to be so until the eighteenth century.) He invented the branch of mathematics known as co-ordinate geometry. It was his idea to measure the position of a point by its distance from two fixed lines – so every time we look at a graph we are looking at something invented by Descartes. In fact, those two familiar lines on a graph are known by his name: 'Cartesian axes', 'Cartesian' being the adjective from 'Descartes'. His most famous works of philosophy are *Discourse on the Method*, which was published in 1637, and *Meditations*, published in 1642.

Descartes never married, though he had an illegitimate daughter who died at the age of five: her death was the greatest emotional blow of his life. He always had an eye to dress, was proud of being an officer, and on the whole preferred the company of men of affairs to that of scholars. However, during the years of his creative work he lived a very solitary life. But when he was fifty-three he was prevailed on by Queen Christina of Sweden, against his will, to go to Stockholm and become her tutor in philosophy. It was a deadly mistake. In the bitter Swedish winter he succumbed to pneumonia, and he died in the following year, 1650.

With me to discuss the first of modern philosophers is Bernard Williams, Professor of Philosophy at the University of California, Berkeley, and author of one of the best-known books on Descartes.

DISCUSSION

Magee I think the best way for us to begin is to get our minds clear about the position from which Descartes started. What, when he began, did he see as his main problem?

Williams Because of the education you referred to, and his experience of the life around him, he had been impressed with the idea that there was no certain way of acquiring knowledge. It looked as though there were some sorts of knowledge around, but there was no reliable method by which people could advance knowledge. To put the situation in a historical context, it is important to realise that science in our sense really didn't exist: there was no science as an organised international enterprise, with research methods and laboratories and so on. Morever, there was room for a great range of opinions about what chances there might be of there being a science. On the one hand there were people, perfectly sensible people, who thought that if you found the right method you could solve all the fundamental problems of understanding nature in a short while. For instance, Francis Bacon, the English statesman, thought that it should be possible to get science on the right road in a very brief period. On the other hand there were people, sceptical people, who thought that there wasn't going to be any knowledge, that there could be no rational way of organising inquiry.

One important reason why there was so much scepticism around stemmed from the religious Reformation. After the Reformation, all sorts of claims were made about how religious truth might be found. These claims conflicted with one another, and there was no way of deciding between them. This gave rise to a great deal of controversy, and one thing that was said, particularly by enemies of religion, was that there was no way of solving any of these questions: there were all these disagreements, and no way of resolving them. Religious people, reacting against that, said in turn that religion was no different in this from anything else. There was no way of putting *anything* on a firm foundation. Scepticism was thus an important current in the intellectual climate of Descartes's time, coexisting in an odd way with very extravagant hopes of what science might be able to do, in particular through what we would now call technology. For instance, there were great hopes that there could be a scientific medicine, and a scientific industry, and so on. But nobody knew how to do it.

Magee For so fundamental a would-be innovator as Descartes the institutions of his day must also have presented severe problems. Almost every serious institution of learning or teaching was in the hands of an authoritarian Church whose own intellectual leaders were in thrall to ancient authority.

Williams That is certainly true. Of course there were many different religious influences, as I just said. One effect of the Reformation had been that some seats of learning had more of a Protestant complexion, while others such as those in Descartes's own Paris were Catholic. But of course the point you mentioned about authority is very important. Although there had been a good deal of research into what we would now call mechanics, or a kind of mathematical physics, in the Middle Ages – and we shouldn't forget that fact – a great deal of what passed for knowledge took the form of commentaries on ancient books, above all (though not exclusively) those of Aristotle. And one thing that Descartes and others of his generation knew for certain was that historical authority was not the same thing as first-order research or inquiry.

Magee Perhaps one can sum it up by saying that Descartes saw his problem as how to find a safe way *out* of this situation. The crucial question was, did a reliable method exist, at least in principle, for getting knowledge and for accumulating knowledge? If it did, what was it? In modern parlance one could say that his quest was for a research programme – and, prior to that, a research method.

Williams Yes, I think that's a correct description of the situation. However, there is one further fact that conditions all of his work and is very important – that science was not conceived as a shared or joint or organised enterprise as it is now. For us it's just taken for granted that science means scientists, a lot of people who communicate with one another, and among whom there's a division of intellectual labour. At that time, the first half of the seventeenth century, it was still a reasonable project for one man to have the idea that he could lay the foundations of all future science. Descartes did really believe that, and it was not a piece of megalomaniac insanity on his part, as it would be in the modern world for anybody to have that idea.

Magee In my introduction to this discussion I said that Descartes became fascinated by the question of whether there was anything we could know for certain. He was clear from the outset that certainty and truth are not the same thing. To put it crudely, certainty is a state of mind, whereas truth is a property of statements which usually relates to the way things are out there in the external world. But Descartes believed that only if you had grounds for certainty could you know you had hold of the truth; and therefore that the pursuit of truth *involves* the pursuit of certainty. This meant that he thought from the beginning that the method he was looking for would have to be one which not only delivered the goods in the form of worthwhile conclusions but could also defend itself successfully against the arguments of sceptics. Now how did he go about meeting that double-barrelled requirement?

Williams Descartes had a set of conditions on inquiry. Some of them were just sensible rules about dividing questions up into manageable parts, trying to get your ideas clear, and things like that. But he had also a rule, very characteristic of his thought, that you shouldn't accept as true anything about which you could entertain the slightest doubt. Now, on the face of it that isn't a sensible rule, because in ordinary life we're constantly seeking true beliefs about things, but we don't necessarily want to make those beliefs as certain as possible, and could not in fact do so. For one thing, we would have to invest too much effort into making our beliefs as certain as we could make them. But Descartes was trying to get the foundations of science: not only the foundations of *a* science, in the sense of fundamental general truths about the world, but also the foundations of inquiry. He wanted to lay the foundations of the possibility of going on to find out more things, and to establish that scientific knowledge was actually possible. To do this, he felt that it was essential that you should start the search for truth with a search for certainty.

He wanted to put the scientific enterprise (as we might call it) into a shape in which it could no longer be attacked by sceptics. So the first thing he wanted to do was to engage in what we might call *pre-emptive scepticism*. In order to put the foundations of knowledge beyond the reach of scepticism he said to himself, in effect: 'I will do everything the sceptics can do, only better. By pressing the sceptical inquiry hard enough, I hope to come out the other side with something that will be absolutely foundational and rock hard.'

It is not that Descartes confused the idea of looking for truth and the idea of looking for certainty. He saw that they were two separate things. But he thought that the right way of searching for truth and, above all, of making the search for truth into a systematic process, was to start by searching for certainty.

Magee This led to the famous 'Cartesian doubt', didn't it – *doubt as method*. This is not the method referred to in the title *Discourse on the Method*, though it is an important part of it. Can you explain how Descartes's methodological doubt worked?

Williams Since he was looking for certainty, he started by laying aside anything in which he could find the slightest doubt. As he famously put it, it's like having a barrel of apples, and some of them are bad and some of them are sound, and you want to separate out the sound ones. So you take them all out first, look at them one by one, throw away the ones that are dubious and put back only the absolutely sound ones. So he started by trying to empty his mind of all beliefs, laying aside anything in which he could see the slightest doubt.

He did that in three stages. He started by laying aside things that just on ordinary commonsensical grounds you might possibly find doubtful. For instance he reminded himself of such well-known facts as that straight sticks can look bent in water or that things may look curious colours to you if you have defects of eyesight, and so on. But he wanted to go beyond those everyday kinds of doubt or grounds of doubt that apply to some of the things we perceive. The next step was to doubt that at any given moment he was awake and perceiving anything at all. He entertained the following thought. He had often dreamt in the past that he was perceiving things, and when he was dreaming, he had thought, just as he does now, that he was seeing people, or tables, or whatever, around him. But, of course, he had woken up and found it was all illusion. Now: how can he be certain at this very instant that he is not dreaming? That is an unnerving kind of sceptical consideration. It had been used by sceptics before, but he gave it an orderly and settled place in his inquiry. Now of course the doubt based on dreaming does depend upon knowing *something*. It depends upon knowing that in the past you have sometimes woken up and found you had been dreaming; it depends on the idea that sometimes you sleep, sometimes you wake, sometimes you dream, and so on. So it does depend on knowing something about the world.

But then he took another step, to the most extreme doubt possible. He imagined a malign spirit (the *malicious demon*, as it's sometimes called in the literature) whose sole intent was to deceive him as much as it could. He then put to himself the following question: suppose there were such a spirit, is there anything he could not mislead me about? This is, of course, a pure thought-experiment. We must emphasise that Descartes never meant this philosophical doubt to be a tool for everyday living. He makes that point over and over again. The Method of Doubt, and particularly the fantasy or model of the evil spirit, is used only as a form of intellectual critique to winnow out his beliefs, and see whether some were more certain than others.

Magee   And of course the ultimate purpose – his long-range strategy in winnowing out everything that he could possibly, in any imaginable circumstances, doubt – is to find rock-hard, indubitable propositions which can then function as the premises for arguments, thus providing unshakeable foundations on which an edifice of knowledge can be built.

Williams   That's right. There are in fact two things. He wants to find rock-hard indubitable propositions, that is to say propositions which in some sense cannot be doubted, which will resist the most extreme doubt. He wants them in part as premises of arguments. He also wants them in a more general role, to provide a background that will validate the methods of inquiry I was referring to before, and we can perhaps say something about how that works.

Magee But meanwhile we have left the ball in the court of the malicious demon, and we must somehow get it back. After peeling away all imaginably doubtable propositions, Descartes found there were some things that it was simply impossible not to be sure of. Will you tell us what they were?

Williams The doubt reaches a turning point; it gets to the end, and Descartes does a U-turn and starts coming back, constructing knowledge as he goes. The point at which the doubt stops is the reflection that he is himself engaged in thinking. As he said, the malicious demon can deceive me as he will, but he can never deceive me in this respect, namely to make me believe that I am thinking when I am not. If I have a false thought, that is still a thought: in order to have a deceived thought, I've got to have a thought, so it must be true that I am thinking. And from that Descartes drew another conclusion, or at least he immediately associated with that another truth, namely that he existed. And so his fundamental first certainty was 'I am thinking, therefore I exist;' or *Cogito ergo sum* in the Latin formulation, from which it is often called simply the *Cogito*.

Magee It's worth stressing the point – which Descartes himself made clear – that by 'thinking' he meant not only conceptual thought but all forms of conscious experience, including feelings, perceptions, pains and so on. This being so, it's not unfair to say that what he was really saying was: 'I am consciously aware, therefore I know that I must exist.'

Williams That's right. In the great work called *Meditations* in which this is most carefully and elaborately set out, he does actually show a great deal of finesse in pushing the boundaries of the *Cogito* forward step by step through various kinds of mental experience. But the sum of what he gets to is exactly that, yes.

Magee Now in the very process of arriving at these fundamental and indubitable propositions Descartes has shown that although we can be certain of them, any inference we may make from them is liable to error, and therefore nothing indubitable *follows* from them. For instance, I cannot doubt that I am at this moment having the experience of seeing you, Bernard Williams, as being, among other things, a material object out there in the external world, but from that it does not follow that there is a world external to myself with material objects existing in it independently of my experience. And the same argument applies right across the board. Although I can always be certain that the immediate deliverances of my consciousness are whatever they are, I can never be certain of the validity of any inference I make from them to something else.

Williams Well, it depends on what sort of inference it is. What he thought was that the mere fact that I have the experience of being confronted with this table, for instance, doesn't guarantee the existence of the table. That certainty was removed even at the dream state of the doubt, and it is made even clearer when Descartes invokes the malicious demon. Using that model, he sees that he might have just this experience and yet nothing actually be there. So one cannot immediately infer the actual world from one's experience. What Descartes tries to do now is to construct a set of considerations that will enable him to put the world back – though it must be said straight away that the form in which the world is put back is rather different from that in which it was originally conceived by common sense. Having moved all the furniture out of the attic in the course of the doubt, we don't simply stuff it all back again in a totally unreconstructed form. We have a different view of the world when we reconstitute it than we did in our original unreflective experience. It is a very important fact about the Method of Doubt that this is so. Descartes conducts the doubt for positive reasons, and when he puts the world back, it has been subtly modified by an intellectual critique of how we can know things. But the question now is how he puts it back.

Magee He seems, in arriving at his indubitable propositions, to have painted himself into a corner. He has his indubitable propositions all right, but in the process of reaching them he has shown that nothing can be inferred from them.

Williams Well, all he's seen at the earlier stage of the proceedings is that the most obvious way of inferring the world from his experiences isn't valid. He's now going to give you a way which he claims is valid. Having got to the point at which he recognises nothing except the contents of his consciousness, it is obvious that if he's going to put the world back he's got to do it entirely out of the contents of his consciousness – there is nothing else available to him. So he's got to find something in the contents of his consciousness that leads outside himself. He claims that what this is is the idea of God. He discovers among the contents of his consciousness the conception of God. And he argues that this is unique among all the ideas that he has; among all the things that are in his mind, this alone is such that the mere fact that he has this idea proves that there really is something corresponding to it, that is to say, there really is a God.

Magee That's a difficult argument for modern readers to swallow – including those who believe in God.

Williams Yes. In fact he has two different arguments, both of which he uses in *Meditations*, for doing this. One is a medieval argument called the ontological argument; perhaps we needn't spend time on that. It presents a logical or metaphysical puzzle, but it's much less characteristic of Descartes. The other argument is more characteristic of Descartes, though it also uses scholastic or medieval materials. It relies on a supposedly necessary principle to the effect that the lesser cannot give rise to, or be the cause of, the greater. Descartes is sure that he has an idea of God, and that idea is the idea of an infinite thing. Although in itself it's only an idea, the fact that it is the idea of an infinite thing demands a very special explanation. Descartes claims that no finite creature, as he knows himself to be, could possibly have given rise to such an idea, the idea of an infinite being. It could have been implanted in him only by God himself: as Descartes memorably puts it at one point, as the mark of the maker on his work. God, as it were, signed him by leaving in him this infinite idea of God himself. When he reflects that the lesser cannot give rise to the greater, he realises that since he has this idea of God, it can be only because there actually is a God who has created him.

Magee And having derived the certainty of God's existence from the deliverances of his own consciousness, he then proceeds to derive the certainty of the existence of the external world from his certainty of God's existence.

Williams That's right. He next considers what he knows about this God. He reflects in the following way: I know that God exists, that he's omnipotent, that he created me, and I know that he's benevolent. (These are of course all traditional Christian beliefs.) Because God created me and is benevolent, he is concerned as much with my intellectual welfare as with my moral welfare. And what that means is that if I do my bit – and that's very important – and I clarify my ideas as much as I should, and I don't assent precipitately to things I haven't thought out properly; if I do my bit in that sense, then God will validate the things which I am then very strongly disposed to believe. Now I find that however much criticism I make of my ideas, however carefully I think out what is involved in my beliefs about the physical world, although I can suspend judgment in the doubt (I wouldn't have got to this point if I couldn't), I do have a very strong tendency to believe that there is a material world there. And since I have this disposition and I have done everything in my power to make sure that my beliefs are not founded on error, then God will at the end make sure that I am not fundamentally and systematically mistaken. That is, I can rightfully believe that there is such a world.

Magee This becomes, doesn't it, Descartes's way of refuting anyone who is radically sceptical about the possibilities of philosophy or science? But in asserting that the world with which they deal is given to us by a God whose existence and benevolence are self-evident he has not so much answered the sceptic as tried to pre-empt him.

Williams Well, it is essential to his position that he believes that these arguments that introduce God will be assented to by any person of good faith who concentrates on them enough. That's *absolutely* essential. It would ruin his whole position if he accepted the idea that whether you believe in God is a matter of culture or psychological upbringing, and that perfectly sensible people can disagree about whether there's a God or not however hard they think about it. For Descartes, to deny the existence of God when confronted with these arguments would be as perverse and as totally in bad faith as it would be to deny that twice two is four. The idea is that if you put these proofs before the sceptic and lead him properly through them, and if the sceptic is an honest person, and is not just mouthing words or trying to impress, he must at the end assent. Some people have not assented because they haven't thought hard enough; they have not treated these questions in an orderly manner. A lot of the sceptics are no doubt fakes, who simply go around making a rhetorical position and don't really think about it. But if you're in good faith and think hard enough about it, then you will come to see this truth and then you cannot consistently deny the existence of the external world. That's what Descartes believed.

Magee One historically important outcome of this set of arguments was the positing of a world consisting of two different sorts of entity. There is the external world, given to me by a God on whom I can rely. But there is also me, observing the external world. Now in arriving at the *Cogito* I found it possible to think away from my conception of myself everything except this very act of thought itself – and this, said Descartes, means that I must irreducibly *be* thought. I can conceive of myself as existing without a body, but I cannot conceive of myself as existing without conscious awareness; so the material which is my body is not part of the quintessential me. This chimes, of course, with the traditional Christian view, held for quite different reasons. And it leads straight to a view of the world as split between subjects which are pure thought and objects which are pure extension. This is the famous 'Cartesian dualism', the bifurcation of nature between mind and matter, observer and observed, subject and object. It has become built into the whole of Western man's way of looking at things, including the whole of our science.

Williams In many ways that is true. At the extreme point of the doubt, Descartes can be said to think that the external world may not exist. But the 'external world' is a phrase that has many things packed into it. The 'external world' is outside what? – outside *me*. But 'outside me' does not mean 'outside my body'. My body is part of the external world, in Descartes's sense: it is itself one of the things outside me. In the end, when through knowledge of God the external world has been restored, I indeed get my body back. It then turns out that I indeed *have* a body. But it never turns out that I *am* a body. What I ordinarily call *me*, according to Descartes, is actually two things: on the one hand, an immaterial – and he also believed immortal – soul, which, as you say, was purely intellectual, purely mental, had no physical extension at all; and, on the other, a body. It follows that when in ordinary life we talk about ourselves in the first person we happily put together statements of quite different kinds. One can say to somebody else quite cheerfully, 'I am embarrassed, I am thinking about Paris, and I weigh a hundred and fifty pounds.' For Descartes, that's just what the grammarians used to call a zeugma – I'm actually talking about two quite different things. When I say I'm thinking about Paris, that's a statement about my mind – that is to say, according to Descartes, about what is really *me*. When I say I weigh a hundred and fifty pounds, that's only a way of speaking –

Magee   – about your body, which is not *you*, really, at all.

Williams   That's right. An American philosopher put it well: in Descartes's view, to say 'I weigh a hundred and fifty pounds' is much like saying 'on the way here I had a puncture'.

Magee   At the beginning we said that Descartes's strategic aim was to establish the possibility of what we now call science; and you have shown us the arguments by which he arrived at his particular view of the external world. How is that a world that can be treated scientifically?

Williams   I mentioned earlier that when through the help of God we put the world back again, we didn't put back the same world that we'd thrown away; it has been criticised in the process. In our reflections we come to the conclusion not only that there is an external world, but that, just as thought is my essence as a thinking thing, so the external world, too, has an essence and that is simply extension. All there is to it essentially is that it takes up space and that it is susceptible to being treated by geometry and the mathematical sciences. All its more colourful aspects – the fact that it *is* coloured, and that there are tastes and sounds – are really subjective. They're on the mental side; they are subjective phenomena that occur in consciousness, caused by this physical, extended, geometrical world.

Magee   He had a striking example of the essential separateness from a continuing substance of all its sense-dependent properties, an example well worth citing. Pick up in your hand, he says, a piece of wax. It has a certain size and shape, a certain solid feel to the hand, a certain texture, temperature, colour, smell and so on; and to us it seems to be the combination of those properties. But if you put it in front of the fire every single one of them changes: it becomes liquid, falls into a different shape, gets hotter, turns dark brown, gives off a different smell, and so on and so forth. Yet we still want to say it's the same wax. What is there about it that's the same? Surely, there is now *nothing* about it that is the same? Answer: yes there is, namely one and the same continuous history of space-occupancy. And this is measurable jointly in terms of space and of time. And both forms of measurement are essentially mathematical.

Williams Yes. It is disputed what exactly Descartes thought the wax argument proved, just by itself. But he certainly used that example to illustrate, if not actually to prove, what he thought was a fundamental idea, that a material thing just is something that occupies space – indeed, in a sense, is a piece of space. He thought that a material body was itself a piece or volume of space, rather than just being *in* space, in part because he didn't believe in a vacuum. He thought that the whole physical world was one extended item, and that separate things in it, tables or whatever, were local areas of this in certain states of motion. This is a foundation for the mathematical physics of the seventeenth century. In its own terms it didn't come off. Eventually it was going to be replaced by the classical dynamics of Newton which had a different conception of the physical world. But Descartes's picture did a great deal to establish the notion of a physical world which is fundamentally of a mathematical character and permits mathematical physics to be done. It is a very significant fact about the scientific revolution that started in the period we're discussing, in Descartes's lifetime and through his work, that the first of the great sciences to get going was mathematical physics. Chemistry, the science that deals with sorts of things in greater particularity, is much more a product of the eighteenth and nineteenth centuries than of the seventeenth century.

Magee Wouldn't it be fair to say that Descartes, in his day, did more to establish the possibility of science as such, and to 'sell' it to the general educated public of Western Europe, than anyone else, with the possible exception only of Bacon?

Williams I think that is probably so. There is a figure who is also enormously famous and whose actual physics is nearer to classical physics as it came out in the end, and that is Galileo. But Galileo was more notorious, perhaps, than respectable, because he was tried and condemned by the Inquisition. Descartes's intellectual influence in this respect was very great, even though the details of his physics were eventually to be, in good part, repudiated.

Magee Up to this point in our discussion, Descartes hasn't provided us with any physics: what he has done is show that a mathematically based physics is possible, that is to say intellectually within our powers and at the same time applicable to the real world. Can you expand on this distinction between doing the science and showing it to be possible?

René Descartes (1596–1650)

Williams Yes. What he hopes to have shown by the manoeuvres that we have followed so far is that the world is so constructed that man is capable of knowing about it. In a sense, man and the world are made for each other, by God. For Descartes, man in his essence is not actually part of nature, because man is this immaterial intellectual substance which isn't part of the natural world, or subject to scientific laws. Man is not part of nature in that sense but nevertheless his intellectual powers are well adjusted to it. That means we can conduct a mathematical physics. Now Descartes thought that some of the fundamental principles of physics could themselves be known by what we would call philosophical reflection. He thought in particular we could know by such reflection that physics has to have a conservation law. There has to be some quantity that was conserved. Descartes actually picked on, as the quantity that was conserved, something, namely motion, which wasn't conserved, and indeed in terms of classical physics later was not even well defined. But the idea was there and it was supposed to be *a priori*; known by reflection. There were some other fundamental physical principles that he thought could be known *a priori*. But beyond that, he thought that truths of physics had to be discovered empirically.

This is quite important because Descartes is, rightly, said to be a rationalist philosopher. He thinks that fundamental properties of the world and of the mind can be discovered by reflection. He does not think that everything is derived from experience. But it's sometimes supposed that he was such a strong rationalist that he thought that the whole of science was to be deduced from metaphysics by purely mathematical or logical reasoning: that if I sat and thought hard enough about the *Cogito* and matter and God I'd arrive at the whole of science. He thought no such thing. In fact, he is absolutely consistent in saying that experiments are necessary to distinguish between some ways of explaining nature and others. You can build different models. This is a very modern aspect of his thought. You can build or construct different intellectual models of the world within his laws, and experiment is needed to discover which truly represent nature.

Magee Is experiment seen by him as designed to test our theories about nature, or as giving us the data out of which those theories are themselves constructed?

Williams It's designed for a number of different things, actually, but the basic point is the following. If you take the fundamental laws of nature, the principles on which matter moves, there are a lot of different mechanisms you could imagine which would produce superficially the same effect. You then make differential experiments, arranging a set-up in which one thing will happen if one model corresponds to reality, and something else will happen if a different model does. So you select between models. And that really is quite a good description of quite a lot of what physicists do.

Magee Essentially, it's the modern notion of the crucial experiment.

Williams Descartes was very keen on that idea. One of the things that he admirably insisted on was that it was no good blundering around the world trying out experiments simply to see what you could find out. You had to ask the right questions. This is another application of a principle we have already mentioned, that God is on your side if you do your bit. God will not allow you to be systematically deceived if you don't systematically deceive yourself. So what you have to do is to think of the right questions: God has arranged things so that nature will give you the answers.

Magee I think it's time we made the point that although God was indispensable to Descartes in arriving at 'the method', once you're in possession of the method you don't have to be a believer in God to use it.

Williams That's right. It is a very important point, that Descartes wanted to free the process of science from theological constraints, theological interference. In one way, he wanted to free it from theological foundations, if that means foundations that can be provided only by theologians. But, as we have seen, God was at the foundation of his system, and he was extremely keen to say that his inquiry did not leave us with a Godless world. His world was made by God, and our knowledge of it is guaranteed by God. Where you have to appeal to God in your intellectual life, however, is not (as you rightly say) in conducting science, but in proving to sceptics that it can be conducted. Moreover, Descartes very sensibly thought you shouldn't spend a lot of time proving to sceptics that it can be conducted. It needs to be done only once, and he thought he'd done it.
Descartes laid great emphasis on God, and it is my own belief that he was absolutely sincere in doing so. I don't think he was a faker of any kind in this respect, although he did conciliate the priests in various ways: he was not a man for getting into trouble with the Church. But although he was sincere himself, the construction he produced is one that made it easier for God to disappear from the world and from people's understanding of the world.

Magee Some people have claimed that Descartes was not a sincere believer in God at all, and they point to passages in his works which are unquestionably ironic. But I do not think their claim can be upheld, for the simple reason that Descartes's entire life's work would fall to the ground if it were true. For all I know, he may have been an insincere Christian, but that would be an entirely different matter. He certainly took an unillusioned view of the Church. But that he sincerely believed in the existence of God is something about which, in my view, there is no room for serious doubt. People who think the opposite are, I suspect, confusing disbelief in Christianity with disbelief in God – a thing which far too many Christians have been apt to do, both then and now.

But I want to turn to something else. A little while ago we touched on Cartesian dualism, the division of total reality into spirit and matter, but then somehow we failed to follow it up. Can we do that now? The most obvious problem it presented was how to explain the interaction between the two. How does Descartes account for spirit's ability to push material objects around in space?

Williams Frankly, the answer is that he never really did. Leibniz somewhat scornfully said on this subject of the interaction, 'Monsieur Descartes seems to have given up the game so far as we can see.' Just before Descartes went to Sweden, he wrote a book in which he did, curiously, try to localise the interactions between mind and body in the pineal gland, which is to be found at the base of the brain. But it barely even makes sense. The idea that this abstract non-material item, the mind, something that is almost though not quite in the same category as a number, could induce a change in the physical world by redirecting certain animal spirits, which is what he believed, is so difficult to conceive even in principle that it was a scandal for everybody. A lot of the philosophy of the seventeenth century, and indeed subsequently, addressed itself to trying to find some more adequate representation of the relation of mind and body than Descartes left us with.

Magee Even so, Cartesian dualism in some form or other got embedded in Western thought for three hundred years.

Williams Well, I think that some distinction between subject and object, knower and known, is a distinction that it is simply impossible for us to do without. There are philosophical systems that try to say that we have no conception of the known independently of the knower, that – in effect – we make up the whole world. But that sort of view, even in its more sophisticated forms, is quite difficult to believe. We use, and certainly science uses, some kind of dualism between the knower and the known, the idea of a world that is independent of our process of knowing it. What very few people now assent to is the absolute dualism between the completely pure mind and the body. The knower has to be understood as an essentially embodied creature, and not just as a pure spirit. This had been accepted in philosophy earlier than Descartes, for instance by St Thomas Aquinas or by Aristotle.

Magee   Are there any other really crucial flaws in the Cartesian system?

Williams   The argument for God seemed one of the weakest parts of the system as time went on, and this had an important historical result because, as you said earlier, it looked as if Descartes, in using the method of doubt, had painted himself into a corner. If he can't get out of the corner by using theological means, there was not any way of doing it, so that if you travel with him down the road of the doubt, it seems that you end up in this idealist position where you're left with nothing except the contents of consciousness.

There's another feature of Descartes's position that should be mentioned. Even in his own lifetime his system was attacked for being circular. God is supposed to validate everything. We've emphasised in the course of this discussion the role of God, particularly in validating our beliefs about the external world, but Descartes also thought that God played an important role in validating our belief in argument in general. But of course it is by argument that he arrives at the belief in God itself. So even at the time his work appeared, people objected that he was involved in a circle.

Magee   Only because he 'clearly and distinctly' apprehends that God exists can he make any progress from the *Cogito* at all. But only because he knows that God exists and is no deceiver does he have any assurance that what he 'clearly and distinctly' apprehends is true.

Williams   The details of this are very much a matter of particular interest for the study of Descartes. But there is a very general problem, of which this is an example, which is the question of philosophy's relation to its own existence. The Cartesian circle, as it's called, is a particular example in this context of the difficulty that philosophy has in stating the possibility of its own existence. It has to allow for its own discovery, its own validity and so on, and it is difficult for it to avoid some sort of circle or some regress there.

Magee   This is a point of such general importance that it's worth pausing over for a moment. Every general explanatory framework claiming validity must be able to explain both its own validity and how we are able to arrive at it. To take an example a long way removed from Descartes: if a philosophy maintains that philosophical beliefs have nothing to do with truth but serve merely to promote the class interests of the people subscribing to them, then it is maintaining that it itself has nothing to do with truth but serves merely to promote the class interests of the persons subscribing to it. Thus it is self-disqualifying as a serious philosophy. Or if another approach holds as its central principle that all meaningful statements must either be tautologically true or be empirically verifiable then it itself is, again, instantly disqualified, because that statement itself is neither tautologically true nor empirically verifiable. Many belief-systems raise difficulties of this kind for themselves: if they were true we should be barred from regarding them as such, and in some cases we would not even be able to formulate them. *A theory has to make room for itself*. It has to be able to provide a non-self-contradictory legitimation of itself, and of the means whereby we have arrived at it. If it cannot do that it is self-contradictory or incoherent, and in either case untenable.

But to return to Descartes: his influence on philosophy has been simply immense, hasn't it? Can you say something about that?

Williams If you summarise it in one thing, it was Descartes, and almost Descartes alone, who brought it about that the centre of Western philosophy for these past centuries has been the theory of knowledge. He brought it about that philosophy started from the question 'What can I know?' rather than questions such as 'What is there?' or 'How is the world?' Moreover, the question is not 'What can be known?' or even 'What can we know?' but 'What can *I* know?' That is, it starts from a first-person egocentric question. I mentioned right at the beginning that it was possible in his time to think that science could perhaps be done by one person. But even when you lay that historical context aside, it is a very important part of his enterprise that it is autobiographical. It is no accident that his two great works, *Discourse on the Method* and the *Meditations*, are written in the first person. They are works of philosophical self-inquiry. This first-person and epistemological emphasis has been the principal influence of Descartes.

Magee After Descartes, it is not until our own century that any significant number of philosophers have disputed that 'What can I know?' is the central question of philosophy.

Williams Well, there is a question about what you make of Hegel in that respect. There are various ways of taking Hegel, in one of which you can see Hegel as trying to get back to a kind of Aristotelian view of philosophy in which this question is less dominant. But it is certainly important that at the end of the nineteenth century, and in our own century, people have moved away from the epistemological emphasis of Descartes more to a logical and linguistic emphasis and have tried to make the philosophy of language rather than the theory of knowledge the centre of philosophy.

Magee Given that the philosophy of Descartes has the faults we have mentioned – and others which we have not mentioned – and given that the central focus of philosophers' concern has in any case moved away from the problem of knowledge, why is the study of Descartes still so valuable?

Let me express this personally. You worked, on and off, for a period of over twenty years at a book about Descartes: why did you consider it worth that enormous investment of your life?

Williams I think for two reasons. Let us leave on one side the case for an historical understanding of the role that Descartes has played in getting us into our present situation. Just to know what he said in a little bit of detail is, I think, very important simply to understanding who we are and where we've come from. But the reason why I think that his work – when I say 'his work' I have particularly in mind the *Meditations* – is something that, if one's interested in philosophy, one wants to read now, is that the path it follows, the path of asking 'What do I know?', 'What can I doubt?' and so on, is presented in an almost irresistible way. It is not an accident that this emphasis in philosophy has been so overwhelmingly important. It isn't that Descartes, just because he was a dazzling stylist, can perform long-distance mesmerism on the mind of Europe. That isn't the reason. The reason is that he discovered something intrinsically compelling, the idea that I say to myself: I have all these beliefs, but how can I get behind them to see if they're really true? How can I stand back from my beliefs to see which of them are prejudices? How much room is there for scepticism? These are really compelling questions, and it needs a great deal of philosophical imagination and work to get oneself out of this very natural pattern of reflection; and, as Descartes said, when you have been through that process you do not merely end up where you were at the beginning. It is not just a matter of recovering from a self-inflicted philosophical illness.

Another question that is put to you dramatically by Descartes is 'What am I?' We can imagine ourselves as other than we are. We have a power of extracting ourselves imaginatively from our actual circumstances. We can imagine ourselves looking out on the world from a different body. We can imagine looking into a mirror and seeing a different face – and, what's important, looking into a mirror, seeing a different face, and not being surprised. And this gives me the idea, a powerful idea, that I am independent of the body and the past that I have. That is an experience basic to the Cartesian idea that I am somehow independent of all these material things. If you look at Cartesian dualism from the outside, as a theory, it is very difficult to believe, for the reasons that we've touched on. But at the same time there is something in it that is hard to resist, if you come to it through a certain set of reflections. The set of reflections that Descartes with unexampled clarity and force lays before you and which lead you down that path – as I think, a mistaken path – are not only very striking, but, as it were, near to the bone. Here again, you cannot return unchanged from trying to overcome Descartes's reflections. It is a prime philosophical task to try to arrive at an understanding of oneself, of one's imagination, of one's ideas of what one might be, that can free one from his dualistic model.

SPINOZA and LEIBNIZ

Dialogue with
ANTHONY QUINTON

INTRODUCTION

Magee For a long time now it has been usual to see Western philosophy in the seventeenth and eighteenth centuries as divided between two opposing schools, British empiricism and Continental rationalism – the chief of the empiricists being Locke, Berkeley and Hume, the chief of the rationalists Descartes, Spinoza and Leibniz. Of the many issues that divided them the most important, put at its crudest, was this. The rationalists believed that we human beings can acquire important knowledge of reality by the use of our minds alone, by thinking, by pure reason. The empiricists denied this. They insisted that experience was always a necessary ingredient, and that all our knowledge of what actually exists must in the end, in some way or other, be derived from experience. Again, the traditional view has been that these two opposing schools finally came together at the end of the eighteenth century and were combined in the work of Immanuel Kant.

In this discussion we are going to consider Spinoza and Leibniz, the two greatest of the rationalist philosophers after Descartes. The first in time was Spinoza, born in Amsterdam in 1632. His family were Portuguese Jews who in the aftermath of the Spanish Inquisition emigrated to Holland in search of religious freedom. He was brought up and educated in an enclosed Jewish community, but he rebelled against religious orthodoxy, and at the age of only twenty-four he was excommunicated by the Jewish authorities. Fortunately for him, he was a loner by temperament as well as circumstances, and he chose a solitary mode of life in order to do his work. When he was offered a professorship at the University of Heidelberg he turned it down. He earned his living grinding lenses for spectacles, microscopes and telescopes. It is believed that the daily inhaling of glass dust from this occupation aggravated the lung ailment that killed him at the early age of forty-four. His acknowledged masterpiece, a book entitled *Ethics* but in fact dealing with the whole range of philosophy, came out after his death but in the same year, 1677. A striking feature of this book is that it is modelled directly on Euclid's geometry: starting from a small number of axioms and primitive terms it proceeds by deductive logic to prove a long succession of numbered propositions which, taken together, lay out the total groundplan of reality. It is often held up as the supreme example of a self-contained metaphysical system whose object is to explain everything.

In only the year before his death Spinoza had a series of meetings with the other philosopher we are going to consider, Leibniz – one of comparatively few instances of two of the greatest of philosophers actually meeting each other and having face-to-face discussions. As a personality Leibniz was a complete contrast to Spinoza: courtier and diplomat, always travelling, honoured in many countries. He was one of the great polymaths of our culture. It was he who coined the notion of kinetic energy. He invented calculus not knowing that Newton had already done so, and he published it before Newton did: in fact it is his notation, not Newton's, that we use to this day. And he was among the greatest of philosophers.

Leibniz was born in Leipzig in 1646 and died in Hanover in 1716. So brilliant was he as a student that he was offered a professorship at the age of twenty-one, but like Spinoza he turned it down, though for the opposite reason: he wanted to be a man of the world. He spent most of his life at the Court of Hanover in the service of successive Dukes, one of whom became King George I of England. Leibniz carried out almost every task imaginable for a person in such a position, so his philosophy was, as one might put it, written in his spare time. He wrote an enormous amount, even so, mostly in the form of quite short papers; but he published scarcely any of his work during his lifetime. He also maintained a voluminous international correspondence, which is now of philosophical importance. Among his outstanding works are *The Monadology*; *The Discourse on Metaphysics*; and a book called *New Essays Concerning Human Understanding*, which is a point-by-point argument with his English near-contemporary, John Locke.

To discuss the work of both Leibniz and Spinoza I have invited someone who is well known both as a philosopher and as a historian of philosophy: Anthony Quinton, Chairman of the British Library.

DISCUSSION

Magee   Obviously we are going to want to discuss our two philosophers separately, but before we do, is there anything that can usefully be said about the two of them together?

Quinton   I think there is: the thing you mentioned right at the beginning. It is a standard piece of tidy, convenient classification. We are presented with opposed trios of thinkers: the three British empiricists, Locke, Berkeley and Hume, and the three Continental rationalists, Descartes, Spinoza and Leibniz. The rationalist trio, as much as the empiricist trio, had a community of style and purpose. Descartes defined the terms and laid down the agenda for the group. But the conception of the world that Descartes produced by the exercise of pure reason is a fairly straightforward affair. He preserves the human self in a recognisable form, as a distinct, autonomous individual. He affirms, indeed claims to prove, the existence of God, in terms at any rate intelligible to his age, for his God is hardly personal. And he preserves the material world in a recognisable form, even if it is deprived of some of its more vivid and colourful and odoriferous attributes. In the conception of the world arrived at by the application of the procedure of rationalism you start from some apparently self-evident propositions, in the manner of somebody working out a system of geometry, and you go on to carry out straightforward logical deductions from the self-evident premisses. Now what that led to in the cases of Spinoza and Leibniz is something very far removed, in different and largely opposed ways, from the everyday understanding of the world. By comparison with them Descartes is in the business of saving the appearances. But both Spinoza and Leibniz say that what the world is really like is very different from what it appears to the ordinary person to be.

Magee In other words, both of them were saying that there is an underlying reality to the world which everyday observation and experience do not perceive but which philosophy can reveal.

Quinton That is right; and a very odd world it is, in each case. Although it is utterly different in each case, the two philosophers purport to be following the same procedure, under broadly Cartesian guidance. Spinoza's world is a unitary one. He maintains that there is only one true thing, which is the world as a whole. It is both extended – spread out in space – and at the same time mental, a system of connected ideas. With Leibniz, on the other hand, the real world consists of an infinity of things that are purely spiritual. Everything material – and space itself, the home of matter – is merely a phenomenon or appearance, a by-product of the real world, which is this infinite array of spiritual centres.

Magee The world is a very odd place, so the truth about it is pretty well bound to be odd too. Bertrand Russell wrote in *The Problems of Philosophy*: 'The truth about physical objects *must* be strange. It *may* be unattainable, but if any philosopher believes that he has attained it, the fact that what he offers as the truth is strange ought not to be made a ground of objection to his opinion.' I agree very strongly with that.
  Well, now: let's start considering Spinoza and Leibniz separately. And let us start with Spinoza. His philosophy is, as you more or less implied, one single hugely elaborate system of ideas which is supposed to correspond to the reality of the world. Now it is always difficult, when expounding a system, to know where to start, because everything in it depends on something else. How would you begin?

Quinton Before getting down to the substantial detail of his system I think one had better say something more about Spinoza's method. He says himself that his book *Ethics* is 'demonstrated in the geometrical manner'; and, as you mentioned in your remarks at the beginning, he sets it out with all the traditional apparatus of geometry: Axioms and Postulates, Definitions and Corollaries, and at the end of each piece of argument we find the letters QED, as if it were an ordinary tract of geometrical reasoning. But the curious thing is that on the whole philosophers have not taken a very great interest in Spinoza's actual arguments. He is not thought of as a reservoir of interesting deductions, whereas Leibniz is thought of in just that way. So perhaps his method – this very explicit and conscious geometrical mode of proceeding – although it is the stylistically most obvious feature of Spinoza's work, is not what really matters about it. What is important is a vision, the vision of the world as an absolutely unitary entity, any division of which – either into parts, such as souls or physical objects, or into kinds, like the mental and the material – is a mutilation, embodying some kind of misunderstanding.

Magee It is a very difficult idea for many people to grasp, this notion of total reality as one single item of which all apparently different objects, including human individuals, are merely facets, aspects, modes. Can you unpack it for us a little more?

Quinton Here again – and I promise not to go on doing this – I think we need to go back to Descartes for a moment. Descartes defined substance in a very influential way. In philosophy the idea of substance is the idea of what really exists, what the real components of the world are, as contrasted with secondary or derivative items which are only shadows or footprints of the real thing. Descartes defined substance as 'that which requires nothing but itself in order to exist'. If that is taken quite literally it follows that the only true substance is God – always supposing that there is such a thing as God (and Descartes thought he could prove that there necessarily had to be) – because everything that exists apart from God, such as human souls and material objects, including human bodies, depends on God, who created it, for its existence. The claim of everything but God to the title of substance is thus defective. But although for Descartes God is the only absolute substance, once having made that point he did not, as Spinoza was to do, dwell on it. He allowed that souls and bodies are at least relative substances. Apart from depending on God they are self-subsistent, and thus different from the thoughts and feelings of souls, or the shapes and sizes of bodies, which are not substantial in any sense. Spinoza, however, takes seriously that point of Descartes's about God being the sole true substance. He insists that there really is only one true substance, only one thing which – to give a rough translation of his own phrase – is the explanation of itself, only one thing whose essence explains its existence, whose essential nature it is to exist. His conclusion was, unlike Descartes's, that the only thing of which that is true is not a creator God, distinct from the world he creates, but the totality of what there is, absolutely everything. One element in Spinoza's grand design which vaguely accords with common sense is his contention that the one substance, the totality, absolutely everything, is in fact nature, the spatio-temporal material world – which is, at the same time (somewhat less in accordance with common sense) God.

Magee One argument he used for the essential unity and the essential divinity of everything derived from the notion of God's infinite nature. If God is infinite, then there isn't anything that God isn't. To put this point a little more clearly, if the world is separate from God then God has boundaries, limits, and in that case he is finite, not infinite. If God is infinite then God must be co-extensive with everything.

Quinton That is, I think, the most persuasive way you could find of arguing for Spinoza's position; and it has anticipations in earlier philosophy. He calls in a good many other arguments to establish his general point, but what it really amounts to is that there is only one thing whose explanation lies within itself. As far as everything else is concerned, its explanation lies outside it. And this One Thing, as I said, Spinoza identifies both with nature as a whole and, more surprisingly, with God.

Magee There really is a giant step between those two ideas, isn't there? To see the whole of reality as being essentially a unity is one thing; to see that unity then as divine is something quite else. Why do you suppose he took that last step?

Quinton I suppose it is because of God's perfection that, in Spinoza's view, nature cannot be understood as a passive by-product of God's activity. Nature is the totality of what there is, the self-explanatory thing; and so, to that extent, it is a perfect being, the most perfect thing there could be; and therefore it deserves the name God. The only God Spinoza was prepared to countenance is a God who is identical with the whole array of natural things.

Magee You said that the really important thing we get from Spinoza is not a set of arguments but a vision of how the world is. That vision, I suppose, could be expressed in words by saying that if we call the totality of everything there is 'nature' then we are sure in the knowledge that, in our terminology, there can be no supernatural or supranatural realm, and we are also sure in the knowledge that God cannot be outside nature.

Quinton That is Spinoza's position. God and nature cannot be conceived as distinct things, as in the orthodox religious tradition, because in that case each would be limited by the other. God would be – self-contradictorily – imperfect. And the created world would be imperfect too, with an incomplete being as its creator.

Magee Because he held this view he had a knock-down answer to the

Baruch Spinoza (1632–77)

most notoriously unsolved problem bequeathed by Descartes, the problem of the interaction between mind and matter. He was able to say that there can be no interaction in the sense postulated, because mind and matter are actually the same thing seen under different aspects – and that this is why we perceive the regularities which give us the illusion of causal connection.

Quinton Certainly the relation between mind and body constituted a special problem for Descartes, and he had a bold, if not very satisfactory, solution for it. He saw the two realms of being, although utterly different in kind, as nevertheless interacting. He claimed that the mind, although wholly non-physical itself, could deflect the flow of physical currents in the nervous system. Spinoza, like many of Descartes's successors, would have none of that, and went on in a manner all his own to unite what Descartes had divided. It has often been maintained by historians of philosophy that we can understand Spinoza best if we conceive him as principally concerned with that problem of Descartes, about the relations of mind and body. I think that is rather a limited idea of what Spinoza is up to: he is really after bigger game, a proper, total conception of things. In developing his fundamental assumption that the one substance is infinite he says not only that it contains everything, and has nothing lying outside it – an idea close to, if not identical with, the idea of infinity – but also that God or nature, the single substance, the totality of what there is, has an infinity of attributes. That sounds puzzling. It is puzzling because, as it turns out, only two of these attributes are in any way accessible or intelligible to us. The others have to be taken on trust. We must just swallow the amorphous notion that what there is has infinitely more attributes than we can have any conception of. The two we do know are the attributes of thought, or consciousness, on the one hand, and of extension, or the occupancy of space, on the other. Spinoza goes on to say that in the total, all-inclusive fabric of the one substance, local and temporary formations crop up like wrinkles in a cloth. He calls these wrinkles modes. They are, in his view, the real nature of what we ordinarily think of as self-subsisting things such as tables, chairs, ourselves, our friends, the Himalayas. In everyday life we take such things to be identifiable items with clear, definite outlines. For Spinoza they are just temporary contours taken on here and there by the fabric of everything there is.

Magee Like waves in the sea.

Quinton Exactly, waves in the sea or wrinkles in cloth. Each of these modes is at once conscious and extended, and so the phases or wrinkles of reality have these two aspects, a mental aspect and a physical aspect, at one and the same time. There is no question here of two utterly separated things happening to keep in time with each other, of running parallel. They are one and the same thing viewed from two different directions. A particular implication worth mentioning is that for Spinoza the mind and the body are inseparable, indeed he describes the human mind as the idea of the human body. That leaves no place for the immortality of the soul – something ruled out more generally by the theory that the soul is a mode, and all modes are transient.

Magee We've both made much of the fact that Spinoza models the presentation of his philosophy on Euclidean geometry, and also believes that his system of ideas directly expresses the system of the world. On the face of it there can be no room for indeterminism in a deductive system. How, then, does Spinoza view the vexed question of whether we do or do not have free will?

Quinton He maintains that what he would regard as the everyday, commonsensical notion of freedom – the idea that the human individual can sometimes act as spontaneous, uncaused cause of things, exercising the freedom of pure spontaneity – is impossible, an illusion engendered by our not knowing what the causes of our actions are. On the other hand he says there is such a thing as human servitude or bondage. Since this is a state that men are not always and irrevocably condemned to, a state from which they can be liberated, a kind of freedom is available to them. Human bondage consists in being induced to act by some causes rather than others. There are some causes – we may describe them in general terms as the passive emotions such as hatred, anger and fear – which are generated in us by the frustrating influence of the parts of the world that are outside us. But as well as these, he believes, we have active emotions, those generated by an understanding of our circumstances in the world, a knowledge of what is really going on. The more our activities are caused by active emotions and the less by passive ones, the less we are in bondage, the more we are ourselves. This is the only kind of human freedom Spinoza can countenance.

Magee I think he was probably the first person in European thought to introduce the idea that discovering what the hidden sources of your feelings and actions are will in some significant sense be liberating even though it does not literally increase your freedom. It is liberating because it puts you at one with yourself. It frees you from the frustration – and therefore from the rage and unhappiness to which frustration gives rise – induced by being at the mercy of forces you do not understand. It leads to acceptance, and that in turn to a lack of feelings of constraint, and this greatly increases your happiness – indeed, it is the secret of how to be happy. This thought has cropped up again and again in different guises ever since. For instance, it is central to the ideas of Freud and psychoanalysis.

Quinton I think you are right. Or one could see Spinoza's attitude to man's position in the world as a stoic one. It is the idea that the world around us is not particularly interested in us, so we must diminish its power to make us suffer by controlling the emotions it excites in us. But you are right in saying that there is something more in Spinoza. He does not think that by a terrific effort we can repress or overcome these sad and unfortunate passive emotions. His position is that by the exercise of the intellect in gaining an understanding of the world we can make these emotions fade away so that their place comes to be occupied by the active emotions. The most elevated of these is what he calls 'the intellectual love of God', the emotion that attends metaphysical understanding, a comprehensive grasp of the nature of the world as a whole.

Magee In a way there is a touch of something paradoxical in the fact that Spinoza is commonly thought of as a religious or quasi-religious thinker when in fact he did not believe in the existence of a personal God, did not believe in the immortality of the soul, and did not believe that we have free will. He has often been described as a pantheist – indeed, he is thought of as *the* pantheist among the great philosophers, in the same sort of way as Schopenhauer is thought of as *the* pessimist, or Hume as *the* sceptic, or Locke as *the* liberal, and so on. Do you think we are right to see him in this way?

Quinton I think that it is certainly right to think of him as a pantheist, and that to think that is not in the least to deny that he is genuinely religious. To come at the point negatively first, there is a good deal of correspondence between the views of Spinoza and many of the views of the roughly contemporary British philosopher Thomas Hobbes. Now Hobbes was a man of indestructible cheerfulness even though he took a gloomy view in principle of the universe in general and of human nature in particular. Despite occasional polite or cautious references to God he was clearly an atheist. The crucial difference from Spinoza is that his attitude is unswervingly secular, perfectly devoid of anything like piety or reverence. But although Spinoza saw the actual nature of the world much as Hobbes did, his attitude towards it is entirely different. It is an essentially religious one of awe and respect, of dignified humility and withdrawal into contemplation. We fail to recognise the genuineness of Spinoza's religious attitude because of Christian parochialism. We tend to lay down requirements which are not universally applicable. We should not see Spinoza as irreligious simply because the attitudes adopted in our cultural background towards a personal, wrathful, intrusive God are in his case directed on to the whole scheme of things. He is religious in something like the way Wordsworth is religious.

Magee He once expressed his identification of God and nature in a dramatic way which appeals to me very much. No one has any difficulty, he said, in understanding that a person has a passionate love of nature, yet we should consider such a person mad if he wanted nature to love him back. Now because nature and God are one and the same, the same thing is true about God. It is conducive to our happiness to love God, but meaningless and absurd for us to expect God to love us.

Quinton That is quite right. There is a parallel to his kind of view of man's place in the universe in the more elevated and sophisticated types of Buddhism. We must admit that in the emotional economy of human life as a whole these attitudes are genuinely religious, even if they are directed towards objects which are not the familiar objects of religious attitudes in our culture.

Magee Do you suppose that Spinoza's orthodox Jewish upbringing and education contributed to the fact that he held these ideas?

Quinton Spinoza's ideas about two of Kant's great metaphysical trio of topics – God, freedom and immortality – are close to those of Judaism. The Jewish God, unlike Spinoza's, is personal, almost overpoweringly, but immortality is not emphatically central to Jewish religion. As for freedom, in the general domain of man's ethical relationship to God the Jewish religion does not have a place for petitionary prayer, for asking God to do things for you. The Jewish attitude is one of grateful acceptance of what God offers, rather than the Christian posture of cringing mendicancy. One accepts what God has to give one with such patience, submission and fortitude as one can bring to bear. That is an entirely Spinozist point of view.

Magee I think we must move on now to a consideration of Leibniz if we are not to give him unfairly short shrift. Like Spinoza, Leibniz produced a huge interlocking metaphysical system; but, unlike Spinoza, he did not put it forward in one single expository work. In Leibniz's case it came out in bits and pieces in a mass of separate papers and letters, and to some degree the reader has to put the system together for himself. Where do you think is the best place to start in an attempt to expound it?

Quinton If one were writing a serious professional treatise on Leibniz, one would probably start from certain logical doctrines which he holds. But for the comprehension in fairly short order of what he is up to, the place to start is the idea of the monad. It is his version of substance, and, as I mentioned earlier, it is utterly opposed to Spinoza's. Monads, for one thing, are infinitely numerous. They do not occupy space but are unextended spiritual things – metaphysical points, so to speak. God is a monad; so is each human soul; so are all the ultimate constituents of the world.

Magee   Can you give us more of a descriptive definition of what monads are?

Quinton   'Monad' is Leibniz's word for substance. It is a single, indivisible, elementary unit. It has a number of properties, but because it is simple it has no parts. There is an argument at the beginning of Leibniz's *Monadology* on which a great deal seems to depend, but which is surprisingly unsophisticated for a man as clever as Leibniz. Whatever is complex, he says, is made of what is simple, and the ultimate simple components of the complex are the real constituents of the world, while the complexes are just by-products of the aggregation of the simples. Now whatever occupies space is extended, and therefore divisible, and therefore complex. So the ultimate components of the world must be non-extended and, because not extended, not material. The real world, therefore, is made up of an infinity of metaphysical points; and since these unextended, indivisible items are not material they must be mental. So the world consists of an infinity of point-like spiritual items, or, as is sometimes said – by Leibniz himself, at times – of souls, everything from the most important of them, God, on whom all the rest depend, down through the human soul, which is the particular monad we get the idea of substance from in the first place, down to the ultimate constituents of what we conceive, confusedly, as matter.

Magee   That is a lot for people to take in at once, so I'd like to go over the main points of it just to be sure we've made it clear. Leibniz argued that everything in the world that is complex must be analysable into simpler elements. If the simpler elements are still complex then they must be further analysable. Eventually we must come to utterly simple elements which are not further analysable, and these are the ultimate constituents of the world. However, these cannot be material, because part of the very definition of matter is that it is something extended, and extension is by definition subdivisible. Obviously the not-further-divisible cannot be subdivisible. So the ultimate constituents of the world must be non-material, and cannot occupy space.

But now, I think, you want to criticise that argument.

Quinton   In the first place one does not really have to say that however far you go on dividing things you must reach a point where they are no longer in principle divisible. Why should not things be infinitely divisible, even if at any given time there is a point beyond which we are not practically

QUINTON · MAGEE 109

capable of dividing them further? But we need not dwell on that. Leibniz's really weird manoeuvre begins when he gets to the point of saying that everything is made of indivisible, unextended points. Now these points are indeed immaterial in the sense that they do not occupy space, do not spread over a tract of space. But that does not in the least mean that they are immaterial in the sense of being things of a mind-like nature. They could perfectly well be in space without occupying any of it. Leibniz assumed that these ultimate points or monads were minds because he accepted without question Descartes's principle that everything that exists is either space-occupying or conscious. Of course, in holding monads to be conscious Leibniz did not go on to suppose that they were universally self-conscious. He thought monads had perceptions, awareness of things other than themselves. But he denied them what he called apperception, the capacity a consciousness may have of being aware of what is going on within it, in particular of its own awareness of things outside itself.

Magee To do Leibniz justice, this vocabulary we are using is making his ideas sound very much weirder than they need. After all, one of the fundamental doctrines of twentieth-century physics is that all matter is reducible to energy – that it is energy that is the ultimate constituent of the physical universe. Now it seems to me that Leibniz was trying to express something astonishingly close to this idea. He was saying that all matter was made up of propensities for activity which are not themselves material – and indeed this is something we now know to be true. But in the seventeenth century the only vocabulary available to people for talking about non-material centres of activity was the vocabulary of minds, souls, spirits; and that is what Leibniz used.

Or do you think I am falling over backwards to salvage his ideas?

Quinton No, not at all. I think one could say that as far as that line of argument goes he had a bit of luck, of prophetic good fortune. Not that he had not got an important idea in the back of his mind, the one you ascribe to him: the idea that nature, the topic of physical science, is a dynamical state of affairs, with motion or activity as part of its intrinsic character – not a huge, stiff, dead contraption requiring a push from outside. The predominating view of many people in his time, and indeed since, while admitting that nature consisted of matter in motion, was that motion is not intrinsic to matter itself but has to be imparted to the material world from an external source. Leibniz did not make that assumption. He took the position that motion or energy or *activity*, which is perhaps the most suitable general term, is intrinsic to the ultimate constituents of the world.

Magee I think that Leibniz is in many striking ways a startlingly modern

Gottfried Wilhelm Leibniz (1646–1716)

thinker, and that we have not yet really brought this out. Reading him is often not like reading a figure from another age at all, but rather like reading a brilliant near-contemporary – in fact, the combination of high logical horse-power with unusual clarity and all the equipment of a great mathematician is reminiscent of Frege and Russell, for example.

Let me offer a fresh instance of what seems to me his modernity for us. He was the first person to formulate explicitly and at length a doctrine which has played a centre-stage role in philosophy ever since, and continues to do so to this day. He argued that all true or false statements must be of one of two kinds. First, a statement may be true in the way a definition is true. If I say: 'All the bachelors in England are unmarried', there is no need for anyone to carry out a social survey to see whether that is true or not. It can be pronounced true without having to look at the facts of the matter at all, because it is *necessarily* true, by virtue of the meanings of the terms employed. But there is another kind of statement which can be pronounced true or false only after the facts have been established. If I say: 'There's a monkey in the next room' – well, there may be or there may not be, and the only way to find out is to go and have a look.

So we have this extremely important distinction between statements whose truth or falsehood can be established by analysis of the statement itself, and which have therefore come to be known since Leibniz as 'analytic statements', and statements whose truth or falsehood can be established only by going beyond the statement and setting it against something outside itself. These have come to be known as 'synthetic statements'.

Now Leibniz, surely, was the first person thoroughly and clearly to expound this, was he not?

Quinton That is perfectly correct. You mentioned earlier that Locke was a near-contemporary: there is a kind of adumbration of the distinction between truths of reason and truths of fact in Locke; but it is a bit indeterminate and unclearly formulated. In Leibniz's case it is clear and lucid. On the one hand there are the truths of reason, things it would be an evident self-contradiction to deny, and so true in virtue of the principle of contradiction, that is to say on logical grounds alone. On the other hand there are truths of fact, statements which it is not a contradiction to deny and which thus report states of affairs that could possibly have been otherwise. The trouble is that under the pressure of Leibniz's metaphysical commitments the distinction between the two comes close to evaporating at the margin. For he goes on to distinguish between *finite* truths of reason, which *we* can see it would be a contradiction to deny, and infinite truths of reason, which look contingent to us but are self-evidently undeniable to the infinite intellect of God. This development arises from

Leibniz's idea that each thing has what he calls its complete individual notion which contains everything that can be truly said about it, all the properties that can be truly ascribed to it. Anything with a different complete notion would necessarily be a different thing. It follows that every property a thing has is necessarily possessed by it. There is just one property which Leibniz's complete notions do not generally contain.

Magee You are referring, of course, to the property of existence. For Leibniz, only God necessarily exists. The existence of anything else depends on God's choosing to assign existence to that possible thing.

Quinton Exactly. There are infinitely many possible individuals, things whose complete notions are internally consistent. A possible world is a collection of such possible individuals each of whose existence is compatible with that of all the others. Here Leibniz arrives at his conception of God's relation to the created world. God contemplates the endless inventory of possible worlds, of possible systems of things that are consistent with each other, and then, being perfect, chooses the best.

Magee It was this argument of Leibniz's that brought down on his head the immortalising derision of Voltaire, who pilloried him in *Candide* as the philosopher Pangloss, forever prating that 'everything is for the best in the best of all possible worlds'.

Quinton He also provoked the late Victorian philosopher Bradley to say: 'This is the best of all possible worlds, and everything in it is a necessary evil.' In fact, Leibniz's main point here is not that God chooses the humanly, practically, emotionally best world but, rather, the possible world that is best in a more abstract, metaphysical way – the possible world in which there is, roughly speaking, the largest amount of existence. In any case, this line of thought seems to remove the last element of contingency Leibniz had allowed for in the existence of things other than God. For it seems to follow that what actually exists must necessarily exist. It is necessary that God exists. It is necessary, since he is demonstrably perfect, that he chooses the best of all possible worlds. That the best of all possible worlds is the best is also a necessary truth of reason, even if beyond the reach of the finite human intellect. So it is a necessary truth of reason that the best possible world exists.

Magee A number of philosophers today are concerned with what they call 'possible worlds'. But by getting into that we have lost sight of our starting point, which was the distinction between what we now call analytic and synthetic statements. I think we should say a little more about this distinction, which after all has been near the centre of philosophical discussion ever since. Indeed, it would be difficult to think of any philosophical doctrine which has had more influence over the last two or three hundred years.

Quinton You are quite right. It was in terms of that distinction – which he proceeded to muddle up in a fruitful and interesting but, I think, finally mistaken way – that Kant set the main problem of his own theoretical philosophy in the *Critique of Pure Reason*. He held that there is a third kind of assertion, over and above truths of reason and truths of fact as described by Leibniz. Kant included in this third category the propositions of mathematics, certain alleged presuppositions of natural science (such as the laws of conservation and causality) and the basic principles of morality. Then again, for a good deal of this century the distinction between truths of reason and truths of fact has been absolutely central to philosophy. When I was younger some teachers of the subject used to say that whatever else one conveys to one's pupils, if one gets that distinction across to them it has been worth their while to study philosophy. And yes, you are quite right to say it was raised to a new level of clarity and explicitness by Leibniz.

Magee The point that this is Leibniz's contribution is especially worth driving home to an English-speaking audience because, in our intellectual parochialness, we persistently attribute it to David Hume. The doctrine is indeed to be found in Hume, who probably worked it out for himself on the basis of pointers from Locke, but the fact is that Leibniz said it half a century before Hume did, and said it more clearly, and said it several times.

Quinton Yes. In Hume's case the distinction is drawn in a relaxed, colloquial, rather imprecise fashion. The basis of the distinction is not very precisely worked out, largely because of Hume's disdain for formal logic. In Leibniz's case, however, a great deal of energy is expended on making it quite clear what the logical foundations of the distinction are.

Magee As in the case of Spinoza, Leibniz has a solution to offer to the Cartesian problem of how mind and matter can interact. But his solution is entirely different from Spinoza's. What was it?

Quinton In so far as it is a solution it is rather like preventing oneself from losing at chess by kicking the table over. In effect what Leibniz says is that matter is not real but is phenomenal, a mere appearance, so that there is not really any matter for mind to interact with. Everything that *really* exists is to some degree or other mental: in nature, at the lower end, in a very rudimentary style; at our end, quite sophisticatedly mental; and, of course, perfect in the case of God, who is a purely mental being and not at all the extended, all-inclusive physical entity that he is, in one aspect, in Spinoza's system.

Magee Leibniz thought, as we explained earlier in a different context, that everything material was reducible to something non-material, and that the ultimate constituents of the world were therefore non-material. But this meant that for him, as for Spinoza, the problem of interaction was not so much solved as shown not to arise. However, this being so, what sort of explanation has he left himself in a position to offer for causality? After all, on the face of it, the universe seems to consist very largely of things interacting with other things.

Quinton Let me give you a short answer which is likely to provoke further questions. The universe is an infinite array of mind-like entities, and each of these perceives – even if often in a very confused, obscure and limited way – all the others. It perceives the whole world from its own point of view. Now these worlds of perception, the pictures of the world formed by the individual monads, are like cinema films taken of a scene from different points of view. If these films are all shown on a battery of screens there will be a systematic correspondence between what they contain, but they will in reality have no influence or effect on each other. Every individual monad has its own perspective on the world but there is, according to Leibniz, no interaction between monads: merely a correspondence between their contents. Each monad has its own inbuilt history which develops with one quality succeeding another. That is the historical unrolling of the complete individual notion we talked about earlier. A principal part of the content of each monad is its awareness of other monads and, Leibniz says, they are all correlated by what he calls the pre-established harmony. Sometimes he uses the alleged fact of this harmony to argue for God's existence. From another point of view, God seems necessary for this extraordinary contingency to be explained.

Magee A certain conception of God makes belief in causality redundant. If God creates everything, ordaining from the very beginning its entire nature and therefore future development, there is no room left for things or events to have an influence on each other. Events are not bringing each other about: God is bringing everything about. So it is God who is responsible in every moment for the way things are, he who keeps everything going all the time. If things appear to us to be causally interconnected it is because the whole cosmos is, from the beginning and throughout its history, God's unitary creation, and the apparent interconnections are not causal interlockings but a pre-established harmony deriving from that fact.

But if all this is so, how can Leibniz account for human beings' possession of free will? – because he certainly did believe that we have free will in some significant sense.

Quinton His main arguments for the existence of God are fairly traditional and conventional. They have some slight up-to-date adjustments, but on the whole they are very much like those of Descartes or Anselm. So we are dealing here with ideas in the familiar history of the subject. But what Leibniz does with an idea of God arrived at in the traditional way is very striking. He carries the notion of God's omnipotence a long way. He says that God creates all the other monads that constitute the world, and that he equips them with an intrinsic nature – unique in each case – which determines everything they subsequently do. In other words, everything that happens is prepared by God. This theory of the complete programming of the universe rules out real causal interaction between one thing and another, as you rightly say. Apparent causal connection turns out to be no more than some kind of correspondence or parallelism between happenings in one thing with those in another. Leibniz reconciles this, in a way, with free will; and at first glance quite successfully. After all, to lack free will might be thought to be a matter of being subject to the causal influence of things outside one, to be externally compelled to do things against the grain of one's own real nature. In Leibniz's picture of the world every individual's determining force, once it is set going by God, is the nature with which God has equipped that individual. So, in a somewhat debating-society fashion, Leibniz could argue that in no system of the world are individuals freer than in his. Every individual is perfectly self-determining. What more freedom could you ask for? But although I am, in Leibniz's scheme of things, not literally constrained by other created things – by other people, or by the natural environment – I am wholly constrained by the system of correspondence that God has set up, of which the nature with which he has equipped me is an aspect. It is in general very difficult for rationalism, which insists that everything can be explained, to allow for anything that most people would acknowledge as human freedom. If everything has an explanation, it looks as if that explanation is going to be causal: everything that happens is going to be intelligible as part of some vast unitary design or plan.

Magee So what you're saying, then, is that any rationalist philosopher – not only Spinoza or Leibniz – who presents us with a fully worked out metaphysical system which explains everything is likely to be unable to accommodate freedom of the will.

Quinton There does not seem to be any room for manoeuvre for individuals in the world as it is conceived by rationalists.

Magee You began our discussion by making some remarks about Spinoza and Leibniz jointly. How would you assess their relative contributions to the subsequent history of philosophy?

Quinton They contribute to different strands in it. Spinoza was much deplored in his own age. The question of the sincerity of his religious professions was very much present to the minds of his contemporaries. Free-thinkers like Hume (who wrote of 'the hideous hypothesis of the atheist Spinoza') and Bayle distracted attention from their own impieties by casting slurs, which he deserved much less than they did, on Spinoza. It was not until the romantic movement in Germany at the end of the eighteenth century, with people like Herder and Goethe, that Spinoza came more or less into his own. Since then he has always been an object of veneration to many because of his personal dignity, his unworldly withdrawal from ambition and self-affirmation. The desire to cut a figure in the world was utterly foreign to Spinoza. He was a person of the greatest sincerity. His own life story is perfectly in accordance with his philosophic doctrines, and he is admired on that account. But he does not appeal enormously to the more technical kind of philosopher. Whereas I should be inclined to say that of all the great philosophers of the post-medieval world there is none who makes a more immediate appeal to technical philosophers, at least to those of the Anglo-Saxon world in the twentieth century, than Leibniz.

Magee Just to take one example, Bertrand Russell, who wrote some sixty books, wrote only one about another philosopher, and that was Leibniz. I suspect Russell identified with Leibniz quite considerably in his younger days.

Talking of Russell, there is one thing that strikes me about both Leibniz and Spinoza which differentiates them from the language-oriented philosophers of today, and that is their orientation towards mathematics. Leibniz, of course, was a mathematician of genius, and a mathematical physicist of genius. And that leads me on to another point. Both men were overwhelmingly concerned with the place of God in the total scheme of things. That is something that cannot be said of any major philosopher of the last 200 years, since Kant – unless one wants to make a solitary exception of Kierkegaard, who is only doubtfully a philosopher in the full sense. Nor is it something which in the last 200 years has commonly accompanied an immersion in mathematical science.

There is, it seems to me, an undeclared agenda to much of the philosophy we have been discussing. Spinoza and Leibniz had a deep understanding of the new mathematics and also of the new physics, both of which developed further in their century than in any other, and they both knew that these had to be accommodated in any sustainable view of the world. But both perceived that, on the face of it, they were not easy to reconcile with traditional beliefs about God, the operation of spirits, freedom of the will, and so on. So what they were trying to do, at least a lot of the time, was to produce a total view of reality which embraced both mathematical science and God. Do you think that's true?

Quinton Yes. I think that is certainly true. I would just like to interpose, first of all, that despite all the mathematical-looking apparatus in his writings, Spinoza was not really a mathematician. He had studied the subject, but he is in a completely different class as a mathematician from Leibniz, who, as you rightly said, is a major figure in the history of mathematics. In Spinoza's case the mathematical form is rather like the conventional apparatus of pastoral poetry. (A pastoral poet is not really an expert on the culture of sheep, or lamb-rearing, or anything of that sort.) But, ignoring that, I think you are right about there being a common topic which obsesses them in some way and which they resolve in their very different fashions. It is the matter of finding a place for religion in the world as it had come to seem in the light of the great discoveries about the nature of the physical world made by Galileo and the physicists of the seventeenth century. Descartes's procedure was, more or less, to give ground to the invader, to say that the material world is all unthinking matter and is where the Galilean rules prevail – but that, as well as the material world, there are individual human souls and the infinite soul of God which are purely spiritual entities, detached from, although in various ways associated with, the material world. Descartes's strategy is like that of splitting a country, say Germany, into two demarcated segments: one area is given to science, the other is preserved for religion. Both Spinoza and Leibniz are understandably dissatisfied with that kind of Solomonic carve-up of the cosmic baby, and both are anxious to combine religion and science more harmoniously. Spinoza does it by adopting the world picture of seventeenth-century natural science *and then recommending religious attitudes to the world so conceived.* Leibniz, working the other way round, says that the world is in fact much more as religion represents it, and is a much more spiritual affair than science realises: we can rest the whole of the scientific conception of phenomena on an essentially religious understanding of the world as the working out of the purposes of an infinitely intelligent spirit, namely God.

LOCKE and BERKELEY

Dialogue with
MICHAEL AYERS

INTRODUCTION

Magee One of the most influential philosophers there has ever been was the Englishman John Locke, born in 1632. He has been generally credited with laying the intellectual foundations both of liberal democracy and of modern empirical philosophy. An empiricist is someone who believes that our conceptions about what exists can never pass entirely beyond the bounds of experience – that everything we can conceive of has either been experienced or is constructed out of elements which have been experienced. Some version of this doctrine has been accepted by many of the greatest philosophers since Locke, and philosophy in the English-speaking world has never escaped its dominance for long. So familiar has it become that many people nowadays regard it as obvious – just plain common sense – but when Locke propounded it it was an idea with revolutionary implications. Whether in philosophy or the natural sciences or politics, part of Locke's message always was: 'Don't blindly follow convention or authority. Look at the facts and think for yourself.' In politics this was revolutionary in an almost literal sense. In France it had a dominating influence on Voltaire and the Encyclopaedists, and thus on the intellectual ferment that preceded the French Revolution. In America, the Founding Fathers had Locke consciously in mind, and made repeated references to him, when they were drawing up the American Constitution.

Locke was educated at Westminster School (probably at that time the best school in England) and Christ Church, Oxford, where he became a don until his mid-thirties. He also qualified as a medical practitioner, and when he left university life he became involved in both politics and medical research. (In his own day he was occasionally known as Dr Locke.) In the turmoil leading up to what the English call their Glorious Revolution of 1688 he had, for his own safety, to go into exile in Holland, and he was one of those Englishmen who followed William of Orange over to England to oust the Stuart kings. By this time he had been working for years on what was to be his philosophical masterpiece, the *Essay Concerning Human Understanding*.It was published in 1689, when Locke was fifty-seven, but it had the date 1690 on the flyleaf, and that is often mistakenly given as the year of publication. Also published in 1689 was *A Letter Concerning Toleration*. There followed in quick succession the *Two Treatises of Government* in 1690 and *Some Thoughts Concerning Education* in 1693. Although Locke lived to be seventy-two, and wrote other things, nearly all his influential writings came out in a period of less than five years.

The next philosopher in the English language after Locke who is still of international reputation, George Berkeley, was in part reacting against Locke, and it can therefore be helpful to consider the two together.

Berkeley was born in Ireland in 1685, and educated at Trinity College,

Dublin. All the philosophical works for which he is now famous were published when he was in his twenties: *A New Theory of Vision* in the year 1709; *The Principles of Human Knowledge* in 1710; and *Three Dialogues* in 1713. Some of his other works deserve to be better known than they are, but his fame rests on those I have mentioned. In 1734 he was made a bishop, and to this day he is often referred to as Bishop Berkeley. Much of his life was spent in public activity, some of it in the New World. He had connections with Yale University, where one of the colleges is named after him; and the town Berkeley in California is also named after him. He died at the age of sixty-seven in 1753, and is buried in Christ Church, Oxford, where he had a son as a student, and which of course had been Locke's college.

Here to discuss with me the work of these two philosophers is someone whose writings about them have made his academic reputation: Michael Ayers, Fellow of Wadham College, Oxford.

DISCUSSION

Magee Let's take Locke first. Although he's one of the world's most influential philosophers, anyone studying the history of philosophy chronologically, and therefore coming to Locke after studying his pre-decessors, cannot but be struck by how much of what Locke said had already been said by others, for example Descartes – the view of the whole universe as a colossal machine, the division of the world into matter and minds, and so on. What is distinctively different about Locke's position?

Ayers Like Descartes, Locke was part of a movement in the seventeenth century to oust the previously dominant view of the world, the Aristotelian view, and to work out a new view which, as you say, had at its centre a conception of the material world as a great machine. The world-machine is composed of lesser machines, but all are subject to the same laws of physics, the same mechanical necessity. Locke's theory of thought and knowledge, too, can look superficially like Descartes's. He takes thought to involve a series of ideas which exist 'in the mind', or 'before the mind', and which represent things outside the mind. Reasoning is a sort of mental operation on ideas which leads to knowledge or belief. His definition of knowledge is the perception of a relation between ideas, and the intuitionist view of knowledge is, or can seem, very like that of Descartes. They share the view that in knowing something we as it were grasp or 'see' a truth.

On the other hand, there are very big differences. One of the most important of these is the different status that Locke gives to the senses. For Descartes, the senses deliver certain data, and they incline us to have certain beliefs corresponding to the data, but these beliefs don't count as knowledge. The deliverances of the senses have to be interpreted and explained by reason before we can suppose that the senses have helped us to acquire any *knowledge* of the world. For Descartes, it's reason or intellect that delivers knowledge, or the intellect operating on the data of sense. But for Locke the senses themselves are basic or fundamental faculties which deliver knowledge in their own right, what he calls 'sensitive knowledge'. This opposition is demonstrated in the different approach of the two philosophers to the sceptical doubt as to whether material objects exist. Descartes accepts the sceptic's challenge to supply reasons for believing in an external world. Locke simply dismisses the challenge. In Locke's view the sceptic is casting doubt on one of the fundamental faculties of the human mind, and yet he himself, in producing his sceptical reasoning, is relying on human faculties. In effect Locke rejects the whole sceptical problem. He is prepared to say that if anybody is wild enough to be a sceptic, reasons can be produced for trusting sense experience. But the deliverances of the senses don't *need* such reasons, and are not really strengthened by them. In themselves the senses supply us with knowledge. They have their own independent authority.

Magee Another thing we should mention as being special to Locke is his particular use of the concept denoted by the word 'idea'. He didn't invent this use, but its widespread propagation in modern philosophy really stems from him. In chapter I of the *Essay Concerning Human Understanding* he goes so far as to apologise to the reader for the frequency with which the term appears in his book. Can you go into that a little?

Ayers The word 'idea' had been used in various technical senses as far back as Plato, of course, although for Plato it meant something very different from what it came to mean in the seventeenth century. Then, largely perhaps because of the way it was taken up by Descartes, it became an extremely popular term for what one might in general call a 'mental content'. But despite this broad agreement in their usage of the term, Descartes and Locke hold very different views on the nature of ideas or mental contents. For Descartes an idea is something fundamentally intellectual. For Locke it is something fundamentally sensory. Broadly, it's Locke's view that, whatever we are thinking about, if we are not actually perceiving it with the senses then we are having something *like* a sensation of it, a sensory image of it. He explains even the most abstract thinking in these terms. Of course his theory has to get more complicated at this point, but basically thought is for him the having of images before the mind, together with a variety of ways of combining, considering and employing them. Now this theory of 'imagism', as we could call it, was not an uncommon one in the seventeenth century, when it tended to lead in one or other of two very different directions.

One of these directions was taken by Hobbes. According to Hobbes, since all our knowledge and understanding are dependent on the senses, and all sensible, substantial objects are material, the only intelligible view of the world which is open to us is a materialist one. 'Immaterial substance' is a contradictory notion. He thought, too, that we can in principle analyse experience, with the aid of language, in such a way that we can arrive at a complete scientific, mechanistic understanding of the world – essentially the same sort of understanding that Descartes thought we can achieve by employing pure intellect. But Locke developed a different line of thought, which is in a certain way more sceptical. Although the senses give us knowledge, they give us limited knowledge – knowledge of the existence of things, not knowledge of their nature or essence. And because all our thought about the world is restricted to the concepts that we have acquired through the senses, even our speculations about the world are restricted. He thought that there was nó method by which scientists could expect to arrive at the underlying nature of things. So, despite his rejection of absolute scepticism about the external world, he was himself a sort of modified sceptic. We know that the world is there, but we don't know what it's really like. Descartes and Hobbes are both in Kant's sense 'dogmatic' philosophers, but Locke is an anti-dogmatic philosopher – which doesn't mean to say he's not a systematic philosopher.

Magee His use of the term 'idea' and his particular theory of knowledge were so influential that I would like to pause over them for a moment. Locke believed, didn't he, that *everything* present to the mind was, in his sense of the word, an 'idea': he used the term to cover not only thoughts but sensory images and even pains and emotions.

Ayers Yes.

Magee Now it's essential to his theory of knowledge that all our know- ledge of the external world is mediated to us through ideas. We do not have direct access (whatever that could mean) to things as they are in themselves – a phrase, and a point, which occur in Locke long before they appeared in Kant. If I look at that table it doesn't pop into my brain. What I have inside my head as I look at that table now is not the table but a visual image of the table. Light is reflected from the table on to the retina of my eye; my eye transmits an image to my brain; and I have the experience which I call 'seeing a table'. In a similar way the whole of my experience, through all five of my senses, consists not of being in direct contact with the objects of the external world but of having images and representations of them – all of which Locke terms 'ideas'. So all our knowledge is, in this sense, mediate: we never have *immediate* knowledge of external objects. Isn't that Locke's view?

Ayers One problem with that question is that the principle that we never have 'immediate' knowledge of external objects, or that we know objects only through 'representations' of them, is open to a variety of interpretations, varying from a platitude which hardly anyone would want to question to an alarming sceptical paradox. Let me try to explain. Take first the view of sensations as 'representations' of things. As it stands, it's almost entirely neutral or non-committal. Everyone would agree, I think (except some idealists and perhaps some behaviourists who hold, or used to hold, that psychology can be done entirely in terms of input and output without any thought of what goes on in between), that in normal sense-experience things are acting on us and causing in us what are in some sense or other *representations* of those things. We are acquiring information *about* things through their effects on the sense organs. The interesting philosophical questions and disputes arise with respect to the nature of those effects, and the proper explanation of their representative role.

A connected point can be made about the notion that ideas are the 'immediate' objects of perception and thought, and the distinction between 'immediate' and 'mediate' or 'direct' and 'indirect' objects. One way in which such a distinction was applied in Locke's time is related to a harmless and natural ambiguity in the notion of an 'idea' which was noted and, indeed, emphasised by Descartes and his follower Antoine Arnauld. Descartes says, in effect, that the word 'ideas' may be used either to mean the states of mind which do the representing of things in the course of thought, or the things themselves *as* they are represented. The ambiguity is a bit like the ambiguity of 'statement' in so far as a 'statement' can be either the act of stating something, or what is stated. So if I am looking at the sun, the expression 'my idea of the sun' can be taken to refer either to my sensation, considered as a state of my mind, or to the sun *as* I perceive it. Which it means in any particular context can very much affect the sense and reasonableness of what is being said. If someone were to say that 'Dürer's idea of a rhinoceros was not much like a rhinoceros', we would assume that he did *not* mean that a particular mental state of Dürer's was not like a pachyderm (we all know *that*!), but that a rhinoceros as Dürer imagined it and depicted it is not like a real rhinoceros. The rhinoceros in Dürer's picture or 'in his mind' is not like any rhinoceros in the world, or 'in reality'. Now for some philosophers the distinction between 'immediate' and 'mediate' objects of experience and thought was in effect equivalent to the distinction between things as we experience and think of them and things as they are in reality or in themselves. Consequently the principle that the immediate objects of our experience and thought are all ideas was taken to be a mere tautology. For of course we can experience things only *as* we perceive them, or think and reason about things only *as* we conceive of them. We can't bypass our own cognitive faculties in our cognitive contact with things.

Magee But you're not saying, surely, that Locke's principle that 'the mind, in all its thoughts and reasonings, hath no other immediate object but its own ideas' is a mere platitude with no interesting consequences?

Ayers Well, even as a platitude it serves to remind us that things are not necessarily in themselves just as we experience or conceive of them – a presupposition of Locke's moderate scepticism. But as a matter of fact his theory has features which are liable to make the principle both more questionable and more interesting than that. I mean his general account of how ideas represent, and the way in which his explanation of representation ties in with his account of 'sensitive knowledge'. As far as the first is concerned, he holds that all our thoughts are composed of simple elements acquired in sense experience (including 'inner sense' or introspection, which he calls 'reflection'), and that each element or 'simple idea' represents whatever it is in reality which regularly causes it in sense experience. So the idea or image of yellow existing in my mind represents or stands in my thought for whatever it is in things which regularly causes sensations of yellow in human observers. Locke was reasonably inclined to believe that what is really out there in the object is, in the case of yellowness, a certain surface-texture which reflects particles of light in a certain way. But the role of the idea of yellow in our thought as the representative or sign of something in objects is quite independent of any speculation or theory about what that something is, or how it has its effect on us. Now you can see how this view of the representative role of ideas fits in with Locke's view of 'sensitive knowledge', explaining both the authority and limitations of such knowledge. In sense-experience, Locke held, we are aware that things are acting on us, causing ideas in us. So when we have the sensation of yellow, we know that what the simple idea of yellow represents or signifies exists out there – that some object is what we call 'yellow'. We have that knowledge even though we do not know what 'yellowness' is in the object, beyond the power to cause a certain sensation in us. We have 'sensitive knowledge' of the *existence* of yellowness, but not of its nature. This is philosophically very elegant, but it dangerously narrows the scope of perceptual knowledge to knowledge of the blank sensory effects of things. It is in the context of that kind of theory, I think, that the principle that the immediate objects of experience are all ideas becomes a little alarming, supplying a weapon which philosophers of a sceptical tendency were not slow to take up.

Magee Isn't there another problem? Even if we accept Locke's explanation of our knowledge of sensible qualities, what about material

John Locke (1632–1704)

objects, the things which have or possess qualities? If qualities are all we perceive, and all we ever can perceive, how does Locke account for the fact that we seem to apprehend the world spontaneously in terms of things that are not qualities yet have them, namely material objects?

Ayers He held that 'sensitive knowledge' extends not only to the existence of individual qualities, but to what he calls the 'coexistence' of qualities – we perceive a number of observable qualities as existing together in the same thing. Roughly, his model is like this: there's a unitary thing out there which we are aware of as affecting us through the senses in a variety of ways. It also affects other objects around it in perceptible ways – that is to say, its presence habitually causes changes in them which in turn have an effect on observers. Finally, it undergoes regular perceptible changes itself in response to other objects. So we acquire the notion of a thing or sort of thing (or it might be a stuff) possessing an indefinite number of powers to affect us through the senses either directly or indirectly, through its affecting, or being affected by, other things or stuffs.

That's Locke's account of the traditional notion of a 'substance'. A substance is something known only through its multiple effects. We can think of any particular sort of substance only in terms of the list of its sensible qualities and powers, but in itself it's something other than those qualities and powers, something which explains their coexistence.

Magee But why should we assume that there is something *more* to things than the qualities and powers which we observe, or which we discover by experiment? Why should we postulate an unknown and unknowable 'substance' behind them, a 'something I know not what', as Locke himself confessed?

Ayers Locke thought that it just didn't make sense to suppose that what exists out there are just bunches of sensible qualities, as we perceive them. That's because he believed that the world is an intelligible place, that it consists in things with intelligible natures, governed by necessary laws. It's the kind of place which an ideal science could ultimately explain and understand. Now although there are regularities at the level of observation and ordinary experience, they tend to be only relative and brute regularities. At that level we don't get the kind of absolute and intelligible laws which for Locke would be the sign that we had arrived at the ultimate truth about the world. It's because the world as we perceive it is not amenable to a simple and comprehensive natural science that we can be sure that the senses don't give us knowledge of the nature of things.

Magee Two questions need to be asked here. First, how can Locke postulate the existence of material objects as the sustainers of observational properties without flagrantly breaching the central principle of empiricism? Second, if all our knowledge is intermediate – representational, pictorial, imagist – and we can never have any direct knowledge of the nature of objects, how is a successful science possible?

Ayers What Locke is really saying is that it is *not* possible, at any rate in the situation in which he wrote in the seventeeth century. One of his main aims was to prick a lot of balloons. He was trying to cut down the pretensions of philosophers like Descartes who thought that they had already arrived at a deductive science of things. As far as the ultimate nature of things is concerned, we are in Locke's view restricted to speculation. And not only are we restricted to speculation, but we can employ in that speculation only concepts that we get from experience. There was, he agreed, a very good speculation to hand, namely Boyle's 'corpuscularian' view of the world as a whole lot of little atoms or particles bouncing around and clinging together and interacting mechanically. Locke clearly accepted that the world must be something like that. In fact his account of the notion of substance is based in part on Boyle's explanation of chemical change.

For Boyle, if we take a chemical substance and observe that it behaves in a whole variety of different ways in different conditions, then that's not because it just happens to have an arbitrary or contingent list of powers to affect other things in various ways, but because it has a certain mechanical structure. Just because of that structure, when it meets other things with various mechanical structures, then obviously it's going to behave in various ways as it interacts with them. That's Boyle's explanation of the fact that the same chemical which is inert in one context may dissolve or give rise to an explosion in another. Locke accepted that explanation provisionally, but he thought there were certain fundamental questions which it left unanswered. One of the questions concerned the particles themselves. If they are atoms, why do they cohere as unchanging, rigid things? It's all very well if you postulate such immutables and then go on from there, but why isn't it the case that when one atom hits another it doesn't slice a piece off, or fall apart itself? So the problem of 'coherence' was one of the problems that he raised.

Another problem had been brought into special prominence by Newton's *Principia*, which had been published just a few years before the *Essay*. An important part of Newton's physics is the inverse square law – the law that every object in the universe attracts every other object in the universe with a force which is proportional to their masses and inversely proportional to the square of the distance between them. Locke accepted that Newton had shown that this law holds, and he accepted that the probability was that it holds absolutely universally. But nevertheless it seemed to Locke like a kind of brute fact and not a principle which is intelligible in itself. Some laws seemed to him, as they seemed to Descartes and other philosophers, intrinsically intelligible – for example, the law that a body moving at a certain speed in a certain direction will continue in motion at that speed in that direction unless its motion is interfered with by another body. It seemed that you didn't have to explain why, once an object has got into motion, it doesn't keep stopping or changing direction of its own accord. But the inverse square law, the law of gravity, didn't seem to have that kind of intelligibility.

Magee In other words, what Newtonian science is giving an account of is not the inner nature of things (which we cannot know) but simply how they behave (which is something we can observe and perhaps experiment with).

Ayers Yes, he thought that in the end what Newton had achieved was a spectacularly good description of how things behave, but not an explanation. That interpretation, it should be said, was one that Newton himself was inclined to. In fact in the second edition of his *Principia*, which he published after Locke's death, Newton introduced a number of philosophical passages which were pretty obviously heavily influenced by Locke.

Magee Among Newton's most quoted words is his Latin phrase *'Hypotheses non fingo'* – which might be very freely translated 'I'm not offering explanations'. What he is saying, in effect, is: 'I tell you that there is, say, such a thing as gravity, and I tell you how its effects are, as a matter of fact, to be calculated, but what on earth the *explanation* is of the entire business is something I don't attempt to go into'. This is his attitude to the whole of the new physics: as you say, he thought it was descriptive but not explanatory. There have been major philosophers down to our own time who have continued to hold this view of science very strongly, for instance Schopenhauer and Wittgenstein. Wittgenstein put it pithily when he said: 'The whole modern conception of the world is founded on the illusion that the so-called laws of nature are the explanations of natural phenomena'; and he added that even when *all possible* scientific questions had been answered the problems of life would remain completely untouched.

The foundations of the new science were mathematical. From Galileo to Newton the great scientists had steadily uncovered more and more constant equations embedded in physical reality. This raises deep questions about exactly what the status of mathematics is. What view did Locke take of it?

Ayers His explanation of the possibility of mathematical science, and geometry in particular, is importantly different from Descartes's. For Descartes geometry is part of the science of space, indeed of matter. It's a part of the science of reality. But for Locke it's an abstract science which is created by us. We so to speak pick geometrical properties off things, and we can go on to construct such properties *ad lib* beyond the limits of our experience. In this way we can create the subject matter of a sort of non-empirical science. Such a science is possible precisely because it's not really concerned with the nature of things at all. It's simply concerned, as Locke puts it, with our own ideas.

Magee And he thought that some of the ideas we have of the properties of things are mathematical in character while others are not. This distinction became highly influential, and is therefore worth going into – Locke didn't invent it, but its influence stems largely from him. He divided the properties of objects into two sorts, which he called primary and secondary qualities. Primary qualities are those properties which an object has in itself, independently of being perceived, and include, among other aspects, its shape, size and weight. Secondary qualities are those properties which involve interaction with an observer, and, again just for example, include colour, taste and smell. The idea is that if no creatures with senses or brains existed, flowers would have no smell, but they would still have the same size, shape and position. If one tries to pin down precisely what the characteristic is that makes a primary quality primary, it appears to be its mathematical character. Primary qualities are the mathematically measurable ones, which are therefore in some special sense objective.

Ayers They are the mechanical ones.

Magee Yes, much better: the mechanical ones; though it remains true that mechanics has mathematical foundations. This distinction between primary and secondary qualities has played such an important role in philosophy, not only in Locke's time but since, that I'd like you, if you would, to make further comments on it.

Ayers Well, the distinction between primary and secondary qualities, as Locke drew it, was really dependent on his provisional acceptance of Boyle's theory. The primary qualities are the properties that Boyle attributed to his particles. They were little solid chunks of matter with size, shape, number and so forth. So the distinction is for Locke really a kind of speculative hypothesis. He evidently believed it to be one that, after appropriate reflection, is so rational and so inescapable that we can hardly doubt that it is fairly close to the truth, even if not the whole truth.

But strictly speaking, as we have seen, Locke's view is that all we really *know* about the world is that there are things out there which have powers to affect us. The distinction between solidity and shape as a real attribute of things, and colour as something which is sense-relative, that distinction is in the end for Locke a sort of hypothesis.

Magee We've now covered enough ground to have at our disposal the materials for an outline-sketch of Locke's view of the world. I'd like to pause for long enough to assemble the picture before we take any more forward steps.

Locke thought that the world as we experience it consists of two fundamentally different sorts of entity, namely minds and material objects. In both cases we can never know what these in their inner nature are: in their inner nature they remain permanently mysterious to us. But we do have direct experience of what they do, how they behave; and such knowledge as we can gain of them is built up from that. One of the things that material objects do is affect minds. They do this through the senses in various ways which give the minds, perceiving subjects, *us*, our ideas about those material objects, and from these ideas we build up our conception of the world which those objects constitute. We perceive objects as having properties of two fundamentally different kinds. They have primary qualities, which are mechanical in type and characterise the object as it is in itself, regardless of whether or not it is being perceived by an observer; they are objective characteristics of the ultimate consti-tuents of matter. The mathematical sciences deal with objects under these aspects. And there are secondary qualities, which are to some degree observer-dependent and could not exist as we apprehend them if there were no perceiving subjects. These have much more about them of 'quality' in the ordinary sense, as opposed to quantity.

To go no further, I think one can say with fairness that a view of the world very like this has been at the basis of Western science from Locke's century to our own. And I suspect that to this very day, what we think of as the ordinary commonsense view of the world is very like it.

I want to move on now to something we have not yet mentioned, though it was of great importance to Locke and is of even greater importance to most present-day philosophers, namely language. Locke's *Essay Concerning Human Understanding* is written in four books, and of these one whole book is devoted to the use of words. How did Locke see language as coming into, or relating to, our experience and knowledge of the world?

Ayers Well, I'd first like to qualify your summing up. The way you summed up made Locke seem less consistent than he is. It's true that he's inclined to think that the world is composed of matter and minds, but he's consistent enough to say that since we don't know the nature of either we can't even be sure of that. So he is very ready to accept the possibility that materialism is true and that we thinking things are in fact complex and subtle machines, although how we work we have no idea at all. He is ready to accept the possibility that there is no immaterial, naturally immortal soul, such as that Descartes ascribes to us.

Magee I'm glad you pulled me up on that point because he has an argument about it which is marvellous and should be mentioned – it carries as much weight today as it did when he first used it. He says that one of two things must be true about us human beings, yet both seem impossible for us to grasp: either we must be material objects which think and have emotions, or there must be something immaterial in us which thinks and has emotions and is uniquely related to the material object which is our body. Now, he says, if we try systematically to think our way through to the bottom of each of these alternatives we find both of them in a profound way unintelligible. Yet one of them must be true. I don't know about you, but I'm persuaded by that. I think Locke is right.

Ayers Yes, the argument there is so strong that one wonders why on other occasions he says that dualism is probably true. He never justifies the 'probably'.

Magee Let's now move on, as I tried to a moment ago, to the question of language. How does Locke's view of language fit in with the rest of his view of our knowledge of the world?

Ayers The book on language is really a book about classification in all the various departments of knowledge, and about what makes for good classification. The most interesting part, I think, concerns the classification of the natural world. What Locke wants to do here is to refute and replace the Aristotelian view that the world is composed of natural kinds and that science is a matter of identifying each natural kind and examining its nature more or less separately. On the Aristotelian model, the scientist has to study the essence or nature of horses, cows, dogs, cats and so forth one by one. These natural kinds are out there, with sharp divisions between them.

Magee According to Aristotle, natural kinds have a real existence of their own in the world, and what we human observers do is discover what they are and carry out our observations on each of them.

Ayers Yes. Locke wants to reject that view, of course, and his rejection has implications for the principles of classification.

Magee You say 'of course', but somebody who hasn't thought about this before might not at once see the 'of course'. Such a person might say: 'But surely there just *are* horses, cows, dogs, cats out there in the world. These categories really do exist in their own right. We don't invent them. All we do is name them.'

Ayers The 'of course' followed from what went before. Given the view of the world as a great mechanical system composed of lesser systems, then dogs and cats are little machines which all function according to the basic laws of physics, so that there isn't, at the fundamental level, a separate nature of dogs and a separate nature of cats. There are differences in structure, but the 'nature' involved is really the same – the laws of nature involved are the same. Well, given that view of the world, Locke fairly understandably concluded that there are no natural divisions into kinds. There are resemblances at the level of observation, and these resemblances cause us, quite reasonably, to slice the world up into sorts and species, but in the end the slicing is done by us, it's not done by nature. For the Aristotelian there are natural divisions between natural species which we simply identify and name. For Locke *we* do the slicing up, so that the names we give things, such as 'gold', 'water', 'horse', 'dog' and so on, are in the end arbitrarily defined by us.

Magee According to Locke, then, as against Aristotle, there are no natural kinds. All such categories are man-made.

Ayers Yes. Nevertheless Locke thought that they ought to be based on much closer observation of nature than was usually the case. His argument was part of the great movement in the seventeenth century for improving scientific language. In effect he lists a number of requisites of good classification. It's arrived at only after careful observation and experiment, and as far as is reasonable takes account of subtle differences, but not so as to make it too clumsy for convenient use. It doesn't depart unnecessarily from established usage, it is kept constant and (very important) it is agreed by all concerned. What Locke rejects is the idea of an absolutely natural classification – we can't possibly exclude all arbitrariness. Classification is a pragmatic business.

Magee But what would he have said about his own distinction between minds and material objects? Surely his own point there is that this distinction is fundamental to the natural order? And surely that makes it a distinction of natural kinds, not one just imposed by us through language?

Ayers I'm sure that he would have agreed that *if* dualism is true, then the mind–matter distinction would be a distinction of kind. The kinds that he is attacking are the Aristotelian kinds, which were all material. There isn't in Aristotelian philosophy anything quite like Descartes's immaterial substance.

Magee   The body–mind distinction raises another important question. If Locke thinks that all material bodies, including therefore our own, are in their inner nature mysterious to us, and that minds are equally mysterious, what is his view of personal identity?

Ayers   The discussion of personal identity is one of the most original and interesting parts of the *Essay*. He agreed with Descartes that I know that I am a thinking thing, but he held that I don't know my nature, because I don't know what nature a thing has to have in order to be able to think. Followers of Descartes held it a very powerful argument for their view that it explained personal identity. For them the identity of a person even in life could not be determined by the body, since matter is in continual flux. So it must be determined by the identity of the soul. The same soul can exist after death – indeed they argued that it followed from the soul's being immaterial and unextended that it is also by nature indestructible. So at the resurrection personal identity would go along with the same soul. Now Locke started from a different consideration, which is that immortality has to be *personal* immortality. The whole point of immortality is, to put it bluntly, reward and punishment. But unless the thing that is being punished in the after-life is conscious of the deeds that it has done in life on earth, then Locke thought that punishment has lost its whole point.

Magee   It would be the equivalent of a different person's being punished.

Ayers   Right. Suppose that we grant that there is such a thing as an immortal, immaterial soul; suppose we grant that that is what receives punishment. If that soul has no recollection of what happened on earth, immortality loses its point. So what really matters, in Locke's view, is not the supposed immaterial soul, but consciousness, the unity of consciousness, whatever is its natural basis.

Magee   And the continuity of consciousness.

Ayers   The continuity of consciousness, that is, the individual's consciousness of its past. And of course in this life what matters is the thought that it's going to be oneself who is going to get punished in the world to come.

George Berkeley (1685–1753)

Magee For Locke, then, memory is the key to personal identity: it is more than anything else the fact that I carry within me a living awareness of my own history that makes me the person I am.

Ayers Yes. Locke doesn't deny or doubt that the memory will have some sort of substantial basis. His point is we don't know what that is. Really the point of his whole argument is to allow for the possibility of immortality without going against his anti-dogmatism, without accepting the immaterial soul of the Cartesians as something of which we have knowledge. But what makes his theory so interesting and important, even today, is that it introduced into modern European thought the idea of the self as constituted by a connected, if interrupted, stream of consciousness. That scandalised the orthodox at the time, but has remained ever since a powerful ingredient of the way we think about ourselves.

Magee In my introduction to this discussion I referred to the very great impact made by Locke's political philosophy, both in his own lifetime and ever since – there has never been a time since Locke when it was not influential. So I don't want us to leave discussion of Locke, and start talking about Berkeley, before we've said something about it. What were the main points of contact between Locke's political philosophy and the central body of his philosophy as we have discussed it?

Ayers Well Locke has the interesting idea that ethics (politics is just a part of ethics as far as he's concerned) is an *a priori* science.

Magee I think you'd better explain what is meant by that.

Ayers It's a science that can be pursued without reference to experience, like geometry. Locke extended his account of geometry to all such sciences. Their basic concepts can be freely constructed without any requirement that they correspond to reality. In a natural science, that's not so: for Locke there is something deeply improper about the concept of a centaur or a unicorn just because there is no such thing. But we can very properly form the concept of a geometrical figure, and reason about it, even though no such figure has ever existed on earth. So too we can properly form the idea of some action or political constitution and rationally evaluate it, even though no such action has ever been performed, or no state has ever been governed in just that way. That analogy encouraged Locke to think that a quasi-geometrical ethical theory is feasible.

Magee What form does his theory take? What, for instance, are its axioms?

Ayers The first principles of his theory, I'm afraid, can reasonably be described as archaic. He held that there can be no obligation without a law, and no law without a lawgiver possessing both the right and power to punish infringements of the law. A legitimate ruler or government fulfils that role in the case of human law, and God fulfils it in the case of moral or 'natural' law. I won't go into the well-known logical flaws in this sort of account of obligation. (Briefly, since no lawgiver, even God, can decree his own right to legislate, at least one obligation, the obligation to obey God's will, is independent of the will of a lawgiver.) But within this archaic framework the thought that there are moral and political principles which make intuitive sense is developed fairly persuasively in an analysis of the rights and duties of government and governed. One famous example, though not original to Locke, is his account of the *a priori* core of the institution of property. Prior to any human law, we have a natural right to the product of our own labour, as far as we can use it. If I pick some fruit to eat, and am depriving no one else, then I have a moral right to that fruit. Someone who takes it from me is stealing my labour. That's the sort of principle which Locke regarded as self-evident, and comparable with a theorem of geometry.

Magee What I admire most about Locke's political philosophy is its clarion call for tolerance. And at least one of his arguments for tolerance is based on his epistemology. At one point his exposition of it contains these marvellous sentences: 'For where is the man that has incontestable evidence of the truth of all that he holds, or of the falsehood of all he condemns, or can say that he has examined to the bottom all his own, or other men's, opinions? The necessity of believing without knowledge, nay often upon very slight grounds, in this fleeting state of action and blindness we are in, should make us more busy and careful to inform ourselves than constrain others.'

Ayers There is an important connection between his epistemology and his views on religious tolerance in particular. He has what you might call an individualistic view of knowledge. Nobody else can do my knowing for me. In order to have *knowledge*, rather than borrowed opinion, I have to think things out for myself. For many practical purposes second-hand opinions are as much as we need or have time for, but with respect to the really important questions of life, moral and religious questions, he thought that people ought to spend time, and ought to be given the time to spend, on thinking things out for themselves as far as possible. If you accept that view, coupled with a very strong sense of how difficult it is to get these things right, then you've obviously got a recipe for a tolerant society, at least in certain spheres.

Magee We, of course, are in danger of taking that kind of tolerance for granted, but that we are in a position to do so is due not least to Locke. In his day it was far from being taken for granted – and is not taken for granted in most of the world today.

Before we leave the discussion of Locke, could I ask you to make a general assessment of his lasting contribution to philosophy? Or, if that's too large a question, say what you think his most important contribution has been?

Ayers Well, as you hinted at the beginning, he supplied a historically very important framework within which people could make sense of modern science, in particular Newtonian science, and a way of looking at the world in which we recognise that there's a lot we don't understand. We recognise the speculative nature of science. He had another less intended effect. Some of his arguments, for example his emphatic claim that the knowledge we get through the senses is really just knowledge of the powers of things to act upon us, provided the ammunition for philosophers like Berkeley himself, who were aiming at a very different view of the world from Locke's. They were able to make use of what they regarded as concessions, concessions to idealism or to extreme scepticism, but at any rate to quite different sorts of philosophy from Locke's. Now I think that Locke has still a lot to say to us partly just because he was the last great realist before the tendency towards idealist philosophy. (I think there is something deeply wrong with idealist philosophy myself.) It's very valuable to go back to Locke as a sort of pre-idealist realist, both in order to analyse what went wrong and why, but also to pick up points which we have forgotten, points which we have lost because of the long reign of anti-realist philosophies.

Magee Perhaps I, not being a specialist in Locke, might be allowed a more general perspective. Locke is regarded as the founding father of modern empiricism, and, more specifically, also as the founder of the mainstream tradition of modern philosophy in the English-speaking world. He was a dominant influence in French thought throughout the eighteenth century – Voltaire devoted most of his life to propagating the ideas of Locke and Newton. To quote *The Encyclopaedia of Philosophy*: 'Voltaire, Montesquieu, and the French Encyclopaedists found in Locke the philosophical, political, educational, and moral basis that enabled them to propose and advance the ideas which eventuated in the French Revolution. In America, his influence on Jonathan Edwards, Hamilton, and Jefferson was decisive.' I don't think any other philosopher has had a greater influence in proportion to his merits. And Locke's work is still very much part of the core curriculum in philosophy. It is widely studied by historians, too, because of its political importance.

But let us move on now to Berkeley. In one sense the transition is easy, because Berkeley is most famous of all for rejecting something which Locke accepted, namely belief in material substance. So Berkeley is, among other things, reacting against Locke. His chief logical point, which is profound, is that nothing in experience can ever give us a warrant for inferring the existence of something which is not experience. He would have agreed with Descartes that I know by the most direct and immediate experience that I exist as a consciously aware being, and also that I know that the contents of my conscious awareness are whatever they are; but from this, he asserted, we can never be justified in claiming the existence of inaccessible, unexperienceable, unconceptualisable material objects 'out there' in the external world which cause us to have some of these experiences; and, indeed, we do not even know what it is we are saying when we make such claims. All we can ever know is that there are experiences and experiencing subjects.

Ayers The way you put it you make Berkeley look like a sceptic, whereas he hotly contended that his philosophy was anti-sceptical and that he wasn't doubting either the deliverances of the senses or that there is something out there responsible for them. His claim was that what's out there is not material, not matter. He wanted to assert that the most fundamental and substantial things in the world, and the only real agents or causes, are spirits – the infinite spirit and created finite spirits.

Magee The way *you* put it makes it sound as if Berkeley's primary concern is not to deny something but to assert something, namely that 'real' reality, and the whole of it, is spiritual.

Ayers The sensible world is a part of reality, but it is given a very subordinate role. It exists, he even asserts that it is *real*, but it's a sort of second-class, mind-dependent, inert, non-substantial being. Berkeley's motive is fundamentally theological. To his mind philosophers like Locke and Descartes had turned the material world almost into a kind of God. They had explained matter as something which, although originally created by God, has a nature and independent being of its own. Their material world, he thought, is like a great clock: it would go on ticking even if God went on holiday. This for Berkeley was virtually atheism, setting up a rival to God. A lot of philosophers before him had felt very strongly that materialism was a source of atheism, and had attacked any view which gave matter an equal status to spirit. In England a group called the Cambridge Platonists had argued against the materialist threat in terms of a chain or ladder of Being, with spirit on a higher ontological rung than matter. Berkeley was perhaps the first to have the idea of turning the tables on matter by making the sensible world, of its very nature, mind-dependent. He takes Locke's distinction between the world as it appears to us and the world as it is in itself, and just chops off the world as it is in itself. All that's left is the world as it appears to us, caused directly 'in our minds' by God. He contends that he is not denying the existence of anything that counts or matters to ordinary people. He is simply casting off a perverse construct of philosophers.

Magee I have a sneaking feeling that he may be right. At least, what he says seems to me to accord with the way most people actually think and talk. If you say to any ordinary person, 'How do you know that this glove exists?' he'll say, 'Well here it is, I'm holding it, I'm looking at it, I can put it on, smell the leather, see the colour – here, feel it yourself.' In other words, he takes the glove to be the sum total of its observable characteristics. He does *not* envisage the essential 'glove as it is in itself' as being some unknowable, unconceptualisable substratum which sustains those characteristics. Such a thought, I'm pretty sure, has never occurred to most people – and I suspect they would find it exceedingly difficult to understand. It occurs, in the main, only to philosophers and the people who study them. So when Berkeley claims that his view is in accord with common sense, I have to say I think he is speaking the truth – though that is not, of course, to say that his view is correct. Don't *you* agree that if you say to someone, 'How do you know this glove exists?' *he wouldn't in most cases know what else he could possibly say about it* after he had enumerated what could be observed about it – that those things, to him, *are* the glove? And that they are indeed the glove is Berkeley's central point.

Ayers It is always rather difficult to settle an argument about what the ordinary person thinks in this kind of case, if only because technical views of the world gradually – or even rapidly – become embodied in the way we all think and talk. For example it's now very much a part of the ordinary person's view of thought that we think in some sense with our brains, but it wasn't always so. Nevertheless, it seems to me very unlikely that any intelligent human being, unless a philosopher, has ever supposed that *all there is* to such a thing as a glove or lump of gold is its sensible qualities. Even to the least civilised of those who have to do with the stuff, a lump of gold is something with powers and a 'nature', as well as sensible qualities. Perhaps it was a philosophical achievement to arrive at the presumption that there must be a unitary explanation of all the qualities and powers of such a thing as gold, its unknown 'substance' or 'substrate'; but, as we have seen, it's Locke's not implausible view that that too is an assumption we all naturally and ordinarily make in the course of taking gold to be an independent substantial thing. The philosophical advance on 'common sense', according to Locke, came with a specific, if ultimately inadequate hypothesis as to what the 'substance' of such things *is*, namely solid matter with a mechanical structure. Now the mechanical hypothesis itself certainly did come into conflict with 'common sense' in so far as it denied that colours, smells and so forth are intrinsic properties of things. That certainly did give Berkeley a weapon, and his attack on the distinction between primary and secondary qualities is central to his argument that *all* of a thing's attributes are as sense-relative or mind-dependent as colours and smells. But that general conclusion doesn't strike me as in the least commonsensical – which doesn't mean that his argument is without force at the philosophical level.

Magee If Berkeley believes there's no such thing as independent matter, how does he account for the success of science (in which he was deeply interested)? Indeed, how can there *be* science if there is no matter?

Ayers Berkeley thought that he could account for it better than Locke could. Whereas Locke was left with the worry that the best science available ends up with brute facts like the inverse square law, for Berkeley *all* laws, of their very nature, are just brute facts. They are simply the order in which God affects us with ideas. This orderly sequence of our ideas has a specific divine purpose, which Berkeley explains by an analogy with language. God is so to speak informing us of what is to come: if I have a visual sensation of a fire, then I know that if I stretch out my hand I'll get burnt. Unless the ideas which God instils in us were in this sort of order, they would be useless to us. As it is, they make the moral life possible by enabling us to act in a purposeful way.

Magee So one might sum up Berkeley's view of total reality as follows. There is an infinite spirit, which is God. There are a number of finite spirits, and that's us. God made us, and is in communication with us via his world. It is God who gives us all the experiences that we have. So what we call the world is God's language to us; and the intelligible regularities of the world – the laws of science, the mathematical equations which we find embedded in our experience – are the grammar and syntax of that language, the structure of the divine communication to human minds.

Ayers And there's no need to postulate matter at all. It doesn't do any work.

Magee If all reality is, in this sense, mental, how does Berkeley explain the fact that I cannot perceive what I choose? If I close my eyes now and open them again I see that table there in front of me. And I cannot choose not to see it. I cannot make good a preference for, say, a sofa, or empty space. Yet if all perception is mind-dependent, why not? Locke and others would say, 'Well it's because there *is* a table there, independently of being perceived, and it affects you in such a way that you perceive it.'

But Berkeley can't say that. What is his explanation?

Ayers Well, there's in a sense a physical object which exists independently of being perceived by us, in that there is an idea of a table in God's mind, together with a divine intention to produce certain table-like ideas in our minds if and when circumstances are appropriate – crudely, whenever we are looking in the right direction. So the 'real thing' is explained in terms both of the order of our ideas, and of what exists in God's mind as the basis of that order. Some critics have thought that the leap from the given order of our ideas to a basis of that order in God's mind has made Berkeley just as vulnerable as the realist ever was to sceptical argument. But for Berkeley there is nothing intrinsically problematic about an inference from our ideas to some external cause. What Berkeley regards as important is to give an account of that cause which makes better sense than the allegedly incoherent and self-contradictory story that the external cause is matter. For example, Locke had admitted that it is totally unintelligible to us how matter should act on mind in sense perception, whereas Berkeley sees himself as avoiding any such problem. God's activity, he thinks, is perfectly intelligible. In fact the only genuine and intelligible causality is the activity of spirits, whether ourselves or God.

Magee I think there is more to be said for Berkeley than we are making it sound there is. The insistence that the objects of our knowledge are, and can only ever be, the data of our experience came, long after Berkeley's death, to be one of the orthodoxies of science. But it goes far beyond that. Karl Popper has written a well-known paper called 'A Note on Berkeley as Precursor of Mach and Einstein', in which he extracts no fewer than twenty-one theses from Berkeley's philosophy which he then shows to have been put forward by such modern physicists as Einstein. There is something profound, and far ahead of its time, about Berkeley's thought, quite apart from anything to do with belief in God.

Ayers The argument that our concept of anything must in the end come back to our experience of that sort of thing, however indirectly, is a powerful one, and has had a great influence. Of course that in a way is Locke's argument too, but for Locke it doesn't imply that there isn't something out there, to which our experience may simply fail to do justice. Berkeley just wanted to chalk off that mysterious independent reality. In quite a different way from Descartes, he's a dogmatic philosopher. His natural world is surprising for what's left out – it's a skin-deep world – but for that very reason it's not a mysterious place. Locke on the other hand wanted to emphasise the difficulty in laying hold of the nature of things, and indeed to put before us the possibility that they will ultimately prove, for all our best efforts, inscrutable. Now it's true that a lot of twentieth-century philosophy of science has been in some broad sense Berkeleian, with a tendency to reduce scientific theories to their practical consequences at the level of experience. But by no means all scientists have subscribed to such an interpretation of their work. Einstein himself thought different things at different times. And among philosophers of science realism has been making an effective comeback.

Magee I'm afraid we are going to have to draw this discussion to a close. Can I ask you to balance out Berkeley, as you did Locke?

Ayers Well, Berkeley is also a very important philosopher, although he has had a reputation in some circles for naïvety. He is in fact immensely ingenious and lucid, and very modern in the way he presents his case. His theological motives are no doubt old-fashioned, but his system has stood as a continual challenge to the realist. It has also been a continual source of ideas for anti-realists of many different complexions.

HUME

Dialogue with
JOHN PASSMORE

INTRODUCTION

Magee The philosopher widely regarded as the greatest who has ever written in the English language is David Hume – not an Englishman but a Scot, born in Edinburgh in 1711. He did some of his best work very young. At about eighteen he experienced some sort of intellectual revelation, and over the next eight years he produced a large and revolutionary book called *A Treatise of Human Nature*. It met with little attention and even less understanding: in his own phrase it fell 'dead-born from the Press'. So in his thirties he tried to rewrite it in what he hoped would be a more popular form. This resulted in two smaller volumes: one called *An Enquiry Concerning Human Understanding*, the other *An Enquiry Concerning the Principles of Morals*. These were scarcely any better received; and he seemed to give the impression then of turning away from philosophy. In his forties he wrote a history of Great Britain, which for a hundred years was the standard work – which is why he is still sometimes listed in books of reference as 'David Hume: Historian'. In his own lifetime he even made a name as an economist: in fact his monetarist theories have been reattracting attention recently. And in a modest way he was a man of affairs. In the War of the Austrian Succession he served as a staff officer on two military expeditions; and for a couple of years, in his early fifties, he was Secretary to the British Embassy in Paris – and then, after that, Under Secretary of State in London.

In all the many different circles in which he moved he was popular for his good nature as much as for his genius. So rare was his gift for friendship that he almost brought off the impossible task of befriending his French contemporary, Rousseau, who at one time proposed making his home in Britain because Hume was there. In France, Hume was known as 'le bon David'; and in his native Edinburgh the street he lived in was, and remains, named after him, St David's Street. In view of the latter fact it is perhaps ironical that in secret he had been writing his final philosophical masterpiece, a profound and damaging critique of natural religion which did not come to light until after his death. He died in 1776, and it was in 1779 that his *Dialogues Concerning Natural Religion* was published. Some people consider it his best work.

Hume is an unusually attractive figure who should also be seen as part of that great flowering of intellectual life in Edinburgh in the eighteenth century which we now refer to as 'the Scottish Enlightenment'. In David Hume, Adam Smith and James Boswell the Scottish Enlightenment produced the English language's foremost philosopher, economist and biographer. And they all knew one another. Adam Smith was one of Hume's closest friends, and was greatly influenced by him. Boswell contemplated writing Hume's biography, but alas, never did.

There is now a substantial literature on Hume, and one of the best books in it, *Hume's Intentions*, was written by the person with me to discuss his work, Professor John Passmore of the Australian National University.

DISCUSSION

Magee Whenever Hume put forward a brief outline of his own philosophy, which he did on two or three occasions, he always placed the central emphasis on causality, the question of what it is for one state of affairs to bring about, or cause, another state of affairs. This is an altogether more important and interesting question than people unused to philosophy realise, because the cause and effect relation seems to be what binds the whole of our known world together. Clearly, Hume regarded what he had to say about this as the cornerstone of his philosophy, and indeed, it is what he is best known for to this day.

Can you explain what the nub of his argument about it was?

Passmore A concrete example might help. Imagine a baby boy, an exceptionally bright child, whose parents have always given him soft cotton toys to play with. He has often dropped these toys out of his cot; they have fallen to the ground with a soft thud. One day his uncle gives him a rubber ball. The baby scrutinises the rubber ball from every angle, smells it, tastes it, feels it, and then drops it. For all his careful investigation he has no possible way of knowing that it will bounce instead of, like all his other toys, thudding softly on the floor. That example will serve to illustrate Hume's first point. Just by examining a thing, he constantly tells us, we can never tell what effects it can produce. Only as a result of experience can we determine its consequences.

Now consider the boy's uncle standing by, watching to see how his nephew will play with his gift. When he sees the ball drop, he expects it to bounce. If you ask him what caused the ball to bounce, he will reply: 'My nephew dropped it.' Or, if he interprets our question more abstractly, he might say 'Rubber balls have the power of bouncing' or, perhaps, 'There is a necessary connection between a ball's being dropped and its bouncing'. I am putting Hume's language into the uncle's mouth, but it is easy to translate it into a more everyday idiom. The uncle might say that his nephew *made* the ball bounce by dropping it, that one *characteristic* of rubber balls is that they bounce when they drop, that if they drop, they *must* bounce. But the change in idiom would not affect Hume's argument.

Hume then asks a deep question. What experience has the uncle had that the child lacks? The uncle makes use of such general concepts as 'cause', 'power', 'necessary connection'. If these are not just empty words, they must somehow refer back to experience. Well then, what, in the present case, is this experience? How does the uncle's experience differ from his nephew's experience?

The difference consists, Hume argues, in one single fact. Unlike his nephew, the uncle has been able to observe, in a very large number of cases, first of all a rubber ball's dropping and then its bouncing. Indeed, there never has been in his experience a case where a rubber ball has been dropped on to a hard surface without bouncing, or where a rubber ball has begun to bounce without having first fallen or been thrown. To use Hume's own language, there has been a 'constant conjunction' between the ball's falling and its bouncing.

So far, so good. We seem to have found a difference between the experience of the uncle and the experience of the baby nephew. But Hume then goes on to ask another question. Exactly how does this difference in experience generate such concepts as 'cause', 'power', 'necessary connection'? Admittedly, the uncle has seen a dropped rubber ball bounce on very many occasions, whereas the nephew has seen this happen only once. Nevertheless the uncle has not seen anything his nephew has not seen, he has only had the same sequence of experiences more often. They both observe a ball drop and then bounce – nothing more. Yet the uncle believes that there is a necessary connection between the ball's dropping and its bouncing. This is certainly not something he finds in his experience; his experience, except that it has been often repeated, is exactly the same as his nephew's. Then where does the idea of a necessary connection, of a causal link, come from, if it is never directly observed?

Hume's answer is that although experiencing the same sequence of events on innumerable occasions does not reveal something we did not notice on the first occasion – a causal link – it does affect the workings of our mind in a special kind of way. It *forms the habit in us* of expecting a rubber ball to bounce when it drops. To believe that A causes B, or that there is a necessary connection between A and B, or that A *makes* B happen, amounts, then, to nothing more than this: our minds are so constituted that when, having in our experience found A and B to be constantly conjoined, we meet with an A we expect it to be followed by a B; and when we meet with a B we presume it to have been preceded by an A. Our experience generates in us a habit of expecting; our consciousness of this habit is our idea of necessary connection. However, we mistakenly project it into the world around us, wrongly supposing that we perceive necessary connection there rather than simply feel impelled to make particular inferences.

Magee This is a matter of such fundamental significance that I would like to dwell on it for a moment. It seems to be impossible for us to form any conception of an ordered world at all without the idea of there being causal connections between events. But when we pursue this idea seriously we find that causal connection is not anything we ever actually observe, nor ever *can* observe. We may say that Event A *causes* Event B, but when we examine the situation we find that what we actually observe is Event A *followed by* Event B. There is not some third entity between them, a causal link, which we also observe. It does not save the situation to say: 'We know that Event A is the cause of Event B because B always and invariably follows A.' Day always and invariably follows night, and night always and invariably follows day, but neither is the cause of the other. Invariant conjunction, though it is all we observe, is not the same thing as causal connection. It could be the case, by sheer coincidence, that every time I cough you sneeze, but my coughs would not then be the cause of your sneezes. So we have this indispensable notion of cause at the very heart of our conception of the world, and of our understanding of our own experience, which we find ourselves quite unable to validate by observation or experience. There is no way in which it could be validated by logic either, since it is an empirical and not a logical concept. It actually purports to tell us how specific material events are related to each other in the real world, yet it is not derived from, nor can it be validated by, observation of that world. This is deeply mysterious. And by making us aware of it, Hume put his finger on a problem to which there is still no generally agreed solution. Is that an accurate recapitulation of what you said?

Passmore Yes. Quite a few philosophers, of course, have tried to reply to Hume, often using arguments which Hume had already considered and rejected in the *Treatise*. Some have argued, to take a case, that once we have seen a rubber ball fall and then bounce or, at the very least, when we have seen this happen on a number of occasions, we know that dropping the ball will always make it bounce. This is because nature is uniform. But what does it mean to say that nature is uniform? No more than that the same causes always give rise to the same effects. And that we know this to be the case is precisely what Hume has questioned. To say that the same causes must always have the same effects because nature is uniform is just to say, or so Hume argues, that they must have the same effects because they must have the same effects. That gets us absolutely nowhere.

Magee In other words, to explain causal connection in terms of the uniformity of nature is a disguised way of assuming the point to be proved.

Passmore That's right. His critics do not improve matters, Hume would add, if they put forward a rather weaker thesis, arguing that our past experience at least *makes it very likely* that in the future, as in the past, rubber balls will go on bouncing. For judgments of probability, he tells us, are always founded on our belief in uniformities. Suppose we say of someone who is suffering from a serious disease that he will probably die before the year is out. We pass that judgment because in our past experience people of his sort suffering from that disease have usually died within a relatively short period of time. But the death-rate from the disease may well alter in the future. No more in this case than in any other case does our past experience demonstrate what our future experience is going to be like, that such deaths will continue to be probable. A new medical discovery, to illustrate Hume's point, may make them improbable.

Magee He brought the same *sort* of argument as he had used about causality to another fundamental question, the existence – and continuity – of the self. He pointed out that although we take it for granted that we have selves, and that we are continuous selves, we cannot actually locate this self in observation or experience. When we introspect, what we encounter are thoughts, feelings, memories, emotions and so on, but we do not encounter some other entity, a self, that *has* those thoughts, feelings *et cetera*. This is a disconcerting, indeed startling, thing to be made to realise, is it not?

Passmore I think one should add that Hume was very dissatisfied with his theory of personal identity. He explicitly tells us so and he does not revert to it in his subsequent writings. As you yourself have pointed out, whenever he sets out to give a short account of his philosophical achievement he particularly emphasises his theory of causality. There he *did* feel satisfied. He had done what he set out to do. He had shown, he thought, that there is something about the way in which our minds work which compels us to believe that some things are necessarily connected with other things even although all our experience is of disconnected perceptions – even although, that is, we never directly experience any kind of causal link.

He could use a similar technique to explain why we believe in the continued existence of physical objects, believe in their persistent identity, even although they disappear from our sight every time we close our eyes. When we reopen our eyes what we see is so like what we saw before we closed our eyes that it is as if we had kept our eyes open all the time; thus we are led to confuse, by a trick of the imagination, what is actually no more than a sequence of very similar experiences with a true experience of identity.

In the same manner, too, he could explain why we believe in the continuous identity of other persons. That, indeed, is just a special case of our belief in the continuous identity of physical objects. I saw you yesterday; I am seeing you again today. You look much the same as you did yesterday, so much the same that it is as if I had kept on seeing you for the last twenty-four hours. Not surprisingly, I take you to be the same person I saw yesterday and to have continued in existence during the time I did not see you, even although my actual perceptions of you have been separated in time, with a night intervening, and even separated in space, between your home and this television studio.

Suppose, however, I begin to worry about my own identity, about why I believe that I am the same person I was yesterday. Hume has told us, as you pointed out, that when I go in search of my own identity by looking into my own mind, all I ever find is a passing perception, never any kind of persistent self. Then why do I believe that I am the same person I was yesterday, that there is some sort of persistent 'I'? To say that what happens is that since the perceptions I have today are so like the perceptions I had yesterday I become confused between that great similarity and strict identity takes it for granted that there is some sort of persistent 'I' which falls into this confusion. But the point at issue is precisely why I believe there is such an 'I'. It looks as if his familiar techniques break down at this point. This deeply troubles Hume because, as he confesses, he had begun with the presumption that so long as he was talking about nothing but the mind and its workings, he would not encounter any sceptical paradoxes, that intellectual difficulties would arise only when he tried to move outside his own mind to consider the nature and the relationships of the world outside that mind. But now he has encountered insoluble problems in giving a satisfactory account of the mind itself.

Magee His argument about causality and his argument about the self have a basic feature in common. In both of them he says, in effect: 'Here is an empirical concept which we take for granted: since it is supposed to describe how something actually is in the real world let us find the experience, the observation of how things are in that world, on which it is based.' And in both cases, when we look for the empirical basis of the concept we find, to our astonishment, that it does not exist. Among his other aims it is as if Hume is trying to bring our ways of thinking about the world into line with the facts of observation and experience, in other words into agreement with the evidence for them. Is this what he meant by his famous subtitle to *A Treatise of Human Nature* in which he described it as 'Being An Attempt to Introduce the Experimental Method of Reasoning into Moral Subjects'?

Passmore The phrase 'moral subjects' he, of course, understood very broadly. It included not only moral philosophy and not only what we should now call 'social science' – political theory, economics and politics – but psychology and logic, which he took to be a theory about how the mind works when it is inferring. Even the principles of literary criticism were, for him, 'moral subjects'. He did want to make all these forms of inquiry 'more scientific', in one sense of that phrase. But when he talks about introducing the 'experimental method' into them, we are not to suppose that he was trying to convert them into the sort of thing we should now call an experimental science. The 'experimental method', for Hume, simply means the method of relying on experience. When people start discussing these 'moral subjects', he says, they often make wild statements without any real evidence. They rely on eloquence rather than argument; they preach when they should rather be looking at the facts. Looking at the facts, he argues, is quite as essential in discussing the moral subjects as it is in the natural sciences. One finds this respect for the facts in Hume's own socio-economic writings, whether he is discussing just how populated the ancient cities were or trade in the modern world. Although he is sometimes mistaken, in our present judgment, he is never merely arbitrary.

Magee So what he is really trying to do, then, is inculcate a radically new respect for reality, for the facts of experience, and to discourage all forms of talk about the world which are not based on those. And you stress the important point that when he talks about 'introducing the experimental method of reasoning' he is not referring to experiments, he is referring to experience.

Passmore Yes, that's roughly it. He does, it is true, very occasionally describe what purport to be experiments, but they are not what any scientist would regard as such. It is interesting to compare him with his contemporary David Hartley. They both like to think of themselves as doing for the human mind what Newton did for physics. They both set out to achieve that end with the aid of a particular theory, the association of ideas, according to which ideas which are related to one another in certain ways, as being very similar to one another or as having been, in our experience, spatially or temporally contiguous, are automatically pulled together into complex wholes – association acting, in Hume's own metaphor, as a kind of gravity. Nevertheless, Hartley has a place in the history of psychology, whereas Hume has not. His approach, for the most part, is conceptual, analytical, philosophical, rather than, in our contemporary sense of the world, scientific. He came to be admired by the founder of phenomenology, Husserl, precisely as one who had shown that there are ways of inquiring into the structure of the mind which do not depend on laboratory experiments.

Magee Underlying Hume's general philosophical approach there is an implied theory of language and of meaning. For what he is saying, in effect, is that for a word to have meaning it must relate to a specific idea; and if the idea is an idea about the world then for it to have real content it has to be derived from experience. On this view, then, if you want to know what a word means you must look for the experience from which it is derived. If there is no such experience, the word has no empirical significance.

Passmore That's right. At one point Hume draws a distinction, which is of crucial importance to him, between thinking and talking – under which head he would include, in this context, writing. We are *thinking* only when we are operating with genuine concepts – if not always totally clear – which have their source in experience. Talking or writing, however, we can fall into using quite empty expressions, which ostensibly point to concepts but in fact refer to nothing whatsoever. If somebody replies that he does in fact refer by a particular expression – let us say 'essence' – to a concept, Hume challenges him: very well, he asks, from what actual experience does that concept derive? And if to that question no answer can be given Hume believes he can safely conclude that the expression in question has no sense.

Magee This approach led him to develop something that came subsequently to be known as 'Hume's Fork'. He said of any given body of ideas that when you are looking at it critically you must ask yourself two main questions. Question one: 'Do these ideas concern matters of fact, in which case do they rest on observation and experience?' Question two: 'Do they concern relations between ideas, as for example in mathematics or logic?' If the answer to both questions is 'No', then, he says, commit those ideas to the flames, for they can contain nothing but sophistry and illusion.

He was a marvellous clearer away of intellectual rubbish, not only in philosophy and politics but also in religion, and indeed in other fields too. Do you think that in the history of philosophy this is one of his most important functions, to be a sweeper away of illusions?

Passmore I'm quite sure about that. There is one particular illusion – or what he regards as such – that he is constantly trying to clear away and that is that we can demonstrate the truth of most of the things we dearly believe. The arguments he uses to establish this point often make him sound extremely sceptical. At one point, he even tells us that if we follow philosophical argument to its final point we shall end up with the total extinction of belief and evidence.

But he also argues that it is completely impossible for any human being constantly to maintain a totally sceptical position. Not because there is something illogical about total scepticism – he rejects those arguments which purport to show that scepticism is intellectually self-defeating – but simply because human beings are unable to avoid acting and believing. One cannot *live* as a total sceptic.

It is nevertheless very useful, he thinks, to follow through the sceptical argument to its extreme conclusion. For practical purposes, we shall be left, at the end, with what he calls a 'mitigated scepticism'. Recognising just how little can be established, we shall free ourselves from any kind of dogmatism, from that attitude of mind which the eighteenth century called 'enthusiasm' and we call 'fanaticism', one feature of which is the belief that there are truths which can be established in such a manner that anyone who fails to recognise them must be morally wicked and can therefore properly be exterminated.

Also, Hume rejects the possibility of constructing large metaphysical systems. If we cannot even be totally sure that the sun will rise tomorrow, how can we possibly establish truths about the universe as a whole, and its origins? Hume's *Dialogues Concerning Natural Religion*, which you mentioned earlier, apply this general line of argument to religion, a topic which greatly interested him. That class of beliefs which he calls 'superstitions' are indeed the principal enemy against which his philosophy is directed. Superstitions, he believes, are dangerous, whereas the beliefs of philosophers are at worst only ridiculous.

Magee Wouldn't it be true to say that Hume's scepticism is not about the world at all but about the capacities of the human mind? I don't think he doubted that there is an independently existing world of material objects in space and time, and that the movements of these material objects causally interrelate, and that we have representations of them through our senses, and that those representations are internal to us yet give us a roughly reliable picture of the world around us. I'm quite sure Hume believed in this whole commonsense view of the world. What he did not believe is that any of it can be rationally demonstrated. We simply cannot prove that any of this is so. Yet we have to assume that it is if we are to live at all. He was not showing how the world is, he was showing how reason is, and blowing many of its pretensions sky high. Rational demonstration is helpless and powerless in the face of some of the most elementary realities – that, I think, was his point. . . . Do *you* believe he had genuine doubts about the commonsense view of the world?

Passmore I don't think so, if you mean that he did not seriously doubt, for example, whether other people existed, in the sense in which one might seriously doubt whether a nuclear war can be avoided. There is, however, a tension in his work between two lines of thought: his belief in the possibility of developing a science of human nature and the scepticism into which he finds himself driven. The science of human nature, he tells us, will rest on two things, our observation of the workings of our own mind and our observation of other human beings. These observations are of people who are assumed to exist independently of us and to act in ways

David Hume (1711–76)

which have effects both on us and on other human beings. He does not doubt, in any serious sense of the word 'doubt', that there are such other people and that their actions have effects. Indeed, he would have to be a madman to do so. What he does deny, however, is that these beliefs can be derived by purely logical processes of inference. Indeed, for Hume strict proof plays no part in human life outside mathematics.

Magee And he did not think that mathematics, or even physical science, was all *that* important as a part of human life, did he?

Passmore Hume was interested in mathematics, especially in geometry, and at one time proposed to write more fully on that theme. As far as physics is concerned, he always speaks with great admiration of Newton, holding him up as an exemplar of what can be accomplished intellectually. Nevertheless, you are certainly right. Hume tells us quite specifically that the really important forms of inquiry are political theory, moral theory, literary criticism and logic – a word he uses very broadly, as I have already said, to mean the theory of the human understanding, of what happens when we infer. Anything else – physics, let us say – was, in his eyes, though important, of the second order of importance. Furthermore, even a soundly based physics, so he tells us, will have to be based, as a necessary preliminary, on an adequate theory of the workings of the human mind. 'There is no question of importance', he is therefore prepared roundly to assert, 'whose decision is not comprised in the science of man.' In his eyes, human beings mattered more than anything else – striving, passionate, human beings. That is in spite of the fact that he was only too conscious of the ignorance, violence and superstition, the horrors and the follies, which human history exhibits. Many philosophers have not been at all like this; their emphasis has been on great abstractions, described as ultimate realities, or perhaps on 'humanity' as distinct from you and me.

Magee I suppose you have in mind Plato's Theory of Forms, or Hegel's *Geist*, or Bradley's Absolute – or even just any philosophising at large about, say, the nature of Space and Time?

Passmore Yes. Admittedly, the first lengthy discussion in the *Treatise* is about Space and Time. But that had, I believe, a special purpose. Theologians had argued that Space and Time are so full of mysteries and paradoxes that it was unfair to make the same thing a complaint against theology. Hume set out to show that this was not so, that the apparent paradoxes could be resolved once we recognised that Space and Time are not mysterious entities but simply the particular ordering in which our perceptions present themselves to us. So if we say, to take Hume's own example, that five notes on a flute 'occur in time', we are really saying no more than that they occur successively. But although his discussion of Space and Time is, as I said, quite lengthy, the fact remains that it had a subordinate role in his great enterprise of constructing an adequate theory of the human mind and human society.

Magee An important point brought out by what you've just said is that in that famous subtitle which I quoted a moment ago – 'An Attempt to Introduce the Experimental Method of Reasoning into Moral Subjects' – special significance attaches not only to the phrase which people have always picked on, namely 'the experimental method of reasoning', but also to the phrase 'moral subjects'. It was human beings, and human affairs, that David Hume was really concerned with.

Passmore That's right.

Magee In my introduction to this discussion, when I referred to Hume's moving on from the writing of philosophy to the writing of history, I deliberately used the phrase 'seemed to give the impression then of turning away from philosophy'. I did not say he actually did turn away from it. This was partly because I had his subsequent writing of the *Dialogues Concerning Natural Religion* in mind, but also partly because I know that you, in your book *Hume's Intentions*, argue that there would have been no turning away, even without that, because in Hume's mind his 'philosophy' and his 'history' were part and parcel of a single concern with human affairs. I'd like you now to expand on that point.

Passmore Well, of course, it is only quite recently that philosophy came to have the narrow sense which now prevails. There are still many survivals of that older, broader use according to which any systematic inquiry, especially into the nature of the world, of human beings and of human society, is a variety of philosophy. Very few 'Doctors of Philosophy' have ever studied philosophy in the modern, professional sense of the word; they would never have been called upon to consider the kinds of issue which this discussion has been concerned with. Hume might have been prepared to agree that he had given up metaphysics – although even then one has to remember that he was working on his *Dialogues* – but certainly not that he had given up philosophy.

Magee The fact remains, though, that with the very important exception of the *Dialogues* he gave up what *we* call philosophy. After finishing his *Enquiries* he gave no further thought – or at least no further published thought – to such matters, say, as causality and personal identity.

Passmore I would certainly have to grant that. But remember his situation. The *Treatise* had been largely ignored. He thought at first that this might be because it was too long or too obscure. So he produced the first *Enquiry*. But still there was no criticism of the sort he felt he had to take seriously. He was convinced that in general terms he was right. Remember, too, that he thought of what he was doing as preliminary to detailed work on 'moral subjects'. What would have been the point in his continuing to work at these preliminaries when, in his judgment, no one had produced any serious criticism of them, criticism which would have forced him to reconsider his views? *Now* was the time to embark upon what, he assures us, are the centrally important subjects.

Magee And the centrally important inquiries constituted what we today would term 'the social sciences' rather than what we would term 'philosophy'.

Passmore Only, of course, if one included history under that heading, for, as you began by pointing out, Hume first made his name as an historian. But history was not, in his mind, at all divorced from social theory. Hume tells us that in the first book of the *Treatise* he had completed all that was necessary in the area of logic. We might say, very roughly, that it was his methodology of the social sciences. Or perhaps that there he had sharpened the knives he needed for cutting with; now it was time to do the cutting. It's true that he also turned away from the moral philosophising which makes up the third book of the *Treatise*. But much the same considerations applied there: he now had, especially as he went on to develop it in his *Enquiry Concerning the Principles of Morals*, the moral theory he needed for his later theorising. And again it had not met with the kind of critical attention which might have persuaded him that he needed to reconsider it.

Magee Underlying Hume's very broad concern with human affairs there was a theory – or a certain conception, anyway – of human nature, and you actually made some reference to it a few minutes ago. Can you now bring it to the surface?

Passmore Well, it's a long story because really most of his work subsequent to the *Enquiries* is a study of human nature in action, human nature in practice. One thing he never doubted was that there was such a thing as human nature. This is a point at which he differed from Locke. Locke had been particularly intent on getting rid of the conception of original sin. This was fundamentally important to Locke because he was a religious thinker as well as a philosopher. And he had argued that human beings are born into the world with minds which are like blank sheets of paper. In his writings on education, Locke suggests that, using education as our method, we can convert human beings into any shape we desire. Many of the French enlightenment thinkers accepted this view; education, they concluded, could be used to perfect humanity. Hume was far from believing that human beings were totally malleable, and therefore perfectible, whether by education or by social change. Human beings, he was convinced, possess by nature particular passions – he instances self-love, resentment at injuries, sexual passions – which are constant through human history. Some societies are more successful than others in curbing or encouraging such passions. But the passions remain.

Magee His view that human nature is always essentially the same rested partly on his knowledge of antiquity – which was surprisingly extensive. He was deeply knowledgeable about Greek and Latin literature and history, and one of the things that struck him most forcefully was that *in very considerable detail* human behaviour had been just the same in those quite different places, and those distant times, and those quite other forms of society, as he saw it manifesting itself round him in his own lifetime.

Passmore Yes. He was particularly interested in Tacitus and Cicero, in what they had to say about human beings and human society. But his range of reference, especially to historians but also to such poets as Ovid, is very wide. The Latin writers interested him more than the Greeks, which was typical of his age. They showed him, he thought, that human passions had not greatly changed since Roman times; they provided him, then, with some of his evidence for the permanence of human nature. Nevertheless, this is not a view that he felt he needed a great deal of evidence for; on the contrary, he thought it pretty obvious. After all, he called his principal work *A Treatise of Human Nature*; that title takes it for granted that human beings have a nature. In one of his essays, he considers whether, as some theologians had maintained, human nature is totally corrupt, even its most apparently virtuous acts being tainted by vanity and self-love; or whether, as others had maintained, it is essentially godlike. In his typical fashion he rejects both views. Human nature, he argues, is neither totally corrupt – people he thought, can be genuinely benevolent – nor does it have the characteristics one could reasonably expect only of demi-gods. But Hume does not question that the issue is a real one. The only point at issue is what human nature is like, not whether there is any such thing.

Magee When one looks at Hume's work from the standpoint of our own time, one is struck by the modernity, from *our* point of view, of much of it. We have talked, for instance, of his concern with the problem of the self: well, some of the most interesting philosophy that has been done in Britain in the last few years has been about this, for instance one of Bernard Williams's books is called *Problems of the Self*, and one of Karl Popper's (in collaboration with J. C. Eccles) *The Self and Its Brain*. Or, to take another example, scientists in the twentieth century have been deeply puzzled, notably in connection with quantum physics, about the presence or absence of causal connection: well, this is a problem of which Hume's is the classic formulation. Only yesterday in the history of philosophy, as it were, the chief representative of logical positivism in the English-speaking world, A. J. Ayer, was constantly reiterating that the central doctrines of logical positivism 'derived very much from Hume'. So, throughout our lifetime, one way and another, things that Hume had to say have been pointedly relevant to the philosophy of our contemporaries.

One problem which Hume highlighted, and about which a great deal has been written in the twentieth century, is the problem of induction. We haven't mentioned that so far. Can you say a word about it? Perhaps the problem itself can be formulated in this way: What justification do we have, in our thinking about the world, for basing a universal conclusion on particular instances?

Passmore Well, it is very closely related to what I said previously about causality. Go back to the case of the baby boy and the bouncing ball. Suppose the baby drops the ball on Monday, and then again on Tuesday, Wednesday, Thursday and as long as you like. Every time he does so the ball bounces. Then Hume freely admits that the baby will come to believe that the ball will bounce whenever he drops it, or, what Hume takes to be the same thing, that he will come to *expect* the ball to bounce. The only question is how this belief comes to be formed. Clearly, the baby boy has not deduced it from some *a priori* principle, indubitably certain, some kind of axiom. Not only does the boy not know any such principle; there is no such principle to be known. The only axiomatic principles, on Hume's view, are mathematical. And we cannot immediately deduce from mathematical principles anything of the sort Hume calls a 'matter of fact', facts like 'all rubber balls bounce' or 'that ball is going to bounce', which tell us something about what actually happens in the world.

Magee Many of our contemporary philosophers would argue, would they not, that even if we cannot strictly speaking demonstrate conclusions about matters of fact in the way we can demonstrate mathematical conclusions, it is nevertheless rational in these circumstances for us to make what they call an 'inductive inference' that, say, the next rubber ball we drop will bounce. What would Hume have to say to them?

Passmore He would ask such philosophers to spell out that inference in detail. Then if they were to reply that the bouncing of the ball follows from some general scientific principle about elastic bodies his response would be that our reasons for accepting that proposition are of exactly the same order as our reasons for expecting the next rubber ball we drop to bounce. Our past experience of the behaviour of elastic bodies has created in us a particular expectation about the way they will behave on occasions we have not yet experienced. So the general question still remains: exactly how does past experience justify a conclusion about future behaviour?

If the defenders of induction were to try to invoke some more general principle such as the Uniformity of Nature, he would want to know what their grounds are for believing that principle to be correct. They are nothing more, he would argue, than the fact that in the past our expectations have not always been disappointed. How does that prove that in the future they will not be disappointed? Attempts to justify our matter of fact inferences, indeed, always come back, on Hume's view, to something of the form: 'Well, the ball bounced when I dropped it on Monday, on Tuesday, on Wednesday . . .' and this, he continues to insist, does not give us any logical justification for believing that it will bounce if we drop it tomorrow.

Of course, he is not denying, not for a moment, that we do in fact expect the ball to bounce tomorrow. But that is not, on his view, because some argument justifies us in doing so; we expect the ball to bounce only because it is part of our human nature to expect things to continue to happen in the future as they have happened in the past. He describes how this happens, what psychological mechanisms are involved, in some detail. We share this characteristic habit of expecting, Hume also thinks, with other animals. True enough, Hume admits, animals do not form empirical generalisations of some such form as 'Whenever my master whistles me, he is going to take me for a walk'. But neither do we, most of the time. We simply have certain expectations after having had certain experiences. Because some animals react in this same kind of way, we quite properly ascribe to them the power to think and reason.

Magee That carried Hume a long way from Descartes, who was convinced that only human beings had the power to think – animals, in Descartes's view, when they appeared to be thinking, were merely reacting to stimuli in a mechanical way. But, leaving Descartes aside, would there not be a widely held view to this day that animals rely on instincts whereas human beings can reason?

Passmore Hume is quite unlike Descartes: he supposes it to be obvious that animals can reason – not mathematically, to be sure, but exactly as we normally reason in everyday life when we hear a particular noise and infer that the bus is coming. This shows, he also thinks, that such inferences do not make use of elaborate logical procedures but are made possible, rather, by simple psychological mechanisms. He is prepared to describe reason, indeed, as nothing but 'a wonderful and unintelligible mechanism in our souls' – 'unintelligible' not in the sense that we cannot give an account of what happens when we infer but in the sense that there is no reason why our minds should work in the way in which they do, creating expectations on the basis of experienced conjunctions. So when Hume tells us that animals are much more rational than philosophers have sometimes supposed them he is in the same breath telling us that we are much more dependent on instincts than we commonly suppose ourselves to be.

Hume's admirers have, for the most part, strongly disapproved of his psychological approach. They have therefore stated Hume's position in a much simpler form: 'There is no valid way of arguing from the premiss that things have been conjoined in a certain way in the past to the conclusion that they will be conjoined in the same way in the future.' And that Hume certainly does say, even if it is by no means *all* he says.

Magee What is really penetrating about this point is that scientific laws themselves were thought, until our own time, to be true universal statements which rested on a number of particular observations or experiments or instances – and, as Hume showed, the logical link simply cannot be made. There is a pleasing illustration of this to be drawn from the history of the teaching of philosophy itself. In Logic textbooks which had been in widespread use for many years before Hume's day, one of the most constantly quoted examples included the sentence 'All swans are white'. And, of course, for literally thousands of years every swan that any European had ever seen had been white – thousands upon thousands of them, and never a single counter-example. But when Europeans discovered Australia they discovered also black swans. That's a marvellous illustration of the fact that however many thousands, indeed millions or billions, of times a particular thing has been observed and found to be so-and-so, it does not follow that the next one will be the same. No finite number of observations, however large, can logically entail a universal conclusion. And of course any actual observations that humans do or ever can make in the real world can only ever be finite in number. Now all scientific laws are unrestrictedly universal statements, and this means that they cannot logically be derived from the observations that were for a long time supposed to be their basis. This insight was explosive, and one is tempted to say anarchic: to those who first understood Hume it seemed that he was knocking the bottom out of science.

Passmore They had certainly supposed that Newton's conclusions had been established once and for all. But scientists themselves would now generally agree that scientific theories are never totally incorrigible. They can, in principle, always be overthrown. Trying to preserve the older view, philosophers of science for a time argued that Einstein had not in fact done anything more than produce a wider theory within which Newton's mechanics could find a place as still being correct provided certain special conditions were fulfilled. But that will not do. Useful though Newtonian mechanics still is in a great range of circumstances, on some issues Newtonian and relativity theories are in total opposition. One cannot avoid the conclusion that if Einstein is right there are points at which Newton was wrong. Still less, of course, can Lavoisier's chemistry be reconciled with the earlier phlogiston theory, or Darwin with Lamarck. When Hume's philosophy finally came to be seriously studied, after more than a century of neglect, he certainly helped to form this newer attitude to science, which granted its fallibility.

Magee I don't see how you can say that Hume's philosophy was neglected for a century when one considers its influence on Kant. Neglected in Britain, perhaps.

Passmore Well, admittedly, Hume did in Germany arouse Kant from his dogmatic slumber, by which phrase Kant meant his earlier belief that it was possible to construct a dogmatic metaphysics. But in the years that followed, it was widely believed that since Kant had answered Hume, there was no need to consult Hume further. In England a Kantian, T. H. Green, did much to rescue Hume's philosophy from oblivion. Ironically enough, however, he was principally concerned to use Hume as a weapon against empiricism, taking him to have reduced empiricism to absurdity by showing that it issues in total scepticism.

Magee Bertrand Russell, in his *History of Western Philosophy*, asserts that in many respects we have still not got beyond Hume. Russell's exposition of Hume treats of the same central problems as you and I have done – causality, and whether scientific laws can be inductively based, and the problems of the self – and goes on to say that in each of those areas Hume formulated problems of a fundamental nature which no one to this day has satisfactorily solved. Would you agree with Russell about that?

Passmore I am afraid he is still right, although fresh attempts to solve Hume's problems come from the press almost daily. Of course, it is equally true that Plato pointed to very fundamental questions that no philosopher has yet solved to the general satisfaction. It is much easier in philosophy to ask questions and to raise problems than it is to produce universally accepted conclusions. Nevertheless, it takes genius to formulate the really fundamental questions, to see fundamental problems which had previously been overlooked. Both Plato and Hume did this. Indeed, not to take seriously the questions they asked – in a form modified, of course, by subsequent philosophical work – is not to be a philosopher.

Magee What sort of person was Hume? When I read his work I get the impression of a massive humaneness, immensely attractive. Do you think he was like that in life?

Passmore His friend, the economist Adam Smith, once said that he came as near to perfection as any human being possibly could. Biographers have recently explored his life in considerable detail. They have not found, I should say, a single example of a mean or malicious action. Occasionally, perhaps, he might strike us as being a little timid. That is not unnatural. He had views about religion which were scarcely popular in the society in which he was living. Even then, it was his friends who persuaded him to be more cautious; it was at their instance that his *Dialogues Concerning Natural Religion* was left unpublished until after his death. He is occasionally, too, a little vain. But, in the circumstances, this is a defect it is easy to forgive; he could not but be conscious of his great intellectual powers.

  If I were to be invited to a celestial dinner party for philosophers, David Hume is the philosopher I should choose to sit next to, even although Plato, for example, is in my judgment a greater philosopher. He had such a warm humanity, he was without pretensions, he was at once witty and serious. Dying, and knowing he was dying, of a protracted bowel disorder, he received his friends with his usual cheerfulness until his weakness finally made that impossible. We have an account of his last days from James Boswell. Knowing that Hume did not believe himself to be immortal, Boswell expected to find himself confronted by a terrified man. On the contrary, Hume displayed an equanimity and cheerfulness which Boswell found quite disturbing.

Magee The style was the man. And as a literary style it exerted enormous influence. Schopenhauer, one of the supreme masters of German prose, said that he consciously tried to write German in the way Hume wrote English. And Bertrand Russell, perhaps the outstanding stylist in philosophy in this century (a winner of the Nobel Prize for Literature), was consciously influenced by Hume in the way he wrote. So is A. J. Ayer, one of the best writers in philosophy of our own day.

Passmore Clarity and elegance were the virtues Hume sought after.

These are by no means popular virtues at the moment; I recently heard them dismissed, indeed, as 'old-fashioned'. Didn't Oscar Wilde once remark that if we write intelligibly we run the risk of being found out? That isn't a risk most of our contemporaries are prepared to take, as Russell was and Ayer is. But it isn't only a question of style in the literary sense. Hume, and after him Russell and Ayer – not to mention quite a few other philosophers – carried on a certain manner of British philosophising which is conspicuous from its beginnings in Bacon and Hobbes, or even before that in William of Ockham. Philosophers in this tradition try to be clear, to be critical, to present arguments, to look at what actually happens in the world. They do not set out to persuade us that there are mysterious transcendental entities. In fact, they work with as few entities as possible and these, they tell us, are to be found in ordinary experience or, if beyond that, in the refined experience of science. It is a relatively modest style of philosophising, for all that it may arrive at conclusions which are quite at odds with popular opinion. In particular, it does not seek to aggrandise human beings. Hume is perhaps its supreme exemplar.

Magee There is one basic difficulty raised by Hume's philosophical approach which we ought to consider before we end our discussion. He shows us that most of the things which we take for granted are things we do not in fact know, and will never be able to know. He also says, rightly, that we cannot live without holding, and acting on, a great many beliefs. This being so, what criteria are we to adopt for the acceptance of beliefs? If knowledge is unattainable, how are we to distinguish between the sort of view that it is reasonable to hold and the sort of view that it is not reasonable to hold?

Passmore That is a very difficult question. At one point in the *Treatise*, Hume promises to tell us exactly what the difference is between what he calls a 'poetical enthusiasm' and a 'serious conviction'. But that promise he does not keep. In his more sceptical moods, indeed, Hume writes as if the only difference between the two is that, when we are seriously convinced, our ideas are more vivid, more forceful, than they are when, as we say, we are 'only imagining'. But at other times he distinguishes between the behaviour of 'the wise man' and the behaviour of 'the vulgar'. The 'wise man', he then says, will reject all beliefs, however vivid and forceful they may be, which are not traceable back to constant conjunctions. 'A wise man', he indeed tells us, 'proportions his belief to the evidence.' After all, Hume was a doughty opponent of what he calls 'superstition' and he has to leave himself some way of showing what is wrong with superstitious beliefs – which, he would have to grant, are often held very firmly. The sceptic and the critic make awkward bed-fellows.

Nevertheless, however dissatisfied we may be with what Hume has to say on this matter, it was he who set the problem which still perturbs us. Suppose we agree that scientific laws are not, in any strict sense, demonstrable or, even, highly probable. Why is it still far better to rely on what scientists tell us, as technologists are successfully doing all the time, than on some silly idea which someone thinks up in a best-selling piece of pseudo-science? That is a question which gets harder rather than easier to answer nowadays, when disagreements between scientists, often on matters of vital human importance, are daily publicised in the media.

Magee   Can I carry the question further by asking you what your own answer to it would be?

Passmore   I do not think that there is any simple answer to this question. But one answer is that scientific hypotheses are subject to a close and uncompromising scrutiny, as the teachings of, let us say, the latest Indian sage are not. That is one reason for objecting to the growing tendency of scientists to announce so-called 'discoveries' before these have been subjected to such scrutiny; it weakens the peculiar virtue of science, which is the way in which it has institutionalised criticism. In Hume's time, of course, science was still, in this respect, only in the making. Another point is that scientific findings are systematically related to one another; they exhibit a high level of consistency. Your example of black swans is not a typical one. It was not a proposition of science but an ordinary commonsensical observation that swans are white. We all know, too, that different varieties of a species often differ in colour, as rabbits do, or dogs. So although it upset a favourite piece of poetic symbolism when black swans were discovered in Australia, it was not at all disturbing to science, as it would be disturbing to come across a swan which breathed in carbon dioxide and breathed out hydrogen, or which contained no DNA whatsoever.

This is scarcely the place to explore that fascinating question further. But, of course, nothing I have said suggests for a moment that scientific propositions are incorrigible. All I am suggesting is that there are good reasons for taking the claims of science very seriously – as there are good reasons, for the matter of that, why we should take the claims of historians seriously or the claims of scholars, even although we recognise that they often make mistakes. The same goes for telephone books and railway timetables.

Magee   My impression is that most people today, including most well-educated people, think of science as a body of known, proved certainties, and take it for granted that the growth of science consists in the adding of new certainties to the body of already existing ones. Anyone who has that view of science has a fundamental lesson to learn from Hume, has he not? And that means that Hume retains for us, among so much else, his full power to disconcert.

Passmore There's no doubt about it; Hume is a very disconcerting thinker. He is particularly disconcerting to those very many people, whether they are scientists or humanists, who are firmly convinced that there is no room for the imagination in science – a view often encouraged rather than discouraged by school science courses. Such people believe that while it takes a great deal of imagination to write a novel or paint a picture or direct a film, science is just a matter of looking to see what happens when you conduct an experiment, making calculations on the basis of these controlled observations, and then churning out a scientific generalisation. This, of course, is nonsense. No doubt, there are many rather unimaginative scientists, doing a routine job. But so are there many unimaginative novelists, artists, film directors, doing a routine job. Any of the great discoveries, or even relatively minor discoveries of principles, needs not only careful experimenting and careful reasoning but flights of the imagination. As Hume's thinking develops in his *Treatise* the imagination, which is at first defined as nothing more than the capacity to have relatively faint images of complexes we have not actually perceived – relatively faint, that is, when contrasted with memory – comes to assume an ever more central and creative role. Even our most ordinary observations of the world around us turn out, on Hume's view, to involve an exercise of the imagination. We do not just passively perceive the world around us. If we did, we should be confined to a mere sequence of sensations. We perceive *things* as distinct from sensations only because our imagination is constantly active. Indeed, the centrality of the imagination in Hume, which leads him in the direction of the now current doctrine that there is not an absolute distinction between what we call 'bare facts' and 'theories', is one of the most fascinating, and disquieting, features of Hume's philosophy.

Magee This prising of our so-called 'knowledge' away from the world, and the space which that leaves for new vision, can also be creatively liberating. Einstein once remarked that he would never have dared to overthrow the science of Newton if he had not read Hume. Two things go together here: the power to disconcert *profoundly* and the power to liberate and stimulate imagination. Reading Hume's philosophy does both of these things as freshly today as when he wrote it.

KANT

Dialogue with
GEOFFREY WARNOCK

INTRODUCTION

Magee For several generations now the man most widely regarded as the greatest philosopher since the ancient Greeks has been Immanuel Kant. He was born in the town of Königsberg, East Prussia, in 1724, and died there, at an age of not quite eighty, in 1804. Many jokes have been made about the fact that he rarely left Königsberg, and never went outside his native province in the whole of his life – also about the fact that he stuck so strictly to a daily routine that the inhabitants of Königsberg could, literally, set their watches by him as he walked past their windows. He never married, and outwardly his life was uneventful. However, he was not the dry stick that my description so far would suggest: on the contrary, he was sociable and amusing, elegant in dress and witty in conversation; and his lectures at the University of Königsberg, where he was a professor for more than thirty years, were famed for their brilliance.

Rather surprisingly, Kant was the first great philosopher of the modern era to be a university teacher of philosophy. Descartes, Spinoza, Leibniz, Locke, Berkeley, Hume – none of these taught philosophy. Nor did most of the major philosophers in the century after Kant, the nineteenth century: the obvious exception is Hegel; but Schopenhauer, Kierkegaard, Karl Marx, John Stuart Mill, Nietzsche – none of these were academic philosophers. In fact Nietzsche gave up being an academic in order to be a philosopher. In the modern era it is only when one gets to the twentieth century that nearly all important philosophers are academics. Whether this recent professionalisation of the subject is a good thing is a moot point – I suspect it is inevitable.

However, to get back to the first of the great professors: although the writings of Kant's youth and early middle age made him widely known, all but a few of them are now virtually unread. His lasting fame rests on a series of publications which did not begin until he was fifty-seven, and which continued into his seventies. We have here a rare spectacle, that of a creative genius of the first order producing all his greatest work in late middle age and old age. His acknowledged masterpiece, *The Critique of Pure Reason*, was published in 1781. At first it was not at all well understood, so two years later he published an exposition of its central argument in a separate, slim volume, usually referred to as the *Prolegomena*, and then brought out a substantially revised edition of *The Critique of Pure Reason* itself in 1787. There followed in rapid succession his second great critique, *The Critique of Practical Reason*, in 1788, and his third, *The Critique of Judgment*, in 1790. Meanwhile he had also published, in 1785, a little book called *The Fundamental Principles of the Metaphysics of Ethics*. Despite its unseductive title, this book has had an immense influence on moral philosophy ever since.

Discussing Kant's work with me is a well-known contemporary philosopher, Sir Geoffrey Warnock, Principal of Hertford College, Oxford, and a former Vice-Chancellor of the University of Oxford.

DISCUSSION

Magee Kant was one of the supreme system-builders of modern philosophy; and one notorious difficulty in expounding any system – precisely because everything in it is held in place by something else – is choosing at what point to break in, in order to make a start; because whatever you begin with already presupposes something else. What do you think is the best point at which to break into Kant's system for purposes of exposition?

Warnock There certainly is that problem. One of Kant's conspicuous merits was that he was very good at making an immense range of views fit together in a comprehensive and systematic way. But in embarking on discussion of Kant I think it is important not to start off in too technical a way; for example, he is sometimes represented as conducting a debate between the merits and demerits of rationalism and empiricism, like a sort of philosophical referee, or discussing how there can be synthetic necessary truths – some technical-looking issues of that sort. Those are indeed issues in which Kant was much interested. But, for a starting point, I think one ought to go further back, to the much wider and simpler concern that really generated these other problems; and that, I would submit, was his concern with an apparent conflict between the findings of the physical sciences in his day and our fundamental ethical and religious convictions. He thought there was at least a *prima facie* conflict or inconsistency there.

Magee What did he think it consisted in?

Warnock I think the central and simplest form of the conflict was that it seemed to be a presupposition – and indeed Kant thought a well-founded and proper presupposition – of the physical sciences that everything that happens is *determined* by antecedent happenings, that there is always a law on the basis of which one can say that, given the antecedent conditions, what happened was the only thing that *could* have happened.

Magee We are talking here about events in the natural world, the physical world . . .

Warnock . . . in the physical world, yes. But of course, when we are thinking about our own conduct, and in particular about moral predicaments we may find ourselves in, we believe that we (and everybody else) have alternative possible courses of action before us – that there are various things we could do, and so for that reason we have to accept responsibility for what we actually do. That was one theme: Kant thought that this was *prima facie* contradicted by a basic presupposition of physical science.

Magee So the problem is: how, in a universe in which the motions of all matter are governed by scientific laws, can any of the motions of those material objects which are human bodies be governed by free will?

Warnock Yes. He was also concerned with the question how God would fit in to an essentially mechanical and physically determined universe. If physical explanations can always, in principle, be both complete and exhaustive, God seems to be left outside, as it were, with nothing to do.

Magee Kant was not the first philosopher, not even the first great philosopher, to see these problems, was he?

Warnock No, certainly not. Those problems had been a main preoccupation of philosophers all through the eighteenth century, ever since the great leap forward, so to speak, in the physical sciences at the end of the seventeenth century. Among the empiricists, for example, Berkeley had been preoccupied with this sort of problem; and, among those in Kant's own Continental tradition, conspicuously Leibniz. No, Kant certainly was not the first.

Magee Why was he so deeply dissatisfied, as obviously he was, with the attempts made by his predecessors to solve these problems?

Warnock Well, he believed – and I think correctly – that his predecessors had typically tried to resolve these conflicts, or bring them to an end, by downgrading the pretensions of the physical sciences. That's certainly true of Berkeley, and I think it's true of Leibniz as well. They had sought to show that the scientists' basic tenets were not really, or at any rate not 'ultimately', *true* – so that the physical sciences could be relegated to an inferior status, and denied any claim to be an equal contestant with metaphysical doctrine and argument. Well, for one thing, Kant thought that the record showed that this was not the right way to proceed; one could say, indeed, that he thought the boot was on the other foot – that, on the one hand, the physical sciences seemed to proceed smoothly and progressively from triumph to triumph, with everybody agreeing what had been established and what hadn't, while on the other hand, philosophy looked to him like a sort of chaotic battlefield. No philosopher agreed about anything much with any other philosopher, no doctrine was accepted for more than a few years before somebody else refuted it, and so on. That's one thing. But then he also thought – and I think this is more important – that Hume, in particular, had raised serious doubts about the credentials of philosophy itself: he had put it seriously in question whether what philosophers purported to be doing was a possible intellectual enterprise. And Kant thought that Hume's challenge, if one can call it that, required would-be philosophers to ask themselves, first of all, whether what they were professing to do was even in principle possible.

Magee   One of his most quoted remarks is about Hume's having awoken him from his dogmatic slumbers. I take it that this is what you are now referring to.

Warnock   Yes.

Magee   What was the awakening, in fact – what did Hume awaken Kant *to*?

Warnock   The problem, to put it in a rather crude nutshell, was this: Hume, and indeed Leibniz and other such philosophers as had thought about it, had accepted a general view to the effect that propositions can be exhaustively divided into two classes. On the one hand, there are what were sometimes called 'truths of reason' (which Kant called analytic propositions) – those being, in a sense, really true by definition, or true in virtue of the meanings of their terms. Simple examples would be the proposition that a square has four sides or that a bicycle has two wheels. Propositions of that sort, they said, could be known *a priori*, that is, independently of experience, and of course were necessarily true. On the other hand, there are substantial, informative, non-trivial propositions which tell us something not simply implicit in the terms we are using; these, they said, were indeed substantial and informative but couldn't be necessary. They were always contingent propositions, might be either true or false, and could be established as true or false only on the basis of experience, observation, or experiment. Now Hume said – and Kant thought he was quite right to say – that, *if that was right*, then philosophy itself was in a serious predicament, because on the one hand it didn't put itself forward as an empirical science based on observation and experiment, and on the other hand it would not wish to concede that all it was doing was elaborating a set of tautologies, analysing the terms in which we speak and think. And Hume's question was: is there anything *else* that a philosopher could possibly be doing, if he isn't doing either of those?

Magee   Didn't Hume realise, and Kant after him, that this claim to divide propositions exhaustively into those two classes created a serious problem not only for philosophy but also for the natural sciences, because unrestrictedly general scientific laws are also propositions that are neither analytic nor straightforwardly factual – they can't be deductively arrived at by logic, nor can they be proved from experience. Both Hume and Kant saw this as a problem for *all* human knowledge, surely?

Warnock Yes, I think so, but they reacted, so to speak, in quite different ways. I think Hume thought that the sciences could carry on pretty well simply as a body of empirical hypotheses – though of course without the claim to establish that anything was necessarily so, and indeed without any sustainable claim to constitute a body of *knowledge*. Kant's view, however, was that this belief in an exhaustive dichotomy of propositions was mistaken. He had no doubt, in fact, that it *must* be mistaken because, while one might well question the credentials of *philosophers* in claiming to put forward propositions that were both synthetic and necessary – not merely analytic but not contingent either – he thought it perfectly clear that propositions of that sort were common form, so to speak, in the natural sciences and in mathematics. So that whatever doubts one might have about philosophy, there certainly were, he thought, undoubted propositions of science and mathematics which were not analytic but were not empirical and contingent either.

Magee In other words, these were propositions which applied to the world yet could not be derived from observation of the world.

Warnock Yes – which we could establish simply by argument. He called them 'synthetic *a priori*'.

Magee If such propositions apply to the world yet are not to be read off from the world by any observation or experience, how do we arrive at them?

Warnock Well, that of course is exactly the crux. One has to introduce here a distinction to which Kant attached the utmost importance – the distinction between what he called 'things-in-themselves', or the world as it is 'in itself', and 'appearances'. Now, on the question of things-in-themselves, Kant would have said, we just can't make any demands – that is, things-in-themselves simply are as they are and there's nothing we can do about that. But if you move to the topic of the world as we experience it, as it presents itself to us as an object of experience, to the world of what he called 'appearances', then, he said, it's a different matter, because there are certain conditions, he claimed, which *any* world must satisfy if it is to be a possible object of experience at all.

Magee For us.

Warnock For us and, it is vitally important to add, anybody and everybody. He thought it a crucial fact that the world is – any 'world' *must* be – a *common* object of experience to an indefinite array of subjects of experience. And if there is to be such a world, one that can be experienced, talked about, and known about in common by a community of subjects of experience, then, he argued, there are conditions which it must satisfy. And so we can say *a priori* that 'appearances' must satisfy these conditions.

Magee Would it be correct to express what you have just said in the following way? What we can experience, or perceive, or know, must of course depend on what there is to experience or perceive or know, but it must also depend on the apparatus we have for experiencing and perceiving and knowing. And what that apparatus is is a contingent matter. To use a modern example, we happen to be equipped to interpret electromagnetic waves of some frequencies but not others: our bodies are able to translate their reception of light rays into perceptions of their surroundings, but we cannot do this with radio waves or X-rays. Yet it is imaginable that we might have been able to apprehend reality in terms entirely different from those in which we do. Now Kant is saying that, this being so, for us to be able to experience anything at all it has to be such as can be coped with by the apparatus we have. This is not to say that nothing else can exist, but it does mean that nothing else can be experienced or perceived or known *by us*.

Warnock Well, I would qualify that in one way. Kant didn't, I think, want to get into purely empirical considerations about what our sensory equipment specifically is, what kinds of eyes and ears and other sense organs we have. I think he was trying to say something more general than that – that the notion of a subject of experience, presented with a world as an object of experience, requires that such a subject should have sensory capacities of some kind, and intellectual and conceptual capacities of some kind. But he didn't want to say that, except in certain very general respects, they must be of this specific kind or that. He wouldn't have been interested in whether our eyes are different from those of kestrels or badgers, for example – his general claim was that an experiencing subject must have some way of perceiving, some faculty of what he called 'sensible intuition'.

Magee So the point, then, is that perceiving subjects *as such* cannot but bring certain predispositions to bear, and only what fits in with those predispositions can be experienced.

Warnock That's absolutely right, yes.

Magee   This, I believe, was something the very nature of which had never occurred to any philosopher before.

Warnock   No, genuinely novel, I think. There are certain passages in Hume which look in a way like anticipations of Kant on this point – passages in which he describes how, on the basis of experienced data or 'impressions', we come to construct our picture of a world of objects. But Hume put all that forward as just a bit of empirical psychology. The idea that we have here not just some facts about experience, but necessary conditions of the very *possibility* of experience – that was Kant's fundamental and genuinely original contribution.

Magee   What was the new view of the nature of human knowledge that this led him towards?

Warnock   Well, he put forward the claim that, if one thought carefully enough and argued long enough, one could specify what he called the Form of any possible experience. He gave to this enterprise the name of the 'Metaphysic of Nature', or sometimes the 'Metaphysic of Experience'. What he called the Matter of Experience, that was a contingent question and there might be this or that actually happening as a matter of sheer empirical fact. But he thought one could spell out, and think out, what the Form, as he called it, of any possible experience must be. And this would be a body of doctrine that would tell you something about the world, of course, because it's telling you what its essential form is, but would also tell you something necessary, that couldn't be otherwise.

Magee   And because there are propositions which do this, Leibniz and Hume had been wrong to insist that all meaningful propositions must be either analytic and *a priori* (true or false by nature of the terms used and the rules governing their use, and thus knowable in advance of their external application) or synthetic and *a posteriori* (true or false according to how things are observed to be in the empirical world, and therefore knowable only after the event, because such knowledge depends on experience). We now have propositions of a third kind, synthetic yet *a priori* propositions which are about the world yet are not validatable by experience: true or false about the world, yet knowable in advance. Can you give any examples of propositions of this sort?

Warnock   Well, putting it in the most general terms, they divide into two broad classes. First of all Kant tried to deal with what he called the Form of Sensibility or rather the two Forms, Space and Time. He argued that these were imposed upon our experience, upon the world as object of experience, by the nature of our sensibility –

Immanuel Kant (1724–1804)

Magee I'm sorry, I want to interrupt you here because I think this is an extraordinarily difficult idea for many people to grasp. Kant was arguing that space and time do not characterise things as they are in themselves . . .

Warnock Yes indeed . . .

Magee . . . but are inescapable modes of experience for us.

Warnock That's right.

Magee So although it is only in those dimensions that we can experience the world, they cannot be said to exist independently of us and of our experience.

Warnock That's certainly right. If you raise the question: 'What about the creation as it is in itself, what kind of spatial and temporal order does it display?', Kant would say: 'Not a discussable topic.' All we can talk about, he insists, is that world which is an object of experience to us, the world as it appears; but the claim is that we can say, of any conceivable such world, whatever objects it may happen to contain and whatever events may occur there, that objects will be spatially extended and located in space, and that events will both take time and occur in an ordered temporal sequence. That must hold, he argues, for any conceivable objects and any possible happenings. And, if that is not ambitious enough, he adds another striking and certainly controversial claim: the detailed specification of the form of Space, he says, is provided by geometry, and that of Time by arithmetic. That, he says, is how geometry and arithmetic themselves are 'possible' – both are bodies of propositions which are neither contingent nor analytic, but 'synthetic *a priori*', and they have that character because they specify Forms of experience – that is, conditions of its possibility.

Magee They are bodies of knowledge, and the knowledge they give us is given to us *in advance of* any possible application in experience.

Warnock Well, that was his view, yes. But it is, I suppose, particularly debatable whether spatial and temporal concepts are really limited, in the rather direct and simple way he seems to suggest, to geometry and arithmetic.

Magee You imply that it is still controversial in our own day.

Warnock Oh absolutely, yes.

Magee Now, given synthetic *a priori* propositions –

Warnock Could I just intervene . . . I was going to say that Kant's synthetic *a priori* propositions divided into two broad classes. We've only dealt with one of them, those that spell out the Forms of Sensibility. If I could just briefly bring in the second. He thought that there are also what he calls Forms of the Understanding, or forms of thought, as one might say. I think the fundamental principle of his argument here is that any possible world of experience, any world about which objective statements can be made and (sometimes) known to be true, must necessarily be in certain respects *orderly*, and predictable. He tries to show that on this basis we can derive, as conditions of the possibility of Understanding, of objective knowledge, the Newtonian principle of universal causal determinism; and then, rather implausibly, he also tries to show that Newton's law of the conservation of matter states a condition of the possibility of experience too. So there he's trying to bring in physics, you see – rather as he sought to bring in mathematics in relation to the Forms of Sensibility, he now tries to bring in the fundamental principles of physical science in relation to the Forms of the Understanding. Ambitious undertaking!

Magee We are beginning to get the outlines of a total picture of human knowledge, but the picture is so large that I want to pause here for a moment to bring out some of its main features. Kant argues that because all our perceptions and experiences come to us through our sensory and mental apparatus, they all come to us in forms which are sense-dependent and mind-dependent. We can have no direct access to things as they are in themselves, by which he means things unmediated by the Forms of our Sensibility and the Forms of our Understanding.

Warnock And it would make no sense to suggest we might have.

Magee I'm glad you emphasised that. Now, no matter what Forms of Apprehension we may happen to have, possible experience must be conformable to them to be able to be experience, for us, at all.

Warnock Yes, absolutely.

Magee Part of the programme which Kant then sets himself is to carry out a thoroughgoing investigation into what the nature of those Forms is. If that investigation is both complete and successful it will tell us what the limits of all possible knowledge are. Is that right?

Warnock Yes.

Magee And anything that falls outside those limits is simply not knowable by us. Among his conclusions are that any experienced world perceived by experiencing subjects must appear to be ordered in the dimensions of space and time, but that space and time have no reality independently of this ordering of appearances, and therefore no reality independently of experience; and the same with causes, that events in such a world must appear to be causally interrelated, but that it makes no sense to speak of causal connections existing independently of experience; and that these facts make possible the success of science, for they are what make it possible for us to have unrestrictedly general knowledge of the world of all actual and possible experience – and science is solely about the world of actual and possible experience, not about the world as it is in itself. All concepts which purport to relate to anything that can be known must be derived from actual or possible experience: otherwise, either they are empty or they can never be validated.

The implications of all this are radical not only for what is asserted but for what is precluded, are they not?

Warnock Yes. That's certainly true, and fundamentally true. Knowledge, for Kant, is bounded by 'possible experience'; and I find it hard to believe that it wasn't, so to speak, something of a disappointment to Kant that this is the position he got himself into. One gets the impression from the way he embarks on his inquiries, that he would have liked, ideally, to build a firm foundation for theological speculation about God and the soul, and metaphysical speculation about the cosmos; having shown, as he thinks, how it is that mathematics and science can constitute impregnable bodies of knowledge, it would have been splendid to be able to do the same for a reformed theology and metaphysics. But what he actually finds himself obliged to say is that there can be no such foundations – all we can establish foundations for is 'possible experience' and what can be an object of possible experience. And if you try to go beyond that, if you try to raise questions about how the cosmos should be characterised quite independently of the limits of any possible experience, or if you try to talk about God and the soul, then your enterprise must collapse and be in principle vacuous. Kant is saying that, certainly, however unhappy he may have been to reach that conclusion.

Magee Now although Kant argues that it is permanently impossible for us to know whether or not God exists, and whether or not we have souls, he did himself believe that God does exist and that we do have souls, didn't he?

Warnock Yes, indeed.

Magee But he was clear that these beliefs are a matter of unsecured faith, not of possible knowledge. Even so, how – on his own premises – can he regard talk about God or the soul as even intelligible? Why is it not vacuous?

Warnock Yes, that is a very good question, and one on which he is in fact slightly shifty, I think. What Kant does could be described as turning the whole issue upside down in a rather interesting way. Some, at any rate, of his predecessors had made the supposition that our moral convictions and attitudes, and our religious convictions, stand in need of some kind of metaphysical foundation, and they tried to provide one in the form of theology and philosophical ethics; whereas Kant finishes up putting the thing exactly the other way up. He says that we are not only *entitled* to moral convictions and religious convictions – he thought it inescapable that we should have them; he also argues that such convictions must lead us inescapably to essentially metaphysical unempirical doctrines about God and the soul. Those doctrines themselves, however, so far as they have any foundation at all, are founded directly in our primitive moral convictions themselves – so that it's those that are the really fundamental thing, while theology and metaphysics are a rather frail, high-flying superstructure on that foundation.

Magee I'd like to go over that again, because it is important, interesting, and startling. Kant is saying this: that it is an undeniable empirical fact that most of us have some moral convictions which we find ourselves unable to ignore even when we want to. Now, for these convictions to have any validity or even significance – and for the basic moral concepts such as *good, bad, right, wrong, ought* and so on, to have validity or significance – we must have some element of freedom of choice. There must be some area, some space, however narrow, within which we can exercise our own discretion. For if there is not – if it is *never* true to say that we could have acted otherwise than we did – any attempt at moral evaluation is empty and meaningless. So if moral concepts possess any significance at all, some degree of free will has to be a reality. And for *that* to be so there must be at least some part of our being which is independent of the empirical world of matter in motion governed by scientific laws, for it must be possible for us to move some of the material objects in that world, namely our bodies, 'at will'. I suspect that 'free', in the context of this discussion, means 'not governed by scientific laws'. And we are forced to the conclusion that we must be possessed of at least partially free spirits or souls.

   Now I see the argument very clearly up to that point, and it seems to be enormously powerful, in fact persuasive. But how does Kant justify the further giant stride from that conclusion to the existence of God?

Warnock Well, in trying to deal with that I'm not quite sure that I'm not going back a stage. You raised the point a minute or two ago that Kant's conclusions appeared to be coming out rather like this: that when we try to talk about God and the soul, what we find ourselves saying is not just not provable in any sort of empirical way, or any *a priori* way either, but actually not really meaningful. I don't think we've quite dealt with that yet, but I think it's absolutely true and something that Kant was very unwilling to admit. What he says about himself in relation to theology and religion is that, in a much-quoted phrase, he had denied knowledge in order to make room for faith – he had simply shown why it was that the subject matter of theology is not a possible topic of knowledge. But then, he says, no one need be alarmed about that, because surely we all have known all along that it's essentially a matter of faith. But, as you rightly say, one could insist that his arguments had really been more radical than that – it isn't just that, when I talk about God, I am saying things that I don't know to be true – his argument really seems to lead to the conclusion that I don't know what I'm saying, or that what I'm saying doesn't really mean anything. It's clear that he was very reluctant to draw that conclusion. What he tries to say is that all he has done is to show it's not a matter of knowledge or proof.

Magee Yes. And I suppose *his* point on that issue is that whereas it is superstitious to rest on faith in a question that can actually be decided, if the question cannot be decided then it is not irrational to entertain a belief on one side of it.

Warnock Absolutely. Yes.

Magee At the very beginning of this discussion you suggested that the problem which really launched Kant on his philosophical enterprise was the apparent conflict between Newtonian physics and the existence of ethics. How, in the light of everything we have said up to this point, did he attempt to solve that problem?

Warnock He resolved it, even in his own view, to a really quite minimal extent, I think – I think this was something of which he himself was perfectly aware. What he would claim is that by making clear the distinction between the world as appearance, as an object of experience, and the world of things-in-themselves, he is in a position to say that, on the one hand, there is the world of appearances, and the physical sciences in principle give us the whole truth about that – as he believed that they did. He had no doubt that Newton had got it absolutely right, and that a physicist's description of the world as an object of possible experience was essentially correct and could be exhaustive. But, he says, bear in mind that we are there talking about the world of appearances. There is also, on the other hand, the topic of things-in-themselves; and there is room there, so to speak, for other sorts of concepts altogether: of free will, of rational agency, right and wrong, good and bad, the soul – there is room for these concepts, not in the world of appearance but outside the world of appearance. Of course he saw that, on his own principles, he would have to say that these other matters couldn't be topics of knowledge. Had you said to him: 'Do you know that there is such a thing as free will?' he would consistently have said: 'No, I do not know any such thing. All I know is that there is room for that possibility.' He claims no more.

Magee But he would also have said that he could not help *believing* that there must be such a thing as free will.

Warnock Oh, certainly. Yes, he would have gone on to say that too.

Magee On this view, ethics comes to us from outside the world of all possible knowledge. Does Kant have a view about where it comes from? How do we get it?

Warnock Well, the short and, by itself, rather unilluminating answer is that he thought it came out of reason. But his removal, so to speak, of moral concepts out of the world leaves him, of course, with a battery of awful problems which in fact he hardly gets round to handling seriously. For instance, if you say that the will, and moral thought and moral consciousness generally, operate in some way outside the world of appearances altogether, then one fairly obvious enormous problem that you have is that of how moral decision, the will, moral thought, impinges on the real world as we experience it at all. How can it make any *difference*? He seems to have separated the will and the world so radically that while perhaps he has created room for moral thought and religious thought to exist, he has made it impossible for them to make any difference to what actually happens. That is one major difficulty which he does not, I'm bound to say, really face.

Magee It will help people to understand the problem further if you say what the main conclusions of his moral philosophy were. It is not possible, in the short space we have left, to go into the arguments with which he supported those conclusions. But if you outline the conclusions themselves it will contribute to an understanding.

Warnock I think one can say something useful, quite briefly, about that. What he really tries to do in his moral philosophy is somehow to extract the essentials of morality from the pure concept of rationality. The essential thing about any agent of whom one can think or speak in moral terms is that he must be a *rational* being, capable of thinking of reasons for and against doing this or that and 'willing' accordingly. Kant tries to argue that the essential requirements of morality are really built into the concept of rationality itself – that those requirements must, *a priori*, be acknowledged by any rational creature as binding. Essentially, he tries to show that only a body of principles of action corresponding to our principles of morality could consistently, and therefore rationally, be universally adopted by a community of rational beings.

Magee And from that he derives his famous Categorical Imperative – which perhaps I should ask you to formulate.

Warnock 'Act only according to that maxim by which you can at the same time will that it should become a universal law.' The idea is that, if as a rational being one cannot (consistently) will that a 'maxim' should be a universal law – that is, should be universally adopted and acted upon by everyone alike – then that maxim cannot be an acceptable moral rule; for a rationally accepted moral rule *must* be such that everyone could adopt it. He wants to say that what morality really imposes on us are conditions on conduct which demand the assent of any possible community of rational creatures; and he further maintains, and rather sketchily tries to show, that there is a single, determinate set of such conditions which alone passes the test, so to speak, of rational acceptability. That, in outline at any rate, is what he is trying to do.

Magee Kant's philosophy is notoriously difficult to understand at first encounter, and I expect some of the people following our discussion are experiencing that difficulty at this very moment. Fundamental to the difficulty is his contention that we simply have no way of acquiring knowledge of things as they are in themselves – that we are, as it were, permanently screened off from them by our own limitations, and that these are partly the limitations of our subject-dependent (and this means us-dependent) forms of sensibility and understanding, which include space and time. Is it helpful, do you think, to say to people who find all this hard to grasp: 'Look, you are already familiar with some of these ideas in a different context. A great many serious religious people have always believed something of this sort, and you know this even if you are not religious yourself. Such people have always believed that this world of our experience is a fleeting world of appearances only, and that what one might call *real* reality, where all permanent significance resides, is outside this world – and that this means, among other things, outside space and time. Now what Kant, being a philosopher, is trying to do is to arrive at these ideas by purely rational argument.' Do you think it's helpful to say that – or do you think it just obscures the issue?

Warnock No, I don't think it does. And one might throw some light on the issue by putting it in this way: consider the question – and don't be put off by its seeming to be an excessively hypothetical and perhaps idle question – what sort of being one would have to be to be acquainted with things as they are 'in themselves', that is, to transcend 'the bounds of sense' and the limitations of possible experience. Well, I believe that the only possible answer you can get out of Kant is that you'd have to be God. For that would involve your being acquainted with things in some completely timeless way, without a point of view in space or any other kind of spatial limitations, with no particular sensory limitations on the mode of acquaintance, and of course not thinking in French or English or any particular language, not even in any specific conceptual form at all. Your acquaintance with the universe would be entirely freed from any of these limitations. And if one asks: 'Well, what would I have to be to be like that?', the only answer is: 'I'd have to be God.'

Magee It is a most striking feature of Kant's philosophy that although he is deeply versed in mathematical physics, and strides forward in the central tradition of science-and-mathematics-based philosophy exemplified by Descartes, Leibniz, Locke and Hume, and sticks strictly to its rules – that is to say, he relies solely on argument, appeals only to rational criteria, rejects any appeal to faith or revelation – he arrives at conclusions which are in line not just with religion but with the more mystical forms of religious belief, Eastern as well as Western.

Warnock Well, yes, except for the uncomfortable fact which we mentioned earlier – that he has to say that, strictly speaking, all discourse on those topics is unintelligible to us. We don't really know what we mean. And that's a proposition that – although Kant claimed to be their ally – theologians have been a bit chary of accepting.

Magee Until recently. May one not say that nowadays many theologians accept precisely that?

Warnock That may be true.

Magee Besides the difficulty of understanding what he has to say, a quite different problem about reading Kant is his prose style. There are great philosophers – Plato, Hume, Schopenhauer – who are beautiful writers, and a pleasure to read. But not even Kant's best friend could claim that for him. Everyone finds his writing difficult; it is nearly always obscure, and sometimes it borders on the impenetrable. Why did he write so badly?

Warnock I think there are three things one might say. I think it's partly due to the fact which you mentioned right at the beginning, that he was by profession – and very single-mindedly by profession – an academic; he certainly does write in a very heavily academic style, with a great taste for technical terminology and jargon, for elaborate dichotomies and tabulations, for what he called 'architectonic' – it's all very academic. But another important point to remember about the *Critiques* – and this again connects with something you said at the beginning – is that by the time he was seriously launched on writing what he knew to be his master works, or at any rate hoped would be his master works, he was nearly sixty, and he was constantly dogged by the thought that he might die before he'd got it all down. There's no doubt that those many hundreds of pages written between the ages of sixty and seventy were written extremely fast. He was working in a hurry, and I think that has a lot to do with the awkwardness, and at times almost impenetrability, of his writing.

Magee Two hundred years ago the expectation of life was so much shorter than it is today that it was in fact perfectly natural for a man of the age Kant was then to suppose he was likely to die soon.

Warnock Yes, his feeling of the need for hurry wasn't unreasonable. Another point – a less obvious one – is that he was writing in German which was still, at that date, a somewhat unusual thing for a man of learning to do. The German language had barely become accepted as a decent language for academic and learned use. Leibniz, for example – I don't believe Leibniz ever wrote a serious work in German.

Magee It was always either Latin or French.

Warnock Either Latin or French, yes. And the effect of that was that there was not an established style, or tradition, of academic, learned German prose for Kant to adopt. The position was quite different for, for example, Berkeley and Hume – in their time English had become a thoroughly manageable, well-established language for that kind of learned use. And I think that must have been a problem to Kant. He had no good models to follow in the language in which he was writing.

Magee The unnecessary difficulty of Kant's writing constitutes an intellectual tragedy, I think, because it places an obstacle, which for many individuals proves insuperable, in the way of understanding the work of possibly the greatest of all modern philosophers. And that means that his work, even after two hundred years, is still unknown territory to most educated people. . . . I referred at the beginning to the fact that he is widely regarded by serious students of philosophy as the greatest philosopher since the ancient Greeks. Why does his reputation stand at quite such a pinnacle?

Warnock I think I would mention chiefly two qualities as entitling him to his pinnacle of fame. I think he was quite exceptionally *penetrating*, in the sense that he was able to see an intellectual problem in something which had previously been taken for granted as not worth much attention. He had an extraordinary capacity to see where the problems were – and that's one of the greatest, most fundamental philosophical gifts – to be able to see that there is a problem where everybody else is going along quite happily, not thinking about it much. Then I think the other thing – and this connects perhaps with his academic professionalism – is that he was extremely good at seeing how the whole compass of his arguments fitted together – how what he says on this topic or that might repercuss, so to speak, on what he'd said somewhere else or in some other connection. He was very self-conscious, and professionally methodical, in that sort of way; there was absolutely nothing piecemeal, or makeshift, or hand-to-mouth about his way of going to work. One has the feeling that the whole huge enterprise is firmly under control. He does, I must say, make writers like Locke and Berkeley, and indeed Hume, excellent though they are, look to me rather like amateurs.

HEGEL and MARX

Dialogue with
PETER SINGER

INTRODUCTION

Magee Few philosophers have more obviously changed the world than Hegel – both personally, through his influence on German nationalism, and indirectly, through the work of his most famous philosophical disciple, Karl Marx (with whose name a great many governments in our own day actually describe themselves). So, if we want to see some of the practical consequences of Hegel's ideas, all we have to do is look around us. Hegel's influence on philosophy itself was correspondingly great: it has been said that the history of philosophy since Hegel can be seen as a succession of varying reactions against his work.

Georg Wilhelm Friedrich Hegel was born in Stuttgart in 1770. A teacher of one sort or another for most of his life, he eventually became Professor of Philosophy at Heidelberg and then in Berlin. As a philosopher he was a late developer, but by the time of his death in 1831 he was the dominant figure in philosophy throughout the whole of Germany. The titles of some of his most influential works are *The Phenomenology of Mind*, *The Science of Logic*, *The Philosophy of Right* and *The Philosophy of History*.

Hegel had several followers who themselves became well known, but far and away the most famous of them is Karl Marx. Marx was born in the town of Trier in Germany in 1818, and as a young student of philosophy was very much a Hegelian. He did not become a Socialist until his middle twenties, when he began to develop that rich and original mixture of German philosophy, French politics and British economics which is Marxism. Together with a wealthy young industrialist, Friedrich Engels, he wrote *The Communist Manifesto* in 1848. The ensuing partnership between Marx and Engels is perhaps the most momentous collaboration in the history of ideas. Engels supported Marx for most of his life so that he could produce his writings; and it was a life spent largely in exile because of Marx's political activities: at the age of thirty-one he went to live in London, and stayed there until his death in 1883. His grave is in Highgate Cemetery. For many years he did his work in the Reading Room of the British Museum, and it was there that he wrote his masterpiece, *Das Kapital*, published in 1867.

Marxism is not exactly philosophy in the accepted meaning of the term, but there is obviously a major philosophical component in it, and that component always remained Hegelian. What I propose to do in this discussion is devote the bulk of the time to Hegel, and then show how some of the most important ideas we shall have discussed were incorporated into Marxism. With me to do this is someone who has published excellent introductions to the works of both thinkers: Peter Singer, Professor of Philosophy at Monash University in Melbourne, Australia.

DISCUSSION

Magee Hegel is widely regarded as being the most difficult of all the major philosophers to read and understand, but your little book about him has the unique merit of conveying some of his central ideas in ordinary language, and I look forward to your doing the same in this discussion. Where, from your point of view, is the best place to start?

Singer I start with *The Philosophy of History*, because Hegel's account of history is quite concrete. Part of the difficulty with Hegel is that his thought is so abstract. But *The Philosophy of History*, because it deals with specific historical events, provides an easy entrée to the more abstract parts of his philosophy.

Magee That in itself is already a new departure as far as Western philosophy is concerned: to none of the great philosophers before Hegel had history, or the philosophy of history, seemed especially important. One may perhaps make a partial exception of Hume, because of his *History of England*, but Hume never produced philosophy of history as we understand the term. Likewise Leibniz wrote the history of a family but never produced any philosophy of history.

Singer Yes, it is a departure. Compare it with Kant, for instance: on Kant's view of human nature, human beings are eternally divided between their reason and their brute desires. It's like the old picture of Man as halfway between the apes and the angels. Now for Kant it is just a fact of human nature that we will always be torn between these two aspects of our nature. But Hegel denied that this was immutable. He looked at human nature in historical terms. In ancient Greece, Hegel said, human nature was more harmonious. People were not conscious of any conflict between their desires and their reason. So the division that Kant saw must be something that has occurred historically. In fact, Hegel said, it developed with the rise of individual conscience in Protestant Europe. Because it has happened historically, it need not be a permanent feature. It could, in some other period, again be overcome and harmony restored.

Magee Hegel looked not just at this but at all important concepts *historically*, didn't he? He saw our concepts as being embedded in ways of life, and thus in societies; and when societies changed, the concepts changed.

Singer Yes, that's absolutely right. He saw that there was *development* in the way history occurred – that it was always moving forward. It was always a process, never static.

Magee And he had a name for the way in which it moved forward; 'the dialectical process', sometimes just referred to as 'the dialectic'. Can you explain what, in Hegel's view, this dialectical process was?

Singer Let's go back to the example I mentioned before. Hegel regarded Greek society as one in which there was a harmony between reason and desire; but this was a simple harmony. It was simple because in ancient Greece people had not developed the modern notion of individual conscience. So there was harmony between the individual and society, because individuals hadn't considered themselves as separate from their city-state, and able to make their own judgments about right and wrong. Then into that simple harmony there came Socrates, whom Hegel considers a world historical figure because it was he who introduced the idea of questioning everything. Socrates went around asking people questions like: 'What is justice?', 'What is virtue?' And when people tried to answer, they realised that they had accepted conventional assumptions about these things which Socrates had no trouble in showing could not be sustained. So the simple harmony of Greek society broke down. Incidentally, Hegel thinks that the Athenians were quite right to condemn Socrates to death. Socrates *was* corrupting and subverting Athenian society. But that was an essential part of the historical process, which ultimately led to the rise of individual conscience. This was the second necessary element of historical development. It was the very opposite of the governing principle of Greek society. So we moved from what Hegel calls the 'thesis' of simple harmony to the 'antithesis' of individual conscience, risen to its height in Protestant Europe. But that too turns out to be unstable. It leads to the destruction carried out by the French Revolution, and the terror that followed the French Revolution; and so that, too, must give way to a 'synthesis'. This is a third stage which combines harmony and individual conscience. Very often, in this process, the synthesis then again serves as the new thesis from which a further antithesis will arise; and so the process will continue.

Magee Why does the process get going at all? Why is there such a thing as historical change? It is, after all, perfectly possible to conceive of societies which come close to being static, like ancient Egypt. Why should not a balanced, harmonious state of affairs, such as Hegel thought ancient Greece was, simply go on going on indefinitely? Why should there *necessarily* be some fly in the ointment which precipitates change?

Singer In the case of ancient Greece it was because it was a simple – perhaps a better word would be 'naïve' – harmony, which could not be sustained once the principle of reason had been developed. Hegel traces the development of this principle of reason in Greek thought, and shows how its development was necessary. Rational beings could not remain content with an unquestioning acceptance of social norms. Exactly why that questioning attitude came at this particular point is a detail of the historical story; but at some stage, as rational beings, we would have to question this simple harmony. Once we question it, individual conscience begins to rise and destroys the naïve harmony on which the society is based.

Magee This notion of 'dialectical change' has been so influential ever since Hegel – and is very much so today, among Marxists – that it is important for us to get it clear. The idea is, isn't it, that the reason why we human beings are involved in a process of perpetual change is that every complex situation is bound to contain within itself conflicting elements; and these are, of their nature, destabilising, so the situation can never continue indefinitely. It breaks down under the strain of these internal conflicts and gives rise to a new situation within which those conflicts are resolved, or at least assuaged. But then, of course, the new situation contains within itself new conflicts. And so it goes on, indefinitely. And that indefinitely continuing process is what constitutes history. Thus the notion of the dialectic is offered to us as the key to the historical process, the underlying explanation of why it is that everything keeps changing. And it tells us what form the change invariably takes: thesis, followed by antithesis, followed by synthesis, which then in its turn becomes a new thesis, to be followed again by its own antithesis, and so on and so forth.

Up to this point in the explanation it has remained open to Hegel to maintain that although change is bound to occur, the actual direction taken by it is indeterminate, the unpredictable outcome of innumerable random conflicts; but he doesn't, does he? On the contrary, he believes it's all actually going somewhere – that it has an aim, a goal.

Singer That's right. The goal for Hegel is the greater development of mind towards freedom. We are moving always towards realising human freedom; and that is a process of increasing awareness of freedom, and of increasing knowledge of ourselves.

Magee You talk as if concepts like freedom and knowledge are *literally* contained in history, and as if historical change *is* the transmutation of these concepts. One is reminded of Russell's jibe that, according to Hegel, history is 'jellied thought'.

Singer History represents the development of these concepts, that's true. History is not a chapter of accidents. It is not a story told by an idiot. It is the purposive moving forward of these principles of freedom and knowledge.

Magee What is this process of change happening *to*? I mean, usually when we talk of change, in any context, we assume there to be something that changes. What is it in this case? Hegel surely can't believe that the concrete stuff of history is abstract concepts – concepts are not a substance, not even an abstract substance. What, then, are we talking about? Human individuals? Societies? Who – or what – is undergoing the change?

Singer The short answer is that he is writing neither about individuals, nor about societies, but about what he calls '*Geist*'. The German word '*Geist*' is a difficult one to translate. The easiest way perhaps would be to say that Hegel is writing about 'mind'. 'Mind' is one normal translation. The German word '*Geisteskrankheit*', for instance, means 'mental illness'. So we could say that in Hegel's view history happens to 'mind', that is, to your mind and mine, or all our individual minds. But '*Geist*' also has another meaning which goes beyond that, the notion of 'spirit'. We talk about the '*Zeitgeist*', the 'spirit of the times'. Or we talk about '*Geist*' when Germans talk about the Father, the Son and the Holy Ghost. So it has also a spiritual or religious flavour – which suggests that in some sense there's a reality above and beyond my individual mind. You could say it is happening to Mind, but to Mind with a capital 'M', not just mind in the sense of individual human minds.

Magee Is Hegel saying that total reality is a unity and is something mental or spiritual, and therefore that all the processes we have been talking about are processes in that mental or spiritual something?

Singer Yes, ultimately Hegel's view is that reality is *Geist*. It is ultimately mental, or intellectual. The processes we have been talking about happen to *Geist*, to Mind as it develops in history.

Magee To some of the people following this discussion it might be beginning to sound bizarre. So I think it's worth pointing out that we are already familiar with ideas very similar to these when it comes to religious beliefs, even though we ourselves may not be religious as individuals. Many religious believers, including many Christians, believe that all reality is ultimately spiritual, and that all reality ultimately has a spiritual significance. I suppose Hegel is saying something closely related to that, though not necessarily religious in the conventional sense.

Singer The difference is that the orthodox Christian holds that God is spiritual and separate from this world, which is mundane and material. On the Christian view the world has a spiritual significance, certainly, but it is not itself spiritual. So the Christian contrasts God and the world. One could present Hegel as saying the very opposite of this – that is, one could say that Hegel is a pantheist, that he believes that God *is* the world and everything is spiritual because it is part of God. But that's not quite true either. The correct intepration of Hegel places him somewhere between the traditional Christian conception and the pantheistic one. According to Hegel, *Geist*, or spirit, is *manifested in* everything, although it is not *identical with* everything that exists.

Magee The truth is that ever since Hegel there has been dispute among Hegel scholars over precisely this question: is Hegel's philosophy ultimately religious or not? Some strenuously maintain that it is, others that it is not. On which side of the dispute do you come down?

Singer I think that it is immensely valuable to try and interpret Hegel as if he were not religious, because then you find that you can make good sense of a large part of his philosophy in a non-religious way. You can understand him as talking about Mind, and when he uses this term in a collective sense to refer to all our individual minds as if they were one Mind, you can read this as referring to the common element in our minds, our common ability to reason, the fact that our minds are structured on similar principles. But I have to admit that though you can push this interpretation a long way, you can't really make a hundred per cent sense of Hegel in that way. The last ten per cent perhaps has to recognise that there is some religious or quasi-religious view of mind or spirit that lies behind what he is saying.

Magee We have now discussed two fundamental ideas which Hegel introduced into Western thought. The first is the idea that the whole of reality is a historical process. The only previous thinker who had come anywhere near putting this view forward was the pre-Socratic philosopher Heraclitus, but with him it lacked the social dimension entirely. All social thought since Hegel, I think it's fair to say, has been influenced by it – and not social thought alone. A second major idea is the dialectic, which is of great importance in our own day through its influence on Marxism. We can add to these a third: the concept of 'alienation'. It was Hegel who introduced it. What did he mean by it?

Singer By 'alienation' Hegel meant the idea that something which is in fact ourselves or part of ourselves seems to us foreign, alien and hostile. Let me give you an example. He presents a picture of what he calls 'the unhappy soul' which is an alienated form of religion. The unhappy soul is a person who prays to a God whom he regards as all powerful, all knowing, and all good, and who sees himself by contrast as powerless, ignorant and base. So this person is unhappy because he demeans himself and puts all those qualities into some Being which he sees as separate from himself. Hegel says that this is wrong. We are in fact part of God, or if you like, we are projecting our qualities into God. The way to overcome this kind of alienation is to realise that we and God are one, and that the qualities we attribute to God are *our* qualities, they are not something separate from, and foreign to, us.

Magee   He wouldn't have said that they were human qualities only, would he, but rather shared ones.

Singer   The claim that they are *only* human was made by one of his later disciples, Ludwig Feuerbach. Hegel wouldn't have said that, but he would have said that we and that kind of Divine Spirit are all part of the same Reality, *Geist* or Mind.

Magee   You have made it clear that Hegel saw total reality as a process of change, and that he saw this change as moving forward dialectically. A moment ago I took the natural next step and asked what this process of dialectical change was heading towards, but we no sooner started answering the question than we got side-tracked. Can we go back to it? Perhaps we're in a better position now to answer it than we were then. Does historical change have a goal?

Singer   The end point of the dialectical process is Mind coming to know itself as the ultimate reality, and thus as seeing everything that it took to be foreign and hostile to itself as in fact part of itself. Hegel calls this Absolute Knowledge. It is also a state of absolute freedom, because now Mind, instead of being controlled by external forces, is able to order the world in a rational way. This can be done only when Mind sees that the world is in fact itself. Then Mind has only to implement its own principle of rationality in the world in order to organise the world rationally.

One remarkable feature of this process arises from the fact that the culmination occurs when for the first time Mind understands that it is the only ultimate reality. Ask yourself: when does this actually happen? The answer must be that it happens when Hegel's own mind, in his philosophical thinking, grasps the idea that Mind is everything that is real. So it's not just that Hegel *describes* the goal, the state of Absolute Knowledge and Absolute Freedom towards which all previous human history had been unconsciously struggling: Hegel's philosophy actually *is* the very culmination of the whole process.

Magee   I wonder if that penny ever dropped with Hegel himself – whether he actually realised that what he was doing was putting himself-as-philosopher forward as the culmination of world history? I doubt it.

You say that the culminating state is seen at one and the same time as a

Georg Wilhelm Friedrich Hegel (1770–1831)

state of Absolute Knowledge and a state of Absolute Freedom. It's not at all evident that knowledge and freedom are the same thing. Did Hegel think they were?

Singer Self-knowledge becomes freedom because for Hegel Mind is the ultimate reality of the world. In all human history *before* that great moment in which Mind recognises itself as the ultimate reality of the world, we have been pawns in the game. We haven't been controlling the historical stage because things have been happening to us without our realising or understanding why they happened. We could not control our destiny because we thought of aspects of our *own* reality as foreign and hostile elements. Once we come to see that we are everything in the world, then we understand the process; we've grasped, if you like, the laws of historical development. Then we see that those laws are in fact the laws of our own reason, they are the very laws of our mind and our thinking.

Magee I take it this is the point of the famous citation of Hegel as having said: 'The Real is the Rational, and the Rational is the Real.'

Singer That's right. And when we come to see that, then we are free. Freedom consists in knowledge of reality, because when we see the rationality of reality we no longer struggle vainly against it. We understand that the essence of reality is our own rational principle. Then we are free to flow with it, and indeed to order it and direct it, in accordance with those laws of reason.

Magee One characteristic of Hegel's thought which you have brought out clearly is the way he sees ideas not as existing only in the abstract, nor as being timeless and unchanging (as, say, Plato did), but as always embodied in societies, institutions – historical realities which change. Now, given this fact, what sort of *society* does Hegel see the historical process as culminating in?

Singer As you would expect from what we have been saying, it is a rationally ordered society. But I must make clear what that is for Hegel, because it is not the society of pure reason. Hegel saw the society of pure reason as typified by the ideals of the French Revolutionaries. They didn't just get rid of the king, the nobles and religion; they tried to make *everything* rational. They said: why have months with irregular numbers of days? Why not make them all the same? Why have weeks of seven days? Let's make them ten, like our decimal system of measurement. . . . And so on. Hegel saw this as the result of a madly abstract notion of reason. It was the reasoning of the town planner who looks at a map of

London and says: 'Oh, your streets all run crookedly, and traffic has to make detours. Let's get rid of this mess. Let's tear the buildings down. We'll make nice straight streets and in each block we'll put a big high-rise apartment building. That way we can fit more people in, we can have a smooth green lawn outside for the children to play, and it'll all be beautiful, ordered, and rational.'

Magee   We've had that precisely in London. It has been catastrophic.

Singer   Hegel would have predicted that it would be catastrophic, because it was abstract reason taken to an extreme. For Hegel, a truly rational town planning scheme for London would look at the *real*, that is, London as it exists, find what's *rational* in the real (and of course it has developed the way it did for certain reasons, so there must be a rational element) and then try to follow those reasons through in a way that fulfils the rationale behind London's development. Hegel's rationality would not lead us to raze it down and start anew. It would encourage us to modify some of the arbitrary and capricious aspects of London's development which cause particular problems; but basically Hegelian rationality seeks what's rational in what's real, and enhances it and develops it so as to allow it to fulfil itself.

Magee   One criticism in particular has always been made of this so-called rational conception of the state, especially by liberal-minded philosophers in the Anglo-Saxon tradition. A state which is a single, organic whole, behaving rationally and ordering everything rationally, cannot permit individual enterprise, initiative, eccentricity or dissent to operate, because these would keep ruining its plans. So in practice it always turns out to be intolerant of individual initiative, i.e. not free. What's your comment on that?

Singer   I don't think Hegel was opposed to all individual freedom, but it is true that his view of freedom was not the standard Anglo-Saxon liberal view. To grasp the difference between the two, let's look first at the idea of freedom in the economic sphere, in the market. According to one view, the liberal view, freedom consists of people's being able to do as they prefer. If I prefer to wear an orange shirt this spring for instance, then I am free if I am not prevented from buying a shirt of that colour. If I prefer to buy a deodorant I am free if I can do that. To decide that I am free, that's all the liberal economist needs to know. But some of the more radical economists have questioned this. They've said that this is a very superficial notion of freedom. They want to know *why* I want to wear an orange shirt this season. Why do I want to use a deodorant? Why do I consider natural body odour to be a problem? The radical economists might decide that the reason is that I've been manipulated. There are people who want to make a profit out of my buying their deodorant, out of my thinking that the colours I wore last season are no longer good enough this season. So I've been manipulated, I'm not free. To know if I am free, the radical economist needs to know not only if I can do what I prefer, but why I prefer what I prefer. Are my preferences rational? Are they preferences that satisfy my needs?

Hegel would have sympathised with the radical economist. He said that freedom is more than just the ability to follow your own caprice, or to satisfy desires which others have induced you to have so that they can sell you something. Freedom, for Hegel, must consist in fulfilling yourself as a rational individual.

Magee That sounds all very fine, but just think what it means in practice. I happen to believe that I know what I want: I want, if I like, to be able to wear an orange shirt this spring, and when the weather gets hotter I want to be able to go out and buy a deodorant. But I live under a state which says to me: 'No, no, you only *think* you want those things. They are not at all rational preferences on your part. But we, it so happens, know what you would want if your preferences were rational. So we'll decide what you're to have – or, in this case, not to have. You'll be much happier, really, even though you may not realise it.'

Hegel's approach, surely, is bound to lead to authoritarianism?

Singer I think in practice you are probably right, and I don't know that Hegel has any reply to that objection. The only thing that he can say is that while it might be very difficult in practice to work out how you can have a society in which individuals genuinely realise their rational natures without an authoritarian state, that doesn't mean that you overcome the problem by the liberal *laissez-faire* notion. We still have to face the problem that people's wants and desires might be being manipulated, and to the extent that they are, it's misleading to say that they are really free.

Magee You are saying that the problem is a real one even if Hegel doesn't have the answer to it.

Singer It's still a problem.

Magee Let us pause for a moment and take stock. I started our whole discussion by asking you what was the easiest way in to Hegel's philosophy, and you replied by saying that it was best to start with his philosophy of history. So we did; and we continued on it – in a straight line, so to speak – to the point we've just reached. Well, are we now in a better position to understand other aspects of his philosophy?

Singer I think we've already grasped many of the essentials of Hegel's philosophy. Take Hegel's *Logic* for instance. We've discussed the dialectic, which is the most famous idea in Hegel's *Logic*, the idea of the thesis, antithesis, synthesis. Or take another point: in the *Logic* Hegel contends that logic is not just a matter of form as separate from content, which is how the traditional logic of Aristotle was interpreted. Hegel says that form and content go together. We can now see why he says that. He thinks that dialectic is something that is realised in the actual process of history. Logic, Hegel said, is 'truth without its husk', that is, the eternal, immutable form of truth, irrespective of a particular historical content, though in fact it's always linked to some content. So that's another of the key ideas of the *Logic*. Another point that we've also just touched on is Hegel's idea of ultimate reality and the way in which what is ultimately real is mental rather than material.

Magee With the *Logic*, then, as with those aspects of Hegel's thought we've discussed, we come up against the notion of reason as being embodied in reality – and embodied, what is more, in a historical reality. One seems unable to escape this idea in Hegel: everything always comes back to Mind and its omnipresence in a historical process. I suppose this is why he is regarded as the Idealist philosopher *par excellence*?

Singer Yes, Hegel certainly thought that Mind is the ultimate reality. That strikes us as a very peculiar notion. To understand why Hegel thought that, you have to consider the way in which he develops his thought from the philosophy of Kant. Kant held that our mind shapes the way in which we perceive reality, so that we cannot actually see anything except through the concepts of space and time and causation which our mind brings to it. However, Kant still thought that there was an ultimate reality that was not mental: he called it the thing-in-itself. But for Hegel this was nonsense. For Hegel if there's no way of knowing the thing-in-itself, then we can't really have knowledge.

Hegel also rejected the ideas of the British empiricists. The British empiricists asked how we know that there is a table like this in front of us. They said that there are some kind of sense data that convey the image of the table to our mind, so there's a medium of sense data between mind and material reality. Hegel said that in that case we could still never know the table as it is, we would always know it only through a medium. Hegel used many arguments to show that this doesn't work and that it must lead to scepticism, to the view that we can't really know anything. But Hegel also offered further arguments to demonstrate the impossibility of scepticism. So where is he left? The only solution, Hegel says, is to reject this idea of a knower and what's known, the table for instance, as existing on its own, separate from the mind that knows it. What you have to say is that knowledge, if it's to exist, must be immediate. There must be no medium through which we know things. How can that happen? Only if the knower and the known are one and the same. How can *that* happen? Since the knower is mind, what is known must also be mind, so all of reality must be mental.

Magee When I consider all the ideas of Hegel that you've put forward up to this point, there seems to me to be one core insight out of which all the most important concepts arise naturally one after another. The core insight is that understanding reality means not understanding a given state of affairs but understanding a process of change. From that it seems to me that all the key notions of Hegel's philosophy then arise naturally in the following way, and in the following order. If we ask: 'What is it that changes?' Hegel replies: '*Geist.*' If we ask: 'Why does it change instead of remaining the same?' Hegel replies: 'Because, to begin with, it's in a state of alienation.' If we ask: 'What form does the process of change take?' Hegel replies: 'The dialectic.' If we ask: 'Does the process of change have a goal?' Hegel replies: 'Yes, Absolute Knowledge (which is Absolute Freedom) on one level, the Organic Society on another.'

Now because it's possible to make Hegel's most basic ideas clear in this way, a question which naturally arises is 'Why did Hegel not do it?' His writing is almost uniquely obscure – it positively repels the reader. So obscure is it that many outstanding philosophers from Schopenhauer to Russell have sincerely maintained that it didn't say anything at all, that it was nothing but charlatanry. They were wrong, of course, but it's partly Hegel's own fault that they took that view. One can read page after page of Hegel, racking one's brains and thinking: 'What the *hell* does he mean?' So much like gobbledygook is a lot of it that philosophy students read passages aloud to each other just to raise a laugh. Why did Hegel write like that?

Singer Some of his less charitable critics thought he was deliberately obscure in order to cover the shallowness of his ideas. But I don't think Hegel's ideas are shallow. I think that they are profound, and that in fact the difficulty comes from the nature of the ideas. One of his students said that whereas an eloquent lecturer might have had everything off by heart and trotted it out clearly, Hegel was always dredging up deep ideas as he lectured. He was bringing these ideas to the surface with great effort. His is the style of one who is thinking aloud and having difficulty with the material. We may very well regret that he did not then revise and polish it, but in the context of German philosophical style at the time, it is not so surprising that he didn't feel the need for clarity. After all, Kant, Fichte and other contemporaries were also very obscure, and they were still regarded as great philosophers.

Karl Marx (1818–83)

Magee Another question all this gives rise to is how it came about that a philosopher so obscure, so difficult to understand, acquired even in his own lifetime such immense influence.

Singer I think that's partly due to his situation at the University of Berlin, which was the capital of Prussia, the rising state in Germany at the time. It's also due to the fertility of Hegel's ideas in a variety of fields. The influence that Hegel had is not just an influence in philosophy, it's an influence in theology, in history, in politics, in economics, in war. The fact that Hegel's ideas could be applied in these ways shows how useful his approach was, particularly the historical elements of his approach. Hegel's historical vision of everything as having developed, as being the outcome of a process, could fruitfully be applied by scholars in all those different areas.

Magee Can we turn now to the after-life of these ideas, which has been so important? One of the first things that happened after Hegel's death was that his followers split into two movements: the Young Hegelians and the Old Hegelians, or alternatively the Left Hegelians and the Right Hegelians. Can you explain the distinction?

Singer The Right Hegelians were the people who thought that Hegel's philosophy implied that something like the Prussian state was the organic state to which Hegel's ideas were pointing. They thought that Hegel had himself said this in *The Philosophy of Right*, his most explicitly political work. There he described a state, a constitutional monarchy, not very different from the Prussian state, and so they thought that there was no real need for further change. So they were the Conservative, or Right-Wing, Hegelians.

The Left Hegelians insisted that the basic thrust of Hegel's philosophy was much more radical. Hegel talked, as we said at the very beginning, about overcoming the division between reason and desire, or between morality and self-interest. That's a very fundamental change to bring about. No one could believe that that had occurred in the Prussia of 1830. So, the Left Hegelians said, the thrust of Hegel's philosophy is for a much more far-reaching change, a revolutionary change. They had to admit that in *The Philosophy of Right* Hegel hadn't written as if he were a revolutionary; but they pointed out that Hegel's salary was paid by the state of Prussia. They said Hegel had compromised, had sold out, but they wanted to be truer to Hegel than he had been to himself. They sought to carry his ideas forward to the point at which the thesis and antithesis of reason and desire, morality and self-interest, are overcome – the point at which we reach the synthesis of a harmonious society, in which those gulfs and divisions in human nature are reconciled.

Magee And of course that brings us to Marxism and Marx, who for us today is far and away the most important and interesting of the Young or Left Hegelians. (Incidentally, I thought that last comment of yours was most revealing in showing how extreme right-wing and extreme left-wing diagnoses can both validly be derived from Hegel – something which puzzles many people who have not themselves looked into it. Not only are right-wing and left-wing totalitarianism similar in practice, but their intellectual ancestry is also similar. Hegel is the grandfather of both.)

All but one of Hegel's basic ideas which we have discussed so far was taken over by Marx and made central to Marxism: first, the idea that reality is a historical process; second, the idea that the way this process changes is dialectical; third, the idea that this dialectical process of change has a specific goal; fourth, the idea that this goal is a conflict-free society; fifth, the idea that until that goal is reached we are condemned to remain in one form or another of alienation. The great point of difference is that whereas Hegel saw this process as happening to something mental or spiritual, Marx saw it as happening to something material. With that one difference, however, the whole pattern of ideas remains the same. It's as if Marx took over a long sequence of equations from Hegel and substituted a different value for x but kept the equations themselves all the same.

Singer Precisely. You can see it, for instance, in Marx's materialist conception of history. This is the central idea in Marx's thought. He saw the development of history as determined by the forces of material production. So the material side, the forces of production, dominate the mental side of our life. Our ideas, our religion, our politics, all flow from the kind of economic structure that we have in our society. That's an inversion of Hegel's view of history. As Marx himself said, he'd stood Hegel on his head. For Hegel, of course, it was the development of Mind that led to the formation of particular societies and particular historical epochs.

Magee Do you think it can be claimed for Marx that he made an original contribution to philosophy?

Singer I don't think Marx made important contributions to philosophy in the narrow sense in which we talk about problems of the ultimate nature of reality. Marx was certainly a materialist, but he didn't argue for his materialism as a philosopher; he accepted it as something that was pretty obvious. What mattered was the material world, not something remote like *Geist*, which Marx dismissed as a kind of speculative German metaphysical abstraction. So he didn't argue for materialism, and he therefore didn't make contributions to that philosophical discussion. What he did do was give us a kind of a vision, a vision of a world in which we are controlled by our economic circumstances and are *for that reason* not free. It's still rather like Hegel in that we are pawns in the game of history: to become free we must control the economic forces, which after all are our own forces. What is economics, after all, but our own ways of providing for food, providing for shelter, and so on? So it's a vision in which we are unwittingly controlled by something that is really part of us. If we are to be free, we must control these forces. That's a powerful, and broadly philosophical, vision of the human situation; but it's not an important philosophical discovery in the narrow, academic sense of the word 'philosophy'.

Magee Viewing the two closely-linked thought-systems of Hegelianism and Marxism together, what would you say has been their most valuable contribution to human thinking since their time?

Singer Well, it's clear from what we've said that the idea of history as a process which affects every aspect of our thinking and our ideas is a crucial addition to our understanding which has come from Hegel and Marx.

Magee It became almost the dominant new aspect of all thought in the nineteenth century, didn't it? Of course, it was soon to receive a powerful boost from Darwin's theory of evolution, which taught us to look on all life – not just human life, still less just social life – as having evolved, and therefore as having been involved in a process of perpetual change.

Singer We can't now imagine looking at societies or ideas as timeless entities, independent of their history. That's something we owe to Hegel and Marx. So that's one very important thing. The other immensely important idea is this notion of freedom, the idea that is so different from the liberal notion. We cannot be free unless we control our destiny, unless we, instead of being blown about by the winds of economic circumstances (for Marx) or steered by the unseen hand of reason (for Hegel) actually take control, realise our own power, realise the capacity of human beings collectively to control our destiny, and do just that. That idea may in practice, as you said, have very dangerous authoritarian tendencies, but it's a very important idea. Now that we've been presented with it by Hegel and Marx, I don't think it can ever be forgotten.

Magee This brings us to the demerits as well as the merits of these ideas. The chief negative charge against them is that they are, quite simply, the fountainhead of totalitarianism in the modern world. Hegel was always appealed to as the intellectual founder of the idea of the organic state, and more specifically of the kind of German state-worship which culminated in Hitler; and his philosophical disciple Karl Marx has always been appealed to as the intellectual founder of Communism, which produced under Stalin the greatest tyranny of the modern age. Both Hitler's regime and Stalin's murdered many millions of their own citizens. Now I am far from suggesting that either of our two philosophers had anything remotely like this in mind, still less that they would have approved of it. But the fact is that both philosophers regarded the embodiment of ideas in history, in institutions, in social reality, as being the really essential thing about ideas – and yet this is the reality of what happened when their own ideas were so embodied. On their own premisses, then, there must have been some fatal flaw in the ideas themselves. What was it?

Singer Well I think their own ideas were mis-embodied. I don't think you can really trace Hegelian ideas at all in Hitler's kind of racist nationalism. You can't find that kind of racism in Hegel.

Magee So you think the state-worshipping tradition of German nationalism has completely misrepresented Hegel?

Singer It was complete misrepresentation of Hegel in that case, certainly. And also, as perhaps the ultimate irony, in what happened to Marx. Marx, as I've been saying, was a philosopher of freedom. He cherished freedom. He hated subordination. He was once asked by his daughter to write down the vice he most detested. He replied: 'Servility.' Servility, the very thing you needed to survive in Stalin's totalitarianism! And yet it is true that these ideas did get misapplied. They did get distorted.

Magee Why? What was it about them that lent itself to this wholesale misapplication, if such it was?

Singer I think in the end there's a faulty view of human nature. There's an attempt to show a greater unity than really exists between human beings. We could trace this to Hegel's notion of Mind or *Geist*, as something which is above and beyond the differences between individual minds. We find it also in Marx, in the idea that if you change the economic circumstances you change human nature, and we will all then overcome the divisions between one and another. The divisions between my interest and your interest, and between our individual interests and the interests of society will all disappear, Marx says, once we get rid of the economic structure which leads us to compete in the market place. It seems, unfortunately, that this is false. You can change the economic basis, but you don't get rid of the divisions between reason and desire, between my interest and yours, or between individual and society. In fact, what happens once you make it impossible, or very difficult, for people to compete with one another for wealth, is that they then start competing for status, or for power. That's no better than it used to be. In the case of Stalin's society it proved to be worse. So I think that Marx was wrong to believe that human nature would change.

The last word perhaps ought to go to Marx's great nineteenth-century rival, the Russian anarchist Bakunin, because Bakunin criticised just this aspect of Marx's thought. Marx said we should let the workers rule because then they will rule on behalf of the great mass of society, the working class. Bakunin said No. You shouldn't have any rulers, he said, because if the workers are rulers, they will cease to be workers and will become rulers. They will follow the interests of the rulers, not the interests of the working class. Marx thought that was rubbish. Marx thought that people in a different society would be different people, would have different, less self-directed interests, and would work together for the benefit of all. If you look at what's happened in the so-called 'Marxist' societies, perhaps Bakunin's view of human nature was right.

SCHOPENHAUER

Dialogue with
FREDERICK COPLESTON

INTRODUCTION

Magee It might be supposed that philosophy, of all subjects, would be free from the vagaries of fashion, but that is not so. In philosophy, just as in other human activities, there seems to be in each generation a reaction against the values of the preceding generation. As a result, writers who have hitherto been widely studied fall into neglect, and new figures come to the fore. The outcome is apt to be that at any given time and place it is mostly the same few philosophers who are the fashionable objects of study, while a number of other well-known philosophers are, by compari-son, being neglected. But then a new generation comes along and re-evaluates one or two of these neglected philosophers, so that they then come back into fashion. And so the process goes on.

Among the philosophers to whom this has happened most conspicu-ously in the last 200 years is Schopenhauer. For most of his lifetime – very roughly, the first half of the nineteenth century – he was almost totally disregarded. Then, in the second half of the nineteenth century, he became one of the most famous and influential of all philosophers. But then, in the first half of the twentieth century, he fell into a neglect so profound that even most teachers of philosophy no longer bothered to read him. And now, in our own time, he is coming back to notice – not least because he was a shaping influence on one of the most important of all twentieth-century philosophers, Wittgenstein.

Arthur Schopenhauer was born in Danzig, now called Gdansk, in 1788. His family had been rich Hanseatic merchants for generations, and the upbringing he received was aimed not at an academic life but at training him to step into an international business. But he had no interest in the family firm. Instead, he insisted on going to university, and thereafter he used his private means to finance a lifetime of independent study and writing. His doctorate thesis, *On the Fourfold Root of the Principle of Sufficient Reason*, has become a minor classic. He was still in his twenties throughout the four years in which he composed his masterpiece, *The World as Will and Representation*, published in 1818, the year he became thirty. (The date 1819 was printed on the flyleaf, so this often appears erroneously as the year of publication.) From then until his death at the age of seventy-two, in 1860, he published a great deal, but all of it was to extend, elaborate or enrich the philosophical system which he had con-structed in his twenties and from which he never departed. He produced a compendious collection of essays called *Parerga and Paralipomena*, and two short but pungent books on ethics called *The Basis of Morality* and *The Freedom of the Will*. There was also a little book called *On the Will in Nature* whose aim was to show that his ideas were supported by new discoveries in science. Most important of all, in 1844 he published a revised edition of *The World as Will and Representation* which was more than twice the length of the original volume.

There are several remarkable things about him. Although, in direct succession to Kant's, his work was securely in the mainstream of Western philosophy, he was knowledgeable about Hinduism and Buddhism, and is the only major Western philosopher to draw significant parallels between Western and Eastern thought. He was the first major Western philosopher to be openly and explicitly atheist. He placed the arts higher in the scheme of things, and had more to say about them, than any other great philosopher – and, no doubt partly for that reason, his influence on creative artists of the front rank has exceeded that of any other philosopher of the modern era. He was himself among the supreme writers of German prose. Many of his sentences are so brilliantly aphoristic that they have been plucked out of context by the hundred and published separately in little books of epigrams. Intellectually this is a catastrophe, because it obscures the fact that Schopenhauer is first and foremost a system-builder whose philosophy can be understood only as a whole.

Of the books in print about it in the English language at the time this discussion is being held, the longest and most recent is, I'm afraid, by me; but a monologue would be out of place in this series, so I have invited the author of one of the others to let me discuss Schopenhauer with him. My guest is, in any case, the most distinguished living historian of philosophy: Frederick Copleston, Emeritus Professor of the History of Philosophy in the University of London. In addition to the treatment of Schopenhauer in his renowned nine-volume *History of Philosophy* he has written a separate book called *Arthur Schopenhauer, Philosopher of Pessimism*.

DISCUSSION

Magee Perhaps the best way to start is by addressing ourselves to the question: What did Schopenhauer set out to do? What would *your* answer be?

Copleston I think that, like many other original philosophers, Schopenhauer wanted to understand the world in which he found himself, the world in which he lived. Or one could say that he tried to form a coherent, unified interpretation of human experience, or to gain conceptual mastery over the world of phenomena, the plurality of phenomena. To do that, he thought it was necessary to identify the underlying reality. If it were asked why he thought there was an underlying reality to identify, I suppose one main reason was that he started from the premises of Immanuel Kant. He thought that the way in which we see the world is a human perspective, that the human mind is pre-programmed to see the world in certain ways. We can't, for example, experience objects except as situated in space and time, as subject to spatial-temporal relations, and as exemplifying the relation of causality. But it obviously doesn't follow that, because things appear to us in a certain way, that is how they are in themselves, apart from the way in which they appear. The concept of a phenomenon, of something as appearing to a human subject, demands, as a correlative concept, the idea of the thing in itself, the thing as it exists in itself, apart from the way in which it appears to us. Though, however, Kant steadfastly refused to abandon this idea of the thing in itself, he maintained that we could not know anything positive about its nature. In Kant's view, the human being's theoretical knowledge is confined to the phenomenal world. Schopenhauer, on the other hand, aimed at identifying the thing in itself, so far as it was possible to do so.

Magee This is such an important idea – and we shall be referring back to it in several ways – that it is worth our while pausing over it, especially because people to whom it is new sometimes find it difficult to get hold of. Kant had argued that experience can come to us only through our faculties, our sensory and mental apparatus. Therefore what we can experience depends not only on what there is 'out there' to experience but also on the nature of our faculties, and what they can handle and what they do to what they handle. This means that the actual forms which experience takes are subject-dependent. From that Kant went on to argue that we can think of total reality as consisting of two realms. There is the realm of our experience, which is as it is because we are as we are, and we cannot conceive of things otherwise. This he calls the realm of phenomena. And then there is the realm of things as they actually are in themselves independently of us and the forms of our experience. This he calls the realm of noumena, the word 'noumenon' meaning 'the thing as it is in itself'. Of this latter realm we can, in the nature of things, acquire no direct conception. Our world – the empirical world, the world of everyday life and common sense, the world with which science concerns itself – is the former, the phenomenal world. It is important to realise that for philosophers like Kant and Schopenhauer the empirical world and the world of phenomena are one and the same thing. And the forms of that world are subject-dependent. Now Schopenhauer took this whole analysis over from Kant, but racked his brains about what the *connection* could be between the world as it is in itself and the world as it appears to us. He accepted Kant's contention that the former can never be directly known, but he wondered whether a detailed analysis of the latter might not give us important indications of what it *must* be – must because, after all, the latter is in some sense a manifestation of the former. Thus, in this indirect way, he was trying to get at the nature of underlying reality. That's the way his inquiry went, isn't it?

Copleston Yes, it is. I think it's important to remember that for Schopenhauer there can be only one underlying reality. Kant himself took it as a matter of common sense, I think, that if there's the table as it appears then there must be the table as it is in itself; and if there's the carpet as it appears, then there's the carpet as it is in itself – that there are a multitude of things in themselves. But, of course, if we think away spatial and temporal relations, and the causal relation, then there's no means of distinguishing one thing from another. So if the underlying reality transcends space and time and causality, and is quite other than the world of phenomena, then it can only be one. Plurality or multiplicity belongs to the world of phenomena. It would, however, be a mistake to assume that Schopenhauer conceived the underlying reality as the external cause of the world, a cause lying beyond the spatio-temporal world and transcending it. For Schopenhauer, as for Kant, the category of causality applies only within the phenomenal, empirical world. The underlying reality, the thing in itself, the noumenon, would be the inside of the world (of the world as it appears, that is to say). It would, indeed, be that which appears, but that which appears is, so to speak, the inner reality of the world, not something transcending the world altogether.

Magee These ideas are really so difficult that I think it is worth taking them slowly. Schopenhauer argued that for one thing to be different from another – for anything to be different from anything else at all – was possible only, and the idea of it made sense only, with reference either to time or to space, or to both. If two things are identical both in time and in space then they are identical. They are the same thing. This means that the notion of there being different things can apply only in this world of experience, this world of time and space, the world as it appears to us. Outside this world it can make no sense to talk about anything's being different from anything else. Therefore whatever there may be outside this world of our experience must be undifferentiated. By this argument Schopenhauer sought to show that Kant had been wrong in talking about things (in the plural) as they are in themselves – that whatever might lie behind this world must be one and undifferentiated. In asserting this he took an enormous stride towards one of the central beliefs of Hinduism and Buddhism. Those religions also believe that behind this highly differentiated and variegated world of phenomena there is one undifferentiated something which manifests itself as this world. In a way the most striking thing of all is that Schopenhauer did not get this belief from Buddhism or Hinduism, he got it by taking up the central thread of argument that runs through the main tradition of Western philosophy – the tradition of Descartes, Spinoza, Leibniz, Locke, Berkeley, Hume and Kant – and developing it further by the purely rational kinds of argument on which the tradition rests.

Copleston It seems to me that if one starts from the premisses of Immanuel Kant – I wouldn't do so myself, but if one does – then Schopenhauer was quite right. For, once the Kantian premisses have been accepted there seems to be no way left of distinguishing one thing from another, except, of course, within the phenomenal world. If the underlying reality is not subject to spatial, temporal or causal relations – if it makes no sense to say, for example, that it is here rather than there – it follows that there cannot be more than one underlying reality. As for Hinduism, we have to remember that – as you know – there have been a number of different systems of Hindu philosophy, some of them being pluralistic. Even within the Vedanta tradition there have been at any rate three distinct philosophies. It is true, however, that there are some resemblances between aspects of Schopenhauer's thought and the most prominent form of Vedanta philosophy, namely the Advaita system. But perhaps we shall have an opportunity of returning to this theme.

Magee Schopenhauer's argument about differentiation is certainly clear, but it won't do as it stands. Numbers, for example, are not differentiated by space or time or causal connection, so those things cannot constitute the principle of differentiation *as such*, even if they suffice for certain very important purposes. However, let us not pursue this at the moment. Let us instead follow Schopenhauer's argument to its next stage. He hoped, as we have said, that if we analyse this world of phenomena we might get from it some clues as to the nature of the underlying noumenon, despite the fact that the noumenon is not directly accessible itself. Now for what we may choose to regard as the next stage in his argument Schopenhauer picked as his starting point what he took to be a crucial oversight in Kant's analysis of knowledge. Kant had argued – or at least talked as if – all our knowledge of physical objects comes to us through our senses and is ordered by our minds. Schopenhauer pointed out that, for each of us, there is one physical object in the world for our knowledge of which this is a completely inadequate account, namely our own bodies. We *do* gain knowledge of our own bodies through all five of our senses, but in addition to that we have another sort of knowledge of a totally different order. Each of us has an enormous amount of knowledge of this physical object which does not pass through any of the five senses at all. We actually know this physical object *directly from inside*. Now this direct, non-sensory knowledge of a physical object from inside looked to Schopenhauer as if it might be used to light a path towards a knowledge of the inner nature of things in general.

Copleston Personally I think that if one starts with Kant's premisses one must then accept Kant's agnosticism. I don't see that there is any way of getting out of it. But you are certainly quite right in claiming that that is what Schopenhauer thought, namely that there was an access to the underlying reality through the body. A real difficulty, it seems to me, is that our idea of anything, even of an ultimate reality, must belong, on Schopenhauer's premises, to the world of phenomena. And there's no way for knowledge to get outside the phenomenal world. Beyond it simply lies silence, as Wittgenstein was to say in the *Tractatus*. However, it's perfectly true that Schopenhauer thought there was a hint of the nature of the underlying reality given through our experience of our bodies.

Magee Up to this point in the argument I would want to defend Schopenhauer because he quite explicitly makes the point that the knowledge which we have of our bodies from inside is not knowledge of a Kantian thing-as-it-is-in-itself. And he gives more than one good reason why not. First, such knowledge inhabits the dimension of time, even if not of space. Time is the very form of inner sense. And time can be a feature only of the phenomenal world. So inner knowledge is still phenomenal knowledge. Second, we have only partial knowledge of our inner selves – and the greater part is hidden from us. Decades before Freud, Schopenhauer argued specifically and at length that the greater part of our own inner life and motivation is unknown to us, and therefore that our lives, our decisions, our actions and our speech are for the most part unconsciously motivated. Here again, then, our knowledge of ourselves from inside is a knowledge of appearances only and not of reality as it is in itself. And there was yet a third reason. Schopenhauer argued that all knowledge must exhibit a subject-object structure. For there to be any knowledge at all, of anything at all, there must be something that is grasped and something that grasps it; there must be a known and a knower, an observed and an observer. This duality seemed to Schopenhauer inherent in the very nature of knowledge as such, and therefore it seemed to him that wherever there was knowledge there must be differentiation – and therefore that knowledge *as such* could exist only in the phenomenal world. Reality as it is in itself must be knowledgeless. So there are three reasons, each of which alone would be decisive, why our knowledge of ourselves from inside is not knowledge of a thing as it is in itself.

Copleston That Schopenhauer anticipated Freud in remarkable ways is perfectly true, and helps to show the importance of Schopenhauer in the history of thought. But it is also true, I think, that all our ideas of the infra-conscious, including the idea that there is an infra-conscious, must belong to the phenomenal world. And, there we are. I mean, Kant's premises, Kant's conclusion. I find Schopenhauer's metaphysics interesting and thought-provoking. But I doubt whether his metaphysical speculation fits in with the epistemological theories inspired by Kant.

Magee It seems to me that you are attributing to Schopenhauer claims he does not make. Although you talk as if you are criticising him, his view of the status of his argument up to this point is exactly the same as your own – he makes no more claims for it than you would. But I will leave it to you to explain how he thinks our inner knowledge of ourselves might provide a pointer to the nature of ultimate reality. (It seems to me, I must say, to remain consistently Kantian.)

Copleston For Schopenhauer, one's bodily movements are expressions of desire or impulse or of some drive. He used the word 'will' as a general descriptive term, though 'force' or 'energy' might have been preferable. Anyway, though one may sometimes refer to willed movement (willing to move my arm, for example), in Schopenhauer's opinion, as later in Wittgenstein's, it is a mistake to postulate a volition, an act of the will, which precedes and causes a given bodily movement. The volition, the willing, is the inside, as it were, of the physical movement. Schopenhauer does not claim that there is only the physical movement, as distinct from any psychical aspect. There is one process in which we can distinguish, by abstraction, two aspects. If we reflect on this analysis – and also on the process of unconscious motivation and infra-conscious drives to which you have drawn attention – our reflection can give us a hint of, a pointer to, the nature of ultimate reality. This is, in itself – according to Schopenhauer – an unconscious striving, a striving after existence, life, self-assertion, an ultimate force or energy or, as he called it, Will.

Magee He believed that this is further borne out if we look at the objects other than ourselves in the universe. The physical universe consists of matter in motion, and both the matter and the motion are unimaginably great – innumerable galaxies and solar systems hurtling through the cosmos at speeds approaching that of light. He saw the universe as instantiating inconceivably colossal amounts of energy. And he followed Kant in arguing that what is ultimate in the phenomenal world must *be* energy. He argued that matter is instantiated energy, that in principle all matter must be transmutable into energy, and that a material object is a space filled with force. In this, of course, twentieth-century physics has borne out Kant and Schopenhauer in the most extraordinary way; but the philosophers reached their conclusions by epistemological analysis a hundred years before the scientists got there.

All right, then: what is ultimate in the phenomenal world is energy. In that case the hidden, unknowable noumenon must be something all of whose phenomenal manifestations are expressed in terms of, or in terms which can be reduced to, energy.

Copleston Yes, but when one is talking about theoretical physics, should one not bear in mind the reluctance of so many physicists to conceive

Arthur Schopenhauer (1788–1860)

terms such as 'energy' as referring to metaphysical entities? Such terms are certainly of use within the framework of theoretical physics. They have their functions. But a good many philosophers would object, whether justifiably or not, to the construction of a metaphysics on the basis of scientists' use of terms such as 'energy'. Or have I misunderstood you?

Magee Well, yes, you have: you have attributed to me a step I didn't take. Or you have attributed it to Schopenhauer – it doesn't matter which; because I might as well come clean and say that on this, which is the fundamental point of his entire metaphysics, I agree with him. He is not saying that the noumenon is energy. He is saying that the noumenon manifests itself in this phenomenal world of ours as energy. His point is that this world of our experience, of common sense, of science, ultimately *is* energy, and that whatever the noumenon is is therefore something that manifests itself as *that*. So here is something about the noumenon which we can know, even though we have no direct access to it: it is something which manifests itself in the phenomenal world as energy.

Copleston I agree that the term 'energy' would be preferable to 'Will', as the word 'Will' tends to suggest a conscious process.

Magee His use of the term 'Will' was a disaster which has led to endless misunderstanding. He foresaw this misunderstanding and warned against it, but that is not good enough. He should not have used the term in the first place. For, as he repeatedly says, 'Will' in his use of it has nothing to do with conscious energy, life, personality or whatever, and still less to do with aims or goals. There is, he says, as much Will in the fall of a stone as in the action of a man. The entire inorganic cosmos is manifestation of Will, and the task of the physical sciences is to discover the regularities and lawlike movements of those manifestations. The conflagration of the sun is Will, the motion of the earth round it is Will, the movement of the tides is Will. All the go and impulse anywhere and everywhere in the Universe are Will.

   The reason why he chose this ill-fated term for it is that the nearest we human beings come to having a direct, unmediated experience of go or impulse is in our capacity as agents, in so-called willed activity; and also because the deepest of all human impulses is the will to survive. In our experience of these things we directly apprehend impulse. This is still only phenomenal knowledge. But because this tiny special case is the one and only instance of a cosmic manifestation that falls within our experience he decided, hesitantly, to give to the whole concept the name we give to our little glimpse of it in experience. As I say, it has created misunderstanding ever since. No term is adequate, as Schopenhauer himself insisted, and perhaps any would have caused misunderstanding. But 'energy' would have caused less. The trouble is, of course, that the noumenon cannot be 'like' anything in experience, so whatever term is used for it is going to create confusion between it and what that term normally denotes.

Copleston Yes. But then of course Schopenhauer wasn't indifferent to the underlying reality, was he? I mean he adopted quite definite attitudes, negative attitudes, towards it, disvaluing it. 'Energy' is such a neutral word; I mean, it would be odd to say that one approves of energy, or disapproves of energy, likes energy, or doesn't like energy. Schopenhauer, however, as we're both very well aware, had a very definite attitude towards the ultimate reality and its manifestations.

Magee That's true, and perhaps you're beginning to identify some of the different misunderstandings there would have been if he'd used the term 'energy'. But as things stand, even quite a lot of people who've written about Schopenhauer have made the mistake of supposing that he identified the metaphysical substratum of everything with the human will. It's difficult to see how they could possibly make this mistake, since he warns against it so often, and not just in one part of his writings but in many different places. But they have. The very impersonality of the term 'energy', its familiar association with the physical sciences, would have made it less damagingly misleading, it seems to me.

Copleston Well, I think you are quite right in making this claim. The point at which I was getting was that Schopenhauer looked on the ultimate reality as perfectly revolting and that he was willing to speak of it on occasion even in moral terms, as wicked. One wouldn't naturally be led to think of energy as revolting or as not revolting. At least I wouldn't. And certainly not as wicked. Anyway, having this definite attitude towards the ultimate reality, Schopenhauer naturally manifested a like attitude to the empirical world, as the manifestation or appearance of the ultimate reality – though in actual fact, of course, his approach was the other way round. That is to say, he proceeded from appearance, the phenomenal world, to the underlying reality, the noumenon.

Magee Let us now confront directly this question of his attitudes. Up to the present point in our discussion we have been sketching Schopenhauer's picture of reality, the way he thought things are, whether we like it or not. But, as you've now been saying, he himself most certainly did *not* like it. In fact he thought the world was a horrific place. It seemed to him full of cruelty, injustice, disease, repression. The hospitals and prisons of the whole world are at any given time full of people going through the most appalling sufferings and tortures. Animal nature is red in tooth and claw; at every moment of every day, in all five continents, thousands upon thousands of animals are tearing each other to pieces alive, devouring each other alive; the world of nature is a world of perpetual screaming. Schopenhauer's view of this is a nightmare vision. And it is expressed in prose of such extraordinary and dramatic power that no one who reads it is likely ever to forget it. But now, relating this to his metaphysics: a noumenon which manifests itself as *this* world of phenomena must be something inexpressibly appalling. And so we get to Schopenhauer's famous view that the metaphysical substratum of the world is something hateful, something unacceptable; and that not to have existed at all would have been better than existence on the terms that obtain. He is, among all the great philosophers, the supreme pessimist.

Copleston Yes. Of course he didn't just leave it there, though, did he? I mean, he had some suggestions, some ways out – the temporary way being through aesthetic contemplation, art, the creation and appreciation of art, which still desire and selfishness and longing and hostility and conflict, for the time being at any rate. One can go into an art gallery and look at the pictures from a purely aesthetic point of view. But then of course one may come out and make for a café or a pub: need and desire reassert themselves. Aesthetic experience provides only a temporary way out, or escape.

I think that it was a mistake for Schopenhauer to introduce his theory of the Platonic Ideas as intermediate between the ultimate reality and the work of art, because I don't see how there can be any place for them in his system. But he is quite right in making a distinction between the aesthetic attitude towards things and the attitude of trying to appropriate them and use them for own's one advantage. Kant had understood this before Schopenhauer, though the latter obviously made use of the distinction within the framework of a philosophy which was not that of Kant.

Magee Our aesthetic responses can be passionate and powerful, can seize us utterly, and yet at the same time they are disinterested.

Copleston Yes, disinterested but not uninterested.

Magee I think we should explain Schopenhauer's point here. What he's saying is something like this. Normally, if I see a plate of food, I think in terms of eating it – either that I want to or don't want to, or don't particularly mind. In any case I view it as something I can use, if I want to, to satisfy my desire or hunger or greed, or simply my will to survive. But if I see a Dutch painting of a plate of food, however lifelike, I don't see it in that way at all: I see it in an impersonal, disinterested light, as an aesthetic object, and am conscious only of its aesthetic properties. Perhaps I have chosen too crude an example, for Schopenhauer thought our normal attitude to everything was to see it in terms of its possible use, and that the aesthetic attitude was an exception to this. In our aesthetic responses we are, as it were, released from the rack of willing. This, Schopenhauer thinks, explains the experience people have of being taken out of themselves in the creation or contemplation of art, and the experience of time standing still. And it feels so wonderful because the normal state of existence from which it liberates us is a burden to us.

Schopenhauer believed that the key function of art is a cognitive, not an expressive one. It's real purpose is not to express emotion but to convey insight into the universal nature of things (which may, indeed, then move us, profoundly, emotionally). What it does, specifically, is to give us direct knowledge of the Platonic Ideas that are instantiated in the individual phenomena of the world, the general behind the particular, yet in terms of the uniquely specific.

How persuasive do you find his view?

Copleston Well, I think that one can give meaning to the view. When I was an undergraduate in the twenties, the idea of 'significant form', largely propagated, if I remember correctly, by Clive Bell, was being bandied about. Presumably, significant form would be an object of intellectual perception, not simply a matter of emotive reaction. Though, however, the subject of truth in art seems to me interesting and well worth discussion, I cannot say that I have ever made up my mind about the matter. I certainly would not wish to dismiss the idea of the concept of truth's being an analogical idea, understandable in rather different ways, which are all justifiable in relation to their several contexts. For example, while I certainly think that the traditional notion of truth as correspondence has a use, the idea of truth in art would seem to require a theory of non-propositional truth. However this may be, my critical reference to Schopenhauer's introduction of the theory of Platonic Ideas was certainly not intended to imply that I see nothing of value in his aesthetic theory. It seems to me that it contains lines of thought which are well worth considering.

Magee It has made an enormous appeal to some very great artists –

Copleston Oh yes, certainly –

Magee – who clearly thought it corresponded to their conception of what they were doing.

Copleston Or at any rate that it flattered them. . . .

Magee Let us move on to a consideration of what Schopenhauer had to say about ethics. What could possibly be the place of morality or ethics in a world such as is depicted by Schopenhauer?

Copleston As you know, Schopenhauer insists that as there's one ulti-mate reality, and as each one of us is identical with that one ultimate reality, therefore in some sense we are all one, ultimately. And he uses this theory as a basis for advocating compassion, sympathy, agapeic love as distinct from erotic love. All the more power to his elbow. I mean that is an excellent thing, that he should uphold ideas of compassion and sympathy. At the same time I find it difficult to see how, if each one of us is an embodiment of a reality which is self-devouring, torn by conflict, mutual love is a practical possibility. Would not one expect mutual strife, a strife which – given the nature of the underlying reality – could not be overcome? It is, I hope, unnecessary to say that I do not question Schopenhauer's value-judgments that love is preferable to hatred, com-passion to cruelty. On the contrary, I endorse these judgments wholeheartedly. But this does not alter the fact that if we are all one Will, and if this Will is something horrible, Schopenhauer was right in not stopping at the idea of compassion but in going on to propose, as an ideal, a turning against the ultimate reality and –

Magee Can I interrupt you, just in the interest of keeping two topics separate? Let us give people more of an idea what Schopenhauer's ethics are before we try to explain this very difficult notion of turning against reality, or as he expressed it, denying the Will. His ethics are, as you have explained, applied metaphysics, and that is in itself a remarkable thing in the history of philosophy. His view was this. Because everything in the world is a phenomenal manifestation of the noumenon, each human individual is therefore a phenomenal manifestation of the noume-non. And because the noumenon is one and undifferentiated, the same in everything, it means that the ultimate, inaccessible, noumenal nature of all human beings is one and the same thing. We are all, in our inner nature, one. This is the reason for compassion, which would otherwise be difficult to explain: it is why I care what happens to you, and why I share your pleasures and pains, why you are not just an external object in my world. It also means that if I do you an injury I am in some ultimate way injuring myself, damaging my own being. Thus the oneness of our being is the foundation of morality, and compassion is the motive for genuinely selfless moral behaviour.

You make the point, quite rightly, that if the noumenon is evil then our oneness in it, and with it, can scarcely be the basis for morality in an approving sense. I agree with that. And it prompts me to make the biggest of all my reservations about Schopenhauer. I reject his pessimism. It leads to major contradictions within his philosophy, of which this is one, and not the only one. Without it, almost everything he has to say makes better sense.

There is, in philosophy, a famous distinction known as the fact–value distinction. The idea is that the facts are one thing but how we evaluate them another: no value judgment is ever entailed by a purely factual statement. It could be, for example, that you and I would agree that the influence of the Christian Churches over our social life has greatly declined in the course of this century: yet you, I take it, would disapprove of or regret that fact, whereas I applaud it. It is always possible for people to agree about the facts but disagree about how they are to be evaluated. Now this applies to my attitude to Schopenhauer. Whether the noumenon is one and undifferentiated is, or is not, a fact, but whether it is hateful is an evaluation. Now I share a great many of Schopenhauer's analyses without sharing his evaluations. It seems to me that much, perhaps even most, of what he has to say about the descriptive nature of reality is brilliant, full of profundity and insight. But his hostility to reality I regard as pathological. I accept large parts of his analysis of experience as being close to the truth, but I reject his misanthropy and his pessimism. I think it is important for people to realise that one can approve very highly indeed of Schopenhauer's philosophy, as I do, without sharing his emotional attitudes.

Copleston As you know, a good many philosophers now question the fact–value dichotomy. For my own part, I think that the distinction has an obvious use. One must distinguish, for example, between statements which simply describe the ways in which people actually behave and statements which assert how they ought or ought not to behave. The two kinds of statements clearly belong to different types of utterance. At the same time I think that in the past the importance and range of application of the distinction have been greatly exaggerated. For example, I don't believe that one can construct any general interpretation of the world that doesn't contain or presuppose value judgments, judgments about importance, significance and so on. Similarly, in any reconstruction of the historic past which goes beyond mere chronology and which tells a significant, coherent story, judgment of value will certainly be implied. In other words, I don't believe in value-free history, or value-free metaphysics. I would not be prepared, for instance, to claim that world-views are value-free. Some world-views include inbuilt judgments of value, and all imply value judgments or presuppose them. I would therefore wish to question any general claim that from a metaphysical system no ethical conclusions can be deduced. I dare say that this thesis can be made true by definition. But in practice I don't think that things work out in quite the way suggested.

Magee No, I don't think they work out in that way either. The point I wanted to stress was that one can accept a very great deal of Schopenhauer – I was always careful not to say all – without sharing his value judgments. As a matter of fact I don't like talking about 'accepting' a philosophy or a philosopher – I would rather say 'learn from'. I personally have learnt a great deal from Schopenhauer while having quite different values from him in many important respects, and I think a lot of other people could do the same. This was my point – not that I or others should, or even could, adopt Schopenhauerian views in a value-free way, but that we could combine a great many of them with different values from his.

But let us now move on to the final step in his philosophy. Taking as he does the view that the world is a loathsome place, and that the noumenon which manifests itself as this world of phenomena can only be something terrible, he draws the logical conclusion by saying that we should turn away from the world, have nothing to do with it – deny the Will, as he puts it. Can you explain what he meant by this?

Copleston When Schopenhauer expressed approval of the asceticism and self-mortification which were advocated and practised in several of the world religions, he conceived them, I would say, as constituting a series of stages on the way towards what he interpreted as a final rejection of the Will, a final extinction of desire, of the will to existence or life. What Schopenhauer had in mind was not suicide but something more akin to the Buddhist entry into Nirvana. The end result of the process of progressive self-denial would be – as far as our knowledge is concerned – a negation of being and an entry into not-being or nothingness. If there is something more, so to speak, we cannot know it. For us, negation of the Will is negation of being, of reality.

I would like to make two comments. In the first place, in spite of some resemblances between Schopenhauer's idea of turning against the Will and aspects of, say, historic Christianity, there is one fundamental difference between Schopenhauer's attitude and that of the Christian or the orthodox Jew or the Muslim. For Schopenhauer, turning against reality was an ideal, whereas Jewish, Christian and Muslim believers in God would certainly not regard rejection of the Deity (for them the ultimate reality) as desirable. Moreover, this difference has implications in regard to the attitude to be adopted to this empirical world of ours. If the world is believed to have been created by a good God, the believer can hardly recommend turning against it lock, stock and barrel.

In the second place – this comment is independent of the first – the radical rejection of the Will envisaged by Schopenhauer would obviously be – on his premises – a rejection of the Will by the Will itself (as embodied in a human being). It is difficult for me to see how the ultimate reality, conceived as an urge to existence, and self-assertion, is capable of any such radical self-rejection. But I suppose that Schopenhauer would claim that the Will, becoming conscious of itself in and through human beings, perceives its own horrible character and is thus impelled to turn against itself in and through its phenomenal self-manifestation.

Magee In your last set of religious comparisons, or contrasts, it seemed to me that you left out the most important one. You talked about Christians, Muslims and Jews, but surely the crucial comparison is with Buddhists? You know a great deal more about Buddhism than I do, so I'm conscious of stepping on to dangerous ground here, but my understanding is that some (though not all) Buddhists do not posit the existence of a personal God, do not posit the existence of an individual soul, and do not posit the individual's permanent survival of death. If that is so, they have all those fundamental beliefs in common with Schopenhauer. But more to the point of our present discussion, many Buddhists see the most desirable aim of life on this earth as being a release from the need to live at all. Surely this is something close indeed to Schopenhauer's denial of the Will?

Copleston It is difficult to generalise about Buddhism in these respects. In Hinayana Buddhism, which has prevailed in South-east Asia and Sri Lanka and which regards itself as inheriting the original spirit of Buddhism, metaphysics is avoided, as being concerned with insoluble problems. If the existence of a divine reality is not actually denied, it is certainly not affirmed. Similarly, though there is a belief in reincarnation, positive statements about the nature of Nirvana, the final goal, are conspicuous by their absence. As for Mahayana Buddhism, in which there are a number of distinct schools or traditions, we can hardly discuss it here. The subject is too complex. In general, you are quite justified, of course, in finding resemblances between Buddhism and Schopenhauer's philosophy. There is a common emphasis on compassion and a common stress on the changing and transitory character of all phenomena. As for belief in God, nobody would describe Buddhism as a theistic religion, even if in some forms of Buddhism we find the idea of an Absolute of which nothing can be said. Perhaps we should leave the matter there. The reason why I referred to Judaism, Christianity and Islam was that as some writers have drawn attention to certain resemblances between Christianity in particular and Schopenhauer's thought, it is important to redress the balance by pointing out a fundamental difference. Resemblance is much more marked, as you rightly assert, in the case of Buddhism.

Magee Before we bring this discussion to an end I think we should say something about Schopenhauer's influence on other people. He has had an unsurpassed influence on creative artists. Some of the greatest novelists of the last hundred and fifty years reveal his influence in their books: Turgenev, Hardy, Conrad, Proust, Thomas Mann; these are just a few examples. Wagner was more affected by him than by any non-musical influence. However, perhaps in a series of discussions on philosophy we should focus our attention not on his influence on creative artists but on his influence on original thinkers. Here there are three examples that stand out above all others: Nietzsche, Freud and Wittgenstein. Could you perhaps start us off by saying something about his influence on Nietzsche?

Copleston As you know, Nietzsche regarded Schopenhauer as an educator – indeed, one of his early writings bore the title *Schopenhauer as Educator*. This indicates that he thought of Schopenhauer as a man who wasn't content with a superficial view of things, but burrowed beneath the surface and wasn't afraid to look the world and history in the face. In Nietzsche's opinion, Schopenhauer didn't try to gloss over the dark aspects of the world and life; nor talk, as Leibniz did, about the best of all possible worlds. As a man of mental integrity, Schopenhauer depicted human life and history as they are, not as one might like them to be. Nietzsche also entirely agreed with Schopenhauer's subordination of intellect to Will. That is to say, he agreed with the thesis that the mind is originally or in the first instance a servant of the Will. Nietzsche also honoured Schopenhauer as a man of independence of character, who didn't allow his views to be dictated by society, or by other philosophers, past or contemporary, but thought them out for himself. It is true, of course, that Nietzsche later criticised Schopenhauer sharply for turning away from life, for having adopted a No-saying attitude to the world and human life. It has been said of Nietzsche, by Professor Crane Brinton, that the great Yea-sayer, namely Nietzsche, spent most of his life saying No, and this is clearly true. At the same time Nietzsche persistently demanded that life should be affirmed, not denied or rejected. I confess to feeling some sympathy with Nietzsche's attitude. For if the world is as Schopenhauer depicted it, then the best thing is, it seems to me, to try to alter it for the better. To be sure, I wouldn't agree with Nietzsche's idea of what would be for the better, but I certainly think that there is need for creative action, rather than for a rejection of reality. However, Nietzsche never ceased to admire Schopenhauer and to revere him as a man whose philosophy had come to him in his student days as a kind of revelation.

Magee The second of the three thinkers influenced by Schopenhauer whom I picked out for special mention was Freud, so perhaps I should say a word about him. Two of the most important ideas that are generally credited to Freud had been spelled out fully by Schopenhauer before Freud was born. One was the notion of the Unconscious; not just the concept itself but an extended argument about it which Freud repeated. The argument is that most of our motivation is unconscious to ourselves; that the reason why it is unconscious is that it is repressed; the reason why it is repressed is that we do not want to confront it; the reason why we do not want to confront it is that it is incompatible with the view of ourselves which we wish to maintain; and therefore a great deal of motivated energy goes into either keeping it repressed or allowing it to surface only after it has been cleaned up and made falsely presentable to our conscious minds. This argument is the core of Freudianism. And yet not only had it been put forward by Schopenhauer long before Freud; Freud himself acknowledged that this was so. But he claimed to have arrived at it independently. The second seminal idea – and probably the idea for which Freud is most famous after the one just mentioned – in which Freud was clearly preceded by Schopenhauer is that of the omnipresence of sexual motivation. Schopenhauer argued, at a time when it was difficult and shocking for a serious thinker to do so, that sexual motivation comes into almost everything. The reason, he said, relates to the fact that it is sexual motivation that brings human beings into existence. This fact means that sexual activity is far and away the most important activity that most of us ever engage in. It determines not only that the world shall be peopled but by precisely whom it shall be peopled throughout all future time, since each individual is unique and is the possible product of only two particular parents. As beings in the world the twin poles of our existence are conception and death. An incalculable amount has been written about death by philosophers and other writers of every kind; little or nothing has been written by most such persons about conception. Yet conception is, to say the least of it, as important to us as death – being the means whereby we come into existence as individuals – and every bit as mysterious. Thus Schopenhauer argues that the great interest in sex which is characteristic of human beings in general is no more than proportionate to what is at stake.

Let us now turn to the third of our three thinkers. Perhaps you would draw our discussion to a close by saying something about Schopenhauer's influence on Wittgenstein, thereby carrying us down to our own time.

Copleston Wittgenstein's debt to the thought of Schopenhauer is clear from the notebooks containing preparatory material for the *Tractatus*, and indeed, even if to a somewhat less obvious extent, from the *Tractatus* itself. In this work we find, for example, the idea of the correlation between subject and object, between the 'I', as epistemological subject, and its world. This 'I', the epistemological subject, is, as it were, the boundary of my world, not an object within it. I can, of course, think of myself, turn myself into an object up to a point, but there remains the 'I' which is trying to think itself, the I-subject. This idea comes straight out of

Schopenhauer even though, as a matter of possibility, Wittgenstein could have derived it from some other philosopher, such as Fichte. Then there is the famous saying in the *Tractatus* that if all the problems of science were answered the problems of life wouldn't have been touched. This idea too seems to have been derived from Schopenhauer. It's also worth noticing that in the *Tractatus* Wittgenstein makes a distinction between the metaphenomenal Will as the bearer of ethics, of which, we are told, nothing can really be said, and the will as a phenomenon, which is said to form part of the subject matter of psychology rather than of philosophy. This distinction between the metaphenomenal or noumenal Will and the phenomenal will can also be traced back to Schopenhauer. It should of course be added that in the course of time Wittgenstein became less and less Schopenhauerian. For one thing, he became markedly opposed to forming any system, whereas, as you said earlier, Schopenhauer was a notable system builder. There is a kind of embryo system in the *Tractatus*, but it does not figure in the later writings of Wittgenstein. Anyway, in the earlier phases of his thought Wittgenstein was certainly strongly influenced by Schopenhauer. In fact Schopenhauer is about the only major philosopher of the past, in no sense contemporary with himself, whom Wittgenstein had really read, studied and, in part, digested. In other words, Schopenhauer's influence did not end with the close of the last century but was felt by one of the most famous philosophers of our own century and time.

NIETZSCHE

Dialogue with
J. P. STERN

INTRODUCTION

Magee Any short-list of those nineteenth-century philosophers who have had the widest influence outside philosophy would have to include Hegel, Marx, Schopenhauer and Nietzsche, to name no others. In Continental Europe the influence of Nietzsche on philosophers too has been prodigious, though from English-speaking philosophers he has more often had to endure hostility, suspicion or neglect – until recently. Now, however, there is an unmistakable growth of interest in his work, and really for the first time, among analytic philosophers. He always did have a great influence on creative writers, including some of the most eminent in the English language: Shaw, Yeats and Lawrence spring to mind as examples. The quality of his own prose is dazzling, and is second to nobody's.

Friedrich Nietzsche was born in Saxony in 1844. He had an academic career of extraordinary brilliance as a classics scholar, and became a full professor in his mid-twenties, an almost unheard-of thing. But then he threw over his university career, went into isolation, and became a philosopher. For sixteen years he poured out his writings, mostly either short books or books of essays and aphorisms: some of the best known are *The Birth of Tragedy, Human All Too Human, The Gay Science, Beyond Good and Evil, The Genealogy of Morals* and, most famous of all, *Thus Spoke Zarathustra*. At first he was deeply influenced by the ideas of Schopenhauer and Wagner; but he rebelled against both, and went on to produce some notorious anti-Wagner polemics.

Until the last four years of his creative life he made no attempt to build a system of any kind. But then he began to think of drawing all his main themes together into a single, comprehensive work, first to be called *The Will to Power*, then *The Revaluation of All Values*. However, it was not to be. Always plagued by ill health, in January 1889 he collapsed into mental illness, a condition almost certainly caused by tertiary syphilis. He was helplessly insane from then until his death in 1900.

With me to discuss his work is J. P. Stern, Professor of German in the University of London, author of one of the best-known books on Nietzsche.

DISCUSSION

Magee Nietzsche was the first philosopher fully to face up to Western man's loss of faith in religion, or in the existence of any world other than this one. If there are no God and no transcendental realm, then morals, values, truth, rationality, standards of every kind, are not given to man from outside himself but are created by man to meet his own needs. *We choose our values* – or at the very least *we collectively create our values*. It's a highly challenging and deeply disruptive view, and Nietzsche realised that to the full. Can we begin from there?

Stern Yes, I think that this is a perfectly fair way of starting. In addition to what you said about his life I think one might mention that he was a son of the manse – his father, who died when Nietzsche was less than five years old, was a minister of the Lutheran Church. His mother wanted him to be a parson: he went to Schulpforta, the most famous of German Protestant boarding schools, and theology was the subject he studied when he first went to the University of Bonn. His attack on Christianity is not a neutral, disinterested, pacific thing at all, but is violent, dramatic – melodramatic in many ways. It's an attack on Christianity rather than on Christ, and I think the point you made, that he envisages nineteenth-century man's having to stand on his own feet without the support of faith or dogma of any kind, is central, and a good point from which to start thinking about his philosophy. We need to see him as somebody who does not simply profess a flat kind of atheism but who is personally and intimately involved in denying the existence of divine justice, of divine mercy, of religious transcendence altogether.

Magee His approach developed eventually into a programme for radically questioning all the foundations of Western thought. We are slaves to convention, Nietzsche says – we base our whole lives on attitudes and ideas whose premises, if we ever get round to actually examining them, we reject. This makes ours an inauthentic way of living, a dead way of living. We must re-evaluate our values in the light of what we honestly do believe and feel.

Stern That is right. What he believed in, what he tried to show, was that the whole edifice both of Christian values and of idealism, which he saw as derivative from those values, was false, and had to be thrown over, and something else put in its stead. The question what is to be put in its stead is not quite so simple. But that was the basic premiss from which he began. And that makes for the drama, indeed the extraordinary melodrama, of the person, of the style, of the whole phenomenon of Nietzsche. He often seems to me to have more in common with Faust and Peer Gynt, the two exemplary figures of modern drama, than with any of the other philosophers in your series. Now this doesn't, I think, mean that he is not to be taken seriously as a philosopher, but on the contrary, that the idea of what should be included in the notion of philosopher needs widening.

Magee His re-evaluation of all values is, of course, a colossal undertaking. It will make our discussion of it clearer if we divide up our consideration of it into parts. There are four main traditions within Western civilisation which Nietzsche attacked: the tradition of Christian morality, the tradition of secular morality constituted by the work of moral philosophers, the ordinary everyday morality of the unintellectual mass of mankind ('herd values', as he called them), and some at least of the traditions deriving from ancient Greece, especially from Socrates. Let us look at each of these in turn. Can you say something about his fundamental criticism of Christian values?

Stern Well, I think to start with, his attack on the Christian scheme of things is a very simple and straightforward one. All the positive values of Christianity are criticised and rejected: turning the other cheek, loving your neighbour as you love yourself, having compassion for those who are suffering, for those who are in some way deprived and whom we call 'the underprivileged' – a phrase Nietzsche would have loathed. All these are ruled out of court. Not, however, absolutely, because, as we shall see later – and I want to make this point very clearly – Nietzsche is constantly making special rules for special people, and is very much against the notion of simply generalising rules in the way in which Kant had done in the Categorical Imperative. The first thing, then, is the attack not on Christ but on Christianity, as really furthering the underdog, furthering the person who cannot stand on his own feet and requires compassion, requires pity, illicitly requires sympathy from outside himself.

Magee Why was Nietzsche against compassion? Why did he despise it so much?

Stern He's not against it, he does not despise it when it comes from the strong person. What he despises is the supporting of the weak person from outside himself, whatever the outside source may be – whether another person and his compassion, or rules and regulations, or laws, or whatever.

Magee And his reason for being against it?

Stern His reason for being against it lay in his fundamental appeal to authenticity, to selfhood, to the *élan vital*, to the life within the person lived to the full. It is this person, who should be living life to the full, whom the need for pity and compassion dishonours, who is diminished by compassion.

Magee What, then, was his chief objection to secular morality, the great tradition of moral philosophy represented by, shall we say, Kant – or, in Nietzsche's own day, the Utilitarians? That wasn't a specifically Christian morality, but Nietzsche was just as much against it. Why?

Stern I think the main reason is this: all systems, or secular moralities, are based on abstraction from the individual case. They're based on appeal to generality. For Nietzsche the word 'general' is the same as 'common', and by 'common' he means common in the nasty sense of the word. He believed that human greatness, the best in man, was rare – and the concomitant of that is the belief that the appeal to a common denominator in men is necessarily an appeal to the lowest, or to that which is least distinguished in them. In a sense all rules and regulations – one might almost go as far as to say all laws – are for him matters for the common herd, no more. And now we're on the third morality Nietzsche attacked, that of the common herd. He is most emphatically not a democratic philosopher; he is a philosopher of the great and noble, and therefore for him the value and appeal of the democratic ideology is very low.

Magee He believed, didn't he, that the individual great man, the hero, should be a law unto himself, should not be hamstrung by consideration for lesser mortals, and still less by petty rules and regulations.

Stern Precisely. That's the best phrase you can use: each great man a law unto himself. That's not the sentence he used, but it's precisely what he meant.

Magee What about the last of our four traditions, that of ancient Greece? It is worth recalling, in this context, Nietzsche's brilliance as a classical scholar. He was deeply knowledgeable about ancient Greece; and he became implacably hostile, didn't he, towards a whole tradition stemming from Socrates?

Stern Yes. But his classic work *The Birth of Tragedy* – I think it's one of the most remarkable works ever written on the problem of tragedy – is concerned with pre-Socratic tragedy and with pre-Socratic Greece, which for him was a kind of Golden Age. And the whole thing goes flat at the point when Euripides, Aristophanes and Socrates come on the scene. What happens then is that strength and goodwill, warmth and beauty, as well as a full grasp of the tragic being of mankind, are replaced by reason, are replaced by what Nietzsche regards as the trivialising practice of rationalising everything and replacing those ancient insights into tragic existence by the Socratic argie-bargie. He never forgave Plato for setting up a hero whose main qualities are those of talking everybody else into the ground.

Magee His concern with the origins of culture, displayed in such a rich way, was bound up with his notion that we make our own values, the point being that if human values are made by us, and are not given to us by God or any authority outside ourselves, then the question of how we get them becomes of fundamental importance. It is also, we might add, a characteristic nineteenth-century concern, this concern with origins – one need cite only *The Origin of Species*. . . . Was Nietzsche influenced by Darwin?

Stern Yes, but he was anti-Darwinian, and I think he didn't really understand very clearly what the whole theory of the origin of the species came to; or perhaps it would be more just to say that he did not appreciate the kind of evidence Darwin was putting forward in support of his theory. Throughout, he was hostile to the scientist's practice of putting forward evidence regardless of its ethical implications. Like so many nineteenth-century figures Nietzsche was always going to study physiology, going to study chemistry, going to study physics, but never got round to it. So I don't think there's an awful lot to be said about his attitude to Darwinism. But the main point about origins is that – again like some philosophers (like Marx, for instance) – he believes you can determine the quality of the product, especially a product of the mind, by the nature and quality of its origins. This, after all, is very much what Freud did; and I suspect that Freud got it largely from Nietzsche, although he (Freud) isn't very ready to acknowledge his debt to Nietzsche. What that means is really that the background, the genealogy of morals for instance – this is the title of one of Nietzsche's books which you mentioned – is in fact indicative of the quality of morals. Now let me say I don't believe this to be true. But it is very much the nineteenth-century view, over and over again, that you can determine the quality of a mental product by the origins at the back of it.

Magee This view that things somehow *are* their origins is a mistake for which there is an accepted term: 'the genetic fallacy'.

Stern That's right. It is a fallacy of which Nietzsche is only occasionally aware, only occasionally critical.

Magee Your mention of Freud suggests another question. Nietzsche's insistence that we create our values to meet our needs led him to an essentially psychological analysis of values in terms of needs that were both individual and social, perhaps, but above all individual, didn't it?

Stern Yes. That is perfectly true.

Magee So his approach becomes, above all else, a psychological one.

Stern It is a way of psychologising a lot of phenomena, and indeed he was a very remarkable psychologist in many ways; yet he does not produce a system, either in psychology or in anything else, and in that sense he's different from Freud. But he's very similar, in fact very much a precursor of Freud, because he places a great deal of emphasis on the unconscious. For instance: Nietzsche's criticism of German idealism hinges on his view that it fails to take account of the unconscious drives which determine our actions, that German idealism simply takes over from Christianity a wholly negative attitude towards these unconscious drives in us and builds a civilisation on their suppression – and again you can see how close this is to the Freud of *Civilisation and its Discontents*. There is a myth to the effect that Freud discovered the unconscious. Nothing could be further from the truth. The unconscious has been about since the end of the eighteenth century, and Nietzsche is among those who used the term and put tremendous emphasis on it. But he does not have a layer theory of the self, the way Freud did. He is much less systematic. He distrusts systems. He thinks there is something indecent about trying to encapsulate a human being or a human psyche within a systematic account.

Magee One consequence of this attitude is his view that different moralities are right for different people. Nothing could more flatly contradict the standard notion among philosophers – derived most immediately from Kant – that a morality must be universalisable if it is to be seriously defensible.

Stern Yes. He believes that individual people are entitled to individual kinds of behaviour and to individually determined bits of knowledge. This is the most astonishing thing; and also, I think, in many ways a very prophetic kind of insight. He believed that knowledge was not absolute, that the acquisition, the pursuit of knowledge was not to be taken absolutely, but that a given civilisation had its own particular entitlement to the kind of knowledge that it could bear and use fruitfully to positive ends. You see, the emphasis is on 'it could bear'. He did envisage situations where knowledge would destroy the knower, and I wish to emphasise that he was pretty prophetic in this. Because in fact we are facing situations, are we not, in which knowledge – the knowledge we strive for and attain – often turns out to be vastly in excess of what we can make of it, of what we can use, use positively rather than destructively.

Magee What you have in mind is presumably our knowledge of nuclear physics, which has become a mortal threat to us. This is a fact that Nietzsche would very well have understood.

Stern Yes. And he did in fact warn us – I mean not about nuclear physics, of course, but about knowledge generally. You see, we really have only one other theory of knowledge apart from our own. Our own is that all knowledge is worth pursuing regardless. The other is the Marxist idea, which creates a system whereby knowledge is either socially useful and therefore pursued, or not pursued and suppressed if it is not socially useful. Nietzsche's view is somewhat similar to this. He does believe that given civilisations can destroy themselves, and the ground from which this destructive attitude is sustained is, in his view – we're coming back now to Socrates – the Socratic yen for knowledge, that endless driving force which pushes us on.

Magee But just as he believed that a civilisation is entitled to as much knowledge as it can bear, so he believed that an individual is entitled to as much knowledge as he can bear. Freud several times said of Nietzsche that he knew himself better than any human being had ever done or was ever likely to do. Before Freud, Nietzsche carried out something akin to a Freudian self-analysis, didn't he?

Stern Yes, I think that's true, though I think one doesn't want to exaggerate it, because he also saw, as Freud did not, the destructive aspect of self-analysis. After all, here is a man who is constantly speaking up on behalf of action, on behalf of discriminating contacts with human beings, who does nothing to further the old German idea of introspection and self-revelation. He was tremendously strongly influenced by Goethe. Goethe was one of the great characters in his hagiology; and Goethe was very clear that excessive introspection doesn't get you anywhere.

Magee Let me just take stock of the position we've reached in our discussion so far. Up to this point we've talked almost entirely about Nietzsche's critical enterprise. We've discussed his basic view that the morals, values and standards which we have inherited were based in origin on a belief in God or gods who had given them to us and would judge us by our success or failure in living up to them. But, says Nietzsche, we've lost our belief in all these gods, and in religion generally, and *that* means we've lost belief in the very foundations of our value system. Yet, so far, we've failed to face up to the fact. We go on trying instead to relate our lives to a value system whose foundations we have ceased to believe in; and that makes our lives inauthentic, indeed, it makes *us* inauthentic. If we're to have an authentic value system we've got to carry out a complete re-evaluation of our values. All this you and I discussed, and in the course of doing so we touched on some of the individual critiques into which this approach led Nietzsche. But now I want to move on to what seems to be the natural next stage for the discussion to take. Having swept everything away on this colossal scale, what does Nietzsche advocate in its place? What, after all this, are the positive values which he comes out with?

Stern Well, the answer to that is a very simple and a very complicated

Friedrich Nietzsche (1844–1900)

one at the same time. The simple answer is: be yourself, at the top level of everything that you are; to the hilt; live your life fully, live it adventurously – and all the other things which later on come under the heading of *élan vital* (in the human sphere, I mean). Be Thou Thyself, that which thou art, is the major premiss from which he begins, and it is also the goal towards which morality and ethics ought to be directed. Now you may ask, of course, if everybody is himself and himself alone, what will be the consequences in a wider sphere? How is it compatible with a political system? And so on. The answers to that question are, I'm afraid, very unsatisfactory as far as Nietzsche is concerned. His whole attitude towards social questions never does get far. Now, I said also that the answer is very complicated, and it was for this reason: Nietzsche's recommendations make living together in some kind of harmony extremely difficult, especially if you add to this his view that laws are there to make things easy for the weak. It is, on the face of it, a simple system, but basically I think there is a great deal of difficulty facing anyone who is going to put this forward as a guide to living in society. In a sense we can say that some of the more outrageous political doctrines of our time, some of the fascist politics of the early part of this century, are based to some extent – among intellectuals at any rate – on this view that you must create your own values and live by them, regardless of the consequences. It hasn't got us very far, as you can see.

Magee But Nietzsche was fully conscious of the fact that it would create conflict. The thing is, he didn't mind. If anything, he *welcomed* conflict – and I agree with you that he was completely unrealistic about the social implications of it. He saw mankind as a rabble led by an elite, and he thought the elite were entirely right to be selfish, to sweep aside the weak and unable and simply seize for themselves whatever they wanted. How, on this basis, the individual members of the elite were also going to be able to live with each other was something which, as you say, he never considered. But there was one thing he was certainly right about: all this is as flatly contrary to any accepted ideas of morality as can be.

Stern Yes, it is. But then you've mentioned only one half of it. The other part of it – which was *not* taken up by the fascists and national socialists – is that you must also conquer all that is comfortable, all that is cowardly, all that is less than adventurous within yourself. And if you've done that – this is the view he puts forward in *Thus Spoke Zarathustra*, for instance – if you've done that, you won't really want to be so very aggressive towards others. You will have some understanding of their weaknesses; though this understanding – the positive, the tolerant understanding of weaknesses – is not precisely Nietzsche's strong point.

Magee It's not exactly what he's most famous for.

Stern No.

Magee People have always been very shocked by Nietzsche and thought quite rightly that what he was advocating was contrary to all known moral standards. The real point, though, is that Nietzsche agreed with them. And he was happy to shock. As you say, he wanted people to be to the full, be *full out*, be unlimitedly, and he wanted *nothing* to stand in the way of that – no conception of rationality, or truth, or fairness, or anything else. On the contrary, he believed that all other criteria should be chosen to serve the claims of being. But he thought that all moralities which have actually existed have run counter to this approach, and have therefore been, in practice, anti-life. At the heart of what he is saying is that life is the only value and the only source of value, and therefore that we must derive all our values from it. We must assert life, say 'Yes' to life in the fullest sense, which means that not only should we give unbridled rein to all our natural instincts, we should take all our standards, even those of rationality and of truth itself, from the same source.

Stern Or from the great man. From the great man – and among the great men he had in mind, as I already mentioned, Goethe would be one; Napoleon would be another, sometimes Luther, sometimes even some of the great Borgia popes – sometimes even Socrates, because he had the strength of mind to carry through his own project.

Magee And truth itself must be subjugated.

Stern Absolutely.

Magee That is to say, if there are truths that would damage us, or would damage our lives, we positively don't want to know them. Or rather, much more than that, the very criterion of truth, what *counts* as true, must be that which serves life. What does not serve life is to be rejected as false.

Stern Yes. We're back again at the question of entitlement to truth, of what he once called 'the hygiene of knowledge'. There ought to be some kind of hygiene that would tell us what kind of knowledge we *may* face and what kind of knowledge we should reject. And you're quite right that truth itself is subjected to a kind of embargo, a kind of sanction.

Magee If Nietzsche were to defend himself against the manifold outcry that has greeted his philosophy I suppose his defence could go something like this. The whole evolutionary process has consisted of the strong eliminating the weak, the able eliminating the unable, the intelligent eliminating the stupid, the enterprising the unenterprising, and so on; and it is only because these processes have been going on unbrokenly over millions of years that humanity has developed at all, and that civilisation has developed at all. These are indeed the processes that create everything of value we possess. Yet with the ancient Greeks and the Jews, along came so-called moralists who taught that these processes were immoral, in fact wicked. The strong should humble themselves, they taught, and should shelter the weak and the meek, and should submit themselves to the rule of law; the clever should help the stupid; the able should take up the causes of the unable, and so on. But if we had always done that, says Nietzsche, we should never have emerged from the pre-human state. Surely what we ought to do, he says, is continue with – go back to – the values and standards that have created humanity and civilisation, not put those standards into reverse.

Stern Yes. I think that is precisely what he says, on a number of occasions, in different contexts; and his worry about the future is precisely that this kind of assertion and self-assertion will not go on – that the democratic spirit, the spirit of the plebs, of the rabble, will take over and annihilate all these values.

Magee Thereby putting into reverse the whole process that has created civilisation out of barbarism.

Stern Yes. But in addition to that we have to bear in mind that he has a view of history which is really rather different from the view on which your defence of him was based. He sees history as repeating itself. Now what that means we shall talk about a little later, but what it means in our present context is that any historical situation can create and absorb and make use of the highest that man is capable of creating. There aren't any privileged situations, there are no privileged eras, and therefore any era that sees itself as capable of fully understanding, of fully creating these values, should be allowed to do that. And the trouble is that the late nineteenth century and the early twentieth century, as he sees them, may very well be what he calls eras of decadence, in which this strength cannot be fully realised. He was a remarkable prophet in some ways, but the new barbarism, the barbarism to come, didn't frighten him enough.

Magee Your mention of Nietzsche's doctrine of endless recurrence prompts me to make a suggestion. When we move on, as I think we now must, to consider Nietzsche's later work, we find there are four really big themes in it. One of them can be summarised by the phrase 'the will to power', a phrase which indeed he popularised; one is the doctrine of the

Übermensch, usually translated 'the Superman', again a term invented by Nietzsche which has entered the language; thirdly, there is the doctrine of the eternal recurrence of time, which you just mentioned; and fourthly there is Nietzsche's idea about the aesthetic understanding of life. Now I suggest that for clarity's sake we deal with these one at a time. Let us start with the will to power. At one time he was going to use this phrase as the title for the summation of his life's work. What precisely did he mean by it?

Stern Well, he takes the notion of the will from your own special philosopher, Schopenhauer, of course, and he reverses Schopenhauer's evaluation of it. Whereas Schopenhauer regarded the will as the source of all the evil in the world, and the source of man's unhappiness, Nietzsche regards it as the origin and source of man's strength. The cultivation of a freedom for the will to enact what it can enact is part of a healthy culture. Now the difficulty there is that this brings you into conflict with other people, and therefore at this stage the will to power becomes a will to self-assertion, a will to the usurpation of others. But that's not all there is to the will. I think it is to be emphasised – not over-emphasised, as some critics have done, but emphasised – that the will to power also turns itself inward, that is to say it destroys within the self all that is weak, all that is comfortable, all that is simply part of a man's self-indulgence.

Magee A drastic bringing of oneself up to the mark by the scruff of one's own neck.

Stern Up to the mark *which one has created oneself*. And this is the difficulty: one has created the mark oneself. We are back at his insistence on the self-creation of this and all other values.

Magee When Schopenhauer talks about the metaphysical will he means something that manifests itself phenomenally in the drive not only in human beings, or indeed in living things generally, but in everything. The force that makes the moon go round the earth, and the earth go round the sun, is thought of by Schopenhauer as being manifestation of what he calls 'Will'. The entire cosmos consists of matter in motion, and it is all manifestation of 'Will' in Schopenhauer's sense. This has nothing to do with 'Will' in the ordinary sense. But Nietzsche also used the concept in the same way as Schopenhauer, didn't he?

Stern I'm afraid he did, yes. I say 'I'm afraid' because I think the weakest parts of his philosophising are those in which he does after all try to pursue a system of some kind, in which he talks about the will to power in nature, the will to power in the cosmos. I've really never derived any profit from that. I don't think it is interesting because the main maxim with which he works – that you cannot systematise great thought – works for him with particular poignancy. It works for him very strongly indeed.

Magee Well now, let's move on to the next of those four main themes of Nietzsche's later work: to the Superman. Everybody knows the word, and one finds it was originally coined in English to translate Nietzsche's term *Übermensch*. It has been a much misunderstood concept. People have associated it with the pure Aryan of Hitler's mythology and the blond beast of anti-Nazi caricature. But of course that's nothing like what Nietzsche meant by it.

Stern No, I think that's not what he meant at all. I think the Superman can be the product of any civilisation. Remember, I said that any era is capable of bringing forth the maximum values that men are capable of. The Superman is the man who lives all that the will to power will secure for him, lives it to the full, and is capable of repeating his own willing *ad infinitum*. But now we're already arriving at the doctrine – that most controversial of all the things he wrote; the most bizarre, if you like, of his views – the doctrine of the eternal recurrence.

Magee Don't let's get there quite yet, though. I want to unpack a little more this notion of the Superman, which has played such a significant role in the thought of the last hundred years. (Its misuse and abuse by the Nazis is only one example. It had an extensive influence on writers and playwrights – for instance on Bernard Shaw, who called one of his best plays *Man and Superman*.) Wouldn't it be true to say that what Nietzsche was trying to get at was the notion of an unrepressed man, taking the concept of repression in what we now see as its Freudian sense? The Superman is a human being whose natural instincts are not repressed – who has not been 'un-selfed', as Nietzsche puts it – and who is therefore *being* to the top of his bent, in an uninhibited, untrammelled, free-spirited way. He is not living his life according to false values: he has re-evaluated his values. He is each one of us as we would ideally be if we were not hobbled by false ideas about ourselves and our lives. Isn't *that* the real concept of the Superman?

Stern Yes, I think that is so, but it would be a man who without restricting himself would naturally, instinctively, unconsciously avoid doing any of the things that Nietzsche regards as evil. For instance, the one category that he comes out against unequivocally is grudgingness, what he calls *ressentiment*: the grudging admission of warmth and greatness in another, the grudging admission of success, those kinds of things. The Superman is one who naturally does not feel any of those things.

Magee He is, among other things, a wholly generous spirit.

Stern Yes – and there again, you see, the whole notion of the Christian generous spirit is not all that far from Nietzsche's purview.

Magee Let us move on now to the third of our four main themes, the notion of eternal recurrence. Of all the doctrines of Nietzsche, this is the hardest not just for people to understand but even for them to take seriously. He appears to be saying that the whole of history moves in cycles, vast cycles, so that everything comes round again and again and again, literally for ever. You and I have actually sat in this selfsame studio having this selfsame conversation innumerable times before and will do so innumerable times again. Now people find it difficult to believe that he really is saying that.

Stern Well, he's really saying that, and he is trying out what might happen if you took that view seriously. I think we ought to say – altogether, relating to our whole discussion – that a great deal of his thinking is of this experimental kind. I don't mean that it's not serious, or not responsible; I don't mean it's trivial; but I do mean that here is somebody who is facing the whole of human thought and trying out, again and again, different views. There's a saying of his – I think a very tragic saying – in a letter, where he writes, 'I feel as though I were a pen, a new pen' (a quill, presumably) 'being tried out by some superior power on a bit of paper.' It's a strange thing to be feeling for somebody who is advocating the will to power and the Superman. Yet I think he did genuinely feel that. Now this is the way he tries out this thought of the eternal recurrence of the same; and it seems to me not so much a theory of being, not so much a theory of the cosmos: it seems to me to be above all a moral theory. That is to say that our actions, our willing, our intentions, our thoughts should have such generosity and grandeur that we should be able and willing to repeat them over and over again *ad infinitum*.

Magee That's bound, in spite of everything, to remind one of Kant's demand that all moral action should be universalisable. But I suppose in Nietzsche's case it's more akin to his doctrine that we should embrace life unconditionally. If you really are, in any given instant, saying an unequivocal Yes to life you would be willing to go on over and over again doing what you are doing in that instant, and only ever that.

Stern With whatever kind of consequence. Yes. To go very much further and try to produce geometrical or mathematical equations in order to prove either the possibility or the impossibility of this notion of the eternal recurrence, which has been tried, doesn't seem to me to be sensible.

Magee The whole thing, really, is a huge metaphor, isn't it?

Stern It *is* a huge metaphor: and, of course, a great deal must be said about Nietzsche's use of metaphor.

Magee Please say some of it now.

Stern I think we are in the habit of taking things literally in a way which doesn't make sense as far as a great many of Nietzsche's statements are concerned. You spoke earlier about his style, and I think it is an extraordinarily powerful, effective style. If I ask myself where it derives from, I think it derives from a strange invention or discovery he seems to have made of how to place his discourse somewhere half-way between metaphor and literal meaning. And this is something which very few people, certainly very few German writers, have done before him. As far as thinking is concerned, he stands entirely on his own – you have mentioned that, and we've seen how he attacks every tradition of the West. Where he finds precursors is in his style: Montaigne, Pascal and La Rochefoucauld are his favourite authors, and his whole aphoristic style derives a lot from them. And it's not only me saying this; he himself says so. This style, which is pitched half-way between metaphor and literal statement, is something quite extraordinary. And I think that unless we understand it for what it is, we are going to misread him. I have a quotation in mind which gives an example of what I mean. When he talked about the terrible deprivation that nineteenth-century people experienced through what he called luridly 'the death of God', he wrote as follows: 'Rather than cope with the unbearable loneliness of their condition men will continue to seek their shattered God, and for His sake they will love the very serpents that dwell among His ruins.' Now you see this mixture of, on the one hand, conceptual thinking – 'loneliness' and 'condition' are abstract terms belonging to conceptual thought, and the entire argument is part of a historical generalisation – with, on the other hand, serpents glistening through the ruins of the shattered God. Well that, and the refusal to go beyond that – the refusal to write out the theory behind the metaphors – essentially constitutes what he's about.

Magee But it does give readers a serious problem. This fusion of poetry and metaphor on the one hand with intellectual concepts on the other means that you never know quite where you have him. You can't make his writings stand up in terms of rigorous intellectual argument, because then they all come apart at the joints, which are the images. But if you take everything as poetic utterance then it's often unclear and highly disputable what it is he is saying. But perhaps this leads us to the fourth of our four themes. We've talked very briefly about the will to power, about the Superman, and about the doctrine of eternal recurrence: the fourth theme was Nietzsche's idea that life is to be understood aesthetically. I suppose the point here is that if there is nothing outside this world – no God, and no transcendent realm of any kind – then life cannot have any purpose outside or beyond itself. Whatever meaning or justification it has must come from within itself: it must exist purely for its own sake, and have import on its own terms alone. All this makes it rather like a gigantic work of art.

Stern   Well, that certainly is a fair way of coming close to what he's after. In the very first of his books, *The Birth of Tragedy*, he uses this phrase three times: 'It is only as an aesthetic phenomenon that the being of man and the world are eternally justified.' It's a complicated sentence, and I don't think I want to go into all the details of it. But what he's saying, essentially, is this: the greatness of the early Greeks, of the pre-Socratics, lay in their tragedy. Their tragedy was a way of facing the worst aspects of human life, its transitoriness, its impermanence, its curruptness, its dependence upon forces greater than ourselves; and their highest achievement was their gift of making of these things a major tale, a story, a wonderful tragedy. This he applies in the largest and most cosmic possible sense. He's asking, as indeed Shakespeare did occasionally: Is the whole world really to be taken seriously, or is it not a great game, a great play, some kind of drama played out by we do not know whom, as a spectacle for we do not know whom? If there is to be a justification – mind you, 'justification' is the word he uses, which is a very dicey word to use in this context (it's a judicial phrase, isn't it?) – if there's to be a justification for man being here, and being what he is, maybe it is simply as part of this huge cosmic drama. A great deal of Nietzsche's thought, some of his most interesting and greatest thought, goes into rehearsing and trying to make sense of this aesthetic justification of man.

Magee   So there is more than one level, then, on which aesthetic considerations are fused into the substance of Nietzsche's thought. I'm in no doubt that this is one reason why it has had such enormous influence on creative artists. Since your special field of expertise is comparative literature, it would be particularly interesting if you would end our discussion with a word or two about ways in which Nietzsche has influenced creative writers.

Stern   Well, to take the three names that you yourself mentioned: Yeats, Shaw and Lawrence. Yeats read Nietzsche for the first time in a little book of excerpts translated by a man called John Common, of all things – a most inappropriate name for a translator of Nietzsche. And from 1902, when Yeats read him, onwards, there is a clear change in the general tenor and attitude of Yeats's poetry. That slightly sultry, slightly sentimental, yellow-roses kind of poetry of the *fin de siècle* Yeats changes, and the great poetry, which is (as Yeats himself calls it) the poetry of blood and mire, is strongly influenced by his reading of Nietzsche, in fact by his attempts to grasp some of the problems we were discussing earlier. With Shaw, the influence is a different one. It is very much in the biological sphere, the sphere of that *élan vital* which I mentioned before – the sphere of the ruthless life, the life that justifies itself. With D. H. Lawrence, on the other hand, it is the question of authenticity. Authenticity as Lawrence conceives it is a very different kind of authenticity from what Nietzsche had in mind: it's social and sexual, and of course both of these are minor factors in Nietzsche. It was through his wife, Frieda, that Lawrence acquired some knowledge of Nietzsche and was so deeply influenced by him. A very late, and I think rather dreadful, Christ story of Lawrence's called *The Man Who Died* seems to me to derive straight from Nietzsche's psychologising of the Christ figure. But now, if we look on the Continent, Pirandello, Thomas Mann, André Malraux, and many other writers have been strongly under Nietzsche's influence, and have acknowledged that influence. Strindberg had a correspondence, most of it through a common friend, with Nietzsche. There are also immensely powerful influences emanating from the Nietzsche myth that came into being after he died in 1900. But we have also to bear in mind that the aphoristic style, the tremendous attractiveness of the metaphors, the brevity of the message – literary persons don't like to read heavy books: they like to read aphorisms – all these play very much into Nietzsche's hand.

Magee There is one final question, a question which I don't think we can finish our discussion without raising, and it concerns the association in people's minds between Nietzsche and Nazism. The Nazis appropriated – or I would rather say misappropriated – Nietzsche as their house philosopher in much the same way as they misappropriated Wagner as their house composer; and it has had the effect ever since of contaminating the reputation of those two geniuses in the minds of many people. Is it fair, or is it unfair, to associate Nietzsche with Fascism?

Stern I think he must be associated with it to some extent – and Fascism rather than National Socialism. Mussolini read him extensively, and received a copy of the *Collected Works* as a present from the Führer on the Brenner Pass in 1938. Hitler himself probably knew mere phrases – I mean he certainly knew phrases like 'the will to power' – but probably hadn't *read* anything of Nietzsche's. I think in some ways the charge of association with Fascism is a justifiable charge. I would put it this way. To the extent that these political parties depended upon their intellectuals, and to the extent that the intellectuals depended upon some sort of

ill-assorted ideology, Nietzsche was a part of it. But at the same time –
and it's to be emphasised very strongly – there are lots of things in him,
and much more important things in him, which are absolute anathema to
those people, to those gangsters (let's put it quite plainly). Self-control,
and the inward struggle of the self, and the attainment of values – of
generosity for instance – and greatness, of the kind we have described,
have nothing whatever to do with the murderous ideologies that came
into being in the Third Reich, and earlier on among the Italians.

Magee   From the fact that you yourself have devoted so much of your life
to studying and writing about Nietzsche nothing could be plainer than
that you believe doing so to be a hugely valuable undertaking, in spite of
his shortcomings.

Stern   Yes. I certainly think it is an immensely valuable undertaking,
providing we do not go to it with some expectation of getting a panacea,
but go to it with a view to finding out what human beings can do, what
human possibility is, what man is capable of understanding and creating
from within himself alone.

HUSSERL, HEIDEGGER and MODERN EXISTENTIALISM

Dialogue with HUBERT DREYFUS

INTRODUCTION

Magee One philosopher active earlier in this century who was much more important than his reputation outside the subject might suggest was a German called Edmund Husserl, who was born in 1859 and died in 1938. His acknowledged masterpiece is a book called *Logical Investigations*, published in two volumes in 1900 and 1901. Among his other books, *Ideas*, published in 1913, also deserves special mention. Husserl's basic approach was something like this. For each one of us there is one thing that is undubitably certain, and that is our own conscious awareness. Therefore if we want to build our knowledge of reality on rock-solid foundations that is the place to start. Up to this point, obviously, Husserl is in agreement with Descartes. However, as soon as we analyse our conscious awareness we discover that it always is, and can only be, awareness *of something*. Consciousness has to be consciousness of something, it cannot just exist by itself as an object-less state of mind. Furthermore, we find in practice that we are never able to distinguish *in experience* between states of consciousness and objects of consciousness: conceptually we can draw the distinction, but in our actual experience, however attentive, they are indistinguishable. At this point Husserl finds himself in agreement with Hume. But now he makes an original move. Sceptics down the ages have argued that we can never know whether the objects of our consciousness have a separate existence from us, independent of our experience of them, and argument over the question has raged for hundreds if not thousands of years. Husserl points out that there can be absolutely no doubt whatsoever that the objects of our consciousness do exist *as objects of consciousness for us*, whatever other existential status they may have or lack, and therefore that we can investigate them as such without making any assumptions at all, positive or negative, about their independent existence. What is more, we have the most direct and immediate access to them that we have to anything, and therefore we should be in a position to find out more about them than about anything else. This investigation can proceed in complete independence of unanswerable questions about the separate existence of its objects. Such questions can simply be left on one side (put in brackets, so to speak) with the result that philosophers, instead of being stuck for ever in the same impasse, ought to be able to make rapid and worthwhile progress.

Thus Husserl launched a whole new school of philosophy, which was devoted to the systematic analysis of consciousness and its objects. It was known as Phenomenology – and one use of that term 'phenomenology' continues to this day to refer to an analysis of whatever it is that is experienced, regardless of whether there is any sense in which matters *objectively are* as we experience them. Direct experience, of course, includes not only material objects but a great many different sorts of abstract entity; not only our own thoughts, pains, emotions, memories and so on, but music, mathematics, and a host of other things. With all of them the question of their independent existential status is bracketed: they are investigated exclusively as *contents of conscious awareness*, which indubitably they are.

One of Husserl's followers, Martin Heidegger, struck out on his own with a book called *Being and Time*, which was published in 1927 and dedicated to Husserl. This book became the fountainhead of twentieth-century existentialism, although in fact Heidegger never liked having the label 'existentialist' attached to him. He went on to produce a lot more philosophical work in the course of a long life – he died in 1976 at the age of eighty-six – and a good deal of it is influential, but *Being and Time* remains his masterpiece. Other existentialist thinkers, especially Jean-Paul Sartre, have become better known to the general public and done more to propagate existentialist ideas outside the confines of academic philosophy, but Heidegger was always very much their master. Even the title of Sartre's chief philosophical work, *Being and Nothingness* (published in 1943), is an allusion to, and acknowledgement of, Heidegger's *Being and Time*.

So here we have a clearcut line of philosophical development, passing from Husserl to Heidegger and from Heidegger to Sartre. And perhaps we might mention one other figure, Maurice Merleau-Ponty, who in 1945 published an important book called *The Phenomenology of Perception*. At one time Merleau-Ponty and Sartre were great friends: together they founded and edited the influential journal *Les Temps Modernes*. But Merleau-Ponty died early, at the age of only fifty-three, in 1961.

To discuss with me this major tradition within modern philosophy I have invited Hubert Dreyfus, Professor of Philosophy at the University of California in Berkeley.

DISCUSSION

Magee I started by conceding that Husserl is not well known outside academic philosophy. Can you launch our discussion by explaining how it is that someone who is so little known generally is of such importance within philosophy?

Dreyfus Husserl was important in a reactionary way: that is, he was the culmination of a whole philosophical tradition, the Cartesian tradition that thinks of man's relationship to the world in terms of subjects knowing objects. In fact Husserl thought he was the culmination of the whole philosophical tradition from Plato on, because he had discovered the indubitable basis on which one could ground the intelligibility of everything. Setting himself up like that he plays a role similar to the role Hegel played in seeing himself as the culmination of idealism. Kierkegaard rebelled against Hegel in the name of existential-thinking, which developed into existentialism, and Marx set himself against Hegel in the name of dialectical materialism. Similarly, Husserl sets himself up at the very least as the culmination of Cartesianism – his last book is called *Cartesian Meditations* – and thanks to him thinkers like Heidegger and Merleau-Ponty came to see the limits of that tradition and rebel against *it*. Twentieth-century Continental philosophy is intelligible only with reference to Husserl.

Magee In my opening words I hadn't time to provide more than a sketch-map of Husserl's approach, but I think we now need something a little more substantial to get our teeth into. Can you fill out a bit more what I said?

Dreyfus Husserl's basic idea was that the mind is directed towards objects under aspects, so, for example, I am perceiving that object as a table seen from above. I can also remember it, have beliefs about it, desires concerning it and so on. Almost all my mental content is directed (headaches and moods excepted), and Husserl noted that directedness was a feature unique to the mind. The mind and nothing else in the universe has a directedness towards something outside itself, he held.

Magee There is a mystery here. How, if I think about some question concerning astronomy, is it possible for goings-on inside my skull to have a meaningful relationship to distant galaxies?

Dreyfus Husserl thought that was a *wunderbar* phenomenon, and he devoted his life to trying to understand it.
   The aboutness of mental content is called 'intentionality' in the tradition; not because it has to do with our intentions, but because it has to do with directedness. Husserl held that there must be some kind of content in the mind that accounted for this aboutness or directedness. This something in the mind, which he called 'intentional content', was like a description of reality, and it was by virtue of that description that I could perceive, desire, remember and so on, some object under some aspect. It was Husserl who made intentionality one of the main topics of philosophy ever since.

Magee What *use* did he make of his account of mental directedness?

Dreyfus He made of it an amazingly complex and comprehensive philosophical edifice, so impressive and encompassing that one would naturally want to react against it. He thought, and quite rightly, that it didn't matter to his account of intentionality whether there was a table out there or not. He could bracket the table. In fact he could bracket the whole world. All he needed to study was the fact that *he took it that* there was a table in a world of objects out there. He thus performed what he called 'the phenomenological reduction'. He reflected on his own intentional content, and that gave him an indubitable basis to start from. It was not just that he had some kind of everyday empirical evidence that he took there to be a table out there in the world. As he put it, he had indubitable evidence that he had himself produced. In taking there to be a table there he knew he was taking there to be a table there. How else could he do it? Nothing could be more evident. He could not be wrong about that. Secondly, he could use the self-evident intentional content as an absolute ground for everything else. No one could experience anything – music, other people, tables, galaxies, as you mention – except by virtue of directed mental content. So Husserl felt justified in claiming that he had discovered the indubitable foundation of all understanding. Like Kant, he claimed he had discovered the condition of the possibility of anyone's being able to encounter anything at all; and like Descartes, he claimed he had direct evidence, not just transcendental arguments. He found all that by describing the way self-contained, conscious subjects are directed towards objects.

Magee And in doing that, as you say, he was the culmination of the whole Descartes-Hume-Kant tradition of philosophy, which sees the fundamental human situation as that of a subject in a world of objects. But it was this very fundamental conception that Heidegger reacted against, wasn't it?

Dreyfus That's right. That Cartesian tradition became so clear and so powerful with Husserl that Heidegger was driven to ask whether the subject–object relation really was an adequate description of our relation to things. Does our basic way of encountering things and people require subjective experience? Husserl kept saying we must do phenomenology, that is, let things show themselves as they are in themselves; and when Heidegger actually looked at the way people are related to things he found that it was not normally as *subjects* related to *objects*. Awareness and consciousness did not play a necessary role at all. Now that seems very strange. How could it be? Well, Heidegger was good at finding simple illustrations. In this case he took, as his example, hammering. When an expert carpenter is hammering – if the hammer is working well, and he is a master at what he is doing – the hammer becomes transparent for him. He is not a subject directed towards the object, hammer. He does not have to think about it at all. He might be paying attention to the nails, but if he is really good and the nails are going in well he does not have to pay attention to them either. He can think about lunch, or he can talk to some fellow carpenter, and his hammering simply goes on in a 'transparent coping' mode. Heidegger calls this kind of everyday skilful coping 'primordial understanding', and the entities thus encountered 'ready-to-hand'. When we look at our ready-to-hand way of being with things we just do not find conscious subjects directed towards independent objects at all.

Magee This is in such profound contrast to the traditional approach in philosophy that I think it is worth recapitulating it, just to make quite sure we are getting it clear. From Descartes onwards philosophers had thought of the human being as a subject in a world of objects, and because of that the central philosophical problems came to be seen as those concerning perception and knowledge. How do we as subjects gain knowledge of the objects that constitute the world? . . . Can such knowledge ever be certain? . . . On what would such certainty be grounded? . . . and so on. Now Heidegger is saying that these questions are fundamentally misconceived. Or rather, to be more accurate, he concedes that they may legitimately arise at some secondary level of concern, but he considers it a profound misconception to regard them as being the most important questions. Primarily, and in our most characteristic modes of being, we humans are not subjects, spectators, observers, separated by an invisible plate-glass window from the world of objects in which we find ourselves. We are not detached from some external reality which is 'out there', trying to gain knowledge of it as something categorially different from ourselves, and trying to relate to it. On the contrary, we are part and parcel of it all, and from the very beginning we are in amongst it all, being in it, coping with it. In consequence we are not in any primary sense 'observing subjects' or 'knowing beings' in the way traditional philosophers have regarded us. What we are, characteristically, are coping beings – or even, one might feel tempted to say, *being* beings. We are beings in amongst and inseparable from a world of being, existences in an existing world, and it is from there that we start.

Dreyfus That's right. Gilbert Ryle put it well when he reviewed *Being and Time*. He reviewed both *Being and Time* and Husserl's *Logical Investigations*. He thought they were both important, but he thought Heidegger was on to something especially interesting. Ryle distinguished knowing-that, which is what the tradition has always been interested in, from knowing-how, which is what he took Heidegger to be describing. Heidegger is not merely claiming the primacy of practical activity. The pragmatists have claimed that too. Heidegger offers a phenomenological analysis of everyday masterful, practical know-how that dispenses altogether with the need for mental states like desiring, believing, following a rule, and so on, *and thus with their intentional content*.

Husserl, of course, tried to absorb hammering into his subject-object

Edmund Husserl (1859–1938)

model of mental activity. Before I can use something as a hammer, I first
have to take it to be a hammer, Husserl said. But Heidegger observed
that picking up a hammer could be transparent too, and countered with
another simple example. He said to his students, in effect: 'When you
come into the classroom you must turn the door-knob, but you don't
perceive the door-knob, take it to be a door-knob, believe that you have
to turn it to get in, try to turn it, etc. All we observe is, here you are in the
classroom and you couldn't have gotten here without turning the door-
knob. You have no memory of doing so because the whole activity is so
transparent it does not have to pass through consciousness.' We might
add that a driver has the same experience shifting from first to second
gear. He does a lot of fancy footwork with the clutch, but he may, at the
same time, be absorbed in a deep philosophical conversation. His coping
need not enter consciousness.

Magee Although these examples may seem mundane, what they
illustrate is of the utmost importance. They show that much if not most
characteristic human activity is not guided by conscious choices, and not
accompanied by aware states of mind. And that is of great significance
because, among other things, it pulls the rug out from under some of the
most securely accepted analyses of human behaviour.

Dreyfus That's right. Heidegger didn't want to deny that there is a place
for contemplation and consciously directed action, but first and foremost
we are coping beings already involved in the world. If something goes
wrong, however, for instance in the hammer case, if the hammer is too
heavy, then I will notice this aspect. I'll become the sort of problem-
solving subject dear to the tradition. I'll become a rational animal. I'll
direct my mind to the problem, figure out that for this task the hammer is
too heavy, and conclude that another hammer may work better. This
kind of Aristotelian practical logic has its place. Likewise, if the door-
knob sticks I have to *try* to turn the door-knob. But it is a retrospective
illusion to suppose I was trying all along. Heidegger calls the way things
show up for us when there is a problem the 'unready-to-hand', and he
thinks that's the level at which Husserl starts doing his phenomenology –
one crucial stage too late.

    While we are at it, there is yet another way things can be encountered
which Heidegger calls the 'present-at-hand'. It is important too. We can
get in a stance of just staring at an object. If the head flies off the hammer,
for instance, or if the nails are missing, or if we are just feeling in a mood
of contemplation, we can see the hammer as a wooden shank with an iron
blob on the end. Then we see a substance with properties. That's the level
philosophers have studied. There's a whole logic of grammatical subjects
and their predicates worked out in what's called the predicate calculus.

That has its place, Heidegger would say, but that's at third remove from everyday coping. It leaves out the practical situation in which things function and can break down. For this third – objective – way of encountering, the hammer isn't even a broken hammer. It's just a piece of wood with metal on the end. And that's important too, Heidegger would say, because context-independent statements like 'the object weighs one kilogramme' can be related by laws in science and theory, and Heidegger had nothing against science and theory. He offers in *Being and Time* what he calls an existential account of the place of science and its objective predicates and laws in the rest of human practices. What's important to him is to show that to get to the predicates and laws of science you have to leave out the level of practical coping in the world. So you shouldn't expect that scientific theory, which can explain context-free causal relations very well, could ever explain the everyday meaningful world of significance that Heidegger describes. And, of course, Husserl's notion of mental content can't account for this everyday world either.

Magee In effect, what you are saying is that in most cases in our ordinary everyday life we direct our full conscious attention at things only when something goes wrong, when a specific problem arises. But that is not the case for most of the time, and therefore not our characteristic state of mind. Most of the time we are borne along in a life-medium which we take for granted, and are not conscious of, and don't direct our attention to. One consequence of this for Heidegger is that, unlike many traditional philosophers, he does not see the world as something whose existence needs to be inferred, with the further consequence that such inference requires validation. We are used to the traditionally formulated problem of my having immediate access only to the contents of my mind, and having then to infer from these contents the existence of a world external to myself – which I then find cannot be securely done. Heidegger says: But no, that is not actually the problem-situation. For me the world can never be something I infer, still less something I need to infer. I *start* with it, in it, of it.

Dreyfus Right again. Philosophers since Descartes had been trying to prove the existence of the external world. Kant said that it was a scandal that no one had successfully done it. Heidegger in *Being and Time* retorts: The scandal is that philosophers keep trying to prove the existence of the external world, as if we were stuck with some *internal* world and couldn't get out. Instead, philosophers should see that in our everyday transparent coping we don't need mental content and are, as he puts it, 'always already being-in-the-world'. I think I should explain that a little further.

Any particular using of a hammer takes place on a whole background of skills, practices and equipment which Heidegger calls the world. The

Martin Heidegger (1889–1976)

hammer only makes sense in terms of nails and wood and houses – a totality of equipment, which Heidegger calls 'significance' – and my skill in hammering is only possible on a background of other skills, of standing and moving and wearing clothes, and talking and so forth. So it's only on the background of the world and my capacities for being in that world, or really being *of* that world, that anything gets encountered at all. What makes possible my relation to objects, then, is not something *in* my mind, as Husserl held, but something *outside* my mind – the world of shared things and practices. Heidegger calls the shared meaning in our shared practices our understanding of being. And, since this understanding need not, and probably cannot, be mirrored in the mind at all, he holds that philosophers should get over asking in a wholesale, sceptical way whether their mental content corresponds to what's out there. Not that we can't sometimes think and say things which correspond to an independent reality – physicists do so, and so does the man in the street – but our mental content can only correspond to what is out there on a background of skills and practices which is not itself mental content and for which all talk of whether it corresponds or fails to correspond to something else is inappropriate.

Magee These considerations led Heidegger to formulate a view not just of the human situation but of human beings themselves, of what they are, which is radically different from the traditional philosopher's. Can you introduce us to what that is?

Dreyfus Well, certainly he can't begin with subjects or persons, or minds, or consciousness. He needs a new way to refer to our ongoing activity on the background of our shared understanding of being. He chooses brilliantly to use the word '*Dasein*'. In German the word '*Dasein*' means simply 'existence', as in man's everyday existence. But it also means, if you take it apart, 'being-there'. This conveys that this activity of human being is an activity of being the situation in which coping can go on and things can be encountered.

Magee How can I be a situation?

Dreyfus When I'm driving – if we consider that aspect of me which is coping, not my physical body – being-there is actively being taken up into the situation in which my directed activity is going on. My skills are completely geared into the situation. Heidegger says cryptically: '*Dasein* is its world existingly'. That's a completely new understanding of what it is to be a human being. Moreover, *Dasein*, like 'human being', can be used to refer to a general way of being and also to refer to a single human being – an instance of that activity. Heidegger uses *Dasein* both ways, which enables him to talk of us sometimes as completely absorbed in the shared situation and sometimes as standing back as an individual contemplating what is going on – always on a shared background, of course.

Magee In the end, the analysis he comes out with of the way of being that we are relates it in its very essence to time, doesn't it? Hence the title of his most famous book. Can you explain for us what that relationship is?

Dreyfus Yes, we'd better spell that out. Another word Heidegger uses for human being as an openness to things in a situation is 'clearing'. We are the activity of holding open a shared clearing in which entities can be encountered. Of course, in opposition to Husserl, Heidegger holds that it is the understanding of being in the shared, public clearing that makes possible the individual activity of clearing. This activity has a three-fold structure. First, Heidegger says *Dasein* has what he calls attunement, the best example of which is mood. Thanks to this basic characteristic of *Dasein* things show up as mattering – as threatening, or attractive, or stubborn, or useful, and so forth. The tradition has generally overlooked this kind of significance, Heidegger thinks, because it doesn't easily fall into knowing or desiring – contemplation or interest – but is presupposed as the background for both. Because we have this basic way of being, called attunement, our situation always already matters to us in some way. Moreover, moods are not essentially private mental states. Crowds have moods, companies have cultures, whole ages have sensibilities. Individual moods are picked up from what the society has to offer. Of course, we can't get behind our moods – can't start from no mood and then step into one.

The second structural component of *Daseining* – remember it is important to hear *Dasein* as a verb – Heidegger calls 'discourse'. The term is a bit misleading since, according to Heidegger, discourse is more basic than language, but his choice of the term can be explained as an illuminating pun. The world is always already *articulated*. That is, everything is always laid out as a context of functional relations. Various pieces of equipment must interrelate if I am to be able to use any particular piece. Human being has always already articulated the world – that is, broken it up at its joints – and we take over this articulation when we use a piece of equipment. If, out of this totality which Heidegger calls 'the referential totality of significance', I pick up a hammer, I can articulate *its* significance as a hammer by hammering with it, or I can articulate it as a nail puller by pulling a nail. Of course, I can also talk about what I am doing, I can say the nail was easy to hammer or to pull out. Then I will be articulating even further what I have already articulated. All these modes of laying things out are called discourse. Discourse is the articulation of the situation in which we currently find ourselves.

The third aspect of *Dasein* which has been implicit in what we've been saying is that *Dasein* is always pressing into new possibilities. If I'm hammering a nail it's in order, say, to repair a house, for the sake of my job as a carpenter, or perhaps as a homemaker. *Dasein* always uses equipment in order to pursue what philosophers would regard as a goal. Heidegger calls what our activity is directed towards a 'towards-which'. And since I act for the sake of achieving some life plan, Heidegger calls this final towards-which a 'for-the-sake-of'. Now it's important that Heidegger does not speak of goals and life plans. His funny language is necessary because a goal is what you have in mind, as is a life plan, whereas Heidegger wants to point out that in everyday transparent, skilled coping, *Dasein* is simply oriented toward the future, doing something now in order to be in a position to do something else later on, and all this makes sense as oriented toward something which that person is finally up to but need not have, and probably cannot have, in mind. Moreover, what it makes sense to do at any moment depends on the background of shared for-the-sake-ofs available in the culture. By the time we have *Dasein* in us we have already been socialised into some set of for-the-sake-ofs. That is part of what it means for an organism to have *Dasein* in it. So *Dasein* is always already in a space of possibilities offered by the culture, and it normally presses forward into one of these possibilities without standing back and choosing what to do. All this Heidegger calls understanding.

This three-fold structure – being already in a mood so things matter, using things so as to articulate their capacities, and pressing into new possibilities – is the structure of *Dasein* itself. In the second division of *Being and Time* this three-fold structure of being-in-a-situation turns out to be equivalent to the past, present and future dimensions of time itself.

Magee In fact Heidegger seems to me to end up saying that being *is* time. We are, he is virtually saying, embodied time.

Dreyfus *Dasein* in his language is care, and the structure of care is temporality. This is the first step toward understanding the basic connection between being and time.

Magee Up to this point we have talked all the while about the individual human being, *Dasein* in the singular; and everything you have said so far applies to that conception. But there is more than one human being in the world, of course, and no one who is not mad supposes himself to be the only one. How does the analysis you have given us so far accommodate the others? Where do all those millions of other *Daseins* come in?

Dreyfus Well, it's very important that they come in from the very start.

Cartesians like Husserl start with an autonomous, isolated subject, so they have the same sceptical problem about the reality of other minds as they have about the external world. Heidegger starts in an entirely different way, closer to the phenomena, which saves him from this problem. We become *Dasein*, or get *Dasein* in us, only when we get socialised into shared coping skills, moods, possibilities and so on. *Dasein* is always already being-with. Moreover, since these skills are social, a *Dasein* generally does what anyone in the society does. I hammer with a hammer because one hammers with hammers in our culture. I eat the way one eats. I pronounce words the way one pronounces words in our country. . . .

Magee And it's necessary that you should, because otherwise you wouldn't be understood. . . .

Dreyfus That's right. People can't stand distance from the norm, Heidegger says. For example, people subtly lead other people to correct their pronunciation. No one has to be coerced to do things as one does them. People are eager not to deviate from the norm. It's a basic fact about human beings which philosophers have not noted. Heidegger never talks about how people develop, but we could clarify his point by saying that only when a baby starts doing what one does, and saying what one says, does the baby have *Dasein* in it. So conformity to public norms is constitutive of *Dasein*. Of course, this need not mean doing what the masses do. Heidegger says at one point: We flee from the crowd the way one flees from the crowd. Even when we flee from the crowd, we do so the way one does. So finally Heidegger says about *Dasein*: One is what one does, or *Dasein*'s self is a one's self.

Magee If we juxtapose some of the various points you've made, the resultant picture could be very disquieting. Earlier, you were saying that Heidegger repudiates the idea that most of our activity is directed by mentally aware reflection, or by conscious choice or decision. Now you are saying that we simply do what one does, and have very little real latitude. Don't these doctrines, taken together, reduce the human agent to some sort of zombie, someone whose mode of being is simply to respond to the pressures on him from outside in an unreflecting way?

Dreyfus That's quite right – this self that just does in an unreflective way what one normally does sounds pretty zombie-like. But Heidegger is trying to avoid the Cartesian/Husserlian problems which arise from starting with isolated, individual selves by explaining things the other way round. He starts with the conforming public self and then tries to show how autonomous individuals crystallise out of this rather amorphous public us. That's the subject of division two of *Being and Time* – the question of authenticity. This is the part of Heidegger which was taken up by the existentialists. In division two, Heidegger talks about favourite existentialist themes such as guilt, death, falling and levelling, which I don't have time to go into here. In any case guilt and death turn out to be versions of anxiety, so we had better talk about anxiety. *Dasein*, according to Heidegger, any *Dasein*, is always dimly aware that the way the world is is ungrounded. By that I mean there is no *reason* one has to do things the way one does. God has not ordered us to do things this way, nor does human nature require it. Heidegger expresses this existentialist view by saying that the essence of *Dasein* is its existence. This means there is no human nature, we are what we take ourselves to be – how we interpret ourselves in our practices. But that is rather unsettling. '*Unheimlich*' – not being at home – is his precise word for it. Anxiety is our response to the fundamentally unsettling character of being-there, and the question then is 'What do we do about it?' Well, we can either flee anxiety, in which case we go back to the kind of conformity which is required of everyone if they are to be intelligible. We do what one does and talk as one talks, but we use these norms to flee unsettledness. We become conformists. We can try desperately to shape up to the norms, to pronounce things the right way, dress the right way, etc. That's how one flees into inauthenticity. That would be in effect disowning what it is to be *Dasein*. Or we can own up to what it is to be *Dasein*. To own up means, for Heidegger, to hold on to anxiety rather than flee it. If you *choose* to do that – and, in anxiety, your normal unreflective pressing into possibilities has broken down, so you do have to make a reflective choice – you will be thrown into an entirely different way of being human. *What* you do needn't change, and it can't change much, since you can only do what one does or else you'd just be kooky and insane. So you probably go on doing the same thing you did, but *how* you do it changes radically. You no longer expect to get any deep, final meaning out of life or find any rational grounding for anything. So you don't embrace projects with the conviction that now at last this is going to make sense of your life, and you also don't drop projects because they fail to provide the ultimate meaning you're looking for. As one of my students once said, 'You are able to stick with things without getting stuck with them.'

In this authentic activity, Heidegger says, you no longer respond to what he calls the general situation. You respond to the unique situation. He doesn't give any examples, but I take it to be something like this. Take the carpenter Heidegger talks about. When he puts down his hammer at lunch time, he could just eat his sausages and sauerkraut, but if there are beautiful flowers blooming outdoors, and he's authentic, he doesn't have to conform to what a respectable carpenter normally does. He can skip lunch and go out and wander in the flowers. But it's important to remember that he can do only what one does. He can't take off all those clothes and roll in the flowers. One doesn't do that. But there's still space for authenticity, namely, doing the sort of thing that one does in a way that allows a response to the unique situation without concern for respectability and conformity. That kind of life, not trying to get absolute meaning, and responding to the current situation, makes you an individual and no longer zombie-like. Heidegger says it makes you flexible, alive, joyous. That is his idea of how one should live.

Magee You are now, contrary to before, making it sound like a philosophy of personal liberation.

Dreyfus But it's an *existential* liberation philosophy, which makes it the last and strangest of liberation philosophies. We don't liberate, say, sexual drives, or repressed classes. The liberation comes from realising that there's no deep truth in the individual subject, as in Freud, no subject of history, as in Marx, to liberate – no meaning in *Dasein* at all. Rather, bravely accepting the unsettling groundlessness of *Dasein* is what is liberating.

Magee Throughout this discussion you've used some very strange terms – not only '*Dasein*' but terms like 'the unready-to-hand' and 'attunement'. You've talked of one's being a situation and calling a towards-which a for-the-sake-of. You've said things like '*Dasein* is its world existingly'. For most readers of the early Heidegger – and everything we've discussed so far is in *Being and Time* – this vocabulary becomes very difficult indeed to cope with. In fact, I have to say that *Being and Time* is among the most difficult books to read and understand that I ever have struggled through. It is so obscure that many people have taken it to be without any serious content at all. This is far from being the case, as you have made abundantly clear. And that is now my point. You, unlike Heidegger, have succeeded in making clear the ideas involved. What prevented Heidegger from doing the same? Why did he have to be so obscure?

Dreyfus Well, the answer is implied in what I have been doing. If Heidegger could have written a conversation in which he could use a misleading everyday or philosophical term to get across his general idea and then back off and use the right word to fit the phenomenon, that probably would have been the best thing to do. For instance, I talked about goals, and then said, but of course goals are mental and most of the time we have no goals in mind. The same holds for life plans, which are not really plans. Then I introduced Heidegger's peculiar language: the towards-whiches, and the for-the-sake-ofs, to refer to non-mental goals and plans. Similarly we have to have a term of art like '*Dasein*' to point up that we are always a shared, social, situated way of being, and only sometimes a conscious subject directed towards objects. In general, Heidegger would say, the whole philosophical tradition has passed over the world and our usual kind of involved coping with the world, not only because it's something you don't notice if everything is going well, but also because we have no language for it. We need language for pointing out things in the world, for calling attention to a stuck door-knob and asking for a lighter hammer if the hammer we are using is too heavy. We don't normally need language to describe the kind of being we are when everything is going transparently well, let alone for describing the taken-for-granted, shared, background understanding in our everyday practices. So Heidegger would say he has to make up a whole new vocabulary for this. Once you get into it, his seems to be an appropriate and economical vocabulary, and he uses it rigorously. Once he has introduced a new term like 'ready-to-hand', or 'present-at-hand', or 'being-in-the-world', he sticks to it.

Magee Let us move on from *Being and Time* to Heidegger's later philosophy. When *Being and Time* was first published it was presented as the first volume of what was to be a two-volume work. But volume two never came out. It is often said that this is because Heidegger changed his views in a way that made it impossible for him to complete his project. This change of view is frequently referred to in the Heidegger literature and even has a name: it is called '*die Kehre*', the turn. When people talk about 'the later Heidegger' they are referring to the work he did after the turn, and of course 'the early Heidegger' refers to his work before the turn. So far, what you and I have been discussing is the early Heidegger, which is still far and away the more influential part of his output – though, who knows, the later work may one day supersede it. What are the real grounds of difference between the early and the late Heidegger?

Dreyfus There are many different interpretations of Heidegger's 'turn'. It's not a settled question among Heidegger scholars. Some say he went from advocating a resolute, active grasping of things to proposing a kind of passive openness. Others say he shifted from individual to cultural concerns. I think that is all true, but I don't think that's the essence of the shift. At one point he says clearly that he has changed from transcendental interpretation (hermeneutics) to thinking being historically. Historical thinking is what is new. You can see that he wasn't doing it before. Everything I've explained so far was supposed to be about the structure of all human beings anywhere, any time. Even anxiety was supposed to be a universal human experience of unsettledness which every person in every culture at every time either fled from or faced up to.

Jean-Paul Sartre (1905–80)

Later Heidegger sees that our Western understanding of being has a history, and that he had been talking about only the modern epoch, without realising it. He begins to try to describe the epoch before Plato when the Greeks still felt rooted – weren't yet unsettled and anxious. Things showed up for them as produced by man and by nature and they received them with appreciation. Later Christian practices embodied the understanding that all things were creatures, so they could read God's plan off the world. While we, with our modern understanding of being, show up as subjects with desires to be satisfied by objects which are to be controlled and used. Even more recently, Heidegger says, we are beginning to understand everything, even ourselves, as resources to be enhanced and used efficiently. These are all different understandings of what it is to be a thing, what it is to be a person, what it is to be an institution. Heidegger would say they are different understandings of what it is to be, and that when the understanding of what it is to be changes, different sorts of human beings and things show up. For the Greeks of Homer's time and before, heroes showed up, and marvellous things. For the Christians, saints and sinners, rewards and temptations showed up. You can't have saints in ancient Greece. They would just have been weak people who let everybody walk all over them. Likewise, you could not have Greek-style heroes in the Middle Ages. They would have been prideful sinners who disrupted society by denying their dependence on God. So in different epochs of our culture different sorts of people and things show up, and the later Heidegger thinks he should call attention to this underlying changing understanding of being.

One of the ways you can see this change in his philosophy is that the later Heidegger no longer takes anxiety to be a universal structure. The early Greeks didn't experience anxiety in the face of meaninglessness. The Christians didn't either. The later Heidegger thinks our modern experience of anxiety results from what he sees as our rootless, nihilistic, technological understanding of being.

The later Heidegger historises every aspect of human being discussed in *Being and Time*, even the being of equipment. In this way he becomes less like Kant and more like Hegel. Except that unlike Hegel he saw the history of the West as a steady decline in which we have gradually lost an appreciation of beings as independent of our control – something still understood by the pre-Socratic Greeks. We also fail to realise that the understanding of being itself is *given* to human beings. In Heidegger's language it is sent by being itself, which means, I think, that it shows up in our practices. We don't produce it. It produces us as the kind of human beings we are. No philosopher before him, Heidegger thinks, understood this, but at least the pre-Socratics didn't deny it as philosophers from Descartes to Nietzsche have done. Heidegger holds that this movement toward the forgetting of the understanding of being in our practices, which great philosophers have reflected and contributed to, was not necessary. It was the result of many historical accidents, but each stage was necessary before the next could occur.

Magee This change of focus from what Heidegger regarded, at least at the time, as the perennial and universal in human experience to what he himself sees as the contemporary and topical is surely a change from the permanent to the ephemeral? In a couple of hundred years' time, when our society will quite certainly have passed through radical changes from its present, I suspect that the later philosophy will have dated a great deal more than the earlier, and indeed that its concerns might have come to seem quite temporary and superficial.

Dreyfus Well, if this were any old culture, or even any old stage of our culture, Heidegger would agree that what he was doing would soon be passé, as you were saying; but he thinks that this is a unique culture, and that we are in a very special stage of this very special culture. We are the only culture that is historical. Of course, in any culture events follow one after another. But only in ours does the understanding of being change – from the Greeks, to the Christians, to the moderns, to us. That's historicity in Heidegger's language, and we happen to stand in a special place in the history of being. A misunderstanding of being as a general characteristic of all beings rather than as a clearing started with Plato 2,000 years ago. It has gone through many philosophical and practical transformations since then, and it is now 'finished', Heidegger says. That means all the philosophical moves have been tried and played out, completed, and now it's done for. Heidegger gets this idea from Nietzsche, whose claim that the God of philosophy and theology is dead convinced him that our recent understanding of being is nihilistic. We have reached the stage of control for its own sake. We are now taking over the whole planet, and we will eventually have to get over our need of God or of philosophical comfort and direction, Nietzsche thought. Heidegger adds that our understanding of being is wiping out every other understanding of being, and this technological understanding of being has reached a point where it no longer gives guidelines for action. Heidegger calls this nihilism.

Magee One often hears existentialists talk about 'the human predicament', and I take it that this, in essence, is what they are referring to. Does Heidegger point to any possible way out of it?

Dreyfus Well, it's first important to see what he means by nihilism. By nihilism he means that for us there are no meaningful differences any more. He doesn't use this expression, but he talks about how the Greek temple – which I would call a cultural paradigm – held up to the Greeks what was important, and so let there be heroes and villains, victory and disgrace, disaster and blessing and so on. People whose practices were manifest and focused by the temple had guidelines for leading good lives. In the same way the medieval cathedral – another cultural paradigm – showed people the dimensions of salvation and damnation, and one knew where one stood and what one had to do. But as our culture has developed, we have tended more and more to treat everything as an object, and flatten everything into one dimension. Since Plato, Heidegger would say, philosophers have always looked for the one stuff that everything can be understood in terms of, and tried to state the truth about that. That philosophical goal is both a reflection of and a cause of our current understanding of being in which everything is measured on one dimension. We don't even seek truth any more but simply efficiency. For us everything is to be made as flexible as possible so as to be used as efficiently as possible. If I had a styrofoam cup here, it would be a very good example. A styrofoam cup is a perfect sort of object, given our understanding of being, namely it keeps hot things hot, and cold things cold, and you can dispose of it when you are done with it. It efficiently and flexibly satisfies our desires. It's utterly different from, say, a Japanese tea-cup, which is delicate, traditional, and socialises people. It doesn't keep the tea hot for long, and probably doesn't satisfy anybody's desires, but that's not important. We went through a stage about a century ago when to be real or important things had to be useful for satisfying our desires. That was the subject–object stage. But now we are ourselves becoming resources in a cybernetic society where to be real is to be used as efficiently as possible. We want to fit into the system so as to get the most out of our possibilities. That's our understanding of being. I remember in the film *2001: A Space Odyssey*, Stanley Kubrick has the robot HAL, when asked if he is happy on the mission, say: 'I'm using all my capacities to the maximum. What more could a rational entity want?' A brilliant expression of what anybody would say who is in touch with our understanding of being. We thus become part of a system which no one directs but which moves towards the total mobilisation of all beings, even us, for their own welfare.

Heidegger would say that the problem is there are no guidelines any more. There are no goals. Why are we concerned with using our time more and more efficiently? To what end? Just to have time to organise our lives even more efficiently? Heidegger thinks there will soon be no meaningful differences, differences with content, any more, such as heroes and villains, or even differences like local and international, but only the more and more efficient ordering of everything, everywhere, just for the sake of more and more efficiency. That is what he means by nihilism.

Magee What you say leads me to repeat my question with all the more urgency: Is there no way out of this predicament?

Dreyfus Heidegger is not optimistic. He thinks we might be stuck in what he calls the darkest night for the rest of human history. But he isn't pessimistic either, since he thinks that the very lack of local concerns and meaningful differences might make us appreciate non-efficient practices – what he calls the saving power of insignificant things. I think he has in mind such things as friendship, backpacking into the wilderness, running, and so on. He mentions drinking the local wine with friends, and dwelling in the presence of works of art. All these practices are marginal precisely because they are not efficient. These practices can, of course, be engaged in for the sake of health and greater efficiency. That is the dark-night possibility. But these saving practices could come together in a new cultural paradigm, which held up to us a new way of doing things which made these practices central, and efficiency marginal. Rock concerts in the seventies were considered by some to offer hope of such an alternative paradigm. Such a new understanding, if it were to be saving, would have to lead us to appreciate again that human practices are special because they receive a changing, historical understanding of being. This is the one ahistorical truth about human beings which Heidegger recognises from start to finish. Such an understanding could go along with our still using our technological devices – Heidegger does not want to return to pre-Socratic Greece – just as the Japanese keep their VCRs and computers alongside their household gods and traditional tea-cups. Overcoming nihilism is a possibility for Heidegger precisely because it means getting over our technological understanding of being, not our technology.

Magee One aspect of the later Heidegger which we haven't touched on but ought to before we consider the existentialist thinkers after him is his concern with language. The later Heidegger is not just concerned with language, he is almost obsessed by it. Why?

Dreyfus We are in a way set to understand that. Since there is no way the human world is in itself, language need not – in fact, cannot – simply correspond to reality. But we can't just arbitrarily make up any old vocabulary either. Rather, language has the crucial role of reflecting and focusing the current practices in any epoch. It does the same job as a cultural paradigm. For Heidegger a vocabulary, or the kind of metaphors one uses, can name things into being and change the sensibility of an age. When in California somebody said that people were 'laid back', people were already soaking in hot tubs, taking it easy, and using drugs. Thanks to this new use of language they discovered that these practices fitted together. More people joined in, and more such practices developed. Language is a marvellously powerful way to preserve and extend practices by focusing them. For Heidegger it is the poets and thinkers, not the priests or scientists, who are receptive to, and use, new language and so promote and stabilise new ways of being. They alone offer hope of some new, non-individualistic, non-willful world.

Magee Your extraordinarily illuminating introduction to Heidegger's work reassures me that we have been right to devote most of this discussion to it. He is, it seems to me, without any serious question the most important existentialist philosopher of the twentieth century. But I did promise in my introduction that we would touch on others, and I think we must now do so. Those I mentioned specifically were Sartre and Merleau-Ponty, so let us take these two, and in that order, since it is in effect the chronological order. How would you characterise Sartre's career as a philosopher?

Dreyfus Sartre started out as a Husserlian, and as a phenomenologist he wrote a good novel called *Nausea*, which is a first-person description of a person's world breaking down. Then he read Heidegger and was converted to what he thought was Heideggerian existentialism. But as a Husserlian and a Frenchman he felt he had to fix up Heidegger and make him more Cartesian. So he starts with the individual conscious subject, but writes about Death, Anxiety, Inauthenticity, Being and Nothing – all the things that Heidegger talks about. The result, *Being and Nothingness*, is a brilliant misunderstanding of *Being and Time*. If the story that we've been telling is right, Heidegger was precisely trying to free us from our Cartesian assumptions. When I went to visit Heidegger he had *Being and Nothingness* on his desk, in German translation, and I said, 'So you're reading Sartre?', and he responded, 'How can I even begin to read this muck?' (His word was '*Dreck*'.) That's pretty strong, but I think accurate, since if you treat Heidegger as if he were talking about subjects you turn him back into Husserl. What Sartre wrote was an edifying existentialist version of Husserl. Sartre's for-itself (consciousness) is like Husserl's transcendental ego – an individual subject that gives meaning to everything by way of its intentionality. Because consciousness gives all meaning, anything can have any meaning for it. There isn't any restraint, any facticity or thrownness, as Heidegger would call it. It follows that we can give meaning to whatever values we choose. To take Sartre's example, if I decide this moment not to be a gambler, the next moment I can give that decision a new meaning, say that it was a foolish decision, and go right on gambling. I am, in Sartre's terms, pure spontaneity, pure lightness, pure freedom, pure nothingness – absurdly free. Sartre holds that consciousness is 'beyond freedom', and human being is the absurd and doomed attempt to find some stable meaning in life.

Magee I find it difficult to believe that Sartre will survive as a philosopher, though easy to believe that he might survive as a playwright or novelist. . . .

 What, broadly speaking, is the view you take of Merleau-Ponty?

Dreyfus I'm very much more impressed with Merleau-Ponty. I think he's a great philosopher, and will survive. His contribution was to bring in the body as our way of being in the world. To stress our non-mental directedness, Merleau-Ponty sometimes speaks of the body as intentional tissue.

 There are two big gaps in *Being and Time*. One of them is that Heidegger never talks about the body, or even about skills, or practices. I put all that in to explain his abstract notions like the ready-to-hand, unready-to-hand, and the understanding of being. So Merleau-Ponty, because he does talk about the body, and how the body acquires skills, helps us understand and explain Heidegger. He also answers Sartre. He says we're not totally free. Each of us is restricted to a body with a certain size, ability to move, and so on – the same general sort of body that everyone else has. We can form stable meanings, both shared and individual, since what we do becomes skills and habits in our body, which we are not free to change instantly and arbitrarily. It's an irony of the history of Continental philosophy that Merleau-Ponty – intent on answering Sartre, who was like Husserl – re-invented a version of Heidegger, and supplemented *Being and Time*.

 Another gap in *Being and Time* is perception. Heidegger talks about perception as if it were just staring at things, and that is unfortunate, because it does seem as if we spend a lot of time not only using things but seeing things. Merleau-Ponty has an analysis of perception as an embodied activity in which we move to get an optimal grip on things in the world, and that makes it more like the ready-to-hand, thereby completing the Heideggerian picture of practice.

Magee I'm particularly struck by the twin points that Sartre, when he thought he was being like Heidegger, was in fact being like Husserl, and that Merleau-Ponty's response to Sartre proceeded to replicate Heidegger's response to Husserl.

 All four of the philosophers we've been discussing are now dead. Do you regard the striking tradition which they represent within twentieth-century philosophy as one which has worked itself out to a natural conclusion, or do you see it as still an alive and continuing enterprise?

Dreyfus I think it's very much alive. Even the phenomenology of Husserl, which Heidegger was trying to kill off, is very much alive. Husserl is alive in two ways: one is that if you want to describe experiences – what it's like to listen to music, to have sexual desire, any phenomenon – Husserl gives you a licence to try it, and also a method for doing it.

Magee I'm interrupting only to say that in Britain today we have bright young philosophers who are writing about precisely those subjects and in precisely that way.

Dreyfus And in the United States too. The other side of Husserl is, if anything, even more influential. He was interested in the structure of intentional content, of that which enables us to direct our minds to things. Now there's a new discipline called cognitive science which is actually trying to investigate the structure of mental representations, as they would put it. Husserl has laid down the general guidelines that anybody doing that sort of investigation must follow. Or, if you're trying to build a mind, as people using computers in artificial intelligence are doing, Husserl also offers guidelines. Many of his ideas, for example that the mind follows hierarchies of strict rules, are now being cashed out in computer programs. So Husserl's doing fine.

Heidegger's doing fine too. *Being and Time* is not, perhaps, studied as much now as it should be. It has important ideas on language, truth, reference, science, and so on, which would be valuable to contemporary philosophers. For example, if you actually get back to the phenomena of our engaged everyday activity you can criticise the linguistic analysts who either trust their intuitions or trust our linguistic categories. Heidegger would say, and I think a description of skills shows he is right, that if you trust your intuitions you take for granted the exclusive explanatory power of beliefs, desires and so forth to explain people's behaviour, and that's not an adequate description of what normally goes on when people act. It's a description only of breakdown and other moments when we are not transparently coping. Likewise, our language does not reflect the need to bring in our background skills, and the understanding of being they contain, to account for the intelligibility of our everyday coping. So Heidegger's phenomenology gives us a good starting point for criticising some unquestioned assumptions of contemporary Anglo-American philosophy. Finally, in Europe now, particularly in France, the later Heidegger is the father of those who want to, as he already put it, deconstruct the tradition. For instance, Michel Foucault and Jacques Derrida are trying to follow out the Heideggerian project of defining exactly what our Western understanding of being is, in order to help us get over it.

So I would say that there is hardly any area of intellectual activity these days to which these thinkers' concerns do not have an interesting relevance.

THE AMERICAN PRAGMATISTS

Dialogue with
SIDNEY MORGENBESSER

INTRODUCTION

Magee In philosophy, as in so many other respects, it is now the United States rather than Britain that is the chief centre of activity in the English-speaking world. But there has been American philosophy of inter-national importance for a hundred years now. In fact Bertrand Russell, in his autobiography, describes the Harvard school of philosophy as having been the best in the world during the late nineteenth and early twentieth centuries. American philosophy of that period is represented above all by three figures who have since attained classic status: C. S. Peirce, William James and John Dewey. They are sometimes given a group label – 'The American Pragmatists' – but they are more different from each other than that might suggest.

C. S. Peirce was born in 1839, the son of a Professor of Mathematics at Harvard. He was trained from the beginning as a mathematician and scientist, and his paid jobs were as astronomer and physicist. Philosophy was something he did in his spare time, until at the age of forty-eight he retired to devote himself to it entirely. This, I'm afraid, led to his being sunk in poverty and debt by the time he died in 1914 at the age of seventy-four. He never wrote a book, and a great deal of his work came out only posthumously, when his so-called *Collected Papers* were published in eight volumes. In fact, even at this late date, there is more of his work to come.

A near-contemporary of Peirce was William James, born in 1842 and also educated at Harvard, from which he graduated in medicine. James became a Harvard lecturer in anatomy and physiology, then after that Professor of Philosophy, and then after that Professor of Psychology. Among his best-known books are: *The Principles of Psychology*, published in 1890; *The Varieties of Religious Experience*, published in 1902; and *Pragmatism*, published in 1907. He died in 1910. Unlike Peirce, he received international recognition during his lifetime. In this con-nection it is interesting to note that the novelist Henry James was one of his brothers, and Henry, for part if not most of his life, felt himself very much under the shadow of world-famous elder brother William.

The third and most recent of the three classical American philosophers was John Dewey, who was born in 1859 and lived until 1952. He spent the whole of his career as a university teacher, first at the University of Michigan, then at Chicago, and finally at Columbia in New York. Few philosophers of any place or time have had such influence on practical and public affairs. His philosophy of education alone can be said to have had world-wide impact, and of course he was influential in other fields as well. It is difficult to pick a few books from so copious an output, but perhaps I might mention *Democracy and Education*, published in 1916; *Human Nature and Conduct*, published in 1922; *Experience and Nature*, published in 1925; and *The Quest for Certainty*, published in 1929.

Discussing the work of all three of these philosophers with me is Sidney Morgenbesser, Professor of Philosophy at Columbia University, New York.

DISCUSSION

Magee Let's start by clearing away misconceptions about the term 'pragmatism'. A lot of people seem to think of it as denoting a somewhat crude philosophy to the effect that any theory or set of ideas that is useful, or that 'works', can in effect be embraced as 'true'. But it's really a great deal more sophisticated than that, isn't it?

Morgenbesser Though there are some passages in James that suggest that formulation it is, as you imply, misleading. It even suggests that all pragmatists agreed with James's approach to truth. They did not. Peirce had serious objections to James's theory of truth. So we cannot generalise; any single formulation would be misleading. The term 'pragmatic' has been applied to diverse theses and programmes: there have been pragmatic theories of the *a priori*, pragmatic theories of justification, pragmatic approaches to public policy. Many of these theses are, I think, conceptually independent of one another. So I suggest we take our lead from the classic pragmatists, Peirce, James and Dewey. Some philosophers find the following schema helpful. Peirce presented us with a pragmatic theory of meaning, a pragmatic theory of clarification of some concepts; James presented us with a pragmatic theory of truth. Peirce developed a theory of inquiry; Dewey took some aspects of Peirce's theory and generalised it to apply to social and political philosophy as well. Peirce's theory of, or approach to, meaning is related to his theory of belief. For many, the important point is to link belief, meaning, action and inquiry.

Magee You've mentioned three people and three main themes: questions about meaning, questions about truth and questions about inquiry (inquiry being very much regarded as a form of action – we'll come to that later). It will clarify our discussion if we separate out both the people and the themes. Let's start with Peirce, and let's start with meaning. The point of doing that is that it was Peirce who coined the term 'pragmatism' in its philosophical sense, and he did so to denote a particular theory of meaning. Can you take the story up from there?

Morgenbesser Peirce presented his pragmatic maxim: 'Consider what effects – effects which might conceivably have practical bearing – we conceive the object of a conception to have: then our conception of those effects is the whole of our conception of that object.' I hope the following example will be helpful. If I ask you what you mean when you say sugar is

C. S. Peirce (1839–1914)

soluble in water you might say that if I or anyone put sugar in water it would dissolve; you are attributing let us call it a habit to sugar which it would observably manifest if some action were performed. Let us consider the sentence 'This is hard' – a sentence in the indicative. Peirce tells us to construe that sentence in the same way as we understood 'Sugar is soluble in water'. If we are clear about 'This hammer is hard' we could specify a 'would-be' sentence, a suitable conditional, attributing observable habits to the hammer which could be activated by our actions. Peirce was concerned with the status of *conditional* statements – or, speaking loosely, the specification of the properties we are attributing to any object when we say that it would manifest certain behaviour. Notice that here we have a rule of procedure that a rational agent would follow if he wanted to be clear about his ideas.

Magee The nub of the point, really, is that meaning must always relate, or be relatable, to something that happens, or could happen – often to something that we ourselves do, or could do – hence the term 'pragmatism', which derives from the Greek word for a deed or action. To put the same point negatively, if no imaginable occurrence or set of occurrences could provide us with a way for distinguishing between the appropriate use of one term and that of another, then the two terms have the same meaning. If no imaginable occurrence or set of occurrences could provide us with a way for distinguishing between a term's correct and incorrect use, then that term has no meaning. For a term to have any meaning at all its appropriate use must designate some specifiable difference of something, if only hypothetically.

But, now, Peirce was not concerned with meaning in isolation, in a scholastic sort of way, was he? His concern with meaning had its place in a wider framework of concern. Can you tell us about that?

Morgenbesser Peirce was concerned with the nature of belief. Let us try to connect our discussion about meaning and the clarification of terms with his approach to belief. Peirce argues that a belief, at least as a first approximation, may be considered a disposition to act, a certain kind of habit. Now if a belief (as a first approximation) is a habit of action – or, if you like, a law connecting behaviour with experience – then we can go from belief to meaning, to linguistic meaning. For a sentence which purports to transcend experience would be considered devoid of meaning, since it could not be used to represent a belief. All of this, as I keep insisting, is a first approximation, for we don't act on beliefs alone but also on our desires, values or preferences.

Peirce has been called the father of the verifiability theory of meaning. There are hosts of other approaches to the verifiability theory of meaning; it would be idle to try to consider all of them, or even some of the more important ones: suffice it to say that all of those theories are complex and capable of multiple developments. Even so, from what I have said so far we can conclude that Peirce presented a necessary condition for meaningfulness, and a sufficient one for the clarification of some terms.

Magee With belief, as with meaning, Peirce is putting forward a doctrine, that is to say putting forward proposals, which derive their significance from a wider context. Just as the chief reason why he wants us to get our meanings clear is that he wants us to clarify our beliefs, so the chief reason why he wants us to clarify our beliefs is to – well, it has a twofold purpose, really: one is to strengthen the foundations of our knowledge, the other is to strengthen the foundations of our actions.

Let us take the first of these. Peirce's theories of meaning and belief have their place in a theory of inquiry – and by inquiry he means all our attempts to find out about the world and acquire knowledge, of whatever kind. Can you give us some indication of what his theory of inquiry was?

Morgenbesser Here we must, I think, distinguish between Peirce as a theorist of ordinary belief and Peirce as a theorist of scientific inquiry. When he discusses ordinary belief he suggests the following picture. When we are in a doubtful situation our beliefs have proven to be unreliable. Something has to be done. We need some policy for dealing with doubt. Peirce considers various methods – tenacity; appealing to authority – and tries to show that the method of inquiry, of revising our beliefs by inquiry, is superior to them.

When we inquire, when we test hypotheses, we hold certain beliefs constant. We can't begin from scratch. But beliefs held constant in one context may be subject to test in another. So all beliefs are revisable, fallible. Some philosophers have found this approach illuminating. But the philosophical point behind the approach should be made explicit. Peirce was challenging another approach to knowledge: that real knowledge is based on certainty; that, before we can really claim to know, we must show that the sentences we claim to know are in some suitable sense supported by sentences which are certain. He also challenged the view that first-person beliefs about present mental states are incorrigible and are basic to support our knowledge claims. Peirce had a battery of arguments against this approach (an approach which many have labelled Cartesian). Many though not all philosophers have found Peirce persuasive. At all accounts, he is credited with challenging the quest for certainty, to use Dewey's phrase, and with a helpful approach to justification and knowledge. I should add that some pragmatist philosophers would say that nothing in Peirce precludes a view that we *can* be certain when we claim to know. Indeed, something along these lines is necessary to account for the Peircian thesis that we do hold some of our beliefs fixed, even if only provisionally. But we must be careful about the uses to which we put 'certain'. There are senses of certainty which allow for revisability – and we can also talk about *degrees* of certainty. So another addition is in order: even philosophers who agree with Peirce about justification as thus far presented would argue that some beliefs – perhaps perceptual ones – must have some initial credibility even if they are revisable. And I think Peirce would agree.

Peirce's approach to science is different. There we have a picture of a man or woman who enters into a scientific community. He or she engages in inquiry perhaps for its own sake, and does not accept hypotheses necessarily in order to act on them. Here Peirce magnificently depicts the phases of inquiry: the abductive, the deductive, the inductive. In the abductive phase theories are presented for consideration. In the deductive phase they are prepared for test. In the inductive phase the results of testing are assessed. For what he has to say about each of these Peirce may be credited as a forerunner of such figures of our own time as Ernest Nagel and Karl Popper.

Magee You introduced the term 'fallible' a moment ago, and this is of the utmost importance. Almost everyone in Peirce's day regarded scientific knowledge as utterly certain, utterly secure, and for that reason incorrigible and unrevisable. He was one of the first people to see and to say that this is not the case. He was not the first, and did not claim to be – he had one or two interesting forerunners of whom he was aware and whom he acknowledged – but he was among the pioneers, and no one before him got as far as he did. He saw with extraordinary clarity that what we actually do in science is use the best available theory for as long as it works, and then when we start to run into trouble with it we try to get a better theory. And he coined the term 'fallibilism' as applying to the very foundations of science. In the late twentieth century some or other development of this idea is becoming the orthodoxy, but in Peirce's day and for a long time after it was very little understood. In fact Peirce can be said to have held a whole range of strikingly 'modern' views about science, can't he?

Morgenbesser Yes. Peirce is opposed to the view that theories can be looked upon simply as empirical generalisations, that scientists accept hypotheses if and only if they are confirmed and not disconfirmed. He stresses the variety of contextual factors that play a role in the assessment of theories. He stresses the role of statistical hypotheses. And he challenges determinism.

Magee The philosopher who influenced Peirce much more than any other was Kant. And that prompts the following question. Did Peirce believe that what our inquiries are giving us beliefs about and knowledge of is an independently existing material world such as present-day realists believe in, or did he take a more Kantian view that we ourselves to some degree construct this world of our experience?

Morgenbesser Your question is both difficult and important. I'll deal with a few of the issues raised.

There are some philosophers – let us call them extreme realists – who argue, or seem to argue, that we may never know how things really are. After all, our theories depend on us: how things are does not. I think Peirce would call this approach or thesis meaningless, not merely pointless: he would not countenance the non-cognisable. So here he seems to be going further than Kant, at least on one interpretation of Kant. Peirce does talk about the real, inquiry is guided by the real, but in order to know anything about the real we must appeal to our theories and their testing – checking, as it were, our beliefs against each other.

Of course, Peirce goes on from there. His approach to inquiry is social. Theories are tested by a community of investigators. This captures one intuition about the real: it is independent of any single individual agent. It is publicly accessible. Peirce, in his later writings, gives us an account of perception which will accord with the view that in perception we are in some form of contact with the real. But still, if we want to know what the real is we have to attend to our theories, and attending to them we seem to have to conclude that the real may, in the word of one philosopher, be amorphous.

Notice that though Peirce claims that inquiry is guided by the real, he also says that anything we can say about the real must be expressible in our theories. Remembering that Peirce has emphasised the revisability of our theories, he also wants to account for the commonsense view that some beliefs are true. A sentence may be both true and revisable. We still have to allow for our discourse about truth.

Magee But surely the fact that anything we can say about the real has to be expressible in terms of our theories means that we are never able to step outside our frameworks of ideas in order to compare them independently with a reality which is separate from them?

Morgenbesser Peirce argues that we can talk about beliefs being true in a way which is in accord with his thesis about inquiry. To say that a belief or opinion is true is to say that it is destined to be accepted if inquiry continues. Of course, we may hold now a true belief which will withstand testing and remain among the opinions destined to be accepted. But now another question arises. How do we know that inquiry will continue? We

William James (1842–1910)

hope that it will, but the hope may not be realised. Partly to deal with this issue, Peirce turns to his theory of objective idealism. The world is, in a suitable sense, mental, it evolves over time into laws of regularity. It is this view of the world which may give us reason to believe that there is some form of harmony between the world's growth and the evolution of our theories. Peirce, therefore, tried to relate his theory of inquiry to his cosmology. Later pragmatists would not.

There is another interesting difference between Peirce and later pragmatists. Peirce tried to specify basic categories which he thought he could show are applicable to our experience, or to any possible experience. He also tried to show that these categories manifest themselves in perception. Peirce's views on these matters have been criticised by later pragmatists.

Magee Since we've now taken to referring forward from Peirce, let's bring William James explicitly into the picture. Although the philosophical term 'pragmatism' was launched by Peirce it was James who made it known to the educated community at large with his book *Pragmatism*, published in 1907. What were the main themes of that book?

Morgenbesser The book is a very rich one. It begins with a critique of various traditional philosophies on the grounds that they are not relevant for the clarification of the problems faced by members of James's generation, not relevant to helping *deal* with those problems – especially the problem of reconciling science and religion. He also criticises some of these philosophies on pragmatic grounds: some of them seem to be mutually contradictory but in point of fact are not. They are compatible with the same data, and have the same consequences for action. So he is concerned with the problem of choice between theories. And he considers pragmatic approaches to conceptual change and to truth. Many philosophers think it important to realise that he is always considering these issues from the standpoint of the agent.

Permit me to elaborate. There are at least three distinguishable aspects of James's approach. Often he tells us that the agent is not a mere spectator of the world scene but is in the world as a player is in a play. He elaborates and discusses the reality of change and of chance, which alternative theories to his own rule out, or seem to rule out. Patently he thinks his theory is in accord with the facts, but he argues that his commitment cannot be justified by appeal to the facts alone. He has, as it were, a bias for interpreting the facts in a certain way, and argues that others should admit to their bias. For James there is no ready-made world. The way we talk about the world is determined by our cognitive and theoretical activities. Going further, we might say that facts about objects in the world cannot be divested of their conceptual shaping.

James also talks about rational choice, and relates his account of rationality to the will to believe. This is our third theme, which I shall sketch only briefly. There are some philosophers who insist that a rational agent ought to keep his degree of belief in accord with the degree of evidence: the lower the evidence, the lower the degree of belief, and the higher the evidence; the higher the degree of belief. Let me call such a philosopher a simple cognitivist. James often seems to argue against the simple cognitivist on the grounds that he, the simple cognitivist, is not clear about what rationality is. We cannot discuss the rationality of the agent until we consider the goals, desires, preferences of the agent. James further argues that an agent may be considered rational even if he or she does not act in the manner suggested by the simple cognitivist. He asks us to consider an agent who has to decide between believing H or not-H. He has a will to believe one or the other, and the evidence supports both equally. Why should the agent postpone decision? Why should he or she remain agnostic? In these cases James argues that the agent has a right to believe H or not-H, and may even perhaps do so by appealing to various non-cognitive factors. I am indicating a theme, and cannot elaborate, but I note that in the case considered by James he is talking about deciding to do, rather than deciding to believe, and of course rationality of action must consider both beliefs and utilities. There are many pragmatists who would go on to make against the simple cognitivist the point that even the scientist does not attend to the evidence alone. If he has to decide whether a certain theory is worthy of test he considers whether the theory will satisfy certain goals, for example whether it has more potential explanatory value or content than its rivals; and he considers such cognitive goals also when he decides whether or not to accept the theory.

Magee So what is crudely regarded by some of its critics as the doctrine that we are justified in believing whatever it benefits us to believe is in reality something very, very much more sophisticated than that. First and foremost, James thinks our beliefs must accord with the evidence, and where the evidence for one theory is stronger than that for its competitors we have no rational choice but to prefer that theory. It is only where the balance of evidence is equal as between two theories that criteria other than evidence are even allowed consideration. And in those cases James argues that the rational course is for us to accept the theory with the richer consequences.

James presented himself as developing Peirce's ideas – other people's too, but certainly Peirce's. But to what extent did Peirce himself actually go along with James's theories?

Morgenbesser When *Pragmatism* came out Peirce wrote a letter to James congratulating him, praising it highly indeed. But he did have his differences with James, and emphasised them in later lectures. He even came to present himself as a 'pragmaticist' in order to distinguish himself from the 'pragmatist' James. He thought James was too nominalistic, too phenomenalistic. For Peirce lawlike statements are not, as it were, merely summary-sentences about occurrences or experiences: 'A1 occurs, B1 follows; A2 occurs, B2 follows; A3 occurs, B3 follows.' They are sentences about what *would* happen: the conditional statements he considered were not reducible to statements about the actual. To some, Peirce is best understood as talking not merely about the actual but about the possible, about unactualised possibilities.

Magee My immediate, perhaps over-simple reaction to a first reading of Peirce and then James was that Peirce was advancing pragmatism as a criterion of meaning, and that this was a highly suggestive and fertile approach, whereas James tried to develop it as a theory of truth and that this failed to carry conviction.

Morgenbesser In some of his writings James asks whether 'It is true that the facts are so-and-so' really means anything in addition to the basic assertion of the facts alone: 'So-and-so'. Perhaps we could amend James as asking whether there is a pragmatic difference between H and 'H is true'. What is the pragmatic difference? He seems to find one: 'is true', he says, is an evaluative predicate; 'is true' is what it is good to believe. He seems to be saying that we can equate truth with verification: the verified is good to believe. (In other writings he equates truth with the satisfaction of desire.) Whatever the motivation or reasoning may be, James often seems to adopt a verificationist approach to truth, and to identify truth with verification, and to be saying that an agent could exhaustively verify a hypothesis by acting on it. But he has been criticised on a number of grounds. Truth cannot be eliminated in this manner. And an agent cannot exhaustively verify a hypothesis. However, there are other occasions when he brings in not merely verification but also satisfaction of desire. For it might be said that it is good to believe a hypothesis if it satisfies desire. But this part of James too was criticised by many later pragmatists, such as Dewey.

Magee I'd like at this point to bring Dewey on centre-stage in our discussion. But before moving James to one side I really must commend him for something we haven't touched on, and that is the literary artistry of his work. His is one of the most attractively individual voices in the history of philosophy. He writes with all the thrust and excitement, the unexpected metaphor and sheer surprise of a creative writer. Some wag once said that when you looked at their actual books you realised that William James was the natural novelist and Henry James the natural philosopher. If our discussion sends anyone away to read William James for himself that person is in for a serious pleasure.

Morgenbesser Can I add something there? All three of the men we're talking about seem to me in some sense remarkable, and specially worthy of respect. Peirce is an awesome figure: the size and variety of the issues he dealt with – logic, inquiry, certain kinds of metaphysics . . . he has been called the Leibniz of America.

Magee When I checked his dates in the latest edition of the *Encyclopaedia Britannica* I saw that it says of him that he is 'now recognized as the most original and the most versatile intellect that the Americas have so far produced'.

Morgenbesser And Dewey of course was a man true to his word. He didn't merely preach that philosophers should become engaged in public life, he did it. He had this great range. And he was a liberal man, and a kind man. When Bertrand Russell wrote his *History of Western Philosophy* he said he had so much respect and admiration for Dewey that he felt apologetic about having to disagree with him.

Magee The only philosopher living at the time when Russell's *History of Western Philosophy* was written and published to be given a chapter in it was Dewey. Let's now bring him fully into the picture sketched by our discussion. Up to this point we have concentrated on Peirce and James and their attempts to improve the methods by which human beings can acquire new knowledge and understanding of their environment, both in an ordinary-life context and, in a more organised way, through science. We've talked about how this involved them in clarifying the concept of meaning, and the concept of truth, and in finding what the proper functioning of those concepts is within an overall conception of inquiry – again, both in ordinary life and in scientific activity. Now for Dewey, as for Peirce, it was considerations of science that launched his most interesting work. Dewey was struck by the fact that the fields in which human beings have had far and away the most success in the last three or four hundred years are those of science and technology. It is here that we have acquired the most, and most reliable, knowledge, and also the most, and most reliable, mastery of nature. And Dewey was moved to ask: What is it about scientific activity that gives it this marvellous success, these wonderful results? Is it something that can be adapted and applied to other fields of human activity with comparable success?

Morgenbesser Dewey does not give us a complete answer to that question, but he does give us a partial one. Scientific institutions have received

John Dewey (1859–1952)

social support because they have, among other achievements, enabled men and women to be more at home in the world. Science is unified by its method, and has remained stable because of that fact. Scientists who disagree with one another can appeal to a common method to resolve their differences. Of course, some scientists may not live up to scientific norms, but when they don't they can be criticised by appeal to those norms. Doubtless, more has to be said about the method of science, and Dewey attempts to do so in his books *Logic: the Theory of Inquiry* and *The Quest for Certainty*. But in the main he is interested in inquiry, not only scientific inquiry. Of course, we can ask whether science will continue, but to raise that question we may have to raise questions about the justification of induction, questions which Dewey for the most part avoids (though he does have some discussion in *Experience and Nature* which bears on the issue). However, if we accept induction we can rely on our past history to justify our commitment to science: it has proven to be a better predictor, a better manufacturer of knowledge, than its competitors.

Magee I suppose the essential point to make about Dewey's view of science – and this goes for all the pragmatists – is that it was dynamic. He did not see science as a body of reliable and changeless knowledge to which new certainties were being added. He saw it as an *activity*, the process of finding things out. Hence the perpetual use of the word 'inquiry'. In line with this he was very much against what some people have called a 'spectator' view of knowledge. Philosophers have too often talked about 'the observing subject' as if we were separate from the world of objects and were viewing it from without; as if we were here and the world was there and we were reading off knowledge from it by observation. This, said Dewey, is a radically false and misleading model. The reality is quite different. We are living organisms in an environment in which, above all else, our concern is to survive; and one of the most important survival mechanisms we have – perhaps *the* most important – is knowledge, because it confers understanding of the environment and, through that, a degree of mastery of it. So the fact is we are part of the very stuff and substance of the world we are trying to understand, to acquire knowledge of, and our acquisition of knowledge is of the utmost practical importance to us, sometimes a matter of life and death. And we are all the time having to act, whether we like it or not, on the basis of the most reliable beliefs we can muster, imperfect or inadequate though many of them may be. And it is from the middle of *that* situation that we are trying to increase our understanding and our knowledge. The would-be knower is a biological organism struggling for survival – not a spectator but an agent.

Incidentally, and this is a very big matter indeed, it is worth making the point here that the revolt against the Cartesian tradition seems to have emerged as one of the salient characteristics of twentieth-century philosophy. It characterises the American pragmatists, Frege and his followers, Heidegger and his followers, the later Wittgenstein and his followers and, perhaps most radically of all, Popper and his followers. . . . For a long time differences of tradition and idiom disguised from most professional philosophers the fact that although the American pragmatists, Heidegger, and the later Wittgenstein worked very largely without regard to one another they were dealing with some of the same fundamental problems, and what is more , they were saying some of the same basic things about them. Even now there seem to be many who have not woken up to the fact. But the realisation is spreading.

However, let me go back to the last point I was making about the pragmatists. In pragmatic philosophy things are nearly always seen from the standpoint of an agent, and it seems to me that this is just about the most important single insight which pragmatism has to convey: that knowledge is of its nature bound up with activity, and that criteria of meaning and criteria of truth need to have some relation to activity.

Morgenbesser Dewey opposed theories of knowledge which considered knowledge independent of its role in problem-solving inquiry. Inquiry is prompted by doubt, and if a solution to the problem is reached at the outcome of a well-conducted inquiry, coming to the conclusion is the making of a warranted assertion. Of course, in reaching the conclusion the inquirer judges the conclusion true, but this does not require defining truth as warranted assertability. Inquiry is guided by thought and idea, but an idea is a plan for action: there is no conceptual gap between thought and action.

When it comes to scientific inquiry we may have an urge to go further and say that science works because it is true, and that it is true because its statements correspond to the way the world really is; but there is no way of detaching ourselves from our current beliefs and seeing the world from above. We appeal to science to tell us about the way the world is because we cannot have independent access, as it were, to the world. There is no way to justify our beliefs about the world without appealing to other beliefs. We can, of course, say that men and women do what they do or believe what they believe because they are involved in the world, and Dewey does attempt to specify what that means in his various lectures about the interaction between man and nature. In doing this we are using science, perhaps for purposes of explanation, but we cannot say that this is a way of justifying science.

Magee One consequence of the fact that Dewey saw the acquisition of knowledge as a social activity was that he was led to take a special interest in institutions. There were other reasons for this too – for instance, he thought that one of the main reasons why science is so successful is that it institutionalises criticism. Can you say a word about Dewey's special attitude towards institutions?

Morgenbesser Dewey's approach to institutions contains a number of themes. First he tells us that there may be no way of listing the specific needs or instincts which specific social institutions arose to satisfy: other social institutions might have satisfied them as well. Often the needs are specified in terms of institutional arrangements – for example we have a need for a job. And of course, as we all know, needs are modified by institutional arrangements: often institutions create needs. The need for food is basic, but no specific institution can be explained as having arisen to satisfy that need: once again, other institutional arrangements could have satisfied it as well – patently, people don't just need food, they want or need certain kinds of food and will reject others. The fact that they do that has to be explained by reference to the life they are living. And then there is a second thesis. At any given time we can criticise socially recognised institutions on the grounds that they don't satisfy the socially recognised needs they claim they do. Often Dewey criticises America's institutions on these grounds, and asks for new social institutions to satisfy the needs that are socially recognised. Some theories attempt to justify institutional arrangements by appealing to a theory of human nature: the institutions have to continue because specific human beings are the way they are. Specific institutions are necessary because of that fact. Dewey often argues that these theories are of little value. Men and women act the way they do because of their culture and their social institutional arrangements, all of which are capable of change. We must discuss what *people* are capable of doing.

Dewey does not deny that there are invariant features of human life, but he argues that there is no one best way of trying to deal with them. The problem is always a specific one – how to deal with current arrangements. Debates about these can be rational and reasonable. And this leads us to the last point. Dewey challenged the dualism between fact and value, the thesis that matters of fact can be rationally discussed whereas matters of value cannot, the idea that before rational discussion of value can begin or rational deliberation can be undertaken we must make judgments about the intrinsically valuable and keep that judgment fixed. Dewey argued that not only may we deliberate about ends but in the process of deliberation we may change our beliefs about those ends. Again and again Dewey tries to find parallels between the way scientists deliberate and the way people can deliberate rationally and come to rational decisions about matters of value. He often discusses the case of the individual deliberator. And his analysis of the method of rational deliberation has been discussed by many philosophers.

Then he tries to generalise, and talks about intelligent deliberation about social matters in order to direct social change. He agrees that rational deliberation about specific issues under debate requires the debaters to share an agreement to get the debate started. But once again, this is true of scientific deliberation as well: scientists must have enough shared background beliefs and agreement on method to be able to test a hypothesis under dispute. In social matters there is no point in talking about joint deliberation unless we realise that the deliberation is morally serious when, and only when, those affected by the outcome have a voice in it, a voice in deciding about the institutional arrangements that affect their lives. Hence he calls again and again for people not to be excluded from such debates.

Dewey has been criticised on many grounds. Some have claimed that he assumes that reasonable men and women can always agree after debate, and of course Dewey has no proof that this is the case. He agrees he has no proof, but argues that there is no *a priori* reason to believe that it cannot be done.

Magee One point he makes about institutions has always made a special impression on me, namely that institutions can give rise to conflicts which are genuinely important and yet are not the problem of any individual.

The institutions on which Dewey's ideas made the greatest impact were educational: in education his influence can truly be said to have been international. Can you tell us something about it?

Morgenbesser Dewey's theory of education was influential for a number of reasons. It contained interesting analyses of various notions of learning and their effects, and interesting theses about the interconnection between learning and doing. It criticised some traditional theories of education on a number of grounds, for instance that they were based on dubious psychological theories, or were not relevant to solving the problems faced by an industrialised and democratic society. It is frequently said that Dewey advised the members of his generation to face specific problems, and then after that to face others – not to scratch where it doesn't itch. But he was also a problem-instigator. He thought that members of his generation, given their commitment to democracy, ought to *face* certain problems, and ought to reorganise some of their institutions, not least their educational institutions.

Right across the board in education Dewey stresses the continuities between scientific inquiry and other sorts of inquiry. In point of fact, some critics of Dewey argue that it is a defect of his theory that he did not stress the specific cognitive goals pursued in scientific inquiry. But notice that for Dewey, and for all pragmatists, inquiry is a special way of acting and of testing by action. Dewey tried to ground education on that approach. He thinks, for instance, that the school is best viewed as a community in which its members, through study and joint activity, develop their powers and abilities, especially the power to develop habits of thought which can be exemplified in all walks of life. From one perspective there is no fixed end of education. From another the focal goal is growth, a goal which is also central in his theory of democracy. As he said, a society of free individuals in which all, through their own work, contribute to the liberation and enrichment of the lives of others, is the only environment in which any individual can really grow normally to his full stature. As Sidney Hook has said, this is an overstatement, but its very overemphasis should indicate how important for Dewey democracy as a moral ideal is.

Magee Really, I suppose he was the most effective of all the early opponents of the traditional idea that education is something imposed on a child through discipline, imposed from without against the child's natural resistance. He saw children as being by nature energetic and curious, and thought that these drives should be harnessed so that the process of education flowed with the child's energies and was powered from inside the child, so to speak. But one of his great merits was that he did not take a sentimental view of children. He thought that educationists who preached that children should never be compelled to do anything, but should be free to decide for themselves what they are going to learn, were foolish, in that they entirely failed to acknowledge both the ignorance and the emotional immaturity of children. Children need direction and support; and quite an amount of sheer instruction is also required if they are to become able to cope with life and stand on their own feet; but if these things are gone about in the right way they can be done with the children as allies rather than as a captive population. In particular Dewey recommended taking advantage of children's abundant energy to encourage learning by doing, by activity, by becoming involved. It can be regarded as basically a problem-solving approach – always concerned with the rationale of what is being done, and therefore with ideas and theories, but also always in conjunction with practice, with activity. I'm having to put this in general terms in order to state it briefly, but Dewey is usually very concrete in his discussion, and he pays particular attention to the specific institutional arrangements required to put his ideas into practice. He was one of the first great modernists in educational theory, and perhaps he was the best. If much of what he said is now taken for granted by many of us, that is in no small degree a measure of his success: at the time when he wrote, education was entirely different from this all over the world, including America.

FREGE, RUSSELL and MODERN LOGIC

Dialogue with
A. J. AYER

INTRODUCTION

Magee A great deal of the philosophy going on today in the English-speaking world – perhaps even most of it – can be traced back, through intermediate developments, to the work of two men: Gottlob Frege and Bertrand Russell. Working for the most part independently of each other, they laid the foundations of modern logic. More than that: although the work on which they began concerned chiefly the principles of mathematics and the relationship between mathematics and logic, its implications went so wide that in the course of time it came to have a profound influence on philosophy in general. Exactly the same thing happened with the philosopher who most obviously and directly followed on from them, Wittgenstein. Wittgenstein was a pupil of Russell, with whom he went to study on Frege's advice; and though he started by developing Russell's and Frege's work in mathematical logic, he ended up acquiring an influence at large on twentieth-century philosophy which is second to nobody's. In this discussion, without attempting to go into any of the technicalities of either mathematics or logic, I hope we shall succeed in giving an indication of how Frege and Russell came to have their enormous influence on twentieth-century thought, and also in saying something about more recent individuals and groups who have come under that influence.

First, a word about the chief figures themselves: Gottlob Frege, a German, was born in 1848, and spent his entire working life in comparative obscurity in the mathematics department of the University of Jena. It was not until after his death that his name became known at all widely among philosophers. His first major work, published in 1879, was called *Begriffsschrift*, a title retained by the English translation because there is no satisfactory English for it; it means something like 'the putting of concepts into notation', and we shall see later what that refers to. Frege's next major work, published in 1884, is called in English *The Foundations of Arithmetic*. He went on producing important and original work – most notably, in 1893 and 1903, two volumes of a projected larger work whose English translation bears the title *The Basic Laws of Arithmetic* but which is more usually referred to, even in English contexts, as the *Grundgesetze*. However, in spite of his substantial output, Frege's work in general was of such depth and difficulty that it remained comparatively unknown until Bertrand Russell drew attention to it in 1903.

Russell was a totally different sort of person from Frege: grandson of a British prime minister – from whom he was later, via his elder brother, to inherit an earldom – he was always prominent on the political and social scene as well as in philosophy; in fact one can truthfully say that he was a famous public figure nearly all his adult life. He did a tremendous amount of popular writing in the form of both books and journalism, and he was also a familiar broadcaster; and through these activities he significantly influenced the social attitudes of successive generations of British people. His widespread influence on people's social and political ideas has obscured for many the fact that the foundations of his fame as a philosopher lie not in social or political theory at all but in contributions to mathematical logic of a highly professional and technical character. Born in 1872, he lived until 1970. The great bulk of his philosophical work had been done by the 1920s, but he remained politically active almost to the end.

To discuss the work of both Frege and Russell, and their influence down to our own day, I have invited one of the most famous of living philosophers, A. J. Ayer. Ayer knew Russell personally and has written a considerable amount about his work, including the best short popular introduction to it. Even so, I think it will make for greater clarity in the discussion if we start with Frege as being the earlier figure.

DISCUSSION

Magee Usually the best way to begin consideration of any philosopher is to ask oneself what his problem-situation was. When Frege began, what was he trying to do?

Ayer Well, he was trying to make up for what he thought were the deficiencies in arithmetic. He thought that mathematical statements as they were expressed in his day were not sufficiently precise, and in particular that mathematical proofs were not sufficiently rigorous. So he began by trying to develop a notation, the *Begriffsschrift* you referred to, in which this would be remedied. This notation was designed to show exactly what mathematical statements stated, and exactly what their proofs consisted in. It was supposed to make it obvious how one step in a proof succeeded another. In this respect there was a deficiency in the mathematics of his time, applying even to Euclid, where assumptions which were not made explicit were required for the proofs to be valid.

Magee Every argument, including a mathematical proof, has to have premises, and these premises are not themselves proved by the argument, otherwise the argument would be circular. This means that the truth of the conclusion of any argument, however rigorous, rests on initial assumptions which are not proved, or rather whose validation lies outside the argument itself. This fact is one of the commonest sources of serious problems in intellectual work. Now isn't it the case that what Frege tried to show was that the initial assumptions on which mathematics rests can all be derived from the most elementary principles of logic? This would have the effect of validating mathematics as a body of necessary truths on the ground that all its theorems are deductively derived from purely logical premises.

Ayer   Not all mathematics. In Frege's case not geometry but arithmetic. He and Russell proceeded in the same way. It involved two enterprises, first of all defining arithmetical concepts in purely logical terms, and secondly showing that arithmetic was deducible from purely logical premisses. The first part was achieved fairly simply. I think that a quite simple illustration will show how it was done. Take any couple, let's say Tom and Jerry. You can define them as a couple by saying that they are not equivalent but are both members of a set, and that anything which is a member of this set is identical with one or other of them. Then you define the number two as a set of such sets, that is, a set of couples. Evidently the same procedure can be applied to all numbers. There are indeed certain complications about infinity, but in this way you can define any cardinal number in purely logical terms, which is what Frege did. He also effected a great improvement in logic itself. A defect of Aristotelian logic, which had prevailed from ancient times until the nineteenth century, was that it was not wholly general. By remedying this Frege was able to state premisses from which most arithmetic was deducible. It was shown later by another logician, the Austrian Kurt Gödel, that in fact it couldn't be completely done, that a formal derivation of arithmetic couldn't be completed.

Magee   Wouldn't it also be true to say that before Frege the laws of logic had been regarded as laws of thought, which is to say as something to do with human mental processes? Frege realised that this couldn't be so: the validity of a proof – the truth about what does or does not follow from what – cannot depend on the contingencies of human psychology.

Ayer   Yes, this was very important. It was one of the most important things that Frege did. One of his early works was an attack on a book on arithmetic by the German philosopher Husserl, in which logic was represented as the theory of judgment. This was how it was viewed by German idealists. Frege insisted that logic was entirely objective and had nothing to do with psychological processes. In his view, the sets into which you reduced numbers were entirely objective entities, so that logic was quite independent of psychology. The propositions of logic were objective truths, which of course the mind was capable of grasping, but they didn't depend for their validity upon features of thinking.

Magee   So, as far as mathematical proof is concerned, the search becomes one for whatever it is that is conveyed from each step in the proof to the next. . . .

Ayer   That's right.

Gottlob Frege (1848–1925)

Magee And whatever this is validates the conclusion impersonally –

Ayer That's perfectly right.

Magee – regardless of how we ourselves think.

Ayer And this, in a way, accounts for Frege's having a philosophical interest beyond his purely mathematical work – because he also developed a theory of meaning which would show how mathematics could be objectively valid. What he did was to equate the meaning not only of mathematical statements but of statements in general with their truth conditions, that is, with the features in them that made them candidates for truth or falsehood.

Magee The most historically influential distinction introduced by him – and it was central to his theory of meaning – was the distinction between sense and reference. It is used still. Can you explain it?

Ayer It's fairly complicated. The two German expressions are '*Sinn*' which is generally translated 'sense', and '*Bedeutung*', which is in fact the German word for 'meaning' but is usually translated by philosophers as either 'reference' or 'denotation'. The denotation of a name is the object which it names. So the denotation of 'Bryan Magee' is you, the actual person. Whereas the sense of a name is the contribution that it makes to the meaning. For instance, if I just say 'Tom' you may say to me 'Who is Tom?', and then I may say 'Well Tom is so and so's brother', or 'The person who invented such and such', or 'The first person to climb such and such a mountain'. And in this way, by attaching a sense to his name, I enable you to identify him. Now this distinction becomes important in certain contexts. Generally, what you care about in the case of a name is what the name stands for. But there are certain cases where it's important to make a distinction between sense and denotation. One good example would be statements of identity. Frege's own favourite example was that of the Evening Star and the Morning Star, both of which, as you know, are in fact the planet Venus. If someone says, 'The Evening Star is identical with the Morning Star', and one takes the meaning of these two expressions to be the denotation, then he is simply saying, 'Venus is Venus', which is a tautology and of no interest, whereas the fact that the Morning Star is the Evening Star was an important discovery. Therefore, in this usage, what the expressions mean is not their denotation, not the object, but their sense.

Magee In short, then, Frege broke down the concept of meaning into two components; and not only are these different from each other but an expression may possess one without possessing the other: an expression may have a sense but not have a reference.

Ayer Yes, this can happen in two ways. There could be names, or nominal expressions, like 'the present King of France' for example, which has a sense but no reference, because nobody corresponds to it. Also, there is the complicated case of expressions which have a function in a sentence as contributing to its truth conditions, making it capable of being true or false, but don't denote anything. These are predicates like 'is good', 'is bad' and so on, which are what Frege called incomplete expressions, since they don't themselves have a reference yet they contribute to giving the sentence a sense, and through its sense a reference.

Magee These distinctions, and indeed Frege's whole theory of meaning, have been enormously influential in philosophy, haven't they?

Ayer They've become very fashionable in recent years, anyhow in England, and to some extent in the United States. They have brought about a new view of the main concern of philosophy. For a very long time, ever since Descartes and his successors in the seventeenth century, the main concern had been the theory of knowledge – what we can know, how we can know it, and how we are justified in holding the beliefs we do. In recent years this has given way to what is sometimes called the philosophy of logic, which is much concerned with questions about meaning; and here Frege has come into great prominence. For instance my successor as Professor of Logic at Oxford, Michael Dummett, has devoted a very large book to exploring the implications of Frege's distinctions for a theory of meaning.

Magee Michael Dummett, who must be regarded as the leading commentator on Frege, makes exceedingly large claims for him. According to Dummett, Frege has introduced a new era in philosophy. Frege has de-psychologised philosophy, because – in the way you just explained – he has dethroned the theory of knowledge from its dominant position as philosophy's ruling preoccupation and replaced it by logic; and this has caused 300 years of philosophical development to change course. Do you go along with that assessment?

Ayer Well I think that there has been a difference of emphasis, but I think also that Dummett exaggerates in two ways. First of all, philosophers have always been concerned with meaning, ever since Socrates, who went about saying, 'What is Knowledge? What is Goodness?', and so on, which is a way of asking what the Greek equivalents of those terms meant. Secondly, I don't think that interest in the theory of knowledge has totally disappeared. There are still people who are concerned with it. Even in Dummett's own works the theory of meaning is very much bound up with questions about truth and falsehood. And these do not take us entirely away from the theory of knowledge, because after all the theory of knowledge is concerned with what reasons you have to suppose that certain statements or propositions are true, or false. So I think that there has been a shift of emphasis, but not the great break that Dummett suggests.

Magee Before we turn to more recent applications of Frege's work I want to step to one side and talk about Russell for a moment. In introducing our discussion I laid emphasis on the fact that Frege worked in isolation for most of his productive life, and this fact becomes important when one considers Russell: poor Russell spent his first several years as a logician re-inventing work that Frege had already done, because, quite simply, he didn't know of Frege's existence. But at least that should make it easier for you now to explain to us the significance of Russell's early work!

Ayer I don't quite know why you say 'poor Russell', because while it is quite true that Russell did a lot of work that Frege had done before him, Russell also exposed a fatal deficiency in Frege's system. He showed that Frege's system of logic actually contained a paradox. . . . I don't know if you would wish me to expound the paradox – I will if you wish.

Magee Yes, please do.

Ayer Well, the paradox was this. Frege, as I was saying earlier, reduced numbers to sets, a move which has now become fairly commonplace even in school arithmetic. And he made the fairly natural assumption that for any condition you can state on things there is a set of just those things that satisfy the condition. Moreover this assumption was one that he needed in order to prove various propositions in his system of arithmetic. Now Russell hit upon the idea of dividing sets into those that were and those that were not members of themselves. Most sets obviously aren't members of themselves; for instance the set of men is not itself a man; but some sets seemed to be self-membered: for instance, the set of all sets. Then Russell said, 'Well, what about the set of sets that are not members of themselves? Is it a member of itself? If it is, it isn't. If it isn't, it is.' Clearly this was a contradiction, rather like the famous old contradiction of Epimenides about the Cretan who said that all Cretans were liars. This comes into the category of self-defeating propositions.

Magee Although the examples are trivial, what is at stake is not at all

trivial, because what these examples show is that there is, or was, something wrong with our underlying assumptions in mathematics or logic.

Ayer It does. It shows that one of Frege's essential assumptions led to
contradiction. And when Russell, I think it was in 1903, conveyed
Russell's paradox in a letter to Frege, Frege's first reaction was not, 'Oh,
I'm wrong', but rather to return the arrogant reply, 'The whole of
mathematics has been undermined'. Then he thought that this was going
too far, and managed to put together some sort of answer to Russell's
objection. However, it was shown soon after Frege's death by a Polish
logician, Leśniewski, that Frege's answer also was untenable, a fact which
may have been suspected by Frege himself, since he never recovered
from Russell's blow. After the publication of *Grundgesetze*, as you
yourself said earlier, he never wrote the third volume.

Magee It must have seemed to him that his life's work had been
demolished.

Ayer As far as laying the foundations of arithmetic went, his life's work
had been demolished, yes. So in fact it was a very sad story, a tragic story.
But Russell went on to deal with his paradox in his own way, with a
complicated device called the Theory of Types, which made it impossible
– made it senseless – to say that a class was or wasn't a member of itself. It
should be said that not everybody is satisfied with that. And there are
thought to be different ways of getting around the paradox. Even so, in a
way Russell triumphed over Frege.

Magee But I have to press the point: it remains true that an enormous
amount of work which the young Russell spent years over had already
been done by Frege, and Russell didn't know that.

Ayer Yes, that is true.

Magee However, it is also true that although Frege did much of the work
first – and some experts to this day also think that Frege did a lot of it
better – it was through Russell that these ideas became famous and
influential in philosophy.

Ayer That is true. I don't know why it was that Frege's work was so
neglected. Partly perhaps for the absurd reason that interest in the
development of logic was very much an English thing. People like Boole
and De Morgan had already been doing it before Frege in the nineteenth
century. And not many English people – not even, I am ashamed to say,
philosophers – read German, or don't read what might seem to be

obscure German articles. So Frege's work wasn't taken up in Germany because in Germany the mistaken psychological view of logic still prevailed, and it wasn't taken up in England simply because of English insularity and incompetence in foreign languages. And it remained almost unknown.

Magee Until Russell, who I believe had had German-speaking nurses or governesses as a child, and knew German.

Ayer He did know German, yes. But even Russell got it indirectly. What happened was that Russell and his collaborator Whitehead went to a congress in Paris in 1903 and met an Italian logician called Peano; and it was through Peano – whose work enormously impressed them, and who was working in the same direction, though with a less efficient system than Frege's – that they got to realise how important Frege's work was.

Magee And the outcome of all this was that the science of logic, which in its fundamentals had changed surprisingly little during the period of over 2,000 years between Aristotle and the nineteenth century, exploded into a whole new era of its development. And one can say that historically, if not intellectually, this came about mainly through Russell.

Ayer Mainly through Russell and Whitehead's *Principia Mathematica*, which took them together about ten years to complete. Russell published *The Principles of Mathematics* in 1903, where he does make an acknowledgement to Frege in the preface, and also in an appendix. And then he went on with his former tutor at Cambridge, Whitehead, to write a three-volume work called *Principia Mathematica* in which he actually tried to carry out the task of deducing mathematics from logic. It is full of formulae, and it is a stupendous work – although, as you rightly said, it doesn't quite achieve the standards of logical rigour that Frege achieved before it. Even so, this was the work that really popularised the subject. All sorts of people took it up, and from then on mathematical logic has proceeded by leaps and bounds.

Magee With the result that it is now an important field of intellectual activity throughout the Western world, for instance in every major university.

Ayer But an interesting point which should also be mentioned is that one of the effects has been not so much to subordinate mathematics to logic, which is what Frege and Russell wanted, but to subordinate logic to mathematics. And in recent years, since mathematical logic has become more and more mathematical, it has had less and less to do with philosophy in general. Thus even a disciple of Frege like Michael Dummett is more interested in the semantic side of Frege's work, the theory of meaning, than in the purely mathematical side.

Magee Frege himself never explicitly made the step from mathematical logic to general philosophy. But Russell did. Can you give us some indication of how all the mathematical logic he had done affected his philosophical position?

Ayer Well it's very odd how little the two are connected. The one place where I suppose they are connected is something Russell called the Theory of Descriptions. As I have already explained, there was a puzzle about the meaning of statements including expressions like 'the present King of France', which didn't denote anything. If you said: 'The present King of France is bald', there was no King of France, and therefore, since the expression did not denote anything, there was a question how it could be meaningful. There had been philosophers, a notable example being a German called Meinong, who thought that such expressions denoted what he called 'subsistent entities'; but Russell thought that this was rubbish, and he exhibited a way of translating out such expressions by showing that they in fact contained covert existence-claims. In our example this would yield roughly the following false statement: 'There is one and only one thing that now rules over France, and whatever it is that rules over France is bald.' In this way Russell got rid of the apparent paradox, so his logical work had a philosophical implication. But in the main he simply went off on another tack. *The Problems of Philosophy* – a Home University Library book – came out in 1912, and in my view it is still the best introduction to philosophy that there is, because Russell was such a marvellous writer (though the book is a little bit old-fashioned). In it he really takes no account of his logical work at all, but simply continues the British empiricist tradition: it is a book that follows straight on from Locke, Berkeley and Hume, starting off with a theory of perception that is very like Berkeley's. The theory is that what we perceive are not tables and chairs and things of that sort, but what Locke calls simple ideas, and what Russell, following his friend Moore, calls sense data. And then it deals with the old, traditional philosophical question of how, on the basis of being presented with these sense impressions, we arrive at physical objects. After that he deals with various traditional philosophical problems from an empiricist standpoint.

He more or less gave up logic after *Principia Mathematica*. He himself said that it wore him out. He collaborated on that book with Whitehead, but Whitehead was teaching mathematics at Cambridge and was mainly occupied with that. Russell had a lectureship at Cambridge from 1910 to 1915, but in the first decade of the century, when the bulk of *Principia*

310 THE GREAT PHILOSOPHERS

Mathematica was written, he was living on his independent income. Thus he had the actual work of writing out nearly all the proofs, and he said that this really incapacitated him from ever doing any detailed work in future. And that is to some extent true: all his later work is full of brilliant ideas which he never fully works out – at a certain point he gets bored, indicating that it 'goes on like this . . .' without bothering to dot the i's and cross the t's.

Magee Am I mistaken, or do I discern one important continuing concern in the later work? Russell was always, it seems to me, concerned to validate the natural sciences in terms of sense data – that is to say, he always wanted to show that the entire corpus of our scientific knowledge could be derived from, and indeed was derived from, nothing but our observations, and our reflections on our observations?

Ayer Well, not always. I think that you make one very important point here, and one in fact that I overlooked when I was talking a few moments ago, and that is that from the very beginning Russell's approach to philosophy was an interest in justification. There is quite an amusing story that when he was about twelve his older brother Frank – who was sent to school, Russell himself being taught at home – started teaching him geometry, and Russell refused to accept the axioms. He wanted to have them proved; but his brother said that they couldn't get on unless they accepted the axioms, so Russell agreed to, *provisionally*. He always wanted to have everything justified. And this was common to both his approach to logic and mathematics and his approach to other branches of knowledge – and, as you say, also his approach to science: he wanted to have a *basis* for our belief in science. Here, however, his views varied. In the book I mentioned, *The Problems of Philosophy*, it's quite true that he wanted to start with sense data, but he didn't think that all scientific statements – or even all commonsense statements, like 'that is a table' – could be reduced to sensory statements. He adopted a causal theory, namely, that you could assume the existence of the physical world as the best explanation for our sensory experiences. Then he changed his view, and in the next important book he published on the theory of knowledge, *Our Knowledge of the External World*, which came out in 1914, he did take the view you just referred to. He thought you could reduce not only every commonsense statement but every scientific statement to statements about our actual and hypothetical sensory experiences. And this view, which is technically known as phenomenalism (and was the view of Berkeley, if you rob Berkeley of God, and also the view of John Stuart Mill – who incidentally was Russell's godfather, his lay godfather since he didn't believe in God), was developed in *Our Knowledge of the External World* and also in some important essays included by Russell in a

Bertrand Russell (1872–1970)

book called *Mysticism and Logic*, which he produced during the First World War, notably an essay called 'The Relation of Sense-data to Physics'. He continued this trend in another important book called *The Analysis of Mind*, which came out in 1921. There he adopted a theory which had been advanced before him by the pragmatist William James, Henry James's elder brother, in which both mind and matter were composed of what James called 'neutral stuff' and were in fact sense data and images. Mind and matter were held to differ only in being different arrangements of these fundamental data. But then Russell gave this up. In 1927 he published *The Analysis of Matter*, in which there are, indeed, traces of this view still remaining, but mainly he went back to the causal theory he had held in 1912. When he revived his interest in philosophy in the 1940s and published his final, or his next to last, philosophical book, *Human Knowledge, Its Scope and Limits*, he went back entirely to a causal theory. He always thought that the basis of our knowledge lay in sense experience, but he changed his mind about the next step. So it was only during one period of his work that he thought that the whole thing could be reduced to sensory terms. More often, and certainly at the end of his career, he adhered very vehemently to a causal theory which put the physical world beyond our observation. In fact he ended up with a very curious theory indeed, that when I'm looking at you I am in fact only inspecting my own brain.

Magee By which, of course, he meant that you are reacting to the sense data of me that occupy your mind.

Ayer That's right. Yes.

Magee I think we'd better not pursue that particular theory, fascinating though it would be to do so; we have broader concerns in our present discussion. One thing which I think you will agree is constant with Russell is the attempt to bring a new rigour to bear in philosophy. And I am tempted to say not only rigour of a logical kind but also rigour of a scientific kind. He was always concerned, for example – this is something he reiterates again and again – that our beliefs should accord with the evidence for them. This principle, if taken seriously, sweeps away a great deal of traditional thinking, including a great deal of traditional philosophising.

Ayer Oh yes, I think that is true. And as you already mentioned, Russell had an influence on Wittgenstein, who was indeed Russell's pupil. And, as you know, Wittgenstein, and also the group of philosophers in Vienna called the Vienna Circle, whom he influenced, condemned what they called metaphysics. Metaphysics, in their view, consisted at least partly in any attempt to describe the world in non-scientific terms. They thought that the natural world was the only world there is, and that science was a matter of forming theories about it which were verified by observation; and any assumption that there was a superior world, a world inhabited by gods or anything of that sort, was nonsensical. Russell may not have considered it nonsensical but he at least held it to be false. He was always concerned to justify science, and was always worried by what seemed to him the fact that the justification for science was extremely problematic.

Magee It remained problematic to the end.

Ayer Yes, to the end. His last philosophical work, called *My Philosophical Development*, which he published in 1959, is mainly a book of reminiscences; but in his last purely philosophical book, the one he wrote on *Human Knowledge, Its Scope and Limits*, which came out in 1948, he sets out what he thinks are the assumptions required if belief in scientific theories is to be justified. And he makes it quite clear that he thinks these assumptions must, as it were, be taken on faith. He tried to work out what we call a theory of induction, but was never entirely satisfied with it, and more or less said: 'We really can't be sure that science is true, but it has a greater chance of being true than anything else that can be set up as its rival.'

Magee So to the very end he couldn't validate science in the way he would like to have done.

Ayer No, he couldn't validate it in the way he would like to have done.

Magee Let us try to talk in a slightly more orderly way about his influence – for he and Wittgenstein must be just about the two most influential philosophers of the twentieth century, in the English-speaking world at least. Now, I suppose the first significant group of people to be influenced by Russell were his contemporaries, or even people older than himself, such as Moore and Whitehead, with whom he collaborated in Cambridge in his younger days?

Ayer Curiously enough the influence went the other way. Let us put it this way. In the purely logical work in which Russell and Whitehead collaborated, it was I think Russell who had the more interesting ideas. The Theory of Types and the Theory of Descriptions came from Russell. But when it came to trying to apply that sort of technique to philosophy – which to a slight extent Russell did in *Our Knowledge of the External World*, for example, in trying to reduce abstract concepts, like concepts of points and instants, to observational terms – then it was Whitehead who took the lead, and Russell got his ideas from Whitehead. Indeed, they quarrelled over this, because Russell didn't pay Whitehead sufficient acknowledgement. You will find the theory developed in two books of Whitehead's that came out after the First World War, *The Principles of Natural Knowledge* and *The Concept of Nature*. Russell in his very early days was also influenced by McTaggart, who was a disciple of Hegel and got both Russell and Moore to be idealists. It was Moore first of all who rebelled against this, in the interests of common sense. Moore was the great defender of common sense, and he influenced Russell to the extent that he cured him of any belief in idealism. So the influence there went that way. In respect to ethics also, in which Russell then was not greatly interested, he was content, like all Bloomsbury, to accept Moore's *Principia Ethica*. He believed that 'good' was a non-natural, indefinable concept, and so forth. On the other hand, Russell had a very big influence on the later – more my – generation of philosophers, in as much as he convinced us that since science was sovereign in the description of the world, all that philosophy could do was elucidate and analyse; so I think that he can be regarded as the father of analysis. But here he differs profoundly from Wittgenstein – I don't want to go too deeply into Wittgenstein. . . .

Magee I'd rather you didn't, because the whole of the next discussion is going to be devoted to him.

Ayer Well, one thing that will come out in your next discussion is that Wittgenstein thought that philosophy was largely a matter of people's getting into a muddle, and that the business of philosophers like Wittgenstein was, in his own famous phrase, to 'show the fly the way out of the fly bottle', that is, to cure people of all these muddles. Well, Russell held a quite different opinion. He always thought that philosophical problems had a solution. This was why he was so opposed, so very hostile, to the purely linguistic philosophy that, for example, flourished in Oxford after the Second World War under the leadership of J. L. Austin. Russell thought that the mere exploration of language for its own sake, the study of the implications of English usage, was trivial. He really believed that there were questions about the justification of our beliefs which it was the business of philosophy to answer, and that these questions were answerable. He thought that the answers could be discovered if you worked at them hard enough. Otherwise he didn't think that philosophy would be worth doing.

Magee May I put a personal question to you? All your life you have acknowledged that you yourself have been influenced by Russell. This means that you can report from the inside what 'being influenced by Russell' is like. What has his influence on you consisted in?

Ayer On me it has been, first of all, that unlike most of my contemporaries I still think that one should start with what Russell calls sense data – I now prefer the term 'sense qualia', because of a technical difference about whether you begin with particulars or with something more general, but for our present purposes it comes to the same thing. So on the whole I share the starting point of his theory of perception. I also agree with the primacy that he attaches to the theory of knowledge. I am, and I have always been, a thoroughgoing empiricist. I agree with the view which Russell derived from Hume, that there is no necessity other than logical necessity, so that there is no such thing as causal necessity. Causality is just a matter of what Hume originally said it was, namely constant conjunction, and is something purely contingent. I agree with Russell in rejecting any form of theology, or anyhow transcendent theology, and in rejecting metaphysics; and I also, most importantly, agree with Russell that philosophy wouldn't be worth doing unless it posed questions to which we could find the answers. Perhaps not he, perhaps not I, but cleverer persons than I will eventually find the answers.

Magee And are all these examples not just of your being in agreement with Russell but of his having influenced you, and having done so quite directly?

Ayer Yes, yes, quite directly, quite directly.

Magee Haven't you also been influenced by him in the way you write – I mean your literary style?

Ayer Well I do regard him as a master of English prose, and while I am not in the same class as Russell as a philosopher I think that I do write English reasonably well.

Magee And again partly under his influence?

Ayer And, again, partly under his influence. Yes, I think there is an affiliation there, both of ideas and of style, from Hume through Mill to Russell, and – coming down a stage – to me.

Magee You could not have made more incontrovertibly the point that Russell can be an all-pervading influence on philosophers now living. Having done that, can we bring Frege back into the picture and take him up at the point where a revival of interest in his work got under way after the Second World War? This meant that for the first time an interest in Frege and an interest in Russell proceeded side by side in the world of professional philosophy. And this continued into the age that we ourselves now inhabit.

Ayer It is very difficult to account for historical events, particularly in such a short perspective, but immediately after the war there certainly was a decline in Russell's influence here in England. However, I think that this was not due to a revival of interest in Frege, but to the increased importance attached to the work of Wittgenstein and Moore. In Moore's case, although I enormously liked and respected him as a man, I think that philosophically he was overrated. And I think that the Oxford philosophers who were responsible for this were not so much Ryle, who respected Russell, but mainly Austin and his disciples. Austin was a linguistic philosopher in the narrowest possible sense, and he had a great respect for Moore as someone who attached importance to ordinary usage and to common sense, whereas common sense was said by Russell to be the metaphysics of savages. I am suggesting that it was the upgrading of Moore that was responsible at that time for the downgrading of Russell, and I am glad to say that this is a trend that has now been reversed.

Magee In my opinion you go too far in saying that Russell was downgraded after the Second World War. If one thinks back to those post-war years and asks oneself who, in the English-speaking world generally, were the most admired and influential living philosophers, even the very shortest of short-lists would have to include – apart from Russell himself – Wittgenstein, Carnap, Quine, Popper, Ryle and yourself: and all of you openly acknowledged yourselves influenced by Russell, whose stamp was indeed, if in different ways, plain and obvious on all of you.

Ayer Yes. Perhaps I am wrong. You would know better than I, because after all you were up at Oxford in the fifties, when I had already departed for London. But certainly the impression reaching us in London was that Russell was not receiving his due.

Magee But that is to take an Oxford-centred view of things, which in philosophy was always a mistake. It is perfectly true that there were locally fashionable philosophers in the Oxford of those days who disparaged Russell, but their own work – and their own view of philosophy, including their evaluation of other philosophers – have not withstood the test of time.

Ayer I am very glad to hear this. And certainly Russell's reputation has recovered. Perhaps I am influenced by the fact that he himself thought that his stock had fallen. I know this, because I used to see a great deal of him at that time. I organised a little group in London which he attended, and he certainly felt that he wasn't getting his due. Being slightly vain, like all philosophers, he suffered from it.

Magee But in any case we agree that his reputation and influence have now come back. Let us turn, if we may, to the post-war revival of interest in Frege.

Ayer Now the revival of Frege is something that I really can't explain. I don't even know exactly how it happened. Probably it started in America, with the development of a school of logicians led by a man called Alonzo Church, who insisted on very great rigour in logic and mathematics and found it in Frege but didn't find it in Russell and Whitehead (though of course they did find it elsewhere: they found it, for example, in Hilbert, though they disagreed with Hilbert for other reasons). In England the first evidence I can find is in a book published fairly late, about 1962 I think, by William and Martha Kneale, a very impressive history of logic in which great importance is given to Frege. He is put on a level with Aristotle. These are the two great names.

Magee But you've jumped over, in time, one book that was crucial to the Frege revival. And it was produced in Oxford, too.

Ayer I've jumped over one thing: you've suddenly reminded me that there was a translation in the early fifties.

Magee In 1950 itself.

Ayer Nineteen-fifty was it? Made by Austin of Frege's *Grundlagen – The Foundations of Arithmetic*. And then there was also a translation made two or three years later – by Max Black, an Englishman living and working in America, and by Peter Geach – of two of Frege's very obscure but important semantic essays, one of them called 'Sense and Reference' and the other 'Function and Concept'. So there was in the early fifties this sudden interest in Frege. But I'm not quite certain what led to it, or indeed what consequences it had.

Magee But surely quite a few of the bright young people took it up and were influenced by it? Whether that influence will last or not I don't know, but it seems to me to have continued up to our own time, at the very least.

Ayer I find little influence of Frege in current philosophical work apart from the writings of Dummett. Perhaps the most interesting work now being done is being done in America, and if you look at the writings of people like Quine and Putnam, and Thomas Nagel, and Donald Davidson in particular, you don't find such a strong influence of Frege – except perhaps in Davidson's case, indirectly, through the work of the Polish logician Tarski on truth (which in a sense links up with Frege, inasmuch as Frege himself linked meaning and truth).

Magee And what about Russell's continuing influence? Do you feel confident that that will last?

Ayer Yes.

Magee Why?

Ayer Mainly because it sustains the view that I take of philosophy. I think that the questions he asked are the important philosophical questions. And I think that his answers to them, whether right or wrong, will always need to be taken into consideration.

Magee Unless I'm mistaken, you also think that his conception of what philosophy itself is is the right conception, namely that it consists in the clarification (and therefore analysis) and the justification (and therefore argument) of our important beliefs.

Ayer Yes – and written in straightforward prose.

WITTGENSTEIN

Dialogue with
JOHN SEARLE

INTRODUCTION

Magee In philosophy, as in most other fields of human activity, the merits of the living are much more controversial than those of the dead. If you took a world-wide poll today among professors of philosophy on the question 'Who is the best living philosopher?', I'm pretty sure no one candidate would get an overall majority. So any list of the so-called 'great philosophers' had better end with the latest of the generally acclaimed dead – and today, for us, that is Wittgenstein.

Ludwig Wittgenstein was born in Vienna in 1889. His father, from whom he was to inherit a fortune, was the richest steel magnate in Austria. Wittgenstein was fascinated by machinery from boyhood, and his education was strongly weighted in the direction of mathematics, physics and engineering. After studying mechanical engineering in Berlin he spent three years at the University of Manchester as a postgraduate student in aeronautics. During this period he became absorbed in fundamental questions about the nature of the mathematics he was using. Bertrand Russell's book *The Principles of Mathematics* inspired him to give up engineering and go to Cambridge to study the philosophy of mathematics, which he did under Russell himself, and soon learned all Russell had to teach. He then went on to do the original thinking that was to produce his first book, *Tractatus Logico-Philosophicus*, published in 1921 – usually referred to just as the *Tractatus*.

Wittgenstein genuinely believed that in this book he had solved the fundamental problems of philosophy, so he turned away from philosophy and did other things. Meanwhile the *Tractatus* acquired enormous influence, stimulating further developments in logic at Cambridge while on the Continent becoming the most admired text among the famous group of Logical Positivists known as 'the Vienna Circle'. But Wittgenstein himself came to feel that it was fundamentally in error, so he returned to philosophy after all. In 1929 he went back to Cambridge, where in 1939 he became Professor of Philosophy. During his second period in Cambridge he developed a wholly new approach, quite different from his earlier one. During the rest of his life the influence of this later approach spread only through personal contact, for apart from one very brief article he published nothing more before his death in 1951. But two years after his death, in 1953, his book *Philosophical Investigations* came out, and proved to be the most influential work of philosophy to have appeared in the English-speaking world since the Second World War.

So here we have a remarkable phenomenon, a philosopher of genius producing two incompatible philosophies at different stages of his life, each of which influenced a whole generation. The two philosophies, though incompatible, do have certain basic features in common. Both are focused on the role of language in human thinking and human life, and both are centrally concerned to draw the demarcation between valid and invalid uses of language – or, as someone once put it, both try to draw the lines at which sense ends and nonsense begins. For me, the earlier of Wittgenstein's two main books, the *Tractatus*, remains hauntingly readable, but it has to be admitted that it is the later one, the *Philosophical Investigations*, that has turned him into a cultural figure of international significance during the period since his death and now exerts an active influence in many fields outside philosophy.

To discuss Wittgenstein's work with me I have invited John Searle, Professor of Philosophy at the University of California in Berkeley.

DISCUSSION

Magee Since Wittgenstein repudiated his own early philosophy, and since in any case it is now his later philosophy that is much the more influential, I don't think we ought to devote too much of our time to the early work. What do we really need to know about it?

Searle I think the key to understanding the *Tractatus* is the picture theory of meaning. Wittgenstein believed that if language is to represent reality, if sentences are to represent states of affairs, then there has to be something in common between the sentence and the state of affairs. Since the sentence and the state of affairs it represents have to have a common structure, in that sense the sentence is like a picture of a possible fact. Just as the elements in a picture correspond to objects in the world, and the arrangement of elements in a picture corresponds to a possible arrangement of objects in reality, so sentences contain names which correspond to objects in the world; and the arrangement of names in the sentence corresponds to a possible arrangement of objects in the world.

Now, this idea that sentences are really a disguised form of a picture gives him a remarkable kind of metaphysical lever. It enables him to read off the structure of reality from the structure of language. And the reason is that the structure of reality has to determine the structure of language. Unless language mirrors reality in some way, it would be impossible for sentences to mean.

Magee So the crucial point here is that we are able to talk about reality not just because names denote but also because sentences picture. For discourse to mirror the world it is not enough for there to be words that stand for things. For us to be able to say how things are we need also to be able to put words in a particular relation to one another which pictures the relation in which things in the world stand to one another. Thus it is the mirroring of one *structure* by another which is the real key to the possibility of meaningful discourse about the world in language. But now this same fact can be read in the other direction, so to speak. Since we know that for meaningful discourse to be possible the structure of language must mirror the structure of the world, and since we know that meaning-ful discourse is possible, we are in a position to find out about the structure of the world by analysing the structure of language.

Searle Right. Every meaningful sentence corresponds to a possible fact; and every true sentence corresponds to an actual fact. So we can learn about the *structure* of reality from sentences, independently of whether the sentence is true or false, because the mere meaningfulness of the sentence determines that it must correspond to a possible state of affairs in the world.

But it is important to emphasise that Wittgenstein was not talking about the surface features of sentences in ordinary language. He was not talking about the visible or audible structure of the sentences that you and I are now using to talk to each other. He thought that these surface, visible or audible, features of ordinary language sentences actually con-cealed the underlying logical structure of the sentence. If we took ordi-nary sentences and did a logical analysis of how they mean, we could then get down to the ground-floor sentences which constitute the underlying meaningful structures hidden by the ordinary sentences. We would get down to what he calls 'the elementary sentences', and in the elementary sentences we would find the strict picturing relationship between the structure of the sentence and the structure of the fact.

He inherits from Frege the idea that the fundamental unit of meaning isn't the word, but rather the sentence. The word only functions, the word only has a meaning, in the context of a sentence. And, as you suggested earlier, it's because the concatenation of words in the sentence itself constitutes a fact that the sentence is able to picture the structure of facts in the world.

Magee I think people will have little immediate difficulty in seeing how a sentence may mirror a fact when the fact exists. But what when I am asserting that a fact does not exist? If I say, 'There is a cat on the mat' – okay, people will see that this sentence may picture a state (or possible state) of affairs. But what if I say, 'There is not a cat on the mat'? We all know what the sentence means, but what state of affairs can it be said to picture – *picture*, mind you? What would a real picture of the absence of a cat on a mat be like? Would it be different from a picture of the absence of a dog?

Searle Wittgenstein thought that words like 'not' and 'and' and 'or' and 'if', the so-called logical constants, were not actually part of the picture relationship. He says: 'My fundamental thought is that the logical con-stants do not represent.' He thought of these logical words as just ways we have of stringing pictures together, but they aren't themselves part of any picture. And that's not so unrealistic if you think about it. For example, across the street from my house in Berkeley is a small park, and posted in the park is a picture of a dog with a red line drawn through it. Now notice that we quite effortlessly understand the red line in a different way from the way we understand the picture of the dog. We know that the picture is not supposed to depict dogs that have a red stripe painted on them. Rather, the line is the negation sign. The whole sign means 'No Dogs'. So the sign in the park is really a Wittgensteinian sort of picture, at least in the sense that the 'not' symbol is used to operate on the picture but is not itself part of the picture.

Magee So we can expand our first formulation by saying that, in the view of the young Wittgenstein, meaningful discourse about the world can be analysed into elementary statements which picture possible states of affairs, and that these elementary statements are either linked together, or postulated as stating possibilities, or set off against each other as stating alternatives, or negated, or whatever it may be, by the so-called logical constants, which are not themselves pictorial.

Searle Yes. Right.

Magee In my introduction to our discussion I said that Wittgenstein was concerned throughout his career to demarcate talk that made sense from talk that did not make sense. How did he draw this line of demarcation in his earlier philosophy?

Searle In his earlier philosophy, in the *Tractatus*, Wittgenstein thought that the only language which strictly speaking makes any sense is fact-stating language. Now, unlike the logical positivists, he didn't relish this conclusion. He didn't think it was such a wonderful result. On the contrary, he thought that it had the consequence that the really important things in life were unsayable, were unstatable. He thought that ethics, religion and aesthetics, for example, were all in the realm of the unsayable. And he once said about the *Tractatus* that the really important part of the book is the part that is left out, the part that is not there at all. But according to the account of meaning given in the *Tractatus* there is a strict demarcation between meaningful or fact-stating language and the other parts of language which are not used to state actual or possible facts in the world and which are therefore, strictly speaking, nonsense. These parts of language try to say something about the important questions of life, but they fail, because what they are trying to say is unsayable.

Magee This is in keeping with the ordinary view commonly held by people who are not philosophers that although ethics, religion and the arts are of fundamental significance in life, language is completely inadequate to say what it is they convey, or are about, or even are.

Searle They are fundamental; but our efforts to discuss them are meaningless, at least as far as the theory of meaning in the *Tractatus* is concerned. And it isn't simply that we can't do them justice; rather, our attempt to do them justice is itself meaningless; we can't say anything meaningful about them at all.

Magee You've said that the key to understanding the early Wittgenstein is the picture theory of meaning. In what way does the later Wittgenstein depart from it?

Searle Though Wittgenstein's ideas are very complex, there is actually a rather simple answer to that question. In his later work, he abandoned the picture theory of meaning in favour of a use or tool conception of meaning. He urges us to think of words as tools, think of sentences as instruments. To get a correct conception of language we need simply to look at how it functions in real life, we need to look at what people do with words. He says, 'For a *large* class of cases – though not for all – in which we employ the word "meaning" it can be defined thus: the meaning of a word is its use in the language.'

His early view had the consequence that the structure of the real world determines the structure of language. But in his later work, it is, in a sense, the other way round. In the *Philosophical Investigations*, the structure of our language determines the way we think of the real world. It determines what we count as one object or two objects or the same object; it determines what we count as an object at all. We can't discuss the world and we can't even think of the world independently of some conceptual apparatus that we can use for that purpose. And, of course, the apparatus is provided by language.

Now this gives him a completely different conception of the role of language in our lives. In the early work, fact-stating discourse is really all the meaningful discourse there is. But in the later work, it turns out that fact-stating discourse is just one type of discourse among many other types, just one type of 'language game' along with, strictly speaking, an indefinite number of other types of language game. In his later work, as a consequence of emphasising the use of language, Wittgenstein is constantly calling our attention to the multiplicity, the variety, that we find in uses of language.

Magee It's very striking, this shift of the master-metaphor from language as a picture to language as a tool. Now it's in the nature of a picture that it pictures one particular state of affairs, but it's in the nature of a tool that it can be used for a number of different tasks. This aspect of the difference was of great importance to Wittgenstein, wasn't it?

Searle Yes. Wittgenstein is always anxious to insist in the *Investigations* that language is indefinitely extendable, and there isn't any single essence that binds all uses of language together. There isn't any single feature that runs through all of language that constitutes the essence of language. And indeed, for particular words, there needn't even be any particular essence that constitutes the definition of that word. He thinks of many words as having only a 'family resemblance' among their various uses. He gives as an example the word 'game'. And he asks us, what, if anything, do all games have in common? And here, as always, he keeps insisting: Don't just think that they must all have some one thing in common, but rather, look and see what you can find. And then he says that, if you consider the enormous variety of different kinds of games – board games, Olympic games, gambling games, ball games, and so on – what you find is that there isn't any single essence of gamehood, there isn't any single thing that all games have in common, but rather there are a series of criss-crossing and overlapping similarities. It is this phenomenon which he calls 'family resemblance'.

Magee This point about 'don't just take it for granted, but *think*' is always very important with Wittgenstein. Taking your example, one's first reaction is to say, 'Oh but it's obvious, all games are diversions of one sort or another'. But then one reflects that American football, in which players suffer appalling injuries for huge sums of money, is not a diversion. If you say, 'Well it's a diversion for the spectators', that won't do, because most of the various games that are actually played in the world probably never have spectators. And would American football played without spectators not be a game? If you say, 'Well, all games are competitive', that isn't true, because there are games for one person, such as patience and solitaire. And if you say, 'Well at least all games are leisure activities, a change from work', that isn't true either, because there are thousands of professionals who play games for a living. And so on and so forth – Wittgenstein's method requires one to work one's way painstakingly through all the examples one can think of; and although the work is, of its nature, detailed, it also calls for imagination, the ability to think of the un-obvious. Wittgenstein himself showed such ingenuity in his use of examples that many of them have become part of the common currency of philosophy. A prolonged analysis of the concept of a game, which we haven't time actually to carry out in this discussion, would show, perhaps surprisingly, that there is no one thing that all games have in common *by virtue of which they are games*. They have certain features in common with innumerable other human activities – for instance, that they are characteristically learnt from others, and characteristically rule-governed – but of course *these* features are not enough to make something a game. And that means that there is no one thing that the word 'game' stands for.

Searle Right. Now it might seem as if Wittgenstein is just reminding us of certain obvious points here, that what he is saying is all rather common-sensical. And to a certain extent, that's right. But it is also important to remember that he is militating against a very powerful philosophical tradition. He is militating against a tradition that goes back as far as Plato and Aristotle. He is fighting, first, against his earlier theory that words get their meanings by standing for objects, and secondly, he is fighting against an even older tradition that says that words get their meanings by being associated with ideas in the mind. And third, he is also fighting against a tradition according to which in order for a word to have a meaning, there must be some essence which that word expresses. According to that view, if we can call a whole lot of different things games, it can only be because they have some essential feature of gamehood in common. So, the interest of his remarks about language derives from the radical attack he is making on the philosophical tradition.

Magee You talked a moment ago of Wittgenstein's application of the term 'family resemblance' to games. Since this is a term which he applies to the meanings of all concepts, a term which he uses to explicate the notion of meaning *as such*, it would be well worth our while to dwell on it for a moment. Usually, when we say that there is a noticeable resemblance among all the members of a certain family, we don't mean that there is one single feature that they all have in common – the same chin, or the same nose (though of course there are occasional families in which this is the case): more often we mean that each one of them seems to have drawn a different selection of features from a common pool, so that there are varying points of similarity which, as you just put it, criss-cross and overlap.

Now Wittgenstein is saying that this is true of the meanings of words. The meaning of a word is the sum total of its possible uses: but there need be no one thing that is associated exclusively with a particular word and is at the same time common to all its possible uses. These are much more likely to exhibit a family resemblance.

Searle That's right, but two further points need to be made. First, he isn't saying that these words are ambiguous. He isn't saying that the word 'game' has different meanings in the sense that the word 'bank' can mean either the side of a river or a finance house. Rather, the one meaning of the word 'game' gets its strength not from the fact that there is a single essence, but from the family resemblance among the different cases. Second, he isn't saying that all words in every language are like this. There are words that have strict definitions. But he did think it was crucial for philosophers to see the pervasiveness of the family resemblance phenomenon, because many of the words that trouble us in philosophy are words of that type. For example, in ethics and aesthetics, we look at words such as 'good' and 'beautiful', and we tend to think that there must be some essential feature which those words mark, that there must be some essence of goodness or essence of beauty. Wittgenstein insists, on the contrary, that if we look at the actual use of these words, we will see various criss-crossing family resemblance relationships in their uses.

Magee He says something similar, doesn't he, about the use not just of individual words but of whole modes of discourse. We use language for an enormous variety of purposes, and we use it differently for different purposes. If you and I are discussing philosophy we use language differently from the way we use it if we're arguing about politics, and differently again from the way we use it if we're discussing a film we both saw last night. In addition to that there are musical talk, scientific talk, religious talk and all sorts of different kinds of other talk – and in all of them language tends to be used in different ways. So again Wittgenstein says: 'If you really want to understand the meaning of a word, don't ask for a dictionary definition, look closely at how it is actually used *in the particular area of discourse under consideration*.' It's mainly this sort of activity that the title *Philosophical Investigations* refers to: an always particular, always specific inquiry into the *actual* use of an *actual* word or concept in an *actual* situation.

Searle Precisely. One of his favourite slogans was 'Don't ask for the meaning, ask for the use'. And at this point in the argument he introduces another metaphor, one of his few technical terms, the notion of 'language game'. The idea he has is that we should see speaking a language, using words, on the analogy with playing games. And the key point of the analogy is that both using words and playing games are human activities. They are things we do. He thinks there are several features in common between the use of words and the activity of playing games that justify the metaphor of a language game. First of all, both are systematic, indeed, characteristically rule-governed (though the notion of a rule, for Wittgenstein, is problematic – we'll get to that in a minute). And we can't have a Humpty Dumpty attitude towards the use of words, we can't think that anything goes, any more than we can think that anything goes in a game. But at the same time there is a great deal of slack, there is room for interpretation; not everything is determined by the rules.

Now once we get out of the idea that meaning is entirely a matter of introspectable entities in the mind, or that meaning is a matter of words standing for things in the world – once we see the analogy between the use of words and the use of pieces in a game like chess – then we can see that the meaning of a word is entirely given by its use. Just as the 'meaning' of the king in chess is entirely exhausted by its role in the game, so, similarly, the meaning of words – including philosophically puzzling words such as 'good', 'true', 'beautiful' and 'just' – is entirely exhausted by their role in the language games that are played with them.

Now there is another aspect of this analogy that is disconcerting to many traditional philosophers. Wittgenstein insists that we shouldn't look for the *foundations* of language games any more than we should look for foundations of games such as football or baseball. All of these are just human activities. These activities have to look out for themselves. We play a language game of ethical discourse, of aesthetic discourse, of fact-stating discourse, a language game with the word 'cause', and a language game of identifying spatial and temporal relationships. A characteristic philosophical mistake is to think that there must be some foundation, some transcendental justification, for each language game. But Wittgenstein is anxious to insist that we should see these as just types of human behaviour, and the use of words as everywhere tied up with the rest of our behaviour. If we think our present language games are the only possible ones we should remember that if we were different, or if the world were different, we might use words differently. But it is not our task to find some foundation or transcendental justification for our present language games. All we can say is, 'This language game is played, and this is how it's played.'

Magee I must say I think it's something of a disaster that he fastened on this term 'language game'. It makes it sound as if what he's doing, or what he's talking about, is somehow frivolous. And it feeds a very specific anti-philosophical prejudice that is quite widespread outside the subject, the idea that philosophy is all just playing with words, that it's all just a game, and that philosophers are people who are merely concerned superficially with language. I have often heard the term 'language game' used in disparagement of philosophy by people who have jumped to wrong conclusions about what the term means. In universities, at one time at least, that was not at all uncommon. But Wittgenstein wasn't expressing anything remotely like the idea that when we talk we're merely playing some kind of game. What he was doing was drawing a sober, serious analogy between certain structural features which are characteristic of most games and certain structural features which are characteristic of most verbal discourse.

331 MAGEE · SEARLE

Searle Right, and let me just re-emphasise the reasons for the analogy: first of all, playing a game is a human social activity. It isn't something sublime that only goes on in our heads, and it doesn't just consist of an abstract set of logical relationships. Games are characteristically social and they are characteristically rule-governed. Those, I believe, are two of the features he wanted to get at in making the analogy between using words and playing games. The force of the analogy is to emphasise that we should look at language in action, we should see speaking a language as part of ongoing, regular, social, rule-governed behaviour.

Now so far, I think, that may sound pretty uncontroversial, to us at least. But there is a more radical aspect to this that goes beyond the analogy with games: Wittgenstein is anxious to insist that there isn't any point of view from outside the language games where we can, so to speak, stand back and appraise the relationship between language and reality. He doesn't think that we can get outside of language to look at the relation between language and reality from the side and see whether or not language is adequately representing reality. There isn't any non-linguistic Archimedean point from which we can appraise the success or failure of language in representing, coping with or dealing with the real world. We are always operating within some language game or other. So there can't be any transcendental appraisal of the adequacy of language games, because there isn't any non-linguistic, transcendental point of view from which they can be appraised.

Magee But does this not have the consequence that we have no actual contact with a 'real world'? If it does, it's a fundamental breach with Wittgenstein's early philosophy. In that, there's no doubt at all of an independently existing reality: we live in a world of facts, and the function of language is to picture those facts. In consequence, the early philosophy is centrally about the relationship between language and reality – about how language pictures reality, and about what can and what cannot be pictured. But you seem to be saying that according to Wittgenstein's later philosophy we are never able to make any comparison between language and something which is not language, because we can never occupy any position which is not embedded in language – not, so to speak, inside language. All our conceptual structures – our conceptions of the everyday world, of science, of the arts, of religion, everything – are built up by us in linguistic terms that we can never get outside of. On this showing, either there is no external reality at all or, if there is, it is something we can never have independent knowledge of or contact with. Is this really what the later Wittgenstein is saying?

Searle No. I think, in fact, the way that you have stated the position is a characteristic way in which Wittgenstein is misunderstood. Many people think: Surely this view leads to some kind of idealism, perhaps a kind of linguistic idealism. It leads to the view that the only things that exist are words. But that is not Wittgenstein's position at all. Wittgenstein is not denying that there are language games in which we talk about real objects in the real world. We can, for example, talk about this table or the couch we are sitting on or the electrons in orbit in hydrogen atoms. Wittgenstein doesn't deny that these words actually refer to objects. That, indeed, is one of the things we use words to do: refer to objects in the world. But he is saying: When we refer to objects in the world we are operating within a language game, and our concept of 'the world' and how we divide up the world is already conditioned by the structure of our language.

Now, it is a misunderstanding of this last point to think that Wittgenstein is saying, 'Everything is relative to a language game'. Or, 'Truth is relative to the language game'. Such remarks would presuppose that we could get outside of language altogether and look at the relationship between language and reality from the side and then conclude, 'Ah ha! Truth is language relative'. To say that would be to make exactly the same mistake as saying, 'Ah ha! Truth is absolute'. Both of these views make the same mistake of thinking that there is a point of view outside of language from which we can survey the relations between language and reality, and then describe how language represents reality. On Wittgenstein's view, we are always working inside language, even when we describe the workings of language. Let me put this point very briskly: Wittgenstein is not for one moment denying the existence of reality, he is not denying the existence of the real world, or the fact that we can make true claims about the real world. What he is anxious to insist on, though, is that if we have expressions in our language like 'real world', 'reality', 'truth', then they must have a use in language games that is just as humble, just as ordinary, as the use of the words 'chair' and 'table', or 'dog' and 'cat'. For Wittgenstein, our task as philosophers is not to sit back and contemplate the sublime nature of reality and truth, but rather to get busy and describe how we actually use expressions like 'real' and 'true'.

Magee Let me bring this down to something simple and immediate, to be sure we're getting it clear. Is part of what Wittgenstein is saying that for me to see this as a hand I have already to be in possession of the concept 'hand'; for me to see that as a table I have already to be in possession of the concept 'table'; and therefore that what I see reality *as being* is constituted by a whole conceptual structure of which I must already be in possession, and which can be articulated in language? Is that it – or part of it?

Searle That is partly right, but I think that Wittgenstein's point goes even

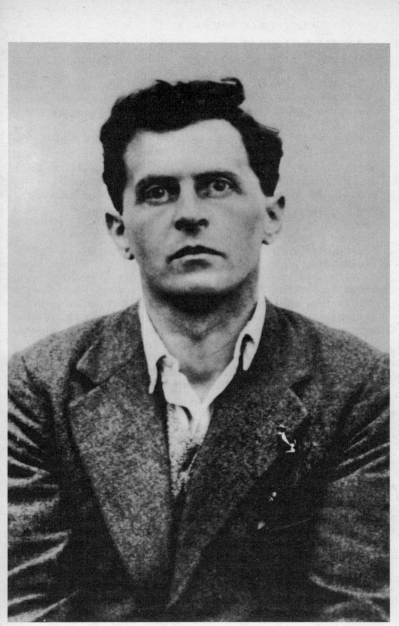

Ludwig Wittgenstein (1889–1951)

deeper than that. If we look at his work historically, it seems to me that we can see that he is part of a larger movement that has occurred in the past hundred years. It is a characteristic feature of twentieth-century intellectual life that we no longer feel that we can take language for granted. Language has become immensely problematic for us. It has moved to the centre of philosophy, and Wittgenstein is one of the great leaders in that movement. At one level, he would certainly agree with what you have just said; that is, he would agree with the point that reality divides up the way we divide it, and that we can think of how we divide it only from within language. We can only think of this as a hand, or that as a table, because we have the relevant concepts, that is the relevant words. But the point he wants to make is even deeper than that. For Wittgenstein, there couldn't be such a thing as thinking, even such a thing as experience, at least as far as we think of experience as a feature of our full-grown adult human lives, apart from the use of linguistic expressions. For him, thinking just is operating with expressions; so language permeates all of thinking, and thus, all of human experience.

Magee Perhaps the sort of independent reality Wittgenstein allows is clarified if one takes the point you've just made in conjunction with one you were making, or implying, earlier, to the effect that each individual language game can be understood only from the inside. The old-style logical positivists, who were extremely influenced by their reading of Wittgenstein's early philosophy, were also extremely dismissive of any form of religious utterance. Because religious utterances are characteristically unverifiable they took them to be, literally, meaningless. But the later Wittgenstein would have had a quite different attitude. He would have said that there is, and has been in every known form of society, religious utterance, and if we want to understand it we must pay close attention to the way concrete examples of it function within given forms of life. Every mode of discourse has its own appropriate logic, and it's simply no good appraising religious utterances as one would appraise scientific utterances – which is what the logical positivists had been doing.

Searle Well, it seems to me, we have to be very careful about how we state this last point. Wittgenstein would say that it is not our task as philosophers to appraise the success or failure of the religious language game. All we can do is describe how it's played. And the important thing for us to see is that it is not played like the scientific language game. He thinks that it is ridiculous to suppose that we should take religious utterances as if they were some sort of second-rate scientific utterances, as if they were theories for which we have inadequate evidence. He was always anxious to insist that we ought to look at the role that different sorts of utterances play in people's lives. For him, that is where we will find the meaning of these utterances. He hated the idea that we should over-intellectualise these matters, and try to make everything into some sort of theoretical enterprise. He disliked the idea that we should examine the claim that God exists as if it were like a claim in physics, and then see if it was up to snuff by scientific standards. Here's the sort of thing that Wittgenstein liked. W. G. Grace, the great English cricketer, once jumped on a chair in a meeting and shouted something like: 'God doesn't want a head, any old cabbage will do for a head. What God wants is a heart.' Now, Wittgenstein liked that because he thought that was the right attitude to have to religion. He thought that was an example of the language game in action. What he hated, on the other hand, was the sort of attitude expressed by his Cambridge colleague A. C. Ewing, who in a philosophy meeting once referred to 'the theistic hypothesis'. Wittgenstein refused to accept that, for example, the Thirty Years War was fought over some mere 'hypothesis'.

To summarise this point: Wittgenstein thought that if you want to understand a type of discourse, such as religious discourse or any other type of discourse, look at the role that it actually plays in people's lives. For him, the characteristic mistake of twentieth-century intellectual life was to try to treat all intellectual endeavours as if they were attempting to be like science. He thought that science had its place like anything else, but that it was a mistake to treat subjects which were plainly not forms of science and technology as if they were second-rate attempts to achieve science and technology.

Magee That point made, I think it's important to add that Wittgenstein did very emphatically *not* adopt an 'anything goes' attitude. He did not think we can just use language how we like and then claim meaning or validity for our utterances on equal terms with anyone else's. On the contrary, he thought we ought to pay the strictest attention to the way we use language. One reason why he thought this was his view that philosophical problems or puzzlements most commonly arise from the misuse of words: specifically, they arise when we take a mode of expression as functioning in one language game when its rightful place is in another. They will arise, for instance, if you treat a religious statement as you would treat a scientific statement.

Searle He puts this very point by saying that philosophical problems arise when we take a word out of the language game where it is at home, and then try to think of it as standing for something sublime. He says that philosophical problems characteristically arise when 'language goes on holiday', that is, when a word is no longer doing the work for which it is properly fitted, and we are examining words apart from the actual language games that give them their meanings; when, for example, we try to inquire into the intrinsic nature of knowledge, or of the good, the true or the beautiful, instead of just looking at how these and other words are actually used in the language games where they get their meanings.

But there is something you said earlier on that I want to take objection to. You might be taken to imply that there is a special philosophical language game. I don't believe Wittgenstein thought that. I think he thought that philosophers should just be engaged in the language game of describing. They should be describing how words are actually used. They should describe how language is used in a way that will enable us to solve, or rather dissolve, the recurring philosophical problems; and they should abandon the idea that philosophy has a special task of *explaining* or *justifying* which goes beyond describing. So, in one sense, philosophy is not a special language game, it doesn't have a special set of rules or procedures. Rather, we should just get inside people's actual practices, especially their linguistic practices, and describe what they do. And we can also describe alternatives to our existing practices in order to get rid of the idea that our practices are inevitable or necessary. We make these various descriptions for specific intellectual purposes. In his conception, we are 'assembling reminders for a purpose'. The purpose is always to remove the intellectual confusions that are created by our inevitable urge to misunderstand the character of language. For example, we are constantly craving for some kind of general theory where there is no general theory, we are craving for foundations where there are no foundations, and we are craving for essences where there are just family resemblances. These are typical of the sorts of mistakes he thinks philosophers characteristically – indeed, inevitably – make, and the aim of philosophical description is to remove the urge to make these mistakes.

Magee In all our talk so far about the analogies Wittgenstein draws between games and the use of language there is one very important point we have not touched on. It concerns the famous 'private language' controversy. Wittgenstein argued that for language to mean anything at all its use has to follow certain rules. But some of the criteria of what constitutes a rule or the following of a rule are inescapably social. From this Wittgenstein concluded that there could be no such thing as a private language. However, not all philosophers have agreed with him, and a controversy has raged over the question ever since. In fact, among professional philosophers it's one of the most controversial aspects of Wittgenstein's philosophy.

Searle Yes, it certainly has been controversial. In fact, I am a bit reluctant to get into this hassle, because there is simply so much junk written about the private language argument. I would rather not get involved in the famous disputes about interpretation. But here goes anyhow. In order to explain Wittgenstein's discussion of private languages, you have to say a little bit about his conception of rules and rule-governed behaviour. We have been talking as if the notion of a rule for Wittgenstein was unproblematic. But of course, it wasn't. In fact, his discussion of rules is one of his most important contributions to philosophy. His first observation is that rules do not account for every possible eventuality. Language isn't everywhere bounded by rules. Indeed, no system is everywhere bounded by rules. There always are many gaps left open by any system of rules. He gives the example of throwing a tennis ball when you serve. There is no rule that says how high you have to throw it. I suppose that if somebody could throw the ball five miles high, and thus delay tennis games, the authorities would have to make a new rule. But the system of rules would never become 'complete', in the sense that there would always be new possibilities which would be unaccounted for by the existing rules.

Now the next point he makes, and it's related to the first point, is that rules are always subject to different interpretations. You can always find some way of interpreting a rule so that it turns out that your behaviour is really in accord with the rule even though at first sight it appears not to accord with the rule. A good historical example of this is the development of the American income-tax laws, where there is a constant struggle between the taxing authorities and people who try to get around the purpose of the rule by reinterpreting it so that their behaviour would seem to be in accordance with the rule. It seems to Wittgenstein that there is a kind of paradox that inevitably arises when we consider the problem of following a rule. If anything can be made to accord with the rule by some interpretation, then anything can also be made to conflict with the rule, given some other ingenious interpretation, and you would get then neither accord nor conflict. It looks as if the rule would simply drop out as irrelevant, that it would play no role in the explanation of behaviour. Now his solution to this problem is to point out that obeying a rule is a social practice, it is something that we do in society and we learn in society. Social groups have ways of making people conform to rules and of training them to conform to rules, and in that way society determines what counts as conforming to the rule. So on his view, there is a way of just responding to a rule which is not an 'interpretation'. We just act on the rule the way we were trained to act.

Now, his discussion of private languages is a discussion of a separate problem from the problem of following a rule, but they are related in that his solution to the problem of following a rule is also his solution to the private language problem. The problem of private languages is this: Could there be a language in which I use words to name my own private sensations, in such a way that no one else could understand the words, because the words are defined ostensively in terms of private experiences,

experiences known only to me? The reason this problem seems so important is that traditional epistemology of the sort one finds in Locke, Berkeley and Hume, for example, is based on the idea that we should build knowledge of the world from the inside out. We start with our inner private sensations and then construct public language and public knowledge on the basis of our inner experiences. Wittgenstein, in his discussion of the private language problem, argues first of all that that is not really how our language for inner sensations works. We don't give private inner definitions to our sensation words, but rather, he points out, our sensation language, our language for describing inner experiences, is tied to public social phenomena at every point. It is only because pains, for example, arise in certain sorts of situations and produce certain sorts of behaviour that we can have a vocabulary for talking about pains at all. Our ordinary sensation language is not really a private language, because we learn and use the terms of this language in conjunction with public criteria, criteria having to do with behaviour and situations.

Secondly, and more controversially, Wittgenstein claims that we *could not* in fact have a private language, we couldn't give a private ostensive definition where we just point inwardly to a private experience, name that experience, and then use the name to refer to the same experience in the future. His argument against this is a *reductio ad absurdum* argument. If we tried to think of a sensation language on this model, we wouldn't be able to make the distinction between actually using the word right and just thinking we are using it right. But if there isn't a distinction between really getting it right and just thinking we have got it right, then we can't talk about right at all. So the idea that we could have a private sensation language reduces to absurdity. His solution to this puzzle, the puzzle of how we can ever use words to refer to inner sensations, is the same as his solution to the general problem about rule following. The rules for using sensation words are public social rules. They are learnt and applied in a social setting. And these external criteria are socially sanctioned and socially applied. It's because we are members of a linguistic community that we can have linguistic rules at all, and it's because we have public social criteria for our inner experiences that we can have a language referring to our inner experiences. He summarises this point by saying: 'An "inner process" stands in need of outward criteria'.

Magee   One point which I would emphasise even more strongly than you have in order to bring out Wittgenstein's argument is that we learn the use of all words, including words for inner sensations, from other people. The words and expressions for tastes, smells, colours, pains, dreams and every other sort of 'inner' experience all existed long before we were born; and so did the criteria for their proper use. And what we do when we come into the world is learn both the words and their proper use from others. When one seriously considers the implications of this it seems that existing words and their meaningful use are inescapably social phenomena no matter how 'inner' and 'private' what they are used to talk about may be. And as you say, the implications of that for epistemology run very deep. For it means that we do not and cannot form our conception of the world by starting from elements which are exclusively private to us and building outwards from those until we reach the 'external' world and other people. And to say *that* is to go against a whole tradition in philosophy, a tradition that started with Descartes.

For the later Wittgenstein, all the criteria of meaning are ultimately social, not personal, and still less private. Words derive their meaning from the contexts within which they are used, and these in turn depend on social practices and thus ultimately on ways of living, forms of life. And he does in fact use that term 'forms of life' a great deal in this context.

Searle That's right. It is very important to emphasise that the notion of the use of words is itself a social notion. Using words is something I do in conjunction with other members of my society. It is only because we are trained in the use of words and trained in the task of following rules generally that we can avoid the form of scepticism according to which anything I do can be made out to be in accord with a rule, because we can always interpret a rule in such a way that any behaviour would be in accordance with it. You are right in calling attention to the fact that Wittgenstein emphasises the idea that a language is a form of life. This has many implications for him, but one of the most important is that we can't carve off language and look at it apart from the rest of human activities. Language is everywhere bound up with the rest of our activities.

Magee An analogy has often been drawn between the philosophy of the later Wittgenstein and Freudian psychoanalysis. According to Freud, neurosis may be caused by psychological hangups of which the patient is unconscious, and in those cases the task of the psychotherapist is to track down the hidden cause of the trouble and bring it to light; and when the patient becomes fully aware of what the cause of his problem was it thereby ceases to be a problem, and the patient is cured. The parallel with the later Wittgenstein is almost exact. According to him, our philosophical problems are caused by conceptual confusions which have their origins in a deep-lying misuse of language. The task of the philosopher is to track down and bring to light the cause of the confusion, and when this has been done the problem is seen to be no longer a problem. There is even the therapeutic element to it: Wittgenstein sees philosophical puzzlement as a kind of sickness to which his method offers itself as a cure.

Searle Indeed. And the word 'therapy' is in fact one Wittgenstein uses.

He compares the philosopher's treatment of a problem with the doctor's treatment of an illness. The comparison with Freud has often been made, but in some ways it is an odd comparison, because, of course, Wittgenstein had very serious objections to Freud. He thought Freud's pretence at science was seriously mistaken. But Wittgenstein's 'therapy' is like psychoanalysis in at least this respect: the confusions that we get into from misunderstanding the logic of our language are profound and largely unconscious. And it is the task of a philosopher, by a variety of therapies, to get us out of these confusions by getting us consciously to see the real character of the facts. Just as Freud thought that the neurotic could overcome his neurosis by bringing to consciousness the repressed impulses that have led to his symptoms, so Wittgenstein thinks that by becoming conscious of the real character of our use of language we can remove the intellectual cramps and hangups, the intellectual obstacles, that have come from our failure to understand how language actually functions.

Magee Unfortunately some people get obsessed by the later Wittgenstein in the way others get obsessed by psychoanalysis. In both cases I am sometimes reminded of Karl Kraus's remark that psychoanalysis is the only illness that mistakes itself for its cure.

Searle Yes. Wittgenstein has become, for better or worse, a kind of cult figure. But so far, at least, the cult is mercifully smaller than Freud's.

Magee I think we should say something about the unusual way Wittgenstein's books are written – after all, this is the very first thing that strikes anyone who picks up one of them for the first time. They are not written in continuous prose. Instead, they are written in separate paragraphs, each paragraph being given a number. There is usually little in the way of connected argument. Often it is downright hard to see what the relationship is between a paragraph and the two on either side of it. The writing is self-evidently distinguished – full of wonderful similes, metaphors and examples, and often offering immediate and startling insights, and yet it is difficult, at least at first, to see what the point of it all is. Why did he choose to write like that?

Searle Well, there are several reasons. But first let me agree with you entirely about the character of the prose. It is both entrancing and exasperating. I was reminded of that when I was preparing for this discussion. I reread almost all of Wittgenstein's published work, and after a time the stylistic charm of it became quite enthralling. Here is a typical example that I like: 'When one is afraid of the truth – as I am now – it is never the *whole* truth that one is afraid of.'

If you read enough of his prose, you start thinking that way yourself. You begin to address your wife in Wittgensteinian aphorisms, which can be very exasperating for her. Also, you have the feeling when you take up one of his later works and read it that it's a bit like getting a kit for a model aeroplane with no instructions as to how you are supposed to put all the pieces together. That also can be extremely frustrating. Each of his later works is something of a do-it-yourself book.

Now why did he write like that? Well first, I think it was the only way he found completely natural. He has often described what a torture it was for him to try even to put the paragraphs together consecutively, much less to write conventional prose in conventional books and articles. But second, I think there is an element in Wittgenstein's style of what one could almost call arrogance. Wittgenstein consciously wanted his work to be different from the standard ways of doing philosophy. He hated the sort of standard articles that appeared in journals, and standard books that were written by professors of philosophy to be read by undergraduate students in the subject. But it isn't just that he wanted deliberately to be different from other people. There is also a third aspect of his style. I think he honestly and sincerely was struggling to say something new and different, and he always had the feeling that he hadn't quite said what he really meant, that he was still struggling to find a mode of expression. And in his own mind, he never really succeeded. Finally, I think we need to say for English-speaking readers that this style, though it looks strange to Anglo-American eyes, is not so unusual in German. There is a tradition in German philosophy of writing aphoristically. You find it in Nietzsche, Schopenhauer and Lichtenberg, to mention just a few.

Magee In spite of some criticisms we may have, which I think you and I in fact agree on, Wittgenstein's writing is at its best superlative – and out of justice to him we ought to say that unequivocally. His prose can be great as well as being always remarkable.

Searle Yes, it's a very great style.

Magee And some of his sentences stay in your mind for the rest of your life once you've read them.

Searle For ever.

Magee In my introduction to this discussion I mentioned the fact that in comparatively recent years – after being for decades almost unknown outside professional philosophy – Wittgenstein has become a figure in our culture at large, and a figure of international significance. One indicator is that his name crops up over and over again nowadays in book reviews in the literary journals. Or to give a more substantial example, he is a serious intellectual influence in anthropology. Can you tell us what the fields are in which he is having most influence outside philosophy?

Searle Well, at present I think most of the references to Wittgenstein in fields outside of philosophy are really a kind of name-dropping. He has become fashionable, and his is an okay name to drop. He certainly is mentioned in a lot of fields. I feel fairly confident that he would himself have felt that he has not been adequately understood. More importantly – I feel, and I believe he would have felt – he has not been adequately understood in philosophy. Some of the other fields where Wittgenstein is often referred to are literary criticism and aesthetics generally. I think his views are likely to become even more influential as his works are absorbed into the general intellectual culture of the time. There is also a great deal of mention of Wittgenstein's works in the social sciences, and indeed, he thought of himself as doing a kind of anthropology. There have been books written about the importance of Wittgenstein's work for political theory. In general, it is in aesthetics and in what the French would call 'the sciences of man' that Wittgenstein has been most influential. This is perhaps paradoxical, because he wrote so much about the philosophy of mathematics. But most of his influence, for better or worse, is not in mathematics. To the extent that he is influential outside of philosophy, his influence is mostly in literary studies and the social sciences.

Magee Do not the structuralists claim Wittgenstein for their own, despite not even being philosophers?

Searle Well, it is the post-structuralists rather than the structuralists who I think have probably misunderstood Wittgenstein the worst. But to get into that would really be material for another discussion.

Magee I have to confess it's not something I know anything about, so let's not get into it.
  I'd like to conclude this present discussion by drawing up the balance sheet. If you set out to evaluate Wittgenstein as a philosopher, what would you see as being the chief pros and cons?

Searle First I want to say some negative things about Wittgenstein's work, and then I will conclude on a more positive note. I believe the single most disappointing feature of Wittgenstein's later work is its antitheoretical character. Wittgenstein is constantly militating against the idea that we should be seeking a general theory or a general explanation of the phenomena which puzzle us, specifically the phenomena of language and mind. Now if some philosopher says to me that I can't have a general theory, let's say of speech acts or of intentionality, then my natural inclination is to regard it as a challenge; my natural inclination is to go out and prove him wrong. And in these two cases I have tried to do just that; that is, I have tried to write general accounts of speech acts and of intentionality. I think it was simply premature of Wittgenstein to say that we could not have general theories of a philosophically enlightening sort about how language functions or how the mind relates to the world. We couldn't possibly know if our attempts at general theories were successful if we didn't try to formulate and test such theories. And the sheer diversity of the phenomena should not by itself discourage us. Think, for example, of physics. If you think of waterfalls, a pot of boiling water, and an ice-skating rink, it seems that the phenomena of water are incredibly diverse. But in fact we now have a good general theory that accounts for all of these and other forms that water can take. Now, I don't see why we shouldn't seek equally general theories in the philosophy of language or the philosophy of mind. Sometimes it almost seems to me that Wittgenstein might have unconsciously thought that since *he* had failed to get a good general theory in the *Tractatus* then any general theory must be impossible. Roughly speaking, he seems to have thought: If my general theory won't work, then no general theory will. In fact, several of his disciples have said to me that since I reject the anti-theoretical aspects of the *Philosophical Investigations* then somehow I must be committed to believing in the *Tractatus*. They seem to think that these are the only two options. I want to suggest that there are many other options.

However, his own earlier failure to get a satisfactory general theory was only one of the reasons for his anti-theoretical bent. I think it rests primarily on a series of massive mistakes. I want to mention two of these because they are crucial to understanding his views on language and mind. In Wittgenstein's philosophy of language he tries to get away from the idea that representation is somehow the essence of language in favour of the view that we should think of language as consisting of different sorts of tools for signalling to one another. And this gives him, as I said earlier, the result that there is an indefinite variety of uses of language, of language games. But if you look closer at these uses of language you discover that representation lies at the heart of nearly every single language game. If I order you to leave the room, if I ask you whether you are going to leave the room, if I predict that you will leave the room, or if I simply express the wish that you should leave the room, in each case I have made a move in a quite different language game from the other cases. But notice that every single language game has to have the capacity to represent the state of affairs of your leaving the room. That common propositional content runs through orders, expressions of wish, predictions, questions and so on. Now once you see that propositional contents run through just about every language game then you can also see that representing lies at the heart of language. Representation is of the essence of language. Now once you see that, you can see that there aren't an indefinite number or an infinite number of things we do with language; there are in fact a rather limited number. There are a limited number of ways we have of representing; and I have tried to give a general theoretical account of how the various modes of representation in different sorts of speech acts actually function. So in the philosophy of language I think the anti-theoretical bent in Wittgenstein is based on a massive mistake. It is based on a failure to see that representation lies at the heart of nearly every single type of language game.

Now in Wittgenstein's philosophy of mind, I believe, there is a similar massive mistake, and that is the failure to see the importance of the brain for the understanding of mental phenomena. Wittgenstein has almost nothing to say about the brain. But many of the things that he does say about the phenomena of mental life are based on a neglect of the fact that causal processes in the brain are sufficient for any of our mental phenomena. So, for example, when he emphasises that mental phenomena such as hope and fear and love and hate are social phenomena that occur in social contexts, it is also important to remember that the purely mental parts of these phenomena are entirely produced by processes in the brain; and that the social context only matters to the extent that it impacts on our nervous systems. When Wittgenstein tells us: 'An "inner process" stands in need of outward criteria', it is a good idea to remind yourself that an inner process, such as feeling a pain, is entirely caused by neurophysiological processes in the thalamus and in the somato-sensory cortex. Roughly speaking, an inner process doesn't stand in need of anything. It just is.

Wittgenstein's aversion to theory and his insistence that philosophy should be purely descriptive and not critical leads him to a kind of waffling in certain crucial areas. Consider religious discourse, for example. I believe Wittgenstein himself obviously had a deep religious hunger. He did not have the middle-class Anglo-American attitude toward religion, that it was just a matter of something for Sunday mornings. There are frequent references in his more personal writings to God and to the problem of getting himself right with God. None the less, I think most people who knew him would say that he was an atheist. Now in a way, when you read his remarks about God, you almost feel that he wants to have it both ways. He wants to talk about God and still be an atheist. He wants to insist that to understand religious discourse we need to see the role that it plays in people's lives. And that is surely right. But of course, you would not understand the role that it plays in their lives unless you see that religious discourse refers beyond itself. To put it bluntly, when ordinary people pray it is because they think there is a God up there listening. But whether or not there is a God listening to their prayer isn't itself part of the language game. The reason people play the language game of religion is because they think there is something outside the language game that gives it a point. You have to be a very *recherché* sort of religious intellectual to keep praying if you don't think there is any real God outside the language who is listening to your prayers.

So much for negative remarks. Let me say what I think is very impressive in Wittgenstein's work. Most contemporary philosophers who admire Wittgenstein would say that his leading contributions have been in the philosophy of language and the philosophy of mind. In the philosophy of language his chief contributions are that he mounted a devastating and, I think, conclusive refutation of the view that words get their meaning either by standing for objects in the world or by being associated with some introspective process in the mind. Furthermore, he gives a very powerful expression to the view that speaking a language should be seen as a form of human activity, that words are also deeds. He is not the only philosopher to have emphasised this, but he is certainly one of the most powerful and most influential. This involves an important break with the philosophical and linguistic traditions, and we are still working out its consequences.

Equally important are his contributions in the philosophy of mind. He mounted one of the most effective attacks against the Cartesian tradition, that is, against the idea that life consists of two parts: a mental part and a physical part. But his attack on Cartesianism is, I believe, so powerful precisely because he doesn't make the mistake of most anti-Cartesians of thinking that if you reject dualism you must reject mental phenomena. Most anti-Cartesians think that in rejecting dualism they have to accept some sort of behaviourism or some kind of crude materialism. Wittgenstein's philosophy of mind proceeds by carefully examining the uses of words for describing mental phenomena. For literally hundreds of paragraphs in his later work he goes through a discussion of how we use psychological verbs like 'mean' and 'know' and 'see' and 'expect' and 'fear' and 'doubt' and 'hope', and many others. He shows in some detail that if you examine the 'depth grammar' of this vocabulary you don't find two separate phenomena, a mental and a physical. The surface grammar, where we have nouns such as 'mind' and 'body' or 'spirit' and 'matter', makes it look as if there are two types of phenomena involved. But an examination of the depth grammar shows how the use of the vocabulary is grounded in actual situations. When we say things like, 'He has been groaning and in pain for the past two hours', we don't feel that we have mixed categories, that the physical groaning shouldn't be conjoined with the mental pain. On Wittgenstein's view our ordinary ways of talking do not lead to Cartesianism if they are properly understood.

So far I think I am probably reflecting the current philosophical ortho-doxy in saying that Wittgenstein's chief contributions are in the phil-osophy of mind and the philosophy of language. But from my own point of view the most powerful part of Wittgenstein's work is one he develops most fully in his very last book, *On Certainty*, though the idea does appear, in a preliminary form at least, in *Philosophical Investigations*. The idea is this. We have a long tradition in Western philosophy, a tradition that goes back to Plato, according to which all of our meaningful activities must be the product of some inner theory. If, for example, I understand your behaviour it can only be because I hold an implicit theory, unconsciously no doubt, about you and your behaviour; if I understand a language, it is only because I have mastered a theory of the language. Now clearly, there is some truth in this traditional view. But Wittgenstein points out that for a great deal of our behaviour, we just do it. We don't need an inner theory in order to behave the way we do in fact behave. As usual, he gives very arresting and colourful similes for des-cribing this phenomenon. For example, he asks us if when squirrels store nuts for the winter it is because they think that they have solved Hume's problem of induction. That is, do they think they have good grounds for supposing the future will be like the past? No, they just do it. Or he says to think of yourself and imagine putting your hand in a fire. Is the reason that you don't put your hand in a fire that you think you have refuted Hume, or you think you have very good inductive evidence about the consequences? Once again, you just don't do it. You couldn't be dragged into that fire; and that is not because you have a theory, it is simply because you have learned to act in certain ways. Wittgenstein urges us to remember that a great deal of what we do ought to be seen as biologically and culturally primitive. We just act in certain ways. We ought to think of these ways of behaving as just animal reactions. Now in my own work I call this set of capacities that we have of a non-theoretical, non-representational variety 'the Background'. And it seems to me that all of our mental life, conscious and unconscious, really goes on against a background of these non-representational, non-theoretical mental capacities and dispositions.

Now it might seem that what I am praising Wittgenstein for, the recognition of a non-theoretical set of background capacities, is inconsis-tent with what I was criticising him for earlier, his resistance to developing a theory. But it's not really inconsistent. The claim that we often in real life proceed without a theory is itself a theoretical claim. So my complaint about Wittgenstein that he is too resistant to theory should not be confused with the separate point that he has correctly seen that in a great deal of our behaviour we proceed without benefit of a theory, we just act.

Magee Do you think there is much more still to be gained by the application of Wittgenstein's ideas, or do you think Wittgenstein himself squeezed most of the juice out of them?

Searle No, I think there is a great deal more to be said. To put it very bluntly, I think Wittgenstein only scratched the surface. This is a very exciting time to be a philosopher, perhaps the most exciting time in the history of the subject; and Wittgenstein, often in spite of himself, is largely responsible for the opportunities which have opened up.

But there is at least some irony in this, because it seems to me Wittgenstein has not been properly understood in philosophy. I think if Wittgenstein had been properly understood and assimilated by the philosophical tradition, a lot of what passes for contemporary academic philosophy would be ruled out of court, would be seen to be mistaken in a very profound way. You see, we have been talking here as if Wittgenstein was an acknowledged genius of contemporary philosophy. To an extent that is true, but it would be more accurate to say that he has simply gone out of fashion in philosophy. It seems to me that what happened was that Wittgenstein emitted certain muffled explosions; distant philosophical alarms were heard, and these led people to think something very important was going on. For a time, mostly in the fifties and early sixties, there was a lot of running about in response to Wittgenstein. But more recently it seems to me people have reassured themselves into thinking that he has been taken care of, that he has been assimilated, and they can now go back to business as usual. So I have two reactions. First, it seems to me we haven't really properly understood Wittgenstein, and secondly, he didn't complete the work. He only just got started.

INDEX

Page numbers in *italic* refer to the illustrations

Abelard, Peter, 59
aesthetics, 342
American Constitution, 120
American pragmatists, 280–97
analytic statements, 111, 112–13
Anselm, St, 59, 61, 68, 70, 74, 115
Aquinas, St Thomas, 35, 58–60, 63–4, 66–7, *69*, 92; Five Ways, 68; *On the Eternity of the World*, 67; and the Roman Catholic Church, 72–3; *Summa Contra Gentiles*, 58–9, 67–8; *Summa Theologia*, 59, 60–1, 67–8
Aristophanes, 237
Aristotle, 30, 34–54, *41*, 58, 60, 80, 92, 201; *Categories*, 42–3; Four Causes, 47–9; and medieval philosophy, 61, 63, 67; *Metaphysics*, 37, 39, 44, 45, 47; moral philosophy, 51–2; *On Psuche*, 49; *Physics*, 47, 64; political philosophy, 53; *Posterior Analytics*, 38–9; Principle of Non-Contradiction, 36–7
arithmetic, 178, 302–3
Arnauld, Antoine, 124
Atomism, 30
Augustine, St, 24, 58–60, 62, 63, 73; *The Confessions*, 58, 59, 74
Austin, J. L., 314, 316
Ayer, A. J., 160, 164–5, 300–18
Ayers, Michael, 120–43

Bacon, Francis, 79, 88, 165
Bacon, Roger, 59, 61
Bakunin, Mikhail, 208
Bayle, Pierre, 116
Bell, Clive, 223

Berkeley, George, 24, 29, 98, 99, 120–1, *135*, 139–43, 172, 310, 338
Bible, 63, 64, 67–8
Black, Max, 317
Boole, George, 307
Boswell, James, 146, 164
Boyle, Robert, 128, 130
Bradley, Francis Herbert, 112, 156
Brinton, Crane, 228
Buddhism, 107, 213, 215, 226, 227
Burnyeat, Myles, 15–30

Cambridge Platonists, 139
Carnap, Rudolf, 316
Cartesian circle, 93
'Cartesian doubt', 81–4
Cartesian dualism, 86–7, 92–3, 95
Cartesianism, 225–6, 257, 284, 294, 345
causality, 147–50, 151, 160–1, 215, 312, 315
chemistry, 88
Chomsky, Noam, 21
Christianity, 23, 63–4, 67, 194–5, 226, 227, 235–6, 239
Christina, Queen of Sweden, 78
Church, Alonzo 317
Church of England, 72
Cicero, 24, 159
cognitive science, 277
Common, John, 249–50
Communism, 207
consciousness, 134–6, 254–5, 275–6
Copleston, Frederick, 212–30
cosmological arguments, 68

Dante, 35
Darwin, Charles, 163, 206, 238
Davidson, Donald, 317–18
De Morgan, Augustus, 307
Democritus, 30

Derrida, Jacques, 277
Descartes, René, 60, 65, 66, 68, 78–95, 89, 98, 99–100, 101, 109, 139, 161; *Cogito*, 83, 86, 90, 93; compared to Locke, 121–2; concept of 'idea', 122, 124; *Discourse on the Method*, 78, 81, 94; dualism, 86–7, 92–3, 95, 104, 117; idea of God, 84–6, 91–2, 93, 101, 115; influence of, 94–5; mathematical physics, 88–90; *Meditations*, 78, 83, 84–5, 94, 95; Method of Doubt, 81–4; on the physical world, 87–8; and science, 81; use of geometry, 98, 105, 130
Descriptions, Theory of, 309, 313
determinism, 74, 285
Dewey, John, 280–1, 290, 291–7, 292; *Experience and Nature*, 280, 293; *Logic: the Theory of Inquiry*, 293; *The Quest for Certainty*, 280, 293
dialectical materialism, 256
dialectical process, 192–4, 195, 196–8, 205
Disputation, 60–1
Divine Grace, 73–4
Dominicans, 59, 72
doubt, Cartesian, 81–4
Dreyfus, Hubert, 255–77
dualism, 86–7, 92–3, 95, 345
Dummett, Michael, 306–7, 308, 317
Duns Scotus, 59, 61, 65
Dürer, Albrecht, 124

Eccles, J. C., 160
economics, 206
education, 159, 296–7
Edwards, Jonathan, 138
Einstein, Albert, 142, 143, 163, 167
empiricism, 98, 99, 120, 138, 163, 201
Encyclopaedists, 120, 138
Engels, Friedrich, 190
Enlightenment, 159
Epicureans, 52
Epicurus, 30
Epimenides, 303
epistemology, 10, 65, 338
ethics *see* moral philosophy
Euclid, 98, 105, 301
Euripides, 237
Ewing, A. C., 335
existentialism, 255, 256, 267, 275–6

fact-value distinction, 225–6
Fascism, 250–1
Feuerbach, Ludwig, 196
Fichte, Johann Gottlieb, 202, 230
Forms, Theory of, 22–3, 27, 38, 42, 45–6, 156
Foucault, Michael, 227
Founding Fathers, 120
free will, 73–4, 105–6, 115, 172, 183
freedom, 199–200, 206, 207
Frege, Gottlob, 65, 111, 294, 300–9, 305, 315–16, 317–18, 324; *Begriffsschrift*, 300, 301; *The Foundations of Arithmetic*, 300, 317; *Grundgesetze*, 300, 304
French Revolution, 120, 138, 192, 198
Freud, Sigmund, 106, 217, 228–9, 238–9, 240, 268, 339–40

Galileo, 88, 117, 129
Geach, Peter, 317
Genesis, Book of, 27, 67
geometry, 98, 100–1, 105, 130, 136, 178
God: in Berkeley's philosophy, 141, 142; in Descarte's philosophy, 84–6, 91–2, 93, 101, 115; Divine Grace, 73–4; existence of, 68–71, 74; in Hegel's philosophy, 195–6; in Kant's philosophy, 180–2; in Leibniz's philosophy, 112, 114–15, 117; in Spinoza's philosophy, 101–2, 106–7, 114; Wittgenstein and, 344–5
Gödel, Kurt, 302
Goethe, Johann Wolfgang von, 116, 240, 243
Grace, W. G., 335
Green, T. H., 163

Hamilton, Alexander, 138
Hartley, David, 152
Hegel, Georg Wilhelm Friedrich, 60, 94, 170, 190–207, 197, 255–6, 271, 314; dialectical process, 192–4, 195, 196–8; *Geist*, 156, 194–6, 202, 205, 207; influence, 204–5; *The Philosophy of History*, 190, 191; *The Philosophy of Right*, 190, 204; *The Science of Logic*, 190, 201
Heidegger, Martin, 256, 257–77, 262, 294; *Being and Time*, 255, 258, 261, 267, 268–9, 271, 275, 276, 277; *Dasein*, 263–9

Heraclitus, 14, 195
Herder, Johann Gottfried, 116
Hilbert, David, 317
Hinduism, 213, 215, 216
historicity, 272
history, 157, 158, 191–4, 196–8, 206–7
Hitler, Adolf, 207, 246, 250
Hobbes, Thomas, 106, 123, 165
Homer, 271
Hook, Sidney, 297
human nature, 158–9, 191
Hume, David, 24, 98, 99, 106, 113, 116, 146–67, *155*, 173–4, 176, 185, 191, 338; on causality, 147–50, 151, 160–1, 315; *Dialogues Concerning Natural Religion*, 146, 154, 157, 164; *An Enquiry Concerning Human Understanding*, 146, 158; *An Enquiry Concerning the Principles of Morals*, 146, 158; on the existence of the self, 150–1, 160; study of human nature, 158–9; theory of language and meaning, 152–3; *A Treatise of Human Nature*, 146, 149, 151, 156, 157–8, 159, 165, 167
Hume's Fork, 153
Husserl, Edmund, 152, 254–61, *259*, 266, 275, 276–7, 302; *Logical Investigations*, 254, 258

'idea', Locke's concept of, 122–5
idealism, 21, 138, 201, 235, 239, 255, 302, 314, 332
identity, 40–6, 134–6, 150–1, 304
imagism, 122–3
immortality, 134–6
induction, 160–2
Inquisition, 88, 98
institutions, 295–6
intentionality, 256–7
Islam, 73, 226, 227

James, Henry, 280, 290–1
James, William, 280–1, *287*, 288–91, 312; *Pragmatism*, 288–90
Jefferson, Thomas, 138
John the Scot, 59, 61
Judaism, 107, 226, 227
just war, 72

Kant, Immanuel, 60, 68, 98, 107, 123,
163, 170–87, *177*, 191, 201, 202, 213–17; Categorical Imperative, 184, 236; *The Critique of Judgment*, 170, 186; *The Critique of Practical Reason*, 170, 186; *The Critique of Pure Reason*, 113, 170, 186; idea of God, 180–2; influence, 286; moral philosophy, 181, 183–4
Kenny, Anthony, 59–75
Kierkegaard, Sören, 116, 170, 255–6
Kneale, William and Martha, 317
Kraus, Karl, 340
Kubrick, Stanley, 273

Lamarck, Jean Baptiste, 163
language: Heidegger and, 274–5, 277; Hume's theory of, 152–3; Locke's view of, 131, 132–3; Wittgenstein's philosophy of, 322–40, 343–4, 345
La Rochefoucauld, Duc de, 248
Lavoisier, Antoine Laurent, 163
Lawrence, D. H., 234, 249–50
Lawrence, Frieda, 250
Leibniz, Gottfried Wilhelm, 29, 68, 92, 98–100, 107–17, *110*, 172, 173, 176, 186, 191; idea of God, 112, 114–15, 117; influence of, 116; and mathematics, 116–17; *The Monadology*, 99, 108; monads, 107–9, 114, 115
Leo XIII, Pope, 72–3
Leśniewski, 304
liberation, 268
Lichtenberg, Georg Christoph, 341
literary criticism, 342
Locke, John, 98, 99, 106, 111, 120, 121–38, *126*, 139–43, 338; concept of 'idea', 122–5; definition of knowledge, 121; on education, 159; *Essay Concerning Human Understanding*, 120, 122, 128, 131, 134; influence of, 138; political philosophy, 136–7; theory of knowledge, 121–4; view of language, 131, 132–3
logic, 63; Hegel and, 201; medieval, 64–5; modern developments in, 65, 300–9
logical positivism, 160, 322, 325, 334
Luther, Martin, 243

McTaggart, J. M. E., 314
Malraux, André, 250
Mann, Thomas, 250
Marx, Karl, 170, 190, *203*, 205–8, 238, 256, 268
Marxism, 190, 195, 205, 206, 239–40
materialism, 30, 46, 205
mathematical logic, 300, 301–4, 308–9
mathematical physics, 88–90
mathematics, 27–8, 116–17, 129–30
meaning, 152–3, 282–4, 304–7, 323–40
medical ethics, 71
medieval philosophy, 58–75
Meinong, Alexius von, 309
memory, 136
Merleau-Ponty, Maurice, 255, 256, 275, 276
metaphysics, definition, 39–40
Mill, John Stuart, 170, 310, 315
monads, 107–9, 114, 115
Montaigne, Michel Eyquem de, 248
Montesquieu, 138
Moore, G. E., 309, 313, 314, 316
'moral luck', 52
moral philosophy: Aristotle, 51–2; Kant, 181, 183–4; Schopenhauer, 244; and warfare, 71–2
Morgenbesser, Sidney, 281–97
Mussolini, Benito, 250

Nagel, Ernest, 285
Nagel, Thomas, 317
Napoleon I, Emperor, 243
Nazism, 246, 250–1
Newton, Sir Isaac, 88, 99, 128–9, 138, 152, 156, 163, 167, 179
Nietzsche, Friedrich Wilhelm, 170, 234–51, *241*, 272, 341; *The Birth of Tragedy*, 234, 237, 249; eternal recurrence, 247–8; influence, 249–51; Schopenhauer's influence on, 228, 234; Superman, 246–7; *Thus Spoke Zarathustra*, 234, 242; use of metaphor, 248–9; will to power, 245–6
nihilism, 272–4
Non-Contradiction, Principle of, 36–7
nuclear weapons, 71–2
Nussbaum, Martha, 34–54

objective realism, 288

Ockham, William of, 59, 61, 63, 65, 165
ontological arguments, 68–71, 84
Ovid, 159
Oxford, 64, 314, 316, 317

Pascal, Blaise, 248
Passmore, John, 147–67
Pastoral Letter of the American Catholic Bishops on Nuclear Weapons and Nuclear Deterrence, 72
Peano, Giuseppe, 308
Peirce, C. S., 280–8, *283*, 289–90, 291
perception, 50–1, 141–2, 276, 309
pessimism, 222, 224–5
phenomenology, 152, 254–5, 257, 277
physics, 88–90, 109, 116–17, 128–9, 156
Pirandello, Luigi, 250
Plato, 14–30, 34, 36, 58, 60, 163–4, 185, 237; *Apology*, 15, 17; concept of 'idea', 122; *Gorgias*, 15, 17; *Laches*, 14, 15, 21; and medieval philosophy, 61, 63; *Meno*, 22, 23; *Parmenides*, 14, 26–7; *Phaedo*, 14, 23, 26, 27; *Phaedrus*, 23; *Protagoras*, 15, 18, 20; *Republic*, 14, 16, 20, 23, 24–5, 28; *Symposium*, 14, 16, 23; *Theaetetus*, 14, 29; Theory of Forms, 22–3, 27, 38, 42, 45–6, 156; *Timaeus*, 14, 27–8
Platonism, 22–3, 30
political philosophy, 53, 136–7
Popper, Karl, 142, 160, 285, 294, 316
post-structuralism, 342
pragmatism, 280–97
private languages, 336–9
psychoanalysis, 106, 339–40
psychology, 63, 124
Ptolemy, 28
Putnam, Hilary, 317
Pythagoras, 14

Quine, Willard Van Orman, 316, 317
Quinton, Anthony, 98–117

rationalism, 90, 98, 99–100, 115–16, 198–9
realism, 143
reason, 161–2
recollection, theory of, 20–1
Reformation, 65, 79, 80

religion *see* Buddhism; Christianity;
    God; Hinduism; Roman Catholic
    Church
Renaissance, 30, 64, 65
Roman Catholic Church, 72–3
romantic movement, 116
Rousseau, Jean Jacques, 146
Russell, Bertrand, 65, 66, 111, 116,
    164–5, 193, 202, 280, 300–1, 303–4,
    307–18, *311*; *The Analysis of Matter*,
    312; *The Analysis of Mind*, 310–12;
    History of Western Philosophy, 163,
    291; *Human Knowledge, Its Scope and
    Limits*, 312, 313; *My Philosophical
    Development*, 313; *Mysticism and
    Logic*, 310; *Our Knowledge of the
    External World*, 310, 313; *Principia
    Mathematica*, 65, 66, 308, 309; *The
    Principles of Mathematics*, 308, 322;
    The Problems of Philosophy, 100, 309,
    310
Russell, Frank, 310
Ryle, Gilbert, 258, 316

Sartre, Jean-Paul, 255, *270*, 275–6; *Being
    and Nothingness*, 255, 275
scepticism, 79, 80–1, 86, 122, 153–4, 201
Schopenhauer, Arthur, 106, 129, 164,
    170, 185, 202, 212–30, *219*, 245, 341;
    influence, 228–30, 234
science, 79–80, 81, 141, 162–3, 291–5
scientific determinism, 74
Scottish Enlightenment, 146
Searle, John, 323–47
self, existence of, 150–1, 160
sense data, 309, 310, 314–15
Shakespeare, William, 249
Shaw, Bernard, 234, 246, 249–50
Singer, Peter, 190–207
Smith, Adam, 146, 164
social sciences, 158, 342
Socrates, 14, 15–22, *19*, 24, 27, 29, 34,
    192, 236, 237, 240, 243, 307
soul, 134–6, 180–1
space, 156–7, 176–8, 215
Spinoza, Baruch, 60, 68, 98–107, *103*,
    113; *Ethics*, 98, 100; on free will, 105;
    idea of God, 101–2, 106–7, 114;
    influence of, 116; and mathematics,
    116–17; modes, 104–5
Stalin, Joseph, 207, 208

statements, analytic and synthetic, 111,
    112–13
Stern, J. P., 234–51
Stoics, 52
Strindberg, August, 250
structuralism, 342
substance, 39, 40–6, 101, 108, 127
Superman, 246–7
syllabus, 61
synthetic statements, 111, 112–13

Tacitus, 159
Tarski, Alfred, 318
teleology, 48–9
Thales, 14
time, 156–7, 176–8, 215, 217
totalitarianism, 206–7
Types, Theory of, 313

unconscious, 228–9, 239
universe, 114, 154, 218
universities, medieval, 60–1, 63
Utilitarianism, 51, 236

Vatican Council, Second, 73
Vienna Circle, 312, 322
Voltaire, 112, 120, 138

Wagner, Richard, 228, 234, 250
warfare, moral philosophy and, 71–2
Warnock, Geoffrey, 170–87
Whitehead, Alfred North, 65, 308, 309,
    313, 317
Wilde, Oscar, 165
William of Orange, 120
Williams, Bernard, 78–95, 160
Wittgenstein, Ludwig, 29, 129, 212,
    218, 294, 300, 312, 314, 316, 322–47,
    333; influence, 341–2; on language
    and meaning, 322–40, 343–4, 345; *On
    Certainty*, 346; *Philosophical
    Investigations*, 322–3, 326–7, 329,
    343, 346; philosophy of mind, 344;
    Schopenhauer's influence on, 228,
    229–30; *Tractatus*, 217, 229–30,
    322–3, 325–6, 343
Wordsworth, William, 107
Wyclif, John, 63

Xenophon, 24

Yeats, W. B., 234, 249–50